A
Life
in
Letters

The Essential Collection

Edited by William H. Shannon
and Christine M. Bochen

ave maria press notre dame, indiana

Originally published in hardcover by HarperOne, an imprint of HarperCollins Publishers, in 2008. ISBN 978-0-06-134832-7

This paperback edition published by Ave Maria Press, Inc., by arrangement with HarperOne.

Letters reprinted by permission of Farrar, Strauss & Giroux, LLC.

Founded in 1865, Ave Maria Press is a ministry of the Indiana Province of Holy Cross. www.avemariapress.com

Paperback ISBN-10 1-59471-256-5   ISBN-13 978-1-59471-256-2

· Cover photograph of Thomas Merton by John Howard Griffin. Used with permission of the Merton Legacy Trust and the Thomas Merton Center at Bellarmine University.

Cover design by Katherine Robinson Coleman.

Printed and bound in the United States of America.

Library of Congress Cataloging-in-Publication Data available upon request.

First Paperback Edition

To Brother Patrick Hart, O.C.S.O.

and

In Fond Memory of Robert E. Daggy

Contents

Introduction

"I do not hesitate to confess that letters from my friends have always and will always mean a great deal to me."
—*Letter to Sister Therese Lentfoehr,*
September 25, 1956

Thomas Merton was one of the most prolific and provocative letter writers of the twentieth century. His letters, archived at The Thomas Merton Center at Bellarmine University in Louisville, Kentucky, number more than ten thousand. The publication of five volumes of selected letters by Farrar, Straus, and Giroux, under the general editorship of William H. Shannon, documented the remarkable breadth of Merton's contacts and interests. Each of the five volumes highlighted a dimension of Merton's life and thought: *The Hidden Ground of Love* (1985), his ideas on religious experience and social concerns; *The Road to Joy* (1989), his exchanges with family and friends, old and new; *The School of Charity* (1990), his reflection on religious renewal and spiritual direction; *The Courage for Truth* (1993), his dialogue with fellow writers; and *Witness to Freedom* (1994), his efforts to confront the many manifestations of what he calls "unfreedom," such as violence and war, by a call to an authentic life of fundamental human and Christian values.

Put simply, Merton's letters offer a rich and nuanced portrait of the monk whose life and writings spoke so eloquently to his contemporaries and continue to speak to readers today. They trace the development of his faith and his grasp of what it demanded of him. They help us see his evolving understanding of the monastic life and what it meant to be a monk, the awakening of his social conscience, the honing of his writer's craft, the emboldening of his voice as critic of society and culture, his grassroots efforts to promote ecumenical and interreligious dialogue, and his growing sense of global consciousness. It is this portrait of the man and the monk that the editors of *Thomas Merton: A Life in Letters* hope to capture in this new volume featuring the best letters selected from the five volumes originally published between 1985 and 1994.

Keeping in Touch

Imagine Merton's letter writing as a way for this monk—living in silence and physical isolation, allowed but few visitors and with almost no opportunities to leave the monastery grounds, much less travel—to initiate and build relationships and enable them to grow. We have a variety of ways of keeping our friendships in good order. We can visit our friends, share a meal with them, attend a concert together, and still have many other possible avenues of contact open to us. Merton's one and only way of reaching his friends was, normally, through his writing. It is true that he did have his share of visitors, considerably more than most other monks. More than once he made the resolution that he would curtail the number of visitors he received. Although he chose a solitary life (and reveled in it), he loved people and craved human contact. His letters helped to fill that need and, in the process, created an extraordinary record of Merton's life and the development of his thought.

Without question, Merton enjoyed receiving letters, as he admitted in one he wrote to Sister Therese Lentfoehr on September 25, 1956: "I do not hesitate to confess that letters from my friends have always and will always mean a great deal to me." And though he occasionally complained that it was impossible for him to respond to all the letters he received, it is clear that he enjoyed both writing and receiving them. Exchanging letters made it possible for him to keep in touch with people who were important to him, providing him conversation partners of all sorts. It was his way of keeping "his friendship in constant repair," to quote Boswell's life of Samuel Johnson.

Paul Pearson, director of The Thomas Merton Center and Archives at Bellarmine University, estimates that Merton had some twenty-one hundred correspondents. Admittedly, his exchanges with some of these were hardly substantive, but the volume of significant letters simply boggles the mind. There were letters to writers from the West and East with whom he enjoyed exploring the mystical, transcendent dimension of human life.

There were letters to activists engaged in the struggle for justice and peace, such as Dorothy Day, Daniel Berrigan, and Jim Forest. There were letters to writers such as Boris Pasternak and a host of Latin Americans, whom he admired for their courage to speak the truth and resist totalitarianism. There were letters to men and women who shared Merton's commitment to monastic life and its renewal. There were letters to correspondents who experienced the joy of faith; to others, such as the Lithuanian-born Polish writer and poet Czeslaw Milosz, struggling to believe; and to some who identified themselves as unbelievers or agnostics.

The Art of Letter Writing

Thomas Merton was an excellent letter writer, as Evelyn Waugh recognized. Waugh, himself a distinguished writer and a master of rhetoric who "translated" *The Seven Storey Mountain* for a British readership under the title *Elected Silence,* admired Merton's excellence in letter writing and advised him to "put books aside and write serious letters and to make an art of it." Merton responded to this advice by writing more books *and* still sending out a huge quantity of letters. Nonetheless, Waugh's insight was perceptive. Merton's style was admirably suited to the art of letter writing: it was personal and intimate, almost always lively and upbeat, almost never heavy or boring. At times he could be deadly serious and deeply perceptive, at other times jovial and even hilariously funny. The impish smile that lights so many photos of him seems to look out through the letters, too. Though his letters often come to grips with substantive issues, they are neither ponderous nor prosaic. When he learned that he had been compared with John Henry Newman, Merton, with characteristic humility and wit, quipped: "I have absolutely nothing in common with Cardinal Newman, except for the fact that we are both converts and both wrote autobiographies. He writes beautiful prose, I write slang." Clearly, this was an exaggeration, as Merton was quite capable of writing excellent prose; yet without doubt the slang is there, too. Slang is, after all, the language of intimacy and an accepted part of the vocabulary of letter writing. His letters, like most good letters, are not polished essays on the topics they address. More often they are flashes of intuition on a topic that is left open-ended. This sense of incompleteness—mildly frustrating at times, one might want to say—prods both writer and reader to follow paths that have been opened but have not yet been fully explored.

The importance of the letters of this remarkable monk can scarcely be overestimated. They reveal aspects of his character and thought that do not appear, at least not with the same clarity and personal touch, in his published works. This is true not only because the very nature of letter writing tends to make it more personal, but also because he wrote with much greater freedom in his letters than in his published works. Almost to the last, the things he wrote for publication were carefully scrutinized by the censors of his Trappist Order and also of the Catholic Church. While the ecclesiastical censors were concerned with maintaining orthodoxy in matters of faith and morals, the censors of the order were concerned with what was fitting form and content for a monk and even what was "opportune" to publish at a particular time. In a letter to poet Lawrence Ferlinghetti, which Merton wrote in August 1961, he put it this way: "These cats are obsessed with a certain image they have of themselves and they don't want anyone disturbing it." And disturb the image Merton certainly did, particularly when he began, in the early sixties, to speak out against the proliferation of nuclear weapons and the mounting threat of nuclear war. After publishing a flurry of poems and articles on war and peace, Merton received word in April 1962 that he was forbidden to publish on the subject. In a letter to Jim Forest, dated April 29, 1962, Merton explained that the reason for this was that, according to the superiors of his Order, writing about war and peace "is not the right kind of work for a monk, and . . . it 'falsifies the monastic message.' Imagine that: the thought that a monk might be deeply enough concerned with the issue of nuclear war to voice a protest against the arms race, is supposed to bring monastic life into disrepute." The chief concern of the Trappist censors was that his writings should conform to the image of what a Trappist monk might be expected to write. The problem, of course, was that, by the 1960s at least, Merton has ceased to be a "typical" Trappist monk (if indeed he had ever been such).

It would be a mistake, however, to think that Merton delighted in being different and in saying what was startling and offbeat (though at times, it must be admitted, he was not above this). He was essentially a man of tradition, striving to recover authentic Christian and monastic values in a time of change and upheaval, during which he often read the signs of the times better and more clearly than others. He never claimed to have the answers to all questions. He did feel that he had discovered some of the right questions; and he probed them relentlessly and with a much greater sense of freedom in his letters than elsewhere. He wrote at a time when the very foundations of Christian life and culture were being shaken. One of the reasons he was sometimes misunderstood is that he was doing a bit of the shaking himself. What is clear is that Merton wanted and needed to be in touch with contemporary women and men as together they struggled with the questions of truth, meaning, and responsibilities that continue to trouble the human spirit.

"A Place in My Solitude . . . An Apostolate of Friendship"

While letter writing was for Merton a way to connect with people, a way to learn from others, a way to try out new ideas, a way to reflect on his work, and a way to engage the issues of the day, it was more than that. Letter writing, as Merton came to see it, was an extension of his monastic vocation. Merton put it this way in his journal: "Mail is one of the things that holds me up. But it is *necessary* to write some letters, even long ones." The necessity, as Merton saw it, stemmed from the fact that he had come to see letter writing as an extension of his vocation. He conceived of his letter writing as "an apostolate," or ministry of sorts. He makes this clear in a letter he wrote to Pope John XXIII in November 1958:

> It seems to me that, as a contemplative, I do not need to lock myself into solitude and lose all contact with the rest of the world; rather this poor world has a right to a place in my solitude. It is not enough for me to think of the apostolic value of prayer and penance; I have also to think in terms of a contemplative grasp of the political, intellectual, artistic, and social movements in this world—by which I mean a sympathy for the honest aspirations of so many intellectuals everywhere in the world and the terrible problems they have to face. I have had the experience of seeing that this kind of understanding and friendly sympathy, on the part of a monk who really understands them, has produced striking ef-

fects among artists, writers, publishers, poets, etc., who have become my friends without my having to leave the cloister. I have even been in correspondence with the Russian writer who won the Nobel Prize in Literature, Boris Pasternak. This was before the tragic change in his situation. We got to understand each other very well. In short, with the approval of my Superiors, I have exercised an apostolate—small and limited though it be—within a circle of intellectuals from other parts of the world, and it has been quite simply an apostolate of friendship.

This "apostolate of friendship" became a way for Merton to engage the issues of his day: the urgent threat posed by the Cold War mentality and the ideology of militarism with its proliferation of nuclear weapons, the threats to human dignity and freedom posed by totalitarian regimes, the dangers of technology and its potential to erode the value of human beings and human work, the use of language to conceal rather than reveal truth. Framing his letter writing as "an apostolate" enabled Merton to see it as an act of faith, a participation in the saving mission of Christ in the world. He had found a place for the world in his solitude.

The Editors' Goals

Thomas Merton: A Life in Letters represents the editors' attempt to put together in a single volume what they consider to be "the best letters" of the five volumes already published. We understand "best letters" to mean the letters that together capture the spirit of Merton the letter writer while representing both the breadth of his interests and the variety of his correspondence. Given the amazing letter output of this remarkable man and writer, the challenge of compiling a single volume of letters was greater than we had anticipated. Which letters should we include? Which correspondences should we highlight? How could we best represent the richness and the range of Merton's concerns? Given the constraint of space, making these hard choices was our major task as editors. Throughout the process, we were committed to two goals:

First, we wanted to communicate a sense of Merton the letter writer, for whom letters were not just a vehicle for exchanging information but a way to initiate, maintain, and deepen relationships. For Merton, letter writing was a personal act of self-revelation and communication. There is an intimacy about his letters, and indeed about any well-written letters—a particularity, if you will—that belongs to no other form of writing. Letters are one-on-one: they exist for dialogue and call for reaction. More than that, the particularity in a good letter often spills over into issues that touch our common human situation. Merton's letters to particular individuals, especially those with whom he corresponded often and with some regularity, reveal something of his own character and the special regard he held for his correspondents as evidenced in tone and, oftentimes, in humor as well. Who Merton was in himself and in relationships comes through best in sustained correspondences. However, "compressing" five volumes into one clearly meant that only rarely could we include the whole of a correspondence or even reprint individual letters in their entirety. Nonetheless, we have tried to preserve the personal quality of the letters, choosing letters not only for the ideas presented there but for the way in which the letters represent Merton, sharing and communicating what was on his mind as well as in his heart.

Second, we wanted to let Merton's letters demonstrate the breadth of his interests and concerns. Merton's letters cover a range of topics and confound facile attempts to cluster and categorize them. Some of the correspondences, far from sticking with one issue, bubble over into many other areas. At the risk of overstating the fact (but not by much), Merton is inclined to talk to everyone about everything. So while he may be writing to peace activists about their resistance to war, he may branch off and talk about issues facing the Catholic Church. Addressing fellow writers about their work and his, he shares thoughts about his life and work and the threats to freedom in the world. Writing to fellow monks about obstacles to an authentic living of the monastic life, he offers critiques of American culture. The scope and variety of his correspondents are staggering. He wrote to poets; to heads of state; to popes, bishops, priests, and lay people; to monks, rabbis, and Zen masters; to Catholics, Protestants, Anglicans, and Orthodox Christians; to Buddhists, Hindus, Jews, and Sufis; to literary agents and publishers; to theologians and social activists; to old friends and young ones, too. The range and contents of his letters are almost as diverse as the number of his correspondents. He wrote about Allah, Anglicanism, Asia, the Bible, the Blessed Virgin; about Buddhism, China, Christ, Christendom, Church, culture, conscience, contemplation, and the Cold War; about Eckhart, ecumenism, God, happiness, his hermitage, his hospital interludes; about illusions, interreligious dialogue, Islam, John of the Cross, Julian of Norwich, Martin Luther King Jr., the Koran, Latin America, liturgy, the love of God, mysticism; about poetry, political tyranny, prophets, psalms, silence, solitude and *sobornost,* Sufism; about Taoism, technology, Trinity, unity, the will of God, his own writings, Zen, and so on. Again, although limits of space forced hard choices, we have tried to represent the richness and depth of Merton's thought.

With these two goals in mind, we have chosen to present the letters in a way that communicates a sense of who Merton was, the significance letter writing had for him, and the development and evaluation of his thinking on subjects of special interest and concern to him. This book is divided into nine parts, each focused on a theme in Merton's life and work. In some parts of the book, we have chosen to present extensive selections from Merton's letters to one or more individuals. In others, we have included shorter selections and excerpts from Merton's letters to a number of correspondents.

This volume offers a glimpse of and insight into one of the most compelling letter writers of the twentieth century—a monk, mystic, and prophet who helped to shape American Catholic thought, fusing spirituality and social justice and pursuing unity beyond difference. We hope that our readers, intrigued by the selections in this book, will seek out volumes containing Merton's letters and will, beyond that, delve into Merton's journals, essays, and books. We like to picture Merton's letter writing as an upward spiral—creating an ever-widening circle of contacts and relationships. The editors will feel amply rewarded if those who read this book become part of that continuing spiral.

William H. Shannon and Christine M. Bochen

PART 1

A Life in Letters

In His Own Words

"There are three gifts I have received, for which I can never be grateful enough: first, my Catholic faith; second, my monastic vocation; third, the calling to be a writer and share my beliefs with others."

—"To My Dear Friend," ca. 1963

While all of Thomas Merton's letters shed light on his life and work, writing a letter was, on some occasions, an opportunity for him to tell his story in brief. The earliest of such letters was one that Merton wrote to Abbot Frederic Dunne in January 1942, a little more than a month after Merton entered the Abbey of Gethsemani. Writing to fulfill the canon law requiring him to identify the dioceses in which he had lived before coming to the monastery, Merton traced the story of his conversion and previewed the narrative line of his best-selling autobiography, *The Seven Storey Mountain*. In brief accounts of his life more than two decades later, Merton struck quite a different chord, as illustrated by the letters and excerpts that follow. In 1963, Merton drafted a form letter that he sent to those requesting information about his life and writings. He sent a copy to Tommie O'Callaghan, a friend in Louisville whom Merton chose as one of three trustees of his literary trust, and quipped: "This might amuse you —I send it to High School kids who want me to write essays for them." In May 1967, he included a short curriculum vitae in a letter to poet Jonathan Williams and prefaced it this way: "I am bad at writing these things, 'born on a chimney top in Strasbourg in 1999' etc., but you can select what you want from this one: there is plenty of choice." In June 1968, in a letter to Sister J. M., Merton offered a cogent reprise of the periods of his life as a monk and writer.

TO ABBOT FREDERIC DUNNE, O.C.S.O.   *Frederic Dunne, O.C.S.O., was Merton's first Abbot. When Abbot Dunne died on August 4, 1948, just two months before the publication of* The Seven Storey Mountain, *the autobiography the abbot had directed Merton to write, Merton noted in his journal that Abbot Dunne "is very close to me and will remain so all the rest of my days. . . . His sympathy was deep and real. . . . I don't know who was ever kinder to me."*

[GETHSEMANI NOVITIATE] JANUARY 2, 1942

At the suggestion of my Father Master, I am writing out for you this outline of the main facts of my life and education, including, in particular, the circumstances of my conversion and vocation.

I was born Jan. 31, 1915, in Prades, France, in the diocese of Perpignan, of Protestant parents. My father was a native of New Zealand, my mother an

American. Both are now dead; my mother died when I was six, my father in 1931. I have no knowledge of having received even a Protestant baptism. It is barely possible that I did: but no record exists of it, and no one is left to tell me.

In 1916 my parents brought me to America. I lived here until 1925 when I returned to France with my father. Then I went to the Lycée of Montauban—a public institution of secondary education, for two years. In 1928 I was sent to England, where from 1929 to 1932 I attended Oakham School at Oakham, Rutland, in the Diocese of Nottingham. This was my address from the age of 14 to 16½. After that I came to America and lived most of 1933 with my grandparents at Douglaston, Long Island, in the Diocese of Brooklyn. During the scholastic year 1933–4 I attended Cambridge University, in England, on a scholarship in modern languages. My home address, however, was my grandparents' residence—50 Rushmore Ave., Douglaston, Long Island, N.Y. In fact this was really my *home address,* although most of the time I was away at school, from 1931 to 1934. But I actually lived there from 1934 to 1939. During that time I attended Columbia University, where I got a B.A. degree, and later I pursued my studies and took an M.A. in English, and even did some work towards the degree of Ph.D. I taught English at Columbia one term.

My next address, 1939–40, was 35 Perry Street, New York City, in the Archdiocese of New York.

After that, from June 1940 to December 1941 my address was St. Bonaventure College, St. Bonaventure, N.Y., in the Diocese of Buffalo. There I was employed as an assistant professor of English.

As to my conversion: I had been brought up without much religious training of any kind. My grandparents gave money to the Episcopal Church, but never attended it. My father was a just, devout and prayerful man, but he did not like the Protestant cenacles in France, and never went to the length of becoming a Catholic. He died a good Anglican. The school I went to in England was Anglican, but I protested against the liberal teaching in religion we received there, and because it seemed to me to have no substance to it, I proudly assumed that this was the case with all religions, and obstinately set my face against all churches. Thus from the time of my leaving Oakham School until 1938, I gradually passed from being anti-clerical and became a complete unbeliever. The consequences of this in my life were disastrous. My only concern was with earthly things: thinking myself passionately devoted to "justice" and "liberty" I began to take an interest in atheistic communism, and, for a while, I held the "doctrines" of radicalism, concerning religious institutions: namely that they were purely the result of social and historical forces and, however well-meaning their adherents, they were nothing more than *social* groups, which the rich made use of to oppress the poor!!!

Suffice it to say that I could not be happy holding such beliefs; and the earthly life, which promised happiness on a purely natural level, had instead brought me great disappointments and shocks and miseries: and I was making bigger and bigger mistakes and becoming more and more confused. I began to realize that my interpretation of the natural order was very mistaken.

As a result of studies and reading which familiarized me with the works of Etienne Gilson and Jacques Maritain, but particularly as the result of the work of God's grace which now began to move me with the most urgent promptings of desire, I began going to Mass at Corpus Christi Church, West 121st Street, New York. And there, I soon began to take instruction and was happily baptized on November 16, 1938.

After that, with many graces from God and many instances of stupidity and ingratitude on my own part, I began, too slowly, the long-needed amendment of my life. In September 1939, considering that my life was still far short of what I desired, I began to pray for a vocation to the priesthood. At that time I was considering the Order of Friars Minor. I even sent an application for admission to that order, and was accepted: however, before beginning the novitiate, I recalled an incident of my past life, and believing this made me unworthy to be a priest, and supported in this belief by a friend who was a priest, I withdrew my application and did not enter the novitiate. Instead, I went to work at St. Bonaventure College, in order to live as nearly as possible the life I would have led if my hopes had not been disappointed. I then discovered that this life also was too easy-going and worldly and relaxed for me; it was well that I had not gone on and entered the Franciscan novitiate! However, I became a Franciscan Tertiary, and by means of daily Communion and other sources of Divine Grace, attempted to advance in the paths of Christian life.

With the passage of time, I was still much unsatisfied, and having heard of the Trappists from a friend [Dan Walsh], I decided to make a retreat here at Gethsemani, which I did during Holy Week, 1941. From the very first moment of entering the monastery I was overwhelmed with the holiness and sanctified atmosphere that filled it, and by the end of that week I was filled with an intense desire to enter this community. However, I still believed that I had no choice in the matter and that, being "unworthy" of the priesthood, it would be useless for me to ever think of applying to be admitted here. Nevertheless I was praying for a Trappist vocation against all hope. The whole situation made me intensely miserable. I returned to my work, and all the impressions I had brought from Gethsemani remained with me all summer—and grew in strength, with my desire to consecrate myself entirely to God as a monk—or if not as a monk, by some other perfect sacrifice of the world: just what, I did not know: but I thought of going as a permanent worker with Baroness de Hueck, in Harlem, where I did actually spend two weeks.

During this time, I was so much at a loss for an answer to my question, for out of shame at the situation in my past which had created this problem, I dared consult no one about it—I finally resolved on saying some prayers and opening the Bible and seeing what answer I would get in this way. With great amazement and fear I read the first words that my eyes fell upon, and they were "*Ecce eris tacens!*" [Behold, you will be silent!]—the words of the angel to Zacharias. Even at this surprisingly clear indication of what I was to do, I remained uncertain for some time, and made a retreat early in September at Our Lady of the Valley [Cistercian Abbey in Rhode Island].

Finally, this fall I decided to consult another friend, a priest, and one more learned and experienced than my former adviser. This time I was told that the problem I had in mind was no obstacle to my becoming a priest—which turned out to be the case when I submitted it to your consideration through Father Master, on my arrival here.

I came to Gethsemani December 10, and was admitted to the community on the Feast of St. Lucy, December 13; and now with many prayers and thanks to Almighty God I beg Him to make me, the least of all His servants, totally His so that my past life of rebellious sins and ingratitude may be burned clean away in the fire of His infinite love—for which I know I humbly share in the merit of your prayers, my Reverend Father!

TO "MY DEAR FRIEND" [CA. 1963]

Forgive me for answering you with a form letter, but I get so many requests like yours that is the only way. It is either this, or no answer at all. You perhaps do not know to what extent correspondence is restricted in a monastery like ours. Even though I have to write many more letters than the Rules provide for, I would never be able to answer everything that comes in. I will put down some notes on the things about which people generally ask, and I hope your question may get answered somewhere along the line.

First: most of the factual information you may need can be found either in the usual reference books (*Who's Who in America, Catholic Authors,* etc.) or in books of my own. *The Seven Storey Mountain* and *The Sign of Jonas* are both autobiographical. More recent information may be found in the preface to a *Thomas Merton Reader* (1962). This *Reader* is probably the handiest way of getting to know what I have written and what I think. There is a *Bibliography* of materials by and about me, edited by Frank Dell'Isola. This however goes only up to 1956.

To give you a quick rundown on the facts of my life: born in France, 1915. I was educated at grade schools in New York, Bermuda, France. In high school and prep school in France and England. I went to college at Cambridge, England and Columbia University, N.Y. I did graduate work at Columbia. I taught at Columbia and at St. Bonaventure University. Entered Trappist monastery of Gethsemani in 1941 and have been here since. Ordained priest in 1949. In the monastery I have been spiritual director of the monks studying for the priesthood (Master of Students) and Master of the Novices, that is to say I am supposed to guide and instruct the new ones who have just entered. I have them for three years, give them classes and so on. This takes most of my time.

People are always asking if I am still here. This is because all sorts of rumors go around to the effect that I have left. I haven't. I am still here. I have not been seen in any New York nightclubs for twenty-five years. I am not teaching at Columbia University now. Nor am I teaching at Georgetown,

Purdue, Chicago, Southern Methodist, Stanford, the Sorbonne or anywhere else except Gethsemani. I am not a priest in a parish in the Bronx or even in Brooklyn. I am not traveling around Chile giving retreats to nuns, etc. If you hear anything of this sort you can assume that it is for the birds.

People often ask why I am here in the first place, and what the contemplative life means to me. It means to me the search for truth and for God. It means finding the true significance of my life, and my right place in God's creation. It means renouncing the way of life that is led in the "world" and which, to me, is a source of illusions, confusion and deceptions. However I say this only for myself, and I have no criticism of anyone who seeks truth elsewhere and by some other way of life, provided that they really seek the truth. There are all kinds of ways to God, and ours is only one of the many. But it seems to be the one for me, and it is the one I have chosen and accepted as God's will. There are three gifts I have received, for which I can never be grateful enough: first, my Catholic faith; second, my monastic vocation; third, the calling to be a writer and share my beliefs with others. I have never had the slightest desire to be anything else but a monk, since I first came here. But I have often thought I would like an even more solitary life than we have in the monastery. I think solitude and silence are very important elements which are sadly neglected in the life of modern man, and if you want to find out more of what I think about this, there are books like *Thoughts in Solitude, New Seeds of Contemplation, The Wisdom of the Desert* and parts of *Disputed Questions.* If you want to find out about the monastic life, besides *The Sign of Jonas* you can also consult *The Silent Life, The Waters of Siloe,* and some of the pamphlets published here at the monastery, like *Monastic Peace.* I would be glad to send you one if you want it, as a present.

For those who ask what I think about poetry (I write poetry), there is an essay published in my *Selected Poems* which deals with poetry and the contemplative life. At one time I thought I ought to give up writing poetry because it might not be compatible with the life of a monk, but I don't think this anymore. People ask me how I write poetry. I just write it. I get an idea and I put it down, and add to it, and take away what is useless, and try to end up with some kind of poem. A poem is for me the expression of an inner poetic experience, and what matters is the experience, more than the poem itself. Some of my favorite poets are St.-John Perse (Alexis Léger), F. Garcia Lorca, Dylan Thomas, Gerard Manley Hopkins, Boris Pasternak, William Blake, John Donne, Dante, Shakespeare, Tu Fu, Isaias, Aeschylus, Sophocles, etc.

To those who ask what I think about art, there are a couple of essays on the subject in *Disputed Questions*. I like modern art. I have always liked such painters as Picasso, Chagall, Cézanne, Rouault, Matisse, and so on. I like expressionists and impressionists and post-impressionists and abstract expressionists and most of the other "-ists" but I don't like social realism. Nor do I like candy-box art or the illustrations in the *Saturday Evening Post*. I am not prepared to enter into an argument in defense of these preferences.

Some may want to know what I think about politics. I think that we citizens of the United States, as a nation, ought to make more serious efforts to act our age and think in proportion to our size. For this, a whole lot of people who never thought about anything serious in their lives are going to have to wake up and start thinking about their moral and political responsibilities. It is no good going on emotions and prejudices and slogans and feelings of righteous indignation. It is no good simply letting our minds become a passive reflection of a television screen. It is no good going around shouting something that someone else has suggested that we shout, no matter what it may be. If we want to become a seriously political nation, the people have got to do some thinking for themselves.

I think two issues in this country are extremely serious: one, the race issue; two, the question of nuclear war. The second one is worse than the first but both of them are pretty bad. I do not believe that people who fight for integration are all Communists. I do not think that people who are opposed to nuclear war are necessarily enemies of America and paid agents of Communism. I do not think that military might is the solution to our problems. It may defend our pocket books, but it will never defend our liberty. Liberty begins inside your own souls. Our souls cannot be free if we believe only in money and power and comfort and having a good time. I do not think that our present line of action is doing anything to keep us free.

Doubtless I could go on to explain what I think about Jazz (I like it); the movies (haven't seen one for years, don't miss them); smoking (don't miss it); TV (never watched it, don't want to); the newspapers (seldom see one);

modern youth (I like them, at least the kind we've got around here—they are the only ones I know); cars (I never had one); wives (never had one, can get along without). There must be some other things about which I ought to have an opinion, but this is enough.

Once again, I am sorry I cannot answer you personally, but I think by now you understand. I will be praying for you. God bless you, pray for me too.

TO JONATHAN WILLIAMS   *American poet and essayist Jonathan Williams visited Merton at Gethsemani in January 1967. They were joined by poet Guy Davenport and photographer Ralph Eugene Meatyard. Merton dubbed the trio "the three kings from Lexington."*

MAY 19, 1967

. . . I have been held up in writing the current curriculum [vitae]. I am bad at writing these things, "born on a chimney top in Strasbourg in 1999" etc., but you can select what you want from this one, there is plenty of choice. . . .

—Curriculum vitae Merton, May 1967

Born 1915 in Southern France a few miles from Catalonia so that I imagine myself by birth Catalan and am accepted as such in Barcelona where I have never been. Exiled therefore from Catalonia I came to New York, then went to Bermuda, then back to France, then to school at Montauban, then to school at Oakham in England, to Clare College Cambridge where my scholarship was taken away after a year of riotous living, to Columbia University New York where I earned two degrees of dullness and wrote a Master's thesis on Blake. Taught English among Franciscan football players at St. Bonaventure University, and then became a Trappist monk at Gethsemani Ky. in 1941. First published book of poems 1944. Autobiography 1948 created a general hallucination followed by too many pious books. Back to poetry in the fifties and sixties. Gradual backing away from the monastic institution until I now live alone in the woods not claiming to be anything, except of course a Catalan. But a Catalan in exile who would not return to Barcelona under any circumstances, never having been there. Recently published *Raids on the Unspeakable, Conjectures of a Guilty Bystander, Mystics and Zen Masters,* have translated work of poets like Vallejo, Alberti,

Hernández, Nicanor Parra etc. Proud of facial resemblance to Picasso and/ or Jean Genet or alternately Henry Miller (though not so much Miller).

TO SISTER J.M.   JUNE 17, 1968

First, your division won't work. The only things I wrote before my conversion were juvenile pieces published in college magazines. And maybe a book review or two. None of it counts for anything.

I'd rather divide as follows: from my conversion in 1938 to my ordination in 1949—that is, up to *Seven Storey Mountain, Waters of Siloe,* etc., when I suddenly got to be well known, a best-seller, etc. Then a long period until somewhere in the early sixties, a transition period which would end somewhere around *Disputed Questions.* During the first period, after entering the monastery, I was totally isolated from all outside influences and was largely working with what I had accumulated before entering. [I drew] on the experience of the monastic life in my early days when I was quite ascetic, "first fervor" stuff, and when the life at Gethsemani was very strict. This resulted in a highly unworldly, ascetical, intransigent, somewhat apocalyptic outlook. Rigid, arbitrary separation between God and the world, etc. Most people judge me entirely by this period, either favorably or unfavorably, and do not realize that I have changed a great deal. The second period was a time when I began to open up again to the world, began reading psychoanalysis (Fromm, Horney, etc.), Zen Buddhism, existentialism and other things like that, also more literature. But the fruits of this did not really begin to appear until the third period, after *Disputed Questions.* This resulted in books like *Seeds of Destruction, Raids on the Unspeakable, Conjectures of a Guilty Bystander, Emblems of a Season of Fury, [The Way of]Chuang Tzu,* etc. It appears that I am now evolving further, with studies on Zen and a new kind of experimental creative drive in prose poetry, satire, etc.

Characteristic books of first period: *Secular Journal, Thirty Poems, Man in the Divided Sea, Seven Storey Mountain, Seeds of Contemplation.*

Characteristic of second: *No Man Is an Island, Sign of Jonas, Thoughts in Solitude, Silent Life, Strange Islands.*

Third period—I've mentioned them above I guess, and (I might add) important to some extent is the introduction to *Gandhi on Non-Violence.* I guess the essay on Pasternak in *Disputed Questions* might throw light on it. Also see Preface to *Thomas Merton Reader* and interview in *Motive* (reprint in *U.S. Catholic* for March [1968]).

Yes, I have a lot of critics, particularly among Catholics. These are usually people who have seen one aspect of my work which they don't like. Most of them are put off by the fact that I sound at times like a Catholic Norman Mailer. I get on better with non-Catholics, particularly the younger generation, students, hippies, etc. At the same time there is always a solid phalanx of people who seem to get a lot out of the early books up to about *Thoughts in Solitude,* and have never heard of the others. These tend to be people interested in the spiritual life and somewhat conservative in many ways. Hence the curious fact that there are by and large two Mertons: one ascetic, conservative, traditional, monastic. The other radical, independent, and somewhat akin to beats and hippies and to poets in general. Neither one of these appeals to the current pacesetters for Catholic thought and life in the U.S. today. Some of them respect me, others think I'm nuts, none of them really dig me. Which is perfectly all right. Where I fit seems to be in the sort of niche provided by the *The Catholic Worker*—and outside that, well, the literary magazines whether little or otherwise. Mostly little. And New Directions, [the publishing house] where I have always been.

I guess that's about it. Looking back on my work, I wish I had never bothered to write about one-third of it—the books that tend to be (one way or the other) "popular" religion. Or "inspirational." But I'll stand by things like *Seeds of Contemplation* (as emended in *New Seeds*). *Seven Storey Mountain* is a sort of phenomenon, not all bad, not all good, and it's not something I could successfully repudiate even if I wanted to. Naturally I have reservations about it because I was young then and I've changed. . . .

PART 2

Becoming and Being a Monk

Reflections on the Monastic Life

"As I reflect over the past and over God's grace in my life there are only two things that are more or less certain to me: that I have been called to be at once a writer and a solitary. . . ."

—To Dom Jean-Baptiste Porion, March 26, 1964

Thomas Merton first visited the Monastery of Our Lady of Gethsemani to make a retreat during Holy Week, 1941. He returned on December 7, 1941—this time to stay. Entering the monastery was but the beginning of Merton's journey. Having chosen to become a Trappist monk, he spent the rest of his life discovering what his monastic vocation demanded of him. For twenty-seven years, until his death on December 10, 1968, Merton lived the simple life of a Trappist monk, striving to be faithful to the vows of obedience, stability, and conversion of life. The letters reprinted here in chronological order offer a glimpse of Merton's experience and deepening understanding of the monastic life. These letters capture the spirit and enthusiasm of the earnest and sometimes naïve young monk, document the tension he felt between being a monk and a writer, and voice his persistent longing for solitude as he confesses his love for and frustrations with life at Gethsemani, shares his dreams and plans to go elsewhere to live as a monk, and revels in being granted permission to live as a hermit on the monastery's grounds.

Deeply immersed in the Christian monastic tradition, Merton became a spokesperson for monastic renewal—a renewal that would at once honor the past and respond to the challenges of the future. Merton's candid reflections on the monastic life include exchanges with fellow monks and men and women religious. The letters of his later years document his attempts to express what it means to be a monk in very contemporary terms to individuals unfamiliar with what the life of a monk entails and, in some cases, skeptical of its value. A sampling of these letters, entitled "Monasticism in Translation," concludes this section.

TO ABBOT JAMES FOX, O.C.S.O. *Dom James Fox, O.C.S.O., succeeded Abbot Frederic Dunne, O.C.S.O., in August 1948 and served as abbot until January 1968. At that time, he retired to a hermitage of his own, where he lived until his death in 1987 at the age of ninety-one.*

[SPRING 1949]

Another protocol from Chop Suey Louie the mad Chinese poet.

It is just to say that I am picturing that immediate goal that Dr. de Quevedo [visiting psychiatrist] wants us all to aim at. What is it? It is this:

a very obscure, quiet, unknown, unnoticed monk: a little guy who goes quietly around without attracting any attention for anything whatever, not complaining about anything and not expressing opinions, doing what he is told and being completely docile and blank as far as the exterior goes—except of course for a happy sort of an expression. I want to be as near as possible to nothing and nobody in the community—and everywhere else too—as a monk can possibly be. The reason for my wanting this is that I am altogether sick of myself and I want to do everything I can to cease existing as an ego outside of God.

I do not aim at the heights, I aim at the depths. Not at what is exalted and spectacular but what is humble and unenviable and unattractive and blank. I aspire to become a nonentity and to be forgotten. In the present situation it will take a little deliberate work to get to be that way and I don't see quite how to go about it, but anyway I'll make an honest effort, and ask Jesus to show me the rest of the way. I have got more to get rid of than anybody else in the community.

May God bless you, Rev. Father, and give you grace to guide and lead this great big community. No man can do it. God has got to do the job. But He will. And I will keep seeing Him there, doing the job. And I'll cooperate by disappearing into His will and being whatever He wants me to become which, I hope, is nothing.

MAY DAY OF RECOLLECTION 1949

I am glad to be having this day of recollection before ordination, instead of after. My personal ideal in the priesthood is one of complete obscurity and simplicity. I ask Jesus to make me a purely contemplative priest. He has plenty of active workers, missionaries, preachers, spiritual directors, masters of novices, etc. But He has so few who are concerned with Him alone, in simplicity, silence, recollection and constant prayer. I beg Him daily that I may always be one of those few, and that I may live the life of pure union with Him that was led by the forgotten saints.

I want to be a forgotten and unknown saint, hidden in God alone. I feel entirely out of sympathy with all the activity and noise of our day and age. Publicity may be necessary for the Church, but I beg God to spare me from it, and from all the constant movement and action and preaching and talking and business and display which seem to have become part of Christian as well as worldly life. All that is not for me. . . .

TO DOM HUMPHREY PAWSEY, O. CART.   *Dom Humphrey Pawsey, O.Cart., a monk of the St. Hugh's Charterhouse in England, became superior of the Carthusian foundation at Sky Farm, in Vermont. Seeking deeper solitude and attracted to the eremetical life, Merton wrote to Dom Pawsey in 1952 to ask if there was "any chance of [his] being accepted as a Carthusian."*

JUNE 21, 1949

. . . One reason why I have not written to you is that I have been too ashamed of myself. Perhaps you have heard some rumor of the awful notoriety that has descended upon me as the result of having suddenly become a "best seller" as an author. My Superiors—meaning especially the late dear Dom Frederic [Dunne], God rest his soul—had me write a book which happened to be my own story. I wrote it, for better or for worse, and it has already sold two hundred thousand copies. An English edition, somewhat chastened by the critical talent of Evelyn Waugh, has now appeared and if you have not seen *Elected Silence*, I shall have the publisher send you a copy. Over here it was called *The Seven Storey Mountain*. What is stranger still, a book on contemplation which is strictly ascetic and mystical and in no sense popular [*Seeds of Contemplation*] is now being devoured by the public of this land, selling especially in Hollywood, of all places. I utterly give up trying to understand what is going on.

Perhaps you can guess, dear Father, that, all joking aside, this situation is extremely painful for me and is the occasion of a deep interior struggle which makes me ask myself if I can possibly continue in an atmosphere of such activity in which, for instance, one is liable to be called up on the telephone by newspaper reporters and in which a house full of retreatants is thirsting for autographs. . . .

TO ABBOT JAMES FOX   [SUMMER 1949]

. . . You can guess that the two hours between 2 and 4 p.m. Sunday afternoon, when you let me go out into the woods, were two of the happiest hours I have ever spent in my life. When I am alone, Jesus is with me at once. I am "never less alone than when I am alone." When people are around, I find it a little difficult to find Jesus. As soon as I am away from others, Jesus is there and all is at peace.

I think that in those two hours I understood things I had never known before about Gethsemani and about my own vocation. It helps a great deal to see Gethsemani from the outside. Inside we are so close to one another and to our own little interests that things get out of perspective. . . .

SEPTEMBER 10, 1949

Hoping this will not be too late to catch you at Citeaux [in France], I am enclosing some notes which I wrote out for Fr. Timothy [Vander Vennet] with suggestions for building up our theological course next year. You may have time to meditate on them on a train or somewhere—and perhaps you might see fit to submit them to someone in the know over there and get their reaction. The idea is of course to make Gethsemani, as you said, a sort of West Point or Annapolis for Cistercians. We should really organize our little seminary and make the house a center of really first-class studies in spiritual theology, especially Cistercian Fathers and mystical theology, with stress also on the canon law and other points so necessary for future superiors. This really involves a sort of long-term plan. It should be something settled and definite and in my opinion it would almost merit a small, separate seminary building where there would be plenty of space for classes and study, quiet atmosphere and so on. It is so hard to get away from organ practicing, power lawn-mowers, tractors, etc., and although I am pretty impervious to noise I still feel the strain of working with the traxcavator going. It would be easier on students' nerves, etc. One extremely important element about this plan would be to expand the range of studies *without putting an inhuman burden* on the students. In many cases the classes would have to be discussion groups in which texts would be read and commented on then and there, with each one offering his own little contribution. This would minimize the danger of boys going off and cramming their heads with facts and cracking their brains with memory work and just generating a whole lot of nervous tension, without any outlet or expression for what is going on inside their heads. I believe that is one of the big sources of nervous trouble in our life. . . .

TO DOM JEAN LECLERCQ, O.S.B. *A Benedictine monk and scholar on Clervaux, Luxembourg, Dom Jean Leclercq, O.S.B., was an authority on St. Bernard of Clairvaux. Merton's letters to Leclercq became more personal as Merton confided that his hunger for deeper solitude had led him to consider becoming a Carthusian and a Camaldolese monk. Merton last saw Dom Leclercq at a conference of monks in Bangkok, Thailand, where Merton died on December 10, 1968.*

APRIL 22, 1950

. . . I might wish that your travels would bring you to this side of the Atlantic and that we might have the pleasure of receiving you at Gethsemani. We have just remodeled the vault where our rare books are kept and have extended its capacities to include a good little library on Scripture and the Fathers and the Liturgy—or at least the nucleus of one. Here I hope to form a group of competent students not merely of history or of texts but rather in line with the tradition which you so admirably represent—men competent in all-round spiritual theology, as well as scholarship, using their time and talents to develop the seed of the word of God in their souls, not to choke it under an overgrowth of useless research as is the tradition in the universities of this country at the moment. . . .

OCTOBER 9, 1950

. . . Cistercian monasticism in America is of a genus all its own. Imagine that we now have one hundred and fifty novices at Gethsemani. This is fantastic. Many of them are sleeping in a tent in the préau. The nucleus of seniors is a small, bewildered group of men who remember the iron rule of Dom Edmond Obrecht [Abbot of Gethsemani, 1898–1935] and have given up trying to comprehend what has happened to Gethsemani. The house has a very vital and enthusiastic (in the good sense) and youthful air, like the camp of an army preparing for an easy and victorious war. Those of us who have been sobered by a few years of the life find ourselves in turns comforted and depressed by the multitude of our young companions of two and three months' standing: comforted by their fervor and joy and simplicity, and depressed by the sheer weight of numbers. The cloister is as crowded as a Paris street. . . .

TO ABBOT JAMES FOX   OCTOBER 7, 1951—FEAST OF THE HOLY ROSARY

This is a report on our private retreat from September 29 to October 6. . . . I spent every afternoon (except Wednesday—all-out work) outside in the woods. The morning was devoted to quiet work, trying to organize things in the vault, typing up some notes, etc. I would go out each day right after dinner and return in time for Vespers. This usually gave me three and a half hours of solid prayer in solitude. I took a book along but scarcely ever read more than a page of it. Most of the time I just entered into the presence of God and stayed quiet and let the silence sink in. Most of the time it was pretty quiet, but sometimes the traxcavator was making a lot of noise. In any case I got a lot of silent prayer. Saturday you gave me permission to try a day in the woods. I was out from Sext until Vespers (that made about seven hours in complete silence and solitude). The effect of this silence and solitary prayer, especially the last day, has been very great.

. . . As the week went on, and especially on the last long day in the woods, something else, something deep, began to get a grip on me inside. . . . I can sum up the last day in the woods by saying that I just got smaller and smaller and dwindled down to nothing in the presence of God. . . .

TO DOM JEAN-BAPTISTE PORION, O. CART.   *A Carthusian monk of Le Grande Chartreuse in France, Dom Jean-Baptiste Porion became the Procurator General of the Carthusian Order.*

FEBRUARY 9, 1952

For my own part, as you know, the betrayal of our deep self that sometimes takes place in our effort to communicate with others exteriorly, has long been a problem. It is not easy for a writer to learn to live, interiorly, without a witness, without a potential reader. But once this intruder is expelled, we truly find ourselves, and find God—and find other men in

God. We betray ourselves and one another in the No Man's Land which exists between human beings, and into which they go out to meet one another disguised in words. And yet without words we cannot find ourselves, without communication with men we do not know God: *fides ex auditu* [faith comes from hearing]. . . .

TO DOM GABRIEL SORTAIS, O.C.S.O.   *Merton served as translator for Dom Gabriel Sortais, O.C.S.O., when the abbot of Bellefontaine in France visited Gethsemani in 1948. Dom Sortais was elected Abbot General of the Cistercian Order in 1951. Merton's extensive correspondence with Dom Sortais documents Merton's vocational crises as well as his struggles with censorship. Merton's writings were subject to the approval of the censors of the Order, who sought to ensure orthodoxy as well as a sense of monastic propriety, which dictated a sense of what was and was not appropriate form and content for a monk. Faced with the censors' objections, Merton made his case directly to Dom Sortais. In 1962, Dom Sortais issued the order forbidding Merton to publish on the subject of war.*

JULY 23, 1952

Our publisher, Harcourt, Brace and Company, has just sent you the manuscript of our journal, *The Sign of Jonas.* At the same time they have set to work to prepare the edition, while awaiting all the changes that your censor will want to suggest to us. Another manuscript is in the hands of one of our American censors. We do believe you will leave intact the essence of this work. To me the essential is this: one must be able to trace the thread of a history, of an interior development unfolding itself in it: the development of a young religious who is moving towards the priesthood, asking himself rather frank questions about his contemplative vocation, about Gethsemani: who sees his questions being solved under the invisible hand of Divine Providence *disponens omnia suaviter et fortiter* [arranging all things sweetly and mightily], and lastly a series of meditations, of "elevations" if you like, or even sort of hymns in prose. . . .

You had told me, in the form of advice, without seeming to attach much importance to it, that perhaps I should not go on writing this journal. If this *is* your will, I shall not write it anymore. But if you see no objection, perhaps I could pursue this very easy work. It is almost the only way to produce something with all my other offices which look like obstacles. The publishers urge me strongly. . . .

. . . The theme of the book is precisely the thirst for God which should be the very heart of Cistercian life, and at the same time I present it all not in ideal terms but in the concrete ambient of an actual monastery, just as it is, with its faults (though I do not dwell on them) and with all the charm of our Cistercian life into the bargain. A word from you would reassure the readers that the Order itself always tries to look at things from a concrete and integrated point of view, that we have never deceived ourselves by pretending to be angels on earth, but that we know that Christian perfection and union with God must be realized in the treadmill of this daily life which is not always the ideal, and that God, in short, allows Himself to be found *in normal life,* provided this life is truly the life of grace and that we endeavor to live it thoroughly, and with no pretense, seeking God and nothing else! I do not say I am more honest than the others. On the contrary, I think this journal is indeed the witness of a perfectly ordinary religious, i.e. ordinarily not perfect! And I think, my Brothers in the Order—at least those who, like me, are not saints—will be able to find themselves in it. . . .

TO ABBOT JAMES FOX   JANUARY 20, 1953

I thought we ought to have a name for the new "refuge" [an old toolshed moved to a wooded hill overlooking the hills to the east] and I chose the name *St. Anne's,* if you approve.

Having been out here almost all day for two days, I find time goes by much too fast, and it is always time to go home much too soon. It is the first time in my life—37 years—that I have had a real conviction of doing what I am really called by God to do. It is the first time I have ever felt that I have "arrived"—like a river that has been running through a deep canyon and now has come out into the plains—and is within sight of the ocean.

Funnily enough, it is out here that I have for the first time discovered the real Benedictine values as they are meant to be. *Silence, simplicity, poverty, peace,* and above all I seem to be much more able to keep my eye on the *will of God.* Out here there is no complexity and no confusion—there is no contradiction between work and prayer, everything is in unity and all is truly centered in God. . . .

to Dom Gabriel Sortais   March 13, 1953

. . . In principle, my Most Reverend Father, any work as a writer should be for us *rare and exceptional*. If you want to know what I frankly think, before God, in my own case, I will tell you this: what I find most embarrassing is to try to do a scholar's job, to speak as an historian, a dogmatic theologian, etc. I also have more or less given up writing as a *poet*, but sometimes an idea may come, it gets written, so to speak, of its own accord, and it helps to *deepen some insight* about God, about the spiritual life, etc. Also fragments of meditations, *impersonal and objective*, upon the truths of faith, our relations with God. It is these fragments (in the line of *Seeds of Contemplation*) that seem to me to be our affair, if we write anything at all. But if I must go on working along this line it will remain, for me, as for the others, *rare and exceptional!* . . .

to Dom Gregorio Lemercier, O.S.B.   *Benedictine monk Dom Gregorio Lemercier was the superior of an experimental monastery in Cuernavaca, Mexico. Merton was interested in the community and, for a time in the late 1950s, considered going to Mexico to live there as a monk.*

October 23, 1953

. . . I have had a chance to verify the effects of machine work on the spiritual life of individuals. . . . It dulls the sense of spiritual things. A monk who spends his work time constantly with a machine has no taste for silence outside his time of work. He is careless about the way he walks, how he handles things, slams doors, throws books down roughly and so forth. There may be a genuine spirit of sacrifice, but the spirit of prayer becomes coarse and thick-skinned. The delicate sensitivity to the inner motions of the Holy Spirit loses all its keenness, and is replaced by another spirit—tense, hard, complicated, cold. . . .

TO ABBOT JAMES FOX   NOVEMBER 29, 1954

. . . The more I see others leaving here, the more I am strengthened in the conviction that I should stay and do what God wants me to do *here*, even though it may seem like being a square peg in a round hole, and may win me the disfavor of some, plus contradiction and criticism. Provided only that I really do God's will and not my own. I hope you will always tell me frankly when I am not doing what you want, because that is my one big safeguard, on which everything depends. . . .

TO DOM JEAN LECLERCQ   JUNE 3, 1955

Many thanks for your letter of May 26. I wish I had received it sooner. Early in May, having consulted the Carthusian Father Dom Verner Moore at Sky Farm, I received from him a very positive encouragement to transfer to Camaldoli and my director here thought I should follow this suggestion, so I applied for a transitus. So far nothing has been heard from Italy however, and Father Abbot is very much opposed to my going to Camaldoli, and I suppose his objections may lead to the refusal of the *transitus*, although the Abbot General says he feels that if it is the will of God he sees no reason for my not going. Things are still in a fluid state however, and with Father Abbot I am earnestly trying to reach the final solution. One thing is certain, everyone more and more seems to agree that I should not stay in the precise situation in which I find myself at the moment. I honestly believe, and so do my directors, that being a cenobite is no longer the thing I need. However, I have no desire to become a preacher of retreats at Camaldoli either, still less an exploited celebrity, although I do feel that even then I would have far more solitude and silence there than I have here. I may be wrong.

However, Dom James is very interested in the question and he has even proposed to place before higher Superiors the possibility of my becoming a hermit in the forest here. If this permission were ever granted it would solve all my problems, I think. The forest here is very lonely and quiet and covers about a thousand acres, and there is much woodland adjoining it. It is as wild as any country that would be found in the Ardennes or the

Vosges, perhaps wilder. I could be a hermit without leaving the land of the monastery. One could begin the project gradually and imperceptibly, for the government is putting up a fire-observation tower on one of our hills and the future hermitage could be in connection with this. One could begin simply by being the watchman on the tower and gradually take up permanent residence there. Unfortunately the higher Superiors, as far as I can see, are absolutely closed to any such suggestion and even refuse to permit a monk to work alone on the observation tower. Dom James is placing the matter before the Abbot General. . . .

I value your prayers in this time of mystery and searching. It is more and more evident to me that someone must go through this kind of thing. By the mercy of God, I am one of those who must pass through the cloud and the sea. May I be one of those who also reach the Promised Land. Whatever happens, I shall certainly write much less and I have no desire to become a "literary hermit." I feel that God wills this solitude in American conversation, even if someone has to leave America temporarily to find it. . . .

AUGUST 11, 1955

. . . At the moment, it does seem that there is a real chance of my being allowed to live in solitude here. Higher Superiors have softened their rigid opposition to some extent, at least admitting the eremitical solution in theory. But Dom James, my Father Abbot, is showing himself more and more favorable to the idea, and I believe that insofar as it may depend on him, I can hope for this permission. Meanwhile on the material side, the way seems to be preparing itself. The State Forestry Department is erecting a fire-lookout tower on one of our big hills, a steep wooded eminence in our forest, dominating the valley by about 400 feet. I have been put in charge of this work with them, and they are going to erect a small cabin there, in which one might conceivably live. It will be an austere and primitive kind of hermitage, if I ever get to live in it. In any case, I depend on your prayers and those of all who are interested in helping me, that Our Lord may be good to me, and if it be His will that I may live alone in our forest. In the meantime I think I can count on a semi-solitary life for part of the year as the watchman on this fire tower. That will be beautiful—unless it is disapproved by higher Superiors. . . .

I have stopped writing, and that is a big relief. I intend to renounce it
for good, if I can live in solitude. I realize that I have perhaps suffered more
than I know from this "writing career." Writing is deep in my nature, and
I cannot deceive myself that it will be very easy for me to do without it. At
least I can get along without the public and without my reputation! Those
are not essentially connected with the writing instinct. But the whole business tends to corrupt the purity of one's spirit of faith. It obscures the clarity of one's view of God and of divine things. . . .

The main purpose of this letter is this: I am cleaning out my files. There
is one manuscript which I think ought to interest you for your "Tradition
Monastique." It is a short, simple collection of meditations on solitude
which I wrote two years ago when I had a kind of hermitage near the monastery. I still have it, but it is no longer quiet. Machines are always working
near it, and there is a perpetual noise. Nobody uses it very much, except
on feast days. But at any rate these pages on solitude are perhaps worth
sending to you. They will make a small volume, better I think than *Seeds of
Contemplation* and more unified. Tentatively I am calling it simply *Solitude*
[published as *Thoughts in Solitude*].

DECEMBER 3, 1955

. . . Will He some day bring me after all to perfect solitude? I do not know.
One thing is sure, I have made as much effort in that direction as one can
make without going beyond the limits of obedience. My only task now is to
remain quiet, abandoned, and in the hands of God. I have found a surpris-
ing amount of interior solitude among my novices [Merton was appointed
Master of Novices in September 1955], and even a certain exterior solitude
which I had not expected. This is, after all, the quietest and most secluded
corner of the monastery. . . .

FEBRUARY 6, 1956

. . . My new life as master of novices progresses from day to day. It is an
unfamiliar existence to which I often have difficulty in adapting myself. I
sometimes feel overcome with sheer horror at having to talk so much and
appear before others as an example. I believe that God is testing the quality

of my desire for solitude, in which perhaps there was an element of escape from responsibility. But nevertheless the desire remains the same, the conflict is there, but there is nothing I can do but ignore it and press forward to accomplish what is evidently the will of God. . . .

TO DOM GABRIEL SORTAIS   JULY 5, 1957

. . . We have at present three priests from South America in the novitiate, and a postulant who as a poet is fairly well-known in Nicaragua [Ernesto Cardenal]. . . .

. . . I think it would be a great grace for me if I could offer myself to help make a foundation in South America, if it is God's will. I tell myself from time to time that maybe I don't have the health, etc., and above all that I don't have enough virtue, and that maybe I am deluding myself, but the Holy Spirit may see to it, and He will settle everything if it is God's will. . . .

TO JAIME ANDRADE   *Ecuadorian artist Jaime Andrade was commissioned to sculpt a statue of the Blessed Virgin and Child for the novitiate library. It mattered to Merton that the sculpture be the work of an Ibero-American artist: "If I have the mission to form contemplative monks—above all some Ibero-American vocations—I have the duty to form them not according to a dead formalism, but according to the inspiration of the Spirit of Truth, who speaks not only in words and abstract ideas but above all in the concrete, in the 'incarnation' of the Divine Logos in humanity."*

MARCH 3, 1958

. . . You are a sculptor: I am a monk and a priest: this means we are both consecrated men, men with a vocation that is more or less *prophetic;* this means that we should be witnesses to the truth, not only to intellectual truth, but to mystic truth, the integral truth of life, of history, of man—of God. We should be witnesses to the *Incarnation,* but that does not mean that we should be occupied with the contemplation of a nice, sentimental [Christmas] "Nativity." The Nativity of God in the world develops in the history of man. The Christ lives in the history of the people, not of rich and powerful people, not of powerful peoples, no, but in that of the poor. The advent of God in the world and the judgment of the world takes place in each moment of history.

So, for me, the "Nativity" of God, of the poor and unknown God, of the powerful and majestic God, Savior and Judge, can be contemplated in the Indian of the Andes, and in all the peoples of South America (as in all the peoples of the world). Here we are "contemplatives"—or we should be. So then, the novice who enters this monastery should see, not the sweet and false image of the Holy Virgin, but the reality—the Virgin Mother of the Indians of the Andes, holding in her arms the Christ incarnated in the flesh and blood of the true America, and of the Indians who received us and fed us centuries ago so that we would be Americans like themselves. . . . we should learn to see God not only in the old forms, almost dead, of a Europe whose historic mission is coming to an end, but incarnated in the forms of the country whose mission is in the future. . . .

JULY 1958

. . . I would like to embark on a new form of monastic life, a very simple kind of life, a small monastery of six or seven very carefully chosen monks with the same aspirations: living for instance in the country near Quito a life fully integrated in the life of the region, and in the soil, yet also fully in contact with the intellectual life of the Capital.

I would *not* carry on any special "work" or "apostolate" (this is where the mistake is generally made by so many). I would not have any arguments to sell to anybody; I would not try to "catch" people and make them go to confession, etc. Preferably I would not even dress as a priest or as a monk, but as an ordinary person. I would live a life of prayer, of thought, of study, with manual labor, and writing, a life not only in contact with God in contemplation but also fully in contact with all the intellectual, artistic, political movements of the time and place. But I would not intrude into the life of the place as one with a "mission" or a "message"; I would not try to sell anybody anything. My function would be (as it must be in any case) to be a man of God, a man belonging to Christ, in simplicity, to be the friend of all those who are interested in spiritual things, whether of art, or prayer, or *anything valid,* simply to be their friend, to be someone who could speak to them and to whom they could speak, to encourage one another, etc. . . .

So I ask you in all simplicity: what do you think of the idea of a small monastery near Quito, a monastery that would be a retreat of silence as it should be, a place of simplicity and work and study, and also a place where ideas and problems could be discussed, or where one could come just for a rest? I would try to make money for it by writing, and there might be a kind of educational project of some kind. But mainly I think just of *being* there with those who are there, and to be in contact with everybody who would want that kind of contact, and without any *arrière pensée* [ulterior motive]. . . .

Basically, also, I am a revolutionist—in a broad, non-violent sense of the word. I believe that those who have used violence have betrayed all true revolution, they have changed nothing, they have simply enforced with greater brutality the anti-spiritual and anti-human drives that are destructive of truth and love in man. I believe that the true revolution must come slowly and painfully, not merely from the peasant, etc., but from the true artist and intellectual . . . from the thinker and the man of prayer.

NOVEMBER 20, 1958

. . . Ideally speaking, the kind of monastery I imagine would have not only a cultural mission but also a social one. Our aim would be to strive, to some extent, to lift up the Indians physically, morally, spiritually by providing a clinic, encouraging education, cooperatives, art-projects. The monastery would be perhaps the nucleus of a farming community of Indians. What I am saying now, of course, is more a project than a definite plan. . . .

On October 29, 1958, Merton sent Dom Gabriel Sortais a copy of a letter he had written to Aleksei Surkov, protesting the expulsion of Boris Pasternak from the Union of the Soviet Writers after Pasternak was named the winner of the Nobel Prize for Literature.

TO DOM GABRIEL SORTAIS   JANUARY 26, 1959

. . . Why did I get interested in Pasternak? Out of sheer curiosity? This
is what you seem to believe. On the contrary, it seems to me that there is
in Pasternak an element that is deeply spiritual and deeply religious. This
is no illusion, everyone acknowledges it. Besides, he has written some religious poems which are among the greatest, the most profound, and the
most Christian of the century. Good enough.

While nearly everyone believed that Pasternak's revolt was political or
literary, the stance that I chose to take in my article was that his revolt was
a-political, anti-political and in truth spiritual. Not only spiritual but Christian. In taking such a position I never for an instant had the feeling that I
was betraying my Christian or my contemplative vocation. On the contrary,
I believe that my vocation as a contemplative writer *demands* this kind of
testimony of me. . . .

It does seem to me, I must add, that the voice of a monk might well
be the one necessary to point out the religious significance of Pasternak's
works. It may be that I am wrong. I am quite willing to accept that. But at
any rate I assure you that, in writing about the Christ of Pasternak, I found
myself face to face with the Christ whom you accuse me of not loving. . . .

                                                          MARCH 2, 1959

. . . I leave the judgment to you, but it seems to me that I have a very serious duty to complete my article on Pasternak and to put the whole truth on
paper. And to publish it. It is a question of giving a Christian explanation
of Pasternak's witness which is both heroic and Christian. This affair has
moved the hearts of everyone, but most profoundly it has touched those
who are writers and intellectuals. It is about an event that has happened in
the very midst of the spiritual life of our time. To dissociate myself from
involvement with this action which is so extraordinary would be for me a
betrayal: a betrayal of my particular vocation, a betrayal of Jesus Christ. At
least this is the way I feel. . . .

TO DOM JEAN LECLERCQ   NOVEMBER 19, 1959

. . . Now I shall tell you, in confidence, something more interesting and
more monastic. I have asked the Congregation of Religious for an exclaus-
tration so as to go to Mexico, and become a hermit near the Benedictine
monastery of Cuernavaca. Dom Gregorio [Lemercier] will take me on and
encourages me very much. This is really what I have been looking for for
a long time. I have good hopes of succeeding with the Congregation, but
the Superiors are dead set against this move. . . . Truly, I am who I am and
I always have the writer's temperament, but I am not going down there to
write, nor to make myself known, but on the contrary to disappear, to find
solitude, obscurity, poverty. To withdraw *above all* from the collective falsity
and injustice of the U.S. which implicate so much the church of this country and our monastery. . . .

TO DOM GABRIEL SORTAIS   APRIL 29, 1960

. . . The Holy Father [Pope John XXIII] has had sent to me, too, very
poor monk that I am, a paternal message to tell me that he approved of a
few discreet meetings in the form of colloquia or of informal retreats with
some distinguished guests who come here from time to time, and with pro-
fessors of Protestant theology, writers, etc. These are discreet, rare contacts,
but which seem to help these souls to understand the Church, or else if they
are Catholic, to deepen their love of God and their Christian faith. I assure
you that I am not launching into a new "career" but I still keep the taste and
the practice of solitude. But these restricted contacts seem to do good and
seem to help me a little, too. Naturally, it is only with Dom James' permission that I make these contacts, and according to his will.

TO MOTHER ANGELA COLLINS, O.C.D.   *Mother Angela Collins, O.C.D.,*
served as Prioress at the Louisville Carmel and later founded a Carmel (a con-
vent of Carmelite nuns) in Savannah, Georgia. Merton visited the Carmel in
Louisville, and the two became friends.

. . . My desires for solitude continue. That is to be expected. Do keep me in your prayers. I don't know what may ever come of it. Work has not yet begun on the little retreat house on the hill [this would become Merton's hermitage], but at least the contractor has been to look at the site. If we get a lot of rain, the work will be held up as they will have a hard time driving through the field up the hill. However I do get what solitude I can.

I am realizing more and more that my big task is within myself. This is imperative. I am seeing what are the depths of my pride, and what an awful obstacle it is. In the old days I used to think about this problem in unrealistic terms: confusing pride with vanity. I know I still have vanity enough, but now for the first time I am beginning to see into the naked depths of pride. There is something one cannot explain in words: this tenacious attachment to self, and the virulence of it, which would make one stop at *nothing* in order to protect this inner root of self. And to see that I do in fact do all sorts of evil, properly camouflaged, in defense of this root of self. The problem is that it is all tied up with our clinging to life itself, which of course is a good thing. The desire to *be*. But the desire in us is not only to be, but to be our own idol, to be our own end. It sounds nice on paper but it is a bit sickening in reality. Do pray for me, and don't go and tell me I am humble, because that is not true except on a superficial, exterior level. Pray for me to be humble, and really humble. Not with the fake, inert sort of humility that excuses all kinds of hidden pride and prevents us from doing God's work. But with humility that is deep and afraid of nothing, of no truth, and which is completely abandoned to God's real will. How hard that actually is. . . .

On April 26, 1962, Dom James Fox informed Merton of a directive from Dom Gabriel Sortais forbidding Merton to publish antiwar articles. On April 29, Merton wrote to James Forest: "here is the ax. . . . The orders are not more writing about peace. . . ."

. . . You have no doubt remarked that the English censors had much less difficulty in accepting an article which protests the nuclear war than the American censors. Besides, it seems to me that the American censor who so formally condemned "Peace . . . Responsibility" ["Nuclear War and Christian Responsibility"] and "Target = City" ["Target Equals City"] has really interpreted my thought wrongly. I am in no way a pacifist in the sense he condemns. On the contrary, I only say that *total* war, *massive* nuclear destruction, without distinction between the combatants and the civilians, is against Catholic moral doctrine. It is what Pius XII says very clearly, as does even the theologian whom this censor quotes textually for two pages of his report without really seeing certain nuances. . . . But it is useless to discuss these things with you. I do not want to discuss. I intend to obey quite simply.

I want to accept wholeheartedly, and with joy, the decision never to write anymore on war. Besides, this does not make me sad at all. This work is enormously difficult, quite repugnant, exhausting and unrewarding. To do nothing is very convenient, and I am relieved of it from that point of view. . . .

I am not asking for indulgence, Most Reverend Father, I only seek God's will. I am not asking you to spoil me. And moreover I will be only too happy to make the sacrifice of a completed book [*Peace in a Post-Christian Era* would not be published until 2004], which cost me a lot. I simply tell you the case, and if you want to stop it at this point, I would be very pleased. One has to finish somewhere all the same.

Anyway, whatever happened I will no longer write anything on war and peace if it is your will. I am going to try and write and publish only things that are clearly the subjects one expects from a monk.

One word to finish with: maybe you wonder why this question of war and peace worries me? In a letter that Dom James showed me yesterday, I think I see a kind of contempt for this kind of monk who strayed into a monastery only to allow his head to be filled with secular preoccupations. Perhaps it is the truth. I do not deny it, for I don't fancy I am a good monk. But may I assure you that it seemed to me I was acting at least as a Christian? I don't claim to be a good Christian: I am altogether unworthy of the graces God has given me. I don't expect to become worthy of them one day, but I try to

love Him with the heart I have, which is not very much, and no doubt for the
true monks it is somewhat a ridiculous thing, this heart, especially when one
knows well that one must not listen to the heart: but anyway I have this weakness. Now I very seriously think there is a real danger of a nuclear war, and a
massive nuclear war. Do you know what that might mean? I don't have to tell
you. The United States might "win" and survive. France and England would
not have the same luck. . . . I wanted to tell you what I thought. No doubt it
was imprudent, unscientific, preposterous. Not all think so, including atomic
scientists. There are quite a lot of very well-informed people who think I am
not altogether wrong. The article "Peace . . . Responsibility" has appeared in
Commonweal in early February. Shortly after, the Lenten pastoral of the Cardinal Archbishop of Chicago was on peace, and this pastoral contained some
ten sentences copied exactly from my article, which shows that the Cardinal
was not altogether in accord with the Father Censor.

I have told you this not by way of defense but by way of explanation. I
have written quite enough on this subject, and people know what I think: so
I am not totally responsible for what is perhaps going to happen. If you ask
for silence on this subject, and you do ask it of me, I obey willingly and with
much joy. As for the book, you can say what you think, I am not attached to
this project one way or another. . . .

MAY 26, 1962

. . . What I said clearly was this: that in war, in any war, either nuclear or
"conventional," the Popes have said that when the destruction is "massive"
and "total" and "uncontrolled," and when thousands and even millions of
human beings who have nothing to do directly with the war and who are
perhaps neutral are annihilated, it is a crime. I thought that that needed to
be said because it is not clear here. What is said by the American theologians
is that one must use strength, even nuclear, to stop the advance of the Communists. For the public, it is understood that distinctions hardly exist, or do
not exist at all. There are American generals who publicly declare themselves
ready to launch a total, massive, nuclear war against Russia any time, and that
it should be done, that we already have good reason to do it, etc.

As far as I know I am nearly the only known American Catholic writer
to have said quite plainly that this situation leaves us in an occasion of very

serious sin. I said so, and people know what I have said. If they believe for that reason that I am a Communist, too bad! . . .

TO FATHER RONALD ROLOFF, O.S.B. *Father Ronald Roloff, O.S.B., was a monk of St. John's Abbey in Collegeville, Minnesota.*

SEPTEMBER 26, 1962

. . . The big thing is, do we really seek God?

Do we really keep our vow of *conversatio morum* [conversion of life], which is the very heart of our monastic consecration? Are we really men of prayer, men living in the Spirit, men given over to the Spirit of God that He may use us as He wills, whether to dwell in us silently, to praise the Father in the liturgical assembly, to announce the message of salvation, to labor in poverty, to study divine truth?

It seems to me that we all need more and more to deepen the grasp we have of our rich monastic heritage, and the closer we get to the source, the more fruitful and splendid our lives will be, in all kinds of varied expressions and manifestations. It seems to me that the monastic life is wonderful precisely for the way it embraces so many varied approaches to God. And it would seem that what we need today are monastic communities that are more and more aware of the opportunities they possess in this regard; opportunities for special kinds of apostolate and for special kinds of contemplation, for eremitical solitude, for community projects in study and research, for special ways of poverty and labor, for peculiar forms of monastic witness, for unusual and pioneering dialogue. We have not scratched the surface of this rich land of ours that our Fathers have left us. . . .

OCTOBER 21, 1962

. . . *Conversatio morum,* then. I think this is the term that needs to be understood, because it is the very heart of the problem. It is what makes the difference between the monk and the non-monk, provided it is taken in a broader than the technical sense. I mean it should include something more than just a pledge to live in a cenobium. (I think the spirit of *conversatio morum* covers solitaries as well as monks who are in parishes.) The great thing is the monastic metanoia, the inner transformation, the newness of monastic life. Where this is effected by the grace of God and by a deep formation in a community, then I think there is nothing the monk cannot handle. The great thing is then making real monks from the inside out, as far as possible in the atmosphere of true monastic silence and prayer in their novitiate and student years, and perhaps longer. A longer, more thorough, more gradual formation in the monastic spirit to give the person a more complete command of himself under God's grace, in all the eventualities he will meet, so that he will meet them always as a man of God, living in the Spirit, and as a true monk. . . .

TO MOTHER MYRIAM DARDENNE, O.C.S.O.   *Mother Myriam Dardenne, O.C.S.O., served as Abbess of the Cistercian Monastery of Nazareth in Belgium and became Founding Superior of the Cistercian Foundation at Redwoods, California. On their way to California in 1962, Mother Dardenne and her sisters stopped at Gethsemani, where she talked with Merton. Merton visited Redwoods twice in 1968.*

DECEMBER 12, 1962

. . . We have not forgotten the joy of your visit with us. It was a grace to see in you the simplicity and good sense of the Cistercian tradition, so to speak incarnate. There is a great deal of talk about monastic tradition and monastic spirituality, but actually the reality of people who live the monastic life in simplicity is much more impressive than words about it. We do not have to have too many splendid programs and doctrines if we seek and find the Lord, and this we do not in ideals only but in the realities of life. Still I am sure that one reason why you are all functioning well is that you have approached the life intelligently and with a little knowledge. Pray that we may do the same. . . .

TO ARCHBISHOP PAUL PHILIPPE, O.P.   *Archbishop Paul Philippe, O.P., was secretary of the Sacred Congregation of Religious in Rome.*

APRIL 5, 1963

. . . It would seem that small contemplative communities are needed which, while preserving jealously their solitude and life of prayer, might also in discreet and limited ways offer opportunities for dialogue and spiritual communication with members of the surrounding society, particularly the intellectual and religious leaders, whether Christian or otherwise. There is a spiritual work of mercy which has almost become a corporal work in our time: offering to others some small share temporarily in the silence and solitude of a monastic setting. This does not mean "closed retreats" only, but a much more informal and human sharing in the benefits of the monastic milieu, perhaps without organized conferences and exercises, indeed perhaps better without them. . . .

. . . I wonder if the problems of religious orders are not really to be solved on a much deeper level than that of organization. Our problems are problems of *spirit* and not merely of *institution*. What we lack is not merely discipline but above all profound and serious *life*. To give these problems our institutional solution which once again stifles the beginnings of life is really no help at all. But to imagine that "life" is to be understood and lived on a merely physical level is another delusion. In short, our problem is not to be solved so much by *rules* as by *men* who are alive with the Spirit of the Risen Saviour and are not afraid to seek new paths guided by the light of perennial tradition and the wisdom of Mother Church. . . .

TO DOM JEAN LECLERCQ   JUNE 10, 1963

. . . Things are developing well here. . . . I received permission to take some time in solitude up at the hermitage, and so far I have had six full days up there, with more to come. Not allowed to sleep there, or say Mass there, but what I have had so far is a great godsend. It has certainly settled any doubts I may have had about the need for real solitude in my own life. Though I realize that I am not the ideal of an absolute hermit, since my solitude is partly that of an intellectual and poet, still it is a very real inclination for solitude and when I have continuous solitude for a more or less extended period, it means a great deal and is certainly the best remedy for the tensions and pressures that I generate when I am with the community. . . .

NOVEMBER 10, 1963

. . . Thanks for your two offprints. I was very touched by many of the beautiful references in your piece on "sedere." Did you know that the 14th-century English mystic Rolle was known as "the sitter"? He has some nice things about sitting as the most favorable position for contemplation. Of course the Buddhists of the Far East have many texts on this too. A Zen artist, Sengai, did a picture of a turnip with this short poem: "Turnips and Zen monks / are best when they sit well."

The one on the early history of eremitism in the West is excellent, and again it has many fine examples, as well as showing that one must not take a stereotyped view of the solitary life. For some people, the solitary life is their only way of truth, and it is *their* truth precisely insofar as it is not imposed on them from the outside . . . people like Dom Augustine Baker and Dame Gertrude More have a wonderful sense of all this. I hope to do a study on Gertrude More for Stanbrook. There is also a piece of mine on her and Baker in the *Collectanea,* coming up soon, I believe. . . .

TO FATHER CHRYSOGONUS WADDELL, O.C.S.O. *Father Chrysogonus Waddell, O.C.S.O., a monk of Gethsemani, studied in Rome and shared with Merton news of the Second Vatican Council.*

NOVEMBER 26, 1963

. . . If there is such a thing as "Mertonism," I suppose I am the one that ought to beware of it. The people who believe in this term evidently do not know how unwilling I would be to have anyone repeat in his own life the miseries of mine. That would be flatly a mortal sin against charity. I thought I had never done anything to obscure my lack of anything that a monk might conceive to be a desirable quality. Surely this lack is public knowledge, and anyone who imitates me does so at his own risk. I can promise him some fine moments of naked despair. . . .

TO FATHER RONALD ROLOFF   FEBRUARY 14, 1964

. . . The root question is the question of the authenticity of our monastic vocation. I mean this in a concrete sense again. I am not talking about the abstract value of our vocation. I am wondering if in fact we come to the monastery and *lose our monastic vocation when we have got there.* I mean, is it somehow squeezed out of us, so that we are left with a husk of outward forms and no inner vocation? Does our monastic life become so artificial and contrived that it is no longer really a life; it is just an existence which we put up with, a set of obligations which we fulfill, having as good intentions as we can muster, meanwhile looking for living interests elsewhere?

That is the trouble with the great overemphasis on monastic institutionalism. In fact, the monk comes to be for the sake of the monastery, not vice versa. The monk is a member of the organization. He cannot be fired, but he can be urged to work hard for the purposes of the organization, whatever they may be: from cheesemaking to liturgical renewal and "contemplation." In order to ensure that the monk will be more or less cooperative, he is told from morning to night that the monastic life consists purely and simply in doing what you are told. Sanctity, doing what you are told. Just do it, and keep you mouth shut, and that is all that is required. That is *everything.* It substitutes for prayer, for the spirit of prayer, for the desire of God (I use that bad word "desire"), it substitutes for meaningful activity, it substitutes for life itself.

This is not to say that obedience is not the "heart of the monastic ascesis." It is. But merely doing what you're told is not obedience. And in order to make it obedience, a "pure intention" is not sufficient either. This unfortunate oversimplification of the monastic life is what drains it of all meaning and spirit. Then, after years of going to choir because one has been told that "this is the most sublime form of prayer you could possibly imagine, just because you have been told to do it," one suddenly wakes up and finds that the official convictions themselves have vanished. Then what? Everything is drained away. There is no interest left. The whole thing is meaningless. . . .

TO FATHER FLAVIAN BURNS, O.C.S.O. *Father Flavian Burns, O.C.S.O., studied under Merton as a scholastic. Following studies in Rome, Father Burns became Master of Scholastics. He served as prior at Gethsemani and, in 1968, succeeded Dom James Fox as abbot.*

MARCH 1, 1964

... A man is not ready for solitary life until he has been able to renounce his own tendency to plan his life, and has completely committed himself to his community in a spirit of total faith. He must no longer insist on working out his own future according to his own attractions and desires. Yet he should be faithful to these desires in all their depth. Only deep faith can bridge this gap, and the faith will not be deep enough if it cannot be faith that God can and does act through the monk's own community. (Obviously there will be cases where this will not be possible at all.) If a monk always has at the back of his mind the proviso that he will one day take off and go somewhere better for a "higher life," he will never in practice make this surrender and this act of faith, and consequently if he does move, he is likely to lose everything. . . .

TO DOM JEAN-BAPTISTE PORION   MARCH 26, 1964

... As I reflect over the past and over God's grace in my life there are only two things that are more or less certain to me: that I have been called to be at once a writer and a solitary *secundum quid* [in some way]. The rest is confusion and uncertainty. At present however I do have a measure of solitude, more than I would have expected in the past, and it is the only thing that helps me to keep sane. I am grateful for this gift from God, with all the paradoxes that it entails and its peculiar interior difficulties, as well as its hidden and dry joys. I think that really there is no solitude but a solitude *secundum quid,* lodged in paradox, and that one becomes a solitary in proportion as he can accept the paradox and the irony of his position. It is the irony that is the expression of God's love in the life of the "monazon" [one who lives alone], the one who practices loneliness on purpose. The joy of the solitary is then the laughter that makes him, as the Fathers said, an Isaac, *risus,* a joke and a delight of the humor of the Lord. I wish you this joy at Easter, and know that I owe my share of it in part to your prayers.

TO FATHER GUERRIC COUILLEAU, O.C.S.O. *Father Guerric Couilleau, O.C.S.O., a Cistercian monk of Bellefontaine in France, was interested, as was Merton, in monastic renewal.*

APRIL 7, 1964

. . . A Quaker friend has said to me: why is it that you monks are not on Freedom Rides and on marches for peace, for civil rights, and so on? I have no answer except . . . shall we say inertia, infidelity or what? The answer that we are supposed to stay enclosed would be all right, if our solitude had a *seriousness corresponding to* the seriousness of the demonstrations. You may not know much about this, but in the Civil Rights movement in this country, a struggle which involves beating, danger of murder (which has frequently been carried out), and perpetual threat of jail and various forms of legal pressure, there have been Christians giving a witness that puts the monks to shame and makes our petty concern with regularity look like a gross evasion. But at the same time I am not asserting that the only thing the monk can do to be "faithful" is to leave his cloister and get involved in these things. That would lead to the most tragic deceptions, without a special charism which no one has the right to expect. But the full seriousness of our monastic life *is* demanded. The full seriousness of the life is not to be realized without an authentic and complete realization of the potentialities and demands of solitude. . . .

TO DOM DAMASUS WINZEN, O.S.B. *Dom Damasus Winzen, O.S.B., a Benedictine monk of Marialaach in Germany, founded Mount Saviour Monastery near Elmira, New York, in 1951.*

SEPTEMBER 8, 1964

. . . Yes, I completely agree that what this country so badly needs and seeks is a personal and "pneumatic" monasticism: to receive the Holy Spirit in the life of the community under a common Father who is truly *pneumatikos* and then to obey the Spirit with the guidance of the Father Abbas and the encouragement of the brethren. The great problem remains that of a system and a way of life that tends to extinguish the Spirit. It all comes to that. One feels everywhere that monks are stifled, and the open window approach of Pope John has not really caught on with the Cistercians, except in places where they are breaking down whole sides of the building (while still not opening the window). . . .

In the end I suppose it turns out that I have been called to be a monk and have somehow become one (of a sort) contrary to all the blueprints. In the end, that is an aspect of the desert *peregrinatio.* But I admit it would be much more comforting to be able to agree with everyone else on all these things. In any event I see no hope whatever of a unity of *doctrina* here. It is just too much to be hoped for and I stopped even thinking of it years ago. One has to be realistic about some things: and this is a community set in fragmentation. I have more in common with friends in China and India than I have with some of the members of my monastic community. It is a rather awful thing to say. And probably means little anyway.

TO DOM IGNACE GILLET, O.C.S.O.   *Having served as Abbot of Dombes and Aiguebelle in France, Dom Ignace Gillet, O.C.S.O., became Abbot General of the Cistercian Order in 1968, following the death of Dom Gabriel Sortais.*

SEPTEMBER 11, 1964

. . . I am, by the grace of God, a monk. A monk of the twentieth century, with his difficulties, which nevertheless are not those of the "young." I am completely convinced of the value of monasticism, and of *traditional* monasticism. (The thing is to understand the "tradition.") I am even more convinced of the role of monasticism in today's world. A prophetic and even charismatic role. I dare to pronounce these terrible words. The monk is a child of God, an instrument of God. Which means that he is poorer than the others, more stripped, less "strong" and not at all a strong-minded person. His life remains hidden in God, mysterious, stripped, but it's a life which should be happy and full because it is a life in the truth and in simplicity, a life before God, with God, in God. Monastic life should be a sign of God in the world, a sign of love, of the truth of the Gospel, a sign of the poor and simple Christ, a brother to the world also but not of this world.

(I am speaking about the monastic ideal, while not being an ideal monk, quite the contrary. I know that I am a poor monk, maladjusted, with necessary indulgences, with a nervous system which plays tricks on me. I am not capable of being a monk who is simply "edifying." I think that I am not a scandalous monk, either, although some might and do think so.). . .

TO FATHER RONALD ROLOFF   FEBRUARY 27, 1965

. . . I do think, and I am more and more convinced of it, that in our situation here a really valid and productive manual labor is of essential importance. The monk has to make his living, and if he can make it by work that also makes him physically tired, that is all the better. I mean the good kind of tired, not just nervous exhaustion. Though of course that cannot be avoided always, in our day. And to try to sidestep it would be an evasion of the cross which everyone else has to carry. But from every point of view I think that the Cistercian has to be a man who works the land and takes a wise and effective care of the natural resources (forest, etc.) which God has given into his charge. This is the kind of work that, for us, helps the "identity" problem to get solved and also takes care of most of the others, too. Stability is much more reasonable and Christian when one has grown roots in the soil of his monastery by work and concern, and when one has been participating in the productive endeavors of the community, sharing in work and in the fruits of work. The business of keeping the monk feeling useless, a non-entity, and so on (Trappist style) is fatal today, and it is just not *true* either. . . .

TO MOTHER ANGELA COLLINS   APRIL 3, 1965

The solitary life is certainly not an idle one. I am quite busy when in the hermitage. At the moment I have found there is an excellent spring nearby but it is choked up, and the woods between the cottage and there are all grown up with vines and brush, which makes a fine fire hazard, too. All this has to be cleared out and the spring opened up. And I can't count on the help of the novices, as they are taken up with work in the monastery. I have electricity now, though, and that is a big help. I am down in the monastery for six or eight hours a day, not more. It looks as if I ought to be able to move in completely at the end of the year, when Rev. Father

[Abbot James Fox] has more or less assured me he will let me out of the novice master's job.

One reason why he is so much in favor of solitude all of a sudden is that I am constantly being asked to get in on meetings such as the one you are going to. He wants in the worst way to prevent me from doing so, and we have had to refuse several already. Or he has refused them for me. . . .

TO DOM ANDRÉ LOUF, O.C.S.O.   *Dom André Louf, O.C.S.O., of the Cistercian Abbey of Sainte-Marie-du-Mont (Mont-des-Cats), became abbot there in 1963. Like Merton, he wrote on prayer and the contemplative life.*

APRIL 26, 1965

. . . In this question of solitude, no amount of theory can substitute for a grain of practice. That is why I write this letter, because already in my life there is a mustard seed of it, and I would like to say what I think of this very small taste of experience in the field of solitude, even though it is limited and relative as yet.

It is known that I have had a hermitage for nearly five years. It began somewhat ambiguously as a place for meetings with non-Catholic retreatants apart from the monastery, in a quiet setting, etc., and a place in which I was permitted to spend the afternoons. Since then, the visits of retreatants have stopped; I have spent more than the afternoons, as much free time as I could get in fact, and finally since last October I have been sleeping here, saying the night office here, taking frustulum or mixt, sometimes supper, going down for work in the novitiate and usually for Prime, Tierce, High Mass, Sext, dinner and perhaps some of the afternoon offices, unless I am completely free, in which case I may return to the hermitage after dinner and not come down again until the following morning at Prime. So you see that at least some solitude is here. What of the fruits?

First of all I can say that for me the experience has been wonderful, and it has dissipated any doubts I may have had about my own need for and happiness in solitude. I have at last the complete sense of having found my monastic vocation. At least in my own mind, I am convinced that I have now found the place which God had destined for me when He called me to the monastic life, and that if before this I was always to some extent unsatisfied and looking for "more," it was simply because this was needed to complete what God had given me before.

Second, there is a sense that this is a complete, inexplicable gift of God to me, without reference to any merit of mine. Frankly I have not been a perfect cenobite and I am by no means a perfect hermit. From the objective point of view one might say that there is a great deal to be desired in my "preparation" and "aptitude" for this kind of life. I am by no means the ideal type of the one called to solitude. But I am not worried by this, since God can do what He wants, and if He wants me here He can see that I make such use of this opportunity as will be pleasing to Him. And in fact I am very happy and busy with Him all the time I am here, though of course I have work to do, manual labor, cutting grass, splitting wood in winter, sweeping, etc., and even some writing (which would scandalize some people) but I try to take three hours a day at least for simple meditative prayer, and in addition to that I have another three hours of *lectio divina* or study when I am here for a good part of the day. When I am here permanently (which I hope will be soon), I hope to spend more time on the Psalter and so on.

This is of course known in the community and on the whole it is quite well accepted, by choir and brothers alike. The cellarer, who is quite critical of the fantasies of the monks, is benign and positive in his attitude toward the hermitage, which he considers quite reasonable in my case, and I have no trouble getting cooperation from the brothers in getting food, or in electrical installation. (I have electric light; I think it is necessary and it is very cheap, about three and a half dollars a month, which includes electric cooking.) The novices of course know it, and there has been no difficulty with the novitiate, as I have an undermaster [Father James Connor] who is willing to spend a lot of time there so as to be available when I am away. But the novices seem to be very content to be alone themselves reading and praying, and some seem willing to wait patiently for the number of years that may be required so that they may perhaps ultimately have a chance to try some solitude. . . .

There have been some difficulties, but nothing very great. It is cold in the winter, and one does not have the comforts of the community. But I prefer this. I have also had some sickness here, but find that I got along all right though quite ill, and when it became bad I was put in the infirmary and recovered quickly. In a word, sickness is no greater problem here than in the monastery. There has been very little *cafard* [in the dumps, the blues]. In fact, much less than in the community, for me!!! But some moments of purification and profound emptiness and loneliness, not so much loneliness for people as metaphysical emptiness and sense of the nothingness of myself and even in some sense of life and of "everything." There are times of purely sickening void. But there is never any feeling that one could or should escape this by returning to the distractions of the community. Quite the contrary, one sees there is no escape except in God Himself who in some way presents Himself as this Void. The Void is then its own fullness. And in fact it generally turns to great light and freedom and joy, much more than anything I ever knew in the monastery. I have never had so true a sense of the nearness of God and of His care for me, yet always in a more inexplicable and less "sensible" manner than in the monastery.

In fact I can say that there is really no special problem at all in the hermit life as far as I now know it. True, I like to go to the conventual Mass in particular, and I would like very much to continue this contact with the community. I certainly feel great love for my brothers and it is a really strong consolation to see them and be with them. It is a very great joy to remain dependent on the community and to feel that I will never have to sever my bonds with my monastic family. I consider this *most important*. It is almost the most important thing about the vocation to solitude for a monk, I believe. The grace of belonging permanently to one's monastic family is irreplaceable. . . .

TO DAME MARCELLA VAN BRUYN   *Marcella Van Bruyn left Stanbrook Abbey in England after twenty-three years to become a hermit. Stanbrook Abbey Press published a number of Merton's books.*

JUNE 16, 1965

. . . As to your questions:

1) I think that the most sensible and desirable thing for one who has a genuine vocation to monastic solitude, in touch with a community, is to really be in solitude. In confidence, I have hopes that after this year I will be permanently in the hermitage. I sleep there now and spend days at a time there when I can, but am almost always there for at least twelve hours out of

the twenty-four and usually more than that. I hope next year to come down perhaps for conventual Mass at first, and for one meal, as this will simplify the problem of cooking and washing dishes.

2) I hope gradually to give up writing. I don't plan to cut it off all of a sudden, because I know myself well enough to realize that this activity is helpful to me and in no way interferes with a genuine life of prayer. It has always been a help, the writing part. The publication [problems are] a little more distracting. But I think eventually the writing will die out by itself. I can see now that I would soon begin to lose interest. But I will probably always write a few little things like meditations or poems, on the spur of the moment.

As to correspondence, that too will gradually work itself out, I hope. At the moment I have a great load of it, with all kinds of letters from strangers, people wanting direction and so on. Most of it I cannot answer and I do not try. Next year I would want to cut it down to just proportions. It seems to me, though that "just proportions" includes keeping up a *monastic* correspondence, within reason. Obviously not a continued barrage, but occasional necessary letters on points of some interest. . . .

3) I would obviously give up the novice mastership and other offices, and I have already spoken of renouncing active and passive voice in the Chapter. I suppose I might have to continue voting, but I firmly intend to refuse all offices, above all that of Abbot, should they ever become so far afflicted as to elect me. Naturally I would not be involved in monastery politics.

4) Secular reading: that covers a wide area. Personally I would perhaps want to keep a bit in touch with philosophy, poetry, art, a little. Again, it would be a gradual affair. I don't think that I am called of set purpose to make a sweeping renunciation of all interest in what is being written and said outside, but on the contrary, I think that it is relevant to me. I don't think a monk can absolutely cut himself off from the really urgent secular problems and ideas, and still be realistic.

5) As things are now, I say the night office in the hermitage, and on many days I am there for None and Vespers. I say Compline there too. I would plan to come to conventual Mass, I think, not more than that, except perhaps Sunday Vespers. Much depends on what they do to the liturgy. If they go over to the vernacular then I doubt if I will find it so attractive. I may just

come down for feast day Masses (and might even continue to concelebrate once in a while). At the moment I have an Ambrosian Gradual and Vesperale in the hermitage and am finding some perfectly lovely things which I add to my own office up there. I say the office silently of course, but I sing a few Ambrosian things, and they are quite a lift.

There is certainly every hope that there will be hermitages here that people can go to for a day or two. This plan is, as Americans say, "in the works." I am sure that some vocations will be saved, and I agree that the thing we need to keep vocations is not to make silly concessions and play around with recreation, TV and what not, but to make the monastic life fully serious and solid, as it should be. The problem is to distinguish between real seriousness and the pettifogging regularism that puts exaggerated emphasis on trivial externals and the letter of outdated usages, thus preventing a real return to the essence of life, which is in solitude, silence, contemplative prayer, reflection, time to penetrate the word of God and listen to His voice, etc., etc. And of course with all this there is absolutely essential humility, compunction, self-stripping and "self-naughting," which people seem to get away from, with their hopes of "self-expression," though I suppose in a way this is a need too, but has to be rightly understood. . . .

TO SISTER MARY LUKE TOBIN, S.L.   *Sister Mary Luke Tobin, S.L., served as the Superior General of the Sisters of Loretto and president of the Conference of Major Superiors of Women. She was one of fifteen women auditors at the Second Vatican Council and kept Merton informed on the progress of the Council.*

JULY 18, 1965

. . . Pray for me to be a real good hermit and listen to the word of God and respond like a man. That is what it really involves. Simply to stand on one's feet before one's Father and reply to Him in the Spirit. Of course this is very much a Church activity. . . .

On August 20, 1965, Merton began living full-time in the hermitage on the monastery grounds.

TO DOM JACQUES WINANDY, O.S.B. *Dom Jacques Winandy, O.S.B., a former Abbot of Clervaux in Luxembourg, founded the Hermits of St. John Baptist in Merville, British Columbia, Canada, in 1964.*

AUGUST 30, 1965

. . . For my own part I am glad to say that I have been relieved of my job as a novice master and am living in the hermitage. I am very grateful to be able to do so, to taste the life in its special character, its emptiness, silence and purifying force. And I have very rapidly discovered that what I am seeking is not eremitism or spirituality or contemplation but simply God. Also that He lets Himself be sought in order to be found, and that all the realities that have been proposed about the desert are real indeed, and not illusion, except that in my case if I think too much about "desert" and "eremitism" it does become a bit of a delusion. It is much simpler just to be an ordinary Christian who is living alone, as it happens. But certainly this ability to expand and move in emptiness, out of the rather confining and limited structure of the community, is an enormous blessing. I am grateful to God every moment for it, and will not spoil it by imagining that my life is in any way special, for that does indeed poison everything. . . .

TO DOM JEAN LECLERCQ   SEPTEMBER 18, 1965

. . . For the first time in twenty-five years I feel that I am leading a really "monastic" life. All that I had hoped to find in solitude is really here, and more. At the same time I can see that one cannot trifle with solitude as one can with the common life. It requires great energy and attention, but of course without constant grace it would be useless to expect these. Hence I would very much appreciate your prayers. But in any case it is good to have this silence and peace, and to be able to get down to the *unum necessarium* [one thing necessary]. . . .

TO DAME MARCELLA VAN BRUYN   FEBRUARY 1, 1966

. . . My own position in the hermitage is really providential, because I would certainly not take gracefully to the changes in the monastery. I go down to say Mass in a chapel quite apart, in the former brothers' novitiate. It is very quiet and undisturbed, except for an occasional tractor outside. I have one meal at the monastery, to save me from my own cooking, and then return to the hermitage. I make my own breakfast and supper, but of course that is quite simple: just a question of bread and butter and something for sandwiches. In fact, since I have been on a diet for years and unable to take milk and eggs, I can have meat which really simplifies things: I often have a meat sandwich for supper and that is all I need. No dishes to wash, nothing to cook except a pot of tea. With an open fire I have the luxury of toast.

We have had quite a bit of snow and the other night it was down to twelve below zero Fahrenheit, which was a bit brisk. But I am snug in bed and after some painful moments got the fire blazing after I got up. I admit it was a bit grim getting up: some water froze inside the hermitage near a window. . . .

Really, though, everything has been going very well indeed. I like the solitude immensely for all the reasons you guessed. Never see anyone except when down at the monastery, can go for days without speaking except to say Mass, but I do have to give one conference a week to the novices and young monks still. It is only half an hour however. . . .

TO MOTHER COAKLEY, R.S.C.J.   *A Religious of the Sacred Heart, Mother Coakley, R.S.C.J., was a novice mistress when she corresponded with Merton.*

NOVEMBER 16, 1966

The hermit life seems to agree with me. I have forgotten all the problems I may have had before and have almost too much peace. But I am not complaining. The life is not easy, but it certainly is a joy and I feel very spoiled—and very free. There is so much that goes on and takes up time and is purely and simply nonsense: and one is well out of it. True, I am not bad at dreaming up nonsense of my own, but somehow it all seems to turn out fruitful, even when it has crazy aspects.

I just wanted to share a word with you and the novices. For the rest let us be united in prayer and joy. God is so much greater than all our thoughts and acts and problems and the best thing we can do is forget ourselves entirely in Him and go along where He wishes. For me an acre of woods seems a wonderful exchange for the entire world and I would never want to trade back. In fact I was allowed to make a profession of a sort on Sept. 8th. Not exactly formal vows but a commitment to the solitary life. So let's keep praying that we will all get lost in His love. And this may help us bring more love into a world that needs it.

TO FATHER I.   *Responding to Father I, an American Benedictine monk, Merton speaks of the "uselessness" of the monastic life.*

DECEMBER 5, 1966

... There has always been and there always will be a conviction in certain minds that the monastic life is useless. Well, it is. It is not meant to serve some practical purpose. It is not "for" something other than itself. On the other hand, the assertion that "reality" is to be found in secular life only is patently foolish: but people will continue to make it. And in the same breath they will lament the fact that they have no time for anything, that they are always nervous and frustrated, that people get on their nerves, that the Negroes are creeping up on them, and so forth. The world has its dignities and heroisms and its servitudes: and for many people life in the world is little more than the latter. The monk should have the courage and patience to keep his life going as a sign of freedom and of peace: he should be in his own way open to the world, and he should even to some extent be able to share some of the advantages of his life with people in the world who seek a little silence and peace to restore their perspectives. The monk can also in his own way be effectively concerned with worldly problems: more effectively for the fact that he is not immersed in them up to his neck.

TO FATHER PETER THOMAS ROHRBACH, O.C.O.   *Father Peter Thomas Rohrbach, O.C.O., was a Carmelite priest and the editor of* Spiritual Life.

AUGUST 13, 1967

... The thing that bothers me is that there is a very real desire for contemplative experience in this country, mostly among non-Catholics, and Catholics are too dense to be aware of the fact that if we don't wake up, the need for contemplation will seek satisfaction everywhere but among

Catholics. In other words, a strong, intelligent movement of renewal in the contemplative Orders and mixed Orders would be very desirable. . . .

TO COLMAN MCCARTHY   *A former monk of Holy Spirit Abbey in Conyers, Georgia, Colman McCarthy wrote for the* Washington Post *and other publications. He was working on an article titled "Renewal Crisis Hits Trappists" (published in the* National Catholic Reporter, *December 13, 1967) when he wrote to Merton. Merton's response was frank and candid.*

AUGUST 15, 1967

. . . I gladly contribute what ideas I can, and here they are. . . .

There is real hope for monasticism in the overall world picture. I find such hope in African monasticism in things like the Indian ashram of Dom Bede Griffiths, in the Protestant monasticism of Taize, in the Little Brothers and the less known, more monastic Brothers of the Virgin of the Poor. But as to the established monastic institutions in America I would not say that I was exactly "hopeful." Some of them seem doomed to complete inertia. Others—like Gethsemani, Conyers, et al—are trying to be progressive but are caught in a bind that makes real originality and creative solutions seemingly impossible. They are committed to the organizational approach, hence to building the institutional image before all else. They are not exactly bad or decadent, but in their decent prosperity, their commitment to permanent security, to their established position, their traditional place of dignity in the Church, they are bound to a certain inevitable rigidity and conservatism, no matter how hard they try to appear progressive. They thought that changes like a vernacular liturgy were revolutionary, and already in less than two years they have discovered that they were not even especially significant. Recent changes in observance will make the life more tolerable but not more meaningful. These monastic institutions have to a great extent failed in their promise to give their postulants deeply meaningful and creative lives. People are now looking elsewhere. These big Cistercian and Benedictine monasteries may survive, but they have no real future unless they show themselves suddenly capable of really radical change.

2) The misfortune of established monasticism, in America as elsewhere, is that for over a thousand years it has been solidly and completely identified

with what Carl Amery calls "milieu Catholicism" and which he analyzed in Germany. Milieu Catholicism is Catholicism which is so completely committed to a social and cultural established milieu that when there arises a choice between the gospel and the milieu, the choice is not even visible. The milieu wins every time, automatically. In such a situation there may perhaps be saints and even prophetic individuals. But the institution will strive in every way either to suppress them or to absorb them. Instead of exercising a prophetic and iconoclastic function in the world, instead of being a dynamic and eschatological sign, such monasticism is occupied entirely in constructing a respectable and venerable image of itself, and thus ensuring its own survival as a dignified and established institution.

3) Can the younger generation in these monasteries really make a dent in the prevailing conservatism? Is the progressivism of the young really in accord with the monastic charism? Or is it merely another version of secular apostolic witness? These are questions I cannot answer. I know there is a real ferment going on in these monasteries. Unfortunately, there is a lot of ambiguity about basic values. For instance the term "contemplative life," already in some ways suspect theologically today, is used more and more negatively as the "non-active" life. In other words "contemplation" is reduced to its juridical significance: cloister and attendance in choir. The term "contemplative life" is being used defensively as an excuse to keep monks in the monastery, to keep them out of contact with the problems and needs of the world, in short to keep them out of dialogue with the world. This is disastrous. Such a use of the term will bring complete discredit on the real value of contemplation. In a clumsy attempt to protect the monastic life, this negativism will only sterilize it and guarantee its demise.

4) What am I doing personally? Without going into details, I can say I am to a great extent living on the margin of life at Gethsemani and concentrating on my own personal task, my own personal development and my contacts with people in my own fields, such as (a) poets and other writers and artists; (b) Buddhists, Hindus, Sufis and people interested in the mystical dimension of religion, whether Christian or other. These contacts remain however very limited. I had a very interesting invitation to go to Japan and visit the chief Zen centers there but permission to go was categorically refused. My Superiors, in a state of almost catatonic shock, said:

"But this would be absolutely contrary to the contemplative life." Comment on this is not necessary. The invitation emanated incidentally from a Jesuit who is a consultor on the Commission for Non-Christian Religions, from a Japanese Bishop and from a Superior of the Order in Japan.

I think that ought to cover the waterfront OK. Any further questions? Feel free to ask. . . .

TO FATHER AELRED SQUIRE, O.P.   *Father Aelred Squire, O.P., an English Dominican, lived the hermit life in Norway before joining the Camaldolese hermits at Big Sur, California.*

SEPTEMBER 25, 1967

. . . The real thing about being a hermit is of course that *hermit* is outside all categories whatever. The hermit who succeeds, or thinks he can succeed, in simply having a recognizable niche—a nest of his own that everyone can account for and understand—may well be lacking an essential element of solitude. The hermit life is a kind of walking on water, in which one no longer can account for anything but one knows that one has not drowned and that this is to nobody's credit but God's. . . .

I agree that solitude is a really essential element in the religious life. One does have to cut loose and float away without ties, in one way or other, and those who try to get away from that aspect of it today are deceiving themselves. Perhaps there could be a less stark, less inhuman kind of loneliness in some communities. . . .

My chief complaint about the hermit life is that a twenty-four-hour day is not long enough to do what one would like to do. Really, didn't you find it slowed you down? I find I simply do not have the power to go on doing many things. I have to stop and vegetate. Eventually I may work, I mean of the "productive" kind, publishable work. But I never know what kind of plan is going to come out. Everything is just what you don't expect. . . .

TO FATHER JULIAN ROCHFORD, O.S.B.   *Father Julian Rochford, O.S.B., was a monk of the Benedictine Abbey of Ampleforth in York, England.*

FEBRUARY 1, 1968

. . . In the long run, it seems to me that the monastic life is ordered to the radical transformation of the one called to it, in and through his common life with his brothers in Christ: the most complete metanoia (*conversatio morum*) ideally ending in complete openness to the Spirit of Love and complete surrender to that Spirit. Which of course could mean all kinds of things: eremitical solitude, pilgrim life, preaching to people of utterly different faiths (or dialogue with same!), works of mercy. . . .

TO SISTER J.   *Sister J., a member of an active religious order, wrote to Merton about her order's experiment of "living in groups of five."*

MARCH 4, 1968

. . . The idea of community really needs reviving: it has got lost in the idea of institution. Community and person are correlative. No community without persons; no persons without community. Too organized an institutional life tends to stifle both community and personality. Primacy tends to be given to an organizational task. Community is an end in itself, not a means to carry out tasks. Community is ordered to life, as a good in its own right. It is life-centered, person-centered. Hence we should not be too anxious about "getting anywhere" with community, except that community itself should "be" and celebrate itself in love. Probably one of the things about it is that it is too simple. We have forgotten how to be that simple. But I am glad your generation is finding out about it again, and maybe the rest of us can learn from you.

TO MOTHER MYRIAM DARDENNE   SEPTEMBER 7, 1968

All I can give is the little that I have, which is certainly nothing. But I can think with you in terms of my own present development and—I won't say crisis, because it is very smooth—but I am completely convinced that for some people the only thing is a solitary and "unattached" life. To simply go where the wind blows them, which is into various new deserts. With absolutely NO plans for any kind of structure, community, what to do, how to do it, but to simply seek the most desolate rock or the most abandoned island and sit there until the tourists move in, then to move on. I have NO ideal, NO program, and the last thing in the world I want is a disciple or anyone to listen or imitate. I'd rather warn everyone to do something else. For me the wind blows to Asia. . . .

The Asians have this only: that for thousands of years they have worked on a very complex and complete mental discipline, which is not so much aimed at separating matter from spirit, as identifying the true self and separating it from an illusion generated by society and by imaginary appetite. At the present moment this illusion has become law, even for Christians. The talk about the goodness of the world, etc., is largely justification of the illusion, though the world is certainly "good." But all the Goodness of the World lingo seems to me to be vitiated by a Madison Avenue consumer-society approach which makes it utterly phony, and bespeaks nothing but the goodness of the market (see Erich Fromm). I don't intend to talk much about this. It is true that the yen for absolute solitude is often vitiated by pure narcissism, regression, immaturity, and is utterly sick. This does not alter the fact that there are vocations to solitude, and for these there remains only the question: when do I start? And how? Once artificial barriers are removed the question tends to answer itself.

In September 1968, Merton traveled to Alaska, where he gave conferences to sisters at the Monastery of the Precious Blood in Eagle River and days of recollection for sisters and for priests in the diocese of Anchorage. In October, he visited Our Lady of the Redwoods Abbey at Redwoods in California and Santa Barbara, where he spoke at the Center for the Study of Democratic Institutions. On October 15, Merton embarked on a journey to Asia, where he met with Hindu and Buddhists scholars and religious leaders, including the Dalai Lama. Merton was participating in a meeting of Buddhist and Christian monks in Bangkok, Thailand, when he died on December 10, 1968.

MONASTICISM IN TRANSLATION

Merton's reflections on the meaning of monasticism and his own experience of the monastic life were not limited to his letters to men and women religious. He also "translated" his monastic way of life into a new idiom as he described it to fellow writers and, on one occasion, to a sixth-grader.

TO HENRY MILLER *American writer Henry Miller began corresponding with Merton in April 1962, when Miller wrote to tell Merton that he was "much moved" by Merton's* Original Child Bomb *and "stimulated" by* The Wisdom of the Desert.

MAY 12, 1963

. . . Yes, I am still at the monastery. There have been all sorts of legends about my being elsewhere, some of them founded on a firm basis of fact: that I did make honest attempts to get permission to live as a hermit in Mexico. But the whole thing was squashed by administrative and political maneuvers which I could not block. However as to my wanting purely and simply to go back to New York, for example, I have never been touched by this insanity even for a moment. I do have times when I wish I could see some of Europe again, and I may do so, since after all, permissions to travel and pretexts for doing so are not absolutely excluded from our life. But normally I am pretty well fixed here, and have no special complaints. I am a monk, and therefore I like the monastic life. If in particular instances it is bound to have a few things lacking, that is only one of the drawbacks of any life. It seems to me that I am here for a reason, just as you are where you are for a reason. And the reason seems to be pretty much the same in both cases. We are here to live, and to "be," and on occasion to help others with the recharging of batteries. I attempt in my own way to keep the monks from getting buried in their own brand of ideological manure, and to maintain at least occasional contacts with the fresh air of reality. On the other hand the manure itself is much less obnoxious and much more productive than what is forked about indiscriminately on the outside. At least it is not lethal. . . .

TO CLAYTON ESHLEMAN *Clayton Eshleman was an American poet who shared Merton's interest in Latin American poets, especially Neruda and Vallejo. Eshleman's questions about the monastic life elicited Merton's frank response.*

NOVEMBER 8, 1965

. . . About the monastery: does it need explaining or justifying? For my own part I have come to the conclusion that if I can live with it my friends can. It is simply a fact. I know that in many ways it seems to be an offensive fact, but I can't help that, and it may change some day. I did not come here for the costume, and there are various ways in which one can accept it: for my part I like it because it is comfortable: and who cares what anybody wears anyway? I assure you that I am not attached in the least to the institutional exterior of the Church. I have committed myself to this, yes, and people know this. All right. But anyone who knows me knows that I am not going to make funny choices when it comes to deciding between something artificial and external and something real and live. I would not be here if I had not found some kind of life in it, and I repeat, I am in no way selling out to whatever may be fictitious about it. I think that is one thing a person learns in a place like this, just as in a Zen monastery you learn to burn Buddhas. But really I don't want to put up an argument for or against it. I am living with it, and certainly I could wish it were different in many ways. I certainly recognize that as far as the relations with people go, it is a forced and arbitrary setup, and moreover I know that I myself have been to some extent harmed and diminished by this. It can't be helped, there are other things which are important enough to counterbalance this, and all life is much the same in that respect. And I am simply not interested in the kind of life I would have to live if I were outside.

All that is a long way round to say if you can possibly forget I am a priest, forget it. And I assure you that I have no interest whatever in pulling any professional priestly magic on you. I pray for you to have life and happiness as I pray for all my friends, and that is it.

Since August I have been living in the woods all the time, going down to the monastery once a day. It is very good for meditation and for being more alive and for my part I am very happy with it. It is really what I came here for. I get some writing done, read a fair amount, chop wood, think a lot. As far as I am concerned, this is where the root is. I do not prescribe it for anybody else, but for me it is a good answer. . . .

TO CID CORMAN   *Cid Corman lived in Japan, where he wrote and pub-lished books of poetry, edited a literary magazine named* Origin, *and trans-lated the poetry of Matsuo Bashô.*

... Initials [*jhs*] on the top of the paper you ask about? That is not a secre-tary, but medieval pious practice to put monogram of name of Christ when you start to write, something like making sign of the Cross when you start doing something. I don't make an issue out of it, it is a habit. Someone helps me with typing when I have stuff to type and can get help, but no secretary. I don't write that many letters anymore since I live in the woods with the foxes. No, there are no monks doing illuminated mass. But there are some nuns in England, good friends of mine, who do some very fancy printing—Stan-brook Abbey. I'll send you a little thing they did for me or I did with them or for them [*The Solitary Life: A Letter of Guigo*]. They are supposed to be doing a bit of Cassiodorus I translated now, but that has been waiting around for a long time. I'll send you that too if I ever get copies and if you remind me in about three months (probably will not be ready even then).

Origin and your letters mean a lot to me somehow. Your allusion to the vow of poverty and the fact that you are broke without a vow while I am broke with it reminds me that something like *Origin* and your letters may well be just as monastic and more so than what we are doing around here. I am very aware of the ambiguities of my kind of monasticism and base no claims of any kind whatever upon it: but on the contrary I am very glad when I find anybody doing anything for love of it, and since that is what I myself seek and need, I respond to it with some liveliness. The essence of monasticism as I see it is this doing something or living in a certain way for pure love of it and without further justification. And without necessarily pointing to any special practical result. Or to anything. Or drawing atten-tion etc. Now that I am alone in the woods (for pure love of it and because life in the community also seemed to me too tangled) I want to think more about writing poetry, though perhaps it is better not to think much about it and write without looking too closely at what is happening. Still it is good to have someone like you articulate about these things and willing to share them. I have been out of contact with that, and remain inarticulate on the subject anyway. I don't know how to talk about poetry. . . .

. . . I respect your feeling that monks, Zen or others, give an impression of hubris by "living detached on a special lane" and then telling everyone else off. Or just claiming to have the answer. I feel that way myself about the monks who really do this and there are plenty. But once again in a despairing plea I hope to get someone at last to see that I am not one of them (but in the past I have been, so I deserve whatever is said about it). This business of chastity is much more complex than that. First of all, it is not a question of negatively scouring out all sexual desire, though many do this or try to. Properly it should be a long hard job of sublimation: and doubtless few of us completely succeed. In any case I have never led or advocated a totally disincarnate life. I was in love before entering the monastery and I have also been in love since (though pretty hampered by the restrictions!) and in the end I have come to a position where I refuse to generalize, and above all I know I don't have the "Big Answers" (who has?). And I do wish everyone would stop inferring that I intend my life to be some sort of reflection on theirs. I don't assume for a moment that the plane on which I live is higher or better than anyone else's, in fact I know it may be a blind alley and a huge mistake, but since I honestly think it is my "fate" (call it that if you like), I have decided, and often, over and over, that is has to be accepted for what it is worth and made the best of. And I suppose I am moderately happy at it and am able to give something to other people from where I am. The point is that this sort of setup does offer a certain kind of freedom of its own, and that if a person wants to choose this and live accordingly, then it would be a bad thing for him to be forced to conform to others who don't want it. People who want and need this kind of solitude (there are always some) should be able to find it and stay in it, though they should do so without looking down on others or being vain of supposed achievements (that vanity immediately empties the whole thing out anyhow). Since this obviously is not your dish, I can see that it would repel you or leave you indifferent: yet the swamp wading you speak of is common to everybody and there is no escape for monks: each one simply has to get through his own swamp as honestly and as completely as he can. The only thing is not to make a virtue out of going under. And I am glad you are getting footway on some rock. Keep it up. . . .

TO SUSAN CHAPULIS   *Susan Chapulis was a sixth-grader, studying monas-*
ticism, when she wrote to Merton requesting "any information whatever" that
she could share with her class.

APRIL 10, 1967

Thanks for your nice letter. You want "any information whatsoever" to help the sixth grade in the study of monasticism. Well, I'll see if I can get the brothers down in the store to send you a little book about the monastery here. That ought to help.

The monastic life goes back a long way. Monks are people who seek to devote all their time to knowing God better and loving Him more. For that reason they leave the cities and go out into lonely places where it is quiet and they can think. As they go on in life they want to find lonelier and lonelier places so they can think even more. In the end people think these monks are really crazy going off by themselves and of course sometimes they are. On the other hand when you are quiet and when you are free from a lot of cares, when you don't have to worry about your car and your house and all that, and when you don't make enough money to pay taxes, and don't have a wife to fight with, and when your heart is quiet, you suddenly realize that everything is extremely beautiful and that just by being quiet you can almost sense that God is right there not only with you but even in you. Then you realize that it is worth the trouble of going away where you don't have to talk and mess around and make a darn fool of yourself in the middle of a lot of people who are running around in circles to no purpose. I suppose that is why monks go off and live in lonely places. Like me now I live alone in the woods with squirrels and rabbits and deer and foxes and a huge owl that comes down by my cabin and makes a spooky noise in the night, but we are friends and it is all ok. A monk who lives all by himself in the woods is called a hermit. There is a Rock 'n Roll outfit called Herman and his Hermits but they are not the same thing.

I do not suppose for a moment that you wish to become a hermit (though now I understand there are some girl hermits in England and they are sort of friends of mine because they are hermits, so I send them stuff about how to be a hermit). But anyway, I suggest that you sometimes be quiet and think how good a thing it is that you are loved by God who is infinite and who wants you to be supremely happy and who in fact is going to make you supremely happy. Isn't that something? It is, my dear, and let us keep praying that it will work out like that for everybody. Good bye now.

TO MARGARET RANDALL   *American-born poet Margaret Randall moved to Mexico in 1961. There, together with her then-husband, Sergio Mondragon, she edited* El Corno Emplumado *(The Plumed Horn), a bilingual literary magazine that published Merton's work.*

JUNE 6, 1967

. . . Every once in a while someone wonders why I am a monk, and I don't want to be always justifying the monk idea because then I get the false idea that I am a monk. Perhaps when I entered here I believed I was a monk, and kept it up for five, ten, fifteen years, even allowed myself to become novice master and tell others what it was all about. No more . . . as far as I am concerned the question "why do you have to be a monk?" is like a question "why do you have to live in Nebraska?" I don't know. It's what the karma added up to, I guess. Here I am, and it would not be physically easy for me to get somewhere else, but on the other hand I have what I want: a certain amount of distance, silence, perspective, meditation, room to do the things I know I must do. I would go nuts trying to do them in a city. Is this better? Certainly only for someone who knows he has to do it this way, more or less, or something like this. But not necessarily for anyone else. I am sure you are quite right about the ordinary life etc. This is a more ordinary life than you think, and also I wonder if I am more out of life or more in it? To me, the woods are life. Of course there is a lot wrong with it. Certainly it would be wonderful to have children to look after and as you say learn from. But I know for my own part that being married would be a very difficult proposition, much too complicated. Loneliness can be terrible too, but somehow I can handle that better. I'm only saying that is the kind of compromise with life that I have ended up with, and not making out it is wonderful: but it is what I can handle. More or less. . . .

PART 3

Living the Writer's Life

From Manuscript to Publication

"Naomi, look, you have a divine mission, no less, which is to keep me in order as a writer and tell me when I am getting completely stupid and cheap and all the rest."

—To Naomi Burton Stone, Holy Thursday, 1950

A s a monk, Merton embraced the solitary life, rarely leaving the monastery grounds and traveling hardly at all until the last year of his life. As a writer, he discovered the inestimable value and necessity of supportive friends outside the monastery walls. Certainly his publishers, particularly Robert Giroux and Jay Laughlin, played significant roles in Merton's life as a writer. So did two women, Naomi Burton Stone and Sister Therese Lentfoehr. They offered him constant encouragement and devoted friendship. Naomi Burton Stone, his lifelong literary agent and first critic, shepherded his books to publication, and Sister Therese Lentfoehr, his first archivist, carefully collected and preserved his manuscripts and books. This section features selections from his letters to Stone and Lentfoehr, letters that span a period of two decades and document the story of Merton's life as a writer.

TO NAOMI BURTON STONE   *Naomi Burton came to America from England in 1939. In 1951 she married Melville E. Stone. A literary agent, she recognized Merton's talents as a writer and represented him in bringing to publication some of the finest works of spiritual writing of the twentieth century, beginning with his best-selling autobiography,* The Seven Storey Mountain. *She became more than a literary agent to Merton. They became close friends. She acted as "sister" and sometimes "mother" to him. He valued her counsel, even the occasional scoldings she found it necessary to give him. In a way he does with no other correspondent, he shared with her his concerns, his needs, his fears. This correspondence sheds a good deal of light on the shadow side of Merton's struggle to achieve personal freedom and maturity.*

JANUARY 2, 1947

Naturally I was delighted to get Bob [Giroux]'s wire [accepting the manuscript of *The Seven Storey Mountain*] and your letter. I will write to Bob when I hear from him. Meanwhile please assure him that I give him a free hand with the editing. There is one idea that I would like to keep or get in somewhere else: the one about the identity of disinterested charity and true freedom, because that is important.... Also I'd like to keep as much as I can of the references to Duns Scotus because even Catholics don't know him, and they should.

About the contract, Father Abbot [Frederic Dunne] says you can send it out here in the ordinary way. He will know what to do about it. Address it to me. I suppose it will be a contract with the monastery because I can't make any contracts.

FEBRUARY 18, 1947

Incidentally I think *The Seven Storey Mountain* would be better not described as a novel, since it was by no means written as one. The others [his premonastic manuscripts] were novels, but this I felt bound to keep as close to literal truth as I could because I felt that some of the impact of the book depended on it. So it is a straight autobiography, and I feel, don't you, that the publicity should make that clear when it gets around to that. I hope all this does not communicate my own mental fog to you, on whom I depend for clarification and clear vision!

EASTER 1947 [MARCH 30]

. . . The Abbot General of the Order [Dom Dominique Nogues] is here now and he told me to go on publishing under the name Thomas Merton, so that is the name I use for all business purposes, contracts, etc. The General likes the idea of the work I am doing.

MAY 13, 1947

. . . And he told me to go ahead and write as I pleased and to use all the slang I wanted. . . .

MARCH 8, 1948

. . . I am nearly finished with a book, *Waters of Siloe,* about the Trappist Order and life which I will shoot along to you. I have promised it already to Bob Giroux. It ought not to be delayed too much because the centenary of the monastery will be celebrated next year and the book ought to coincide with that. . . .

Also, Laughlin is interested in another project that is under way, a book of more or less random thoughts about the contemplative life called *The Soil and Seeds of Contemplation.* That will be ready, I suppose, about mid-summer. The St. John of the Cross project has stalled somehow.

NOVEMBER 8, 1948

This is just to thank you for the wonderful job you and Bob have done on *The Seven Storey Mountain*. It certainly seems to be going quite well. I am getting so much fan mail that it makes me nervous. . . .

HOLY THURSDAY 1950

. . . And so, in the fullness of happiness of this day: Naomi, look, you have a divine mission, no less, which is to keep me in order as a writer and tell me when I am getting completely stupid and cheap and all the rest. And it is easy for me to get that way, as I write in such a hurry when I get the slightest chance to sit in front of a typewriter. Those chances are getting rare. Father Abbot [James Fox] is trying to keep the way clear for me to have time for the two big jobs I am supposed to do—writing and teaching. They dovetail together well, as long as other stuff doesn't land in the middle and disrupt everything. But there are always things cropping up. I need a full-time secretary, I guess. Pray for me to get a lot of sense and to be guided by the Holy Ghost and not my own mad impulses.

APRIL 29, 1950

Well, the settlement is very easy, Naomi. There just isn't any problem anymore. Father Abbot read over part of the *Journal* ms. and got to talking with some prominent Catholics somewhere. The latter were all up in the air with surprise and dismay at the thought of a cloistered monk writing and publishing a *Journal* in his own lifetime. Of course you can't write a *Journal* when you are dead. But they convinced Father Abbot that the *Journal* simply should not be published. At least not while I am still walking around on the face of this earth. Such a thing had never been heard of before. And that is quite true: it hasn't. Maybe it isn't such a wonderful book either, I don't know. Anyway, Father Abbot is quite definite about not wanting it to go into print because he feels that it would get him and the monastery into a lot of nasty criticism from people who just wouldn't understand.

MAY 10, 1951

Several weeks have gone by without my saying a word to you about my happiness to hear that you were married and to send you my very best wishes and my prayers and my blessing. It was not necessary to be in a rush about it. You know I always keep you in my prayers anyway and that I always ask Our Lord to make you very happy.

The reason why I held things up was that I wanted to send you a tangible sort of a wedding present. I knew you would be pleased to hear that Father Abbot had reconsidered his decision about the *Journal* and that he would allow the publication of special selections from it [under the title *The Sign of Jonas*]. I have tentatively made some selections and am sending this copy to you for Bob. . . .

MARCH 3, 1956

. . . It was so good to have you here, and of course I don't mind at all having a sister who is sensible. Not all are. But as a matter of fact that was what I was thinking about sitting up there at Gannon's [the residence for lay visitors]: that I had always secretly regretted not having a sister and now all of a sudden one shows up. There is just the right balance of being the same and being different. I certainly trust your opinions and your observations, since they are the first things I have heard that made sense in a long time. . . .

The bitterness in me comes from the fact that I have at last opened up the area in which it is impossible not to notice that in all this solitude business and in my other outbursts of idealism I have been reliving all the brat experiences of my childhood, magnified and adorned. Secondly, the bitterness comes from realizing that now there is definitely *no hope* of my ideals being realized, that they are more or less fictitious and illusory and that perhaps I don't even want them myself—that indeed I may not even know what I really want, except that I am rather sure I don't want the big pot of spiritual adolescence which is called the monastery of Gethsemani. I mean that I find it distasteful and frustrating—although of course, I "want" it in the sense that I mean to keep my vows. Thirdly, the bitterness centers on my writing. My ambivalence about writing is not as great as I have made it seem. I really have little ambivalence about writing as such, provided I can just write. That I really enjoy and I profit by it and it comes easy, etc. But of course writing against the obstacles we have here is another matter. Then again, I know that my writing has been a safety valve for the neurosis, too. Being without the safety valve is a strain at times, but perhaps it is a good thing. I shudder to think how many pages I have written beating people over the head for not being spiritual and which I now realize to have been just egotistical junk. In fact I am awfully aware of the shallowness and superficiality of most of the writing I did between 1945 and 1950—and some of what I have written since then, too. . . .

Well, I plow through things and seem to come out all the time anyway. I am really very happy that in all this wrestling with myself, I am really getting rid of an awful lot of Merton, but the void that replaces him is a bit disconcerting: except that I know God is there. One thing is sure: I do not particularly want the survival of the person and even the writer I have been. Although I do have enough sense to realize that this is what I shall always probably be. But my true self is not one that has to be thought about and propped up with rationalizations. He only has to be lived, and he is lived, in Christ, under the surface of the unquiet sea in which the other one is busy drowning.

P.S. Please don't stop "bothering" me and don't apologize for it. For heaven's sake I need it. And so do you, I guess.

APRIL 4, 1956

. . . I was in to see the man about those Rorschach tests we took as an experiment, and lo, I discover from my own that I really love everybody and am socially adapted and that all I am really looking for is a chance to help people. I say to him: "But I want to live a solitary life." And he says to me firmly: "Clinically you are social." "No," I gasp, "I am truly a hermit." He replies, inflexibly: "The Rorschach test says you are social." Dom James will be ten years younger when he hears it. But I still hope I can get enough solitude occasionally to continue breathing. But nevertheless this type declared, and I believe it, that there is a whole lot of potential creative and productive stuff in me going to waste because I spend most of my time rejecting everybody and telling myself that they are rejecting me. So, maybe I'll be seeing him again. . . .

Easter was wonderful and today is wonderful, all the way into town the pear trees and cherry trees and redbuds were in bloom and the farms looked clean and fresh instead of being the usual mudholes, and everything was sublime, even the hogs. . . .

APRIL 27, 1956

. . . In May 1939, about six months after my baptism, I remember Fr. Moore grabbed me and said I should be confirmed by Bishop Donohue— which I was. The thing that most occupied me was the choice of a new middle name. That is where I came up with James. (Do you remember, I used to be definitely Thomas James Merton.) (Everything spelled out in all letters.) I don't think it makes any sense to say whether I felt anything or not. We made a procession outside of Corpus Christi, about ten feet along the sidewalk, out one door and in the other, and all the heathens in Teachers College stood at the windows and looked at our Popish pranks, and what I felt was embarrassment or resentment. Yet it was a big day.

In confirmation, we get the strength and the perspective, first of all, to get along with a Spirit Who is our Spirit, as intimate to us as our own selves and more so, and yet the Spirit of God and infinitely beyond our clear knowing. In confirmation we get the strength to keep up with the pace He sets, which is the pace of the wind blowing where it listeth and you don't know where it is going. The thing we have to avoid above all is being untrue to this Spirit by saying He has said something when He hasn't, and saying He has not said something when He has. And first of all, we must not saddle Him with all our own foolishness, and blame Him for our own wacky visions. At the same time, however, we must be able, in a quiet, confident way, to do the seemingly crazy things He asks of us—the craziest of which is, perhaps, to be ordinary. . . .

MAY 2, 1956

First of all, here are a couple of poems. . . . Matthew Scott is sending the long one to Graham Greene [called "The Sting of Conscience," with the subtitle "Letter to Graham Greene"]. I hope Greene will be appropriately edified at the effect of [his novel] The Quiet American on a Trappist monk. . . .

The poem—which Merton later admitted was a projection of his own troubles onto his mother, America, the monastery, and the Church—has eight stanzas. Here is the first stanza:

You have written, Greene, in your last book
The reasons why I so hate milk.
You have diagnosed the war in my own gut
Against the innocence, yes, against the dead mother
Who became, some twenty years ago,
My famous refuge.

MAY 17, 1956

Honestly, you may be surprised to learn that your letter of May 13 surprised me. I don't mean that I imagine I ought never to be scolded, or that I thought you were going to go up into ecstasy over the Graham Greene poem. After all, I said I didn't intend to publish it right now—or ever, if you don't want me to. And I remember vaguely you never liked him.

What surprised me was that you said I had been hurting you by the letters I wrote. That is one I just can't figure out, except of course I know I said a lot of things, about not liking living so much with other people, etc., etc. But haven't you caught on to the fact that that is mostly a line and that when I say it I am automatically filling up paper (which I admit is a very bad habit)? What on earth is there in any of that stuff to hurt you or anybody else? Do you mean to say you take it seriously? Do you take it seriously when everybody thinks rainy days are horrible or nice days are wonderful? Who cares what kind of a day it is? Who cares about solitude? I like it, and if I can have it, all right, and if they ever put me where I get a lot of it, swell. As for living with people, I do find it uncomfortable, and it is not something I can make myself entirely happy about by pressing a button. But I was only rattling the bars of my crib because I thought you liked it. Since you finally tell me that you don't, I'll gladly stop.

The key sentence of your letter appears to me to be this one: "Every time I tell you that I think what you are doing is wrong, this is the way you reply—if you reply."

Okay, so you think the Greene poem is a *reply*. God help us. Do you really think you are my mother? It was sent you purely as a matter of business, and contains no veiled or open message either to you or to someone else except Greene—and God and I suppose my mother, God rest her soul.

It is, by the way, not intended to be read to the Senators in Congress either, or published on handbills and distributed in the subways.

"What I am doing is wrong." Well, what am I doing? I am being novice master. I am not writing much of anything except five million conferences. I am trying to get a little time each day to read a book and think and catch my breath. Oh yes, the dreams. Well, I am *not* typing out dreams and distributing them all over the Middle West either. . . . What else am I doing? I am not griping as much as you think, and I am certainly griping less than I have at any time in the past twelve years. Only during that time I didn't express my gripes much to anyone, certainly not to my agent. The Greene poem contains aggressive thoughts? Well, yes. That is, by the way, one of the reasons why it is a good poem. It contains a lot of things that are in me, rather than a lot of things that are not in me.

Analysis? Yes. I can use some. With the full approval of everyone concerned, including several people who know and who say that I am neurotic enough to stand treatment, I shall be going in to the man in Louisville for a while. Maybe he'll make things nicer for you, as well as for everybody around me. Believe me, groups of people did not "suddenly" start to become a problem just when I stopped writing, and as a matter of fact I have been griping a lot less since I have stopped writing—because I don't have to try to write and listen to machines all over the place at the same time. It is a big relief. . . .

I think fundamentally you are sorry that I am not the person you want me to be. I am fully prepared to admit you want me to be better than I am, and even that you are able to see things that I cannot see about what I ought to be. But you ought to be warned of the fact that I react strongly—and unconsciously—against any thought of being made anybody's ideal. . . .

So what's the conclusion: I am childish, I am selfish, I love to gripe. I want to complain and have someone to complain to, and for a while you were elected. I am sorry. It won't happen again, and at the same time I will make a serious effort to grow up. But please be patient. I am neurotic, you know: and I am not just using that as a convenient cover. . . .

This, for the moment, will have to serve as a reply to yours of the 13th. If you think it is inadequate and unsatisfactory, please let me suggest that communication is not as easy for me as you think: I mean real communication on a really personal level. You don't know yet that for me communication is not communication but a narcissistic gesture of some sort at which I happen to be quite clever. Do you think that I have ever in my life communicated with another person? Sacramentally I hope, but not in writing.

Maybe that sounds horrible, or maybe I am exaggerating because of an ideal of communication that I know will never be attained on earth—or something. But I am trying to tell the truth. That is one of the real problems for me here. It is true I seem to contact people (like novices, etc.) better than others do. But I know that in fact I am not that much in communication with them, in fact very, very little. I wish I could be, and I suppose it is really quite simple, but what do you do about the wall, twenty feet thick, that is in between? ...

June 4, 1956

One of the reasons why I write such bad letters is that I write a lot in a hurry without previously taking a moment to think what I am about to say. I haven't thought about this one either, not directly. So perhaps the best thing I could do would be to make it a little shorter and try to think a little while the paper is in the machine. . . .

Now about me. (At once I get discouraged at such a beginning. You wouldn't think it, but to some extent I freeze up, even though I seem so glib when I talk about myself.) There is something I am groping for, anyway. I hope I can get to it in the next fifteen minutes. Without too much beating around the bush.

First, in a way it seems silly that I should write about myself to you. But I don't think it is. You are my good friend and one I can talk to, and I can't talk to most of those here as I can to you. It is still unconventional. Okay. But I am pretty sure by now that I am not meant to follow any beaten track. Let us assume, anyway, that it makes sense for me to occasionally tell you what is going on. I won't say cry on your shoulder, because actually I don't cry on people's shoulders, I just pretend to because I think they like it. Hence the trouble that comes from the misunderstandings created by my ambivalence. In fact, I am probably too proud to cry on anybody's shoulder, and yet at the same time I need to.

Second, I am really beginning to discover that the solitude I need is a solitude in which I talk less about myself, while staying where I am. That seems to make a little sense, doesn't it? There is such a thing as just clamming up, finally. It will at least save me from experimenting and saying things I don't mean.

Third: in point of fact, let it be known and recorded that I am, I confess, far happier now than I have been at any time since I came here. In the last six months, for the first time, I have consistently felt that I belonged here for days on end. I have been consistently unbothered by the things that used to drive me nuts. I have found a way to fit into the place by being detached from places, in effect. I honestly am ceasing to care much *where* I am or what I am doing.

Fourth, yes, I project my troubles onto everybody else—in the Greene poem, I projected them on (1) my mother, (2) America, (3) the monastery, (4) the Church. An interesting lineup, of which I am conscious, and I think it makes a good poem. What the poem says is not that I really have anything fundamental against 1, 2, 3, or least of all 4, but that I am definitely conscious of being in hidden rebellion against all of them. (I am a fallen man, and I guess there are a few others around.) I am certainly boiling with hostilities and resistances, which are the expression of my pride as they are also of my weakness. And I am also definitely conscious of the fact that for ten years in the monastery when I was following the straight ascetic-mystic line, I was getting nowhere except into a few pretenses with which I did not quite kid myself, but did, apparently, kid a lot of other people. At the present time, by the grace of God, I am starting over again and the going is much rougher, much more colorful, and much more honest, less publishable, more fruitful, I believe. And also I do not doubt, have never doubted for an instant, that I am very much loved by God, and in fact in some way favored by Him, why He alone knows. I am always more and more aware of the fact that I am united to Him, even though, paradoxically, I become more and more aware of the fact that I am sinful enough to be plenty separated from Him. Again, I am in some things rather sure of His will, in a diffuse sort of way (in others I am in black perplexity about the whole business). But the thing that I am surest of is that I am somehow on the right track, and the path that He wants for me is the one I am walking on, and I have no need to seek another. But by the path I am walking on I mean the concrete one I am walking on, not just the institutional Cistercian path—I mean *my* path. Which oddly enough seems to be Cistercian too. And it is going into the desert but not the desert that anyone expects. It is not going anywhere that anyone expects, including myself. And that is where I want to go; and where, by God's grace, I will go.

As for you, you want me in the worst way to be a saint, and that of course gets me upset, because I am not, and it is precisely difficult for me to accept the fact that anyone expects anything of me. That is when I go into one of my tantrums, and is one of the natural roots of my love for solitude—a weak root, and a diseased one. . . .

JULY 30, 1956

[Psychoanalyst Gregory] Zilboorg has been terrific. I am infinitely grateful for the possibility of contact with him. His lectures were terrific (and there is to be another week of them) and the whole thing has been for me like a retreat—not so much a question of picking up a lot of magic technical devices as of getting a real orientation for the human needs of sick people, a sense of how to handle them (*not* manipulate them) and help them to get well. This week Fr. Abbot is here too. And six other Trappists from all over the place.

Finally, Zilboorg is absolutely against publishing "The Neurotic Personality" [the article Merton had written was sent to Zilboorg before the conference]. He says it is sheer trash and can do nothing but harm and I shouldn't even try to revise it. I should put it on the shelf and get busy really learning something about the subject, and that will take time. I thoroughly agree with him about the article.

DECEMBER 29, 1956

. . . He [Zilboorg] gave us a couple of talks, I had some good conversations with him from which it transpires that, though I am indeed crazy as a loon, I don't really need analysis. He now has me all primed and happy with slogans like "Pipe down," "Get lost," etc. Nothing I like better. . . .

APRIL 25, 1960

. . . My own spiritual musings are about as usual, only worse. Never had such troubles with censors, so complicated, so unreasonable, so long-drawn-out. I stand surrounded by the massacred books they have rejected, and both the General (Dom Gabriel Sortais] and I are dizzy. Dom James has given up trying to keep up with us. Mainly they have finally sat on a project of my collaborating with the Zen man [Dr. D. T.], Suzuki. Even when I offered to invite other equally edifying collaborators—Fromm, Tillich, etc. Why not Khrushchev? (There I go again!)

Every time I open my poor trap the least bit about the solitary life the censors set up an anvil chorus that can be heard from here to Brooklyn. After all, I am not agitating about *anything,* just saying things which people in a contemplative order theoretically ought to appreciate. Not Trappists. . . .

JANUARY 7, 1964

The main thing I have on my mind, and I have written about it to J. [Laughlin] and spoken to Fr. Abbot about it, is having you and J. be my literary executors. Of course there are a lot of ins and outs, and the main thing is that you are my publishers, or about to be, but that is an advantage . . . Also Fr. Abbot agrees that up to a point it would be a very good thing to have this matter in the hands of someone outside the Order. Provided that it were guaranteed that the monastery would get the royalties and other monies due to it, and also that someone in the monastery would have a chance to veto the publication of any passage of a book that might bring serious discredit on the monastery or someone in it. . . .

Of course the main problem is that both you and J. are my age. But we could bring into it, as J. suggests, some young lawyer who might be interested. We can discuss it. I just wanted to put the thing before you and see what you thought. If I kick off, or get shot by the local patriots after my latest book, there will be a certain amount of unpublished material, quite a lot, much of which is already stored away at Bellarmine College. It will be made clear that they have no rights, only the "physicality" of the manuscripts. Is that word real? It is the one J. used. . . .

MARCH 3, 1964

Well, the unthinkable has happened. It usually does. A letter from the new Abbot General [Dom Ignace Gillet] came in concerning the articles

on peace in *Seeds of Destruction*. [These articles were part of a manuscript Merton wrote in 1962 that he called *Peace in a Post-Christian Era*
and that was published posthumously in 2004.] I was sure, since these had
been cleared before by the previous Abbot General, with difficulties, but yet
cleared and published, that I had the right to go ahead with them. However,
the new Abbot General dug out all the correspondence, had a meeting with
the definitors, and said that these articles are not to be "republished" in
book form and implicitly in any other form. . . .

Naomi, frankly I must say that this whole thing leaves me a bit dizzy. And
sick. I can't say exactly that it constitutes a temptation against my "vocation," but it certainly raises some pretty profound questions indeed. . . .

MARCH 13, 1964

. . . Naturally I am feeling much more philosophical about it after the
first day. When I wrote you the cut was open and full of salt. Thanks for
your good letter and advice. I suppose there is not much point reflecting on
it and making statements. I know exactly what the thing is. . . . Of course the
worst element in it is that I am getting in so many ways disillusioned with
the Order and the Church even (that is the thing that upsets people). But I
have no intention of making any kind of fuss about it, or starting a row. I
will have to live with this as everybody else has had to live with it since the
beginning. The modernist crisis is long since over and I am not a modernist
in any case. This is a different era. And I am afraid it is a much more dour
and serious era too.

Thanks for everything. Happy Easter.

AUGUST 9, 1965

. . . At the end of this month I am out of my novice job and permanently
in the hermitage. I am of course very glad, and also I see that it will not be
any big joke either. The more I get into it, the more I see that the business of
being solitary admits of absolutely no nonsense at all and when I see how
totally full of nonsense I am, I can see that I could wreck myself at it. Yet I
really think God asks me to take this risk, and I want to do this. So please
pray hard, really. . . .

AUGUST 17, 1965

This is just to thank you very, very much for your really understanding letter. In a thing like this, which is so strange in its way, it is good to have you really catch on immediately. And it is better still to have your support and your prayers. I am grateful for all these things. And I am really very hopeful for the future, even though my system is acting up furiously at times. That is the way it has to be, and I am glad it is so.

One thing that is very clear to me: this going into solitude is really what I must do. I know, if one can ever be said to know, that this comes from God and that I must obey Him. Of course, what my mad stomach tells me is that He has lured me out there to destroy me. But of course I don't "believe" such a thing. And in the long run what is happening is the kind of acceptance where one says: "Look, if you want to destroy me, that's fine because I would rather be destroyed by you and to please you than to have everything else in the world and be pleasing to you." And the funny thing about this is that I absolutely mean it, and I can't think of anything else in the world that makes sense or calls for two seconds of interest, compared with this. Of course I would like to go out and be a hermit in grand style, but I realize that I will probably be a pretty silly one, but I don't care, I'll make the best of it I can, with God's grace, and if it is absurd, well, classify it as an existentialism and forget it. But I think, in my stubborn head, that it is the real fulfillment of my monastic vocation. . . .

Meanwhile, I am really confident that, as you say, if I just plunge in everything will really be fine, and it actually has been so far with the quiet semi-hermit routine I have had all year. What happens now is just that it is taking on the shape of an "event" and I suppose even a drama, though I don't consciously get dramatic about things. This time perhaps, without meaning to, I am. So let's hope I calm down by next week. Saturday is the day I officially "begin." . . .

AUGUST 25, 1965

. . . About the hermitage: the five days I have been here all the time have been simply perfect, and everything seems to indicate that it will go on that way, but of course the original joy of it will doubtless wear off but for one thing I have no doubts: this is exactly right for me. It is all that I ever hoped for and more. . . . And that is really quite extraordinary, I think. I still see that it is going to be hard, but at least it is going to make sense. No one minds doing something difficult if he has sufficient reasons for tackling it. I can see without difficulty that if I really want to live the kind of life I came here for, then this is the sort of situation I must do it in. They have been the best days since I came here to Gethsemani twenty-five years ago, without any shadow of a doubt. That is what I am here for, and thank God I have found it, because it was very likely that I might never have done so. . . .

AUGUST 31, 1965

. . . Am settling down fine, actually I have stopped thinking about whether I am a hermit or what, and am simply living, with plenty to do, lots of reading, work, long meditations, and really this life makes an enormous amount of sense for me. It really does, and is doing me a lot of good in all sorts of ways. I am much less frustrated, spend less time mentally arguing against the ideas of the Abbot, stomach is much better, am utterly simplifying all meals I take up here, cooking practically nothing except soft-boiled eggs, and everything is working out fine, only problem I have had really was that I got into a difference of opinion with a nest full of hornets and was quite badly bitten. Believe me, those things are fierce. But fortunately it seems that I am not allergic to hornet bites so I didn't swell up as some people do. They were painful, however. . . .

OCTOBER 19, 1967

. . . I [will] make a new will (which is probably what will be required). The plan is to set up a Trust with you and J. and a Kentucky resident (Tommie O'Callaghan) as trustees, and to have the Abbey formally agree to this. Then we will be in the clear and everyone will presumably know where everyone stands and be happy with it. And the next Abbot won't have to worry about it.

JANUARY 19, 1968

The new Abbot is Fr. Flavian [Burns]—one of the other hermits and hence obviously all in favor of hermits. That is fine, because other candidates were not! He is the best of the lot, and the one I voted for, the one most people seem to like, the one most in favor of a serious monastic life, not wildly experimental but for real development. I think he still needs to develop, he is young and inexperienced, but has possibilities. . . .

MAY 4, 1968

. . . By the way, my old aunt [Agnes (Aunt Kit) Merton] (the one who visited here four years or so ago and who is in *Conjectures* [*of a Guilty Bystander*]) was lost in the Wahine disaster (big shipwreck in New Zealand). I was awfully sorry about it. Survivors said she was terribly courageous walking about and telling everyone to cheer up. She was among the many who were lost between the ship and the nearby shore, even though they had life belts. Heavy waves, etc. It must have been very wretched for them all. (Life rafts capsized and all the rest.) Do pray for her. She was a very dear person and about the last one in the family really close to me. I'm sure she is in heaven anyway, but I pray for her. . . .

TO SISTER THERESE LENTFOEHR, S.D.S. *A member of the congregation of the Sisters of the Divine Savior, a poet and teacher living in Racine, Wisconsin, Sister Therese began a correspondence with Merton in 1948 that continued for twenty years. She sent Merton gifts and wrote glowing reviews of his books. Merton began sending her manuscripts and drafts of his writing. She searched out everything she could find out about him. Hers was the largest private collection of Mertoniana (it eventually went to Columbia University). In November 1967, she visited him at Gethsemani, accompanied by Tommie O'Callaghan.*

NOVEMBER 3, 1948

. . . Your remarks about *The Seven Storey Mountain* are so exceedingly generous they leave me inarticulate—no book written by me could possibly be that good! But I am happy that you really liked it and I know your prayers will do a great deal to make it bear fruit among the people for whom it was mainly written—my own uncouth tribe, footloose "intellectuals." I am very happy that I am no longer one of them. I only wish I was more of a monk. . . .

. . . Your suggestion about sending something to the Holy Father gives me food for thought. It sounds like a very good idea. Father Abbot is not here now, but I'll ask him. Meanwhile, in order to repay your gift of books with a little token—call it a Christmas present, if you like—I thought you might be curious to see a manuscript of the *Mountain,* since it was much cut. So I'll give you the carbon instead of burning it up. . . .

This time it was my turn to faint! I have never had such a marvelous Christmas present. Your generosity in parting with that relic of St. Therese is certainly heroic. I was afraid Father Abbot might insist on putting it with the other relics here, in the Church. But no: he said, with a sigh of relief and an expression that contained a ray of hope: "Frater Louis, you *need* something like that." He insists that I wear it, in the hope that at long last I may start to be a good Cistercian. . . .

. . . Really, the *Mountain* did need to be cut. Its length was impossible for any publisher. The editor at Harcourt was, is, my old friend Bob Giroux who comes into the book for a line somewhere. He did a very good job. Evelyn Waugh has edited the London edition and tells me he cut a great deal more—mostly for reasons of economy and because what he cut seemed to be more or less "local interest" to Americans. . . .

Well, everything cooperates for good to those who love God. The new Father-Cellarer, at the beginning of the year, took over the room where I was working. That left practically nowhere for me except the rare book vault. And now here I am behind a double iron door in what is the closest thing to being soundproof in this silent monastery, and surrounded by twelfth-century manuscripts of St. Bernard. It is simply wonderful. . . .

. . . I sent the other carbon of the *Mountain* ms. to Fr. Terence Connolly at Boston College and he has put the thing on exhibition in his library, so I want to tell you at once that you must feel free to make use of your copy in any way you please. . . .

APRIL 26, 1949

. . . Thank you also for the card from New York. One thing distresses me: it is the thought that you may have been led to ferret around in the Columbia library until you unearthed some skeleton in the closets of the Columbia of fifteen years or so ago. If you did, then I have no need to assure you that those skeletons are certainly skeletons and there is nothing in those closets to edify a religious. I am only thinking of your own sensibilities. For my own part, I ought at least to be able to accept the humiliation of my past as some kind of penance. After all I ought to do something to make amends.

On the other hand you will be glad to hear that the priesthood is very close now and that they have arranged the ordinations for Ascension Day, May 26th. . . . I am trying to immerse myself in the Mass—and the more I do so, the more I feel that that Holy Sacrifice is the purest and most perfect of prayers and that all contemplation is to be found therein. . . .

MAY 13, 1949

. . . About the ordination—alas, Father Abbot wants everything to be very, very quiet and simple. Here it cannot be otherwise. We have absolutely no accommodations for lady visitors. One or two friends—the close ones mentioned in the book—will be here, I expect. No, we never go out to say a First Mass. That is strictly forbidden. I know that with the slightest encouragement you would probably be willing to camp in a tree with the Kentucky possums, but you must be content to be here in spirit, and I shall profit greatly by your good prayers. How badly I need them. There is practically nothing of the priest about me. I am still a rough diamond, without any gentleness or tact or charity. Well, the first apostles are my consolation. But pray that I may imitate them as they were *after* Pentecost, not before! . . .

JUNE 2, 1949

. . . As to the marvelous grace of ordination at last I have found the place in the universe that has been destined for me by the mercy of God. The priestly character, unworthy as I am to receive it, is so much "mine," in the designs of God and Our Blessed Lady, that I feel as if I had at last awakened to discover my true name and my true identity, as if I had never before been a complete person. . . .

JULY 15, 1949

. . . Thank you very kindly indeed for your beautiful review of *Seeds* [*of Contemplation*]. How like you it is! You have seen deeply into the book and have been very kind to the author, and have neglected the faults of a brash young writer who is perhaps too bold and too careless. . . . I am not surprised that some of the clergy are annoyed at me. There will always be careful and conscientious folk who travel a strictly beaten track who will be upset by people like myself who have too little respect for convention. . . .

AUGUST 28, 1949

. . . When you feel particularly low, and are convinced that you have been abandoned by God because of your weaknesses, remember that He is nearer then than in many an hour of consolation. . . .

. . . About prayer: have you a garden or somewhere that you can walk in, by yourself? Take half an hour, or fifteen minutes a day and just walk up and down among the flowerbeds with the intention of offering this walk up as a meditation and a prayer to Our Lord. Do not try to think about anything in particular and when thoughts about work, etc. come to you, do not try to push them out by main force, but see if you can't drop them just by relaxing your mind. Do this because you "are praying" and because Our Lord is with you. But if thoughts about work will not go away, accept them idly and without too much eagerness with the intention of letting Our Lord reveal His will to you through these thoughts. . . .

NOVEMBER 12, 1949

. . . The double ending [of *The Mountain*]: First I wrote an ending, when I finished the first draft of the book in October 1946. The present ending was written after my solemn profession (March 19, 1947) and was in fact the result of some lights that came to me in prayer on the Feast of the Sacred Heart, June 1947. I wrote the last pages (the conversation with Our Lord) on the afternoon of that Feast. Most of the other parts of the last section of the epilogue (about the monastery) in the new and printed version were written about that time too, in the days before the feast. But the article on "Active and Contemplative Orders" was slipped in there at the suggestion of Dr. Francis X. Connolly of Fordham. . . .

MAY 6, 1950

As usual I have a score of things to thank you for and I am far behind with all of them. Taking the most recent arrival first: your article in the *Catholic World* for this month ["I will be your Monk"] is simply delightful. You have done a superlative job. Needless to say, I wish I could be something of what you make me appear to be on paper! . . . My highest ambition is to glorify Him by throwing all care to the winds and living on His love, without the slightest vain solicitude for anything in the universe. . . .

AUGUST 19, 1950

. . . Thank you, dear Sister, for working on the "Orientation Notes." The title page should read: "Monastic Orientation—Lectures given to the Choir Novices—Abbey of Gethsemani—1950.". . .

Your account of your visit to Ed [Rice] fascinated and charmed me. I rarely get any news from him, and it was good to see into his apartment with you! Don't worry, I didn't bat an eyelash at your knocking on the window—except in surprise at the thought you would think I would be surprised. . . .

FEBRUARY 10, 1951

. . . I am going to become an American citizen some time this year, if I pass the examination! Also—today I finished the book *Fire Cloud and Darkness.* At least the first draft of it. It was your St. John of the Cross relic that did the trick. The book is practically all about his doctrine. From the time I got the new relic, I was so flooded with ideas—especially about transforming union—that the thing went like a breeze. . . .

Many thanks for the wonderful job on the *Journal*. I can easily fill in the spaces. You did a heroic job of deciphering. Meanwhile, I have finished the book for Harcourt Brace. The title is now *The Ascent to Light*. I guess I told you I had finished it, last time. . . .

. . . I have been appointed Master of the Students—a new thing here. I have to form the whole scholasticate, so to speak out of the air. . . .

. . . The job [Master of Students] is a necessary one. It is almost entirely spiritual direction—and they certainly can get problems! But the big thing is this. I earnestly beg your prayers because I am just waking up to the infinite depths of my insufficiency for this job. . . .

. . . The Carmelites everywhere seem to be quite pleased by the book [*The Ascent to Truth*], and Bob [Giroux] tells me it has sold 45,000. I have given up trying to understand why. But I am glad to have the Carmelites with me—I feel I belong more and more to them, even though I belong more and more to my own Cistercians. . . .

Yes, the little volume of Rilke arrived safely and I am delighted with it. I have always liked Rilke anyway. His poems on Our Lady are really meaningful and I relish them. Some of my scholastics are reading them also. . . . Busy editing the *Journal* at present. *Bread in the Wilderness* is scheduled for October. . . .

. . . Bob Giroux was down from New York this week, and we were putting the finishing touches on the *Journal* [*The Sign of Jonas*] which is going to press now.

NOVEMBER 6, 1952

. . . To set your mind at rest about *The Sign of Jonas*—it was objected to by censors and the Abbot General withheld his *imprimi potest,* but matters had gone so far with the printing and publicizing of the book that it was deemed advisable to let it finally be published. . . . The book shows quite frankly that I am not much of a religious—a truth which I have no desire to conceal—and it also gives a clear insight into various problems. By a series of accidents, it turns out that God's will is for the thing to be published. . . .

JULY 10, 1954

. . . Finally finished the work on *Viewpoints,* which has a different title: I have called it *No Man Is an Island*—words taken from one of John Donne's "Devotions." The reference is to the Mystical Body, every man being not an "island" but a "piece of a continent." I don't know what Harcourt Brace will do with the title. I have never thought up so many titles for any one book as I have for this one. . . .

NOVEMBER 29, 1954

. . . The new book? It is called *Existential Communion.* I know you will like the daring title, but I hope the contents are all correct. Pray that they may be so. The book is simply an attempt to show that whatever is good about existentialism is and has been for a long time part of the Christian mystical tradition. . . .

DECEMBER 20, 1954

I have been scrounging around for something to send you this Christmas, and there is little here that is worthy of your attention—or proportionate to my debt to you. However, there is one thing which I treasure and which you will also like. It is an old magazine containing an article on my Father's painting and several reproductions both in color and black and white. It is an old beat-up magazine, and may be in worse shape still by the time it reaches you. But I think you will agree on its worth. . . .

. . . *No Man Is an Island* is on the way to the printers and was scheduled for Lent, but it is too late for that now. If you like the title (as I do) please pray that it may stick. There is opposition to it—not from Bob Giroux, so much as my agent [Naomi Burton Stone] who objects that the Donne text has been mined for titles by other authors (v.g. Hemingway who took *For Whom the Bell Tolls* from a few lines higher up). . . .

JANUARY 18, 1955

I am glad you liked the "Art in N.Z." I thought you would. The picture of Father in the clipping was taken when he was pretty young. Probably about the time he was married, I should think. I never remember him as young as that. . . .

AUGUST 6, 1955

. . . What I am hoping for now is to find some real solitude. Things at last seem to shaping up to provide me with some, after all these years. God works slowly and I am not the most prudent man in the world so I suppose it is a very good thing that He works slowly in my own life. Yet now that I think of it, things are moving faster than one would think. . . . But I do think there is some hope of my becoming at least a quasi-hermit. I have been put in full charge of the forest. . . .

. . . But one more thing—on the eighteenth please say a good big prayer for my old New Zealand grandmother who is really OLD. She is going to be a hundred on that day. I hope it doesn't run in the family. . . .

SEPTEMBER 29, 1955

I have been very busy in the forest, as the time has come to start marking trees for "selective cutting" for the winter's firewood and for forest improvement. Sounds scientific. I have a Jeep which runs furiously once it gets started and the other day I ran into a post and bashed in the radiator, so that the garage man is mad at me and my face is very red. I must learn to use the brake. . . .

OCTOBER 22, 1955

. . . The abbatial election at the [Abbey of the] Genesee has lit on one of the fathers [Walter Helmstetter], the novice master, and I am to replace him, so it seems. I thought I was headed for the fire tower and silence, and I find I am moving in the opposite direction. . . .

However, I shall be in charge of the forest and take the novices out to fell trees and to plant in the spring. I am busy marking the timber we are to cut this winter. There is one quiet little valley full of beech trees which I love very much—it was always cool and quiet in the summer, and very beautiful in the fall with the sun coming through the colored foliage. But the beeches have to go. . . .

FEBRUARY 21, 1956

. . . We have a couple of new postulants, one of whom is a Spanish priest who got here via South America and who does not speak English. I try to give him direction in Spanish. There is another—a Benedictine—from Brazil who, thanks be to God, knows French. Our third South American cleric is fortunately English and it turns out that his sister lives at a village in Surrey two miles from the home of my aunt [Gwynned Merton Trier], where I used to spend Christmas when I was in school in England. Strange, isn't it? . . .

Happy Lent. By the way, don't worry about me. The doctors have told me not to fast and have clapped me into the infirmary refectory. I am not dying, or anything, but they just thought I wasn't getting enough protein which is probably true as I am allergic to milk and cheese and never eat it and that is about our only protein source. For a while I have been getting eggs to help out, though. And now even meat. What a Lent. . . .

JUNE 11, 1956

. . . What keeps me on the jump at this particular time is that it is the season for postulants. They all poured in around June 1st, when the schools were out. None of them could enter immediately as I make them all take psychiatric tests (which are slow in getting scored) and some have to go to summer school for Latin, but they will be drifting in between now and September—around ten of them, I hope. Pray that I may always make good decisions. I can't expect to be infallible but still it is such an important affair. So many are desperately anxious to enter and yet one can see they should not come here. But there are many really solid vocations among them. . . .

. . . I take this occasion, then, not only to wish you a very happy and holy feast, from the bottom of my heart, but to tell you how really and how deeply I have appreciated all you have done, and how much I have relished our correspondence. Although I have always put on a show of being very ascetic, I do not hesitate to confess that letters from my friends have always and will always mean a great deal to me. . . .

. . . The Abbot General is progressively tightening up restrictions and making the censorship tougher and tougher so that writers will be definitely discouraged in the Order. And that too is all right—it is really the spirit of the Order to keep silent!!! However not all the writers have been clamped down on and certainly not everybody has had their mail stopped. . . .

. . . Christmas was in some ways quite hectic here. There is a relatively enormous tree in the novitiate library outside my door, and the branches form a kind of hedge that I have to plough through to get in and out. They took over the undermaster's room in entirety for the crib. It is good to see all the novices happy. . . . Nothing could possibly be more happy and joyful than a Trappist novitiate at Christmas time. . . . The Midnight Mass was wonderful. Of course I remembered you most especially in my three Masses. . . .

. . . We got a big batch of postulants in June, and there are over thirty in the novitiate at the moment. . . . We have a seminarian from Hungary [Laszlo "Ladislaus" Faludi], one who escaped last November, after the police came looking for him. He has not arrived yet, was here for an interview and will enter in September. A good soul, I think. I have a young Nicaraguan poet [Ernesto Cardenal] who is also a good man, and has an interesting background. Through him I am finding out about Latin America and a lot of interesting people in it. . . .

. . . About the visit: I am always up the same tree in that regard. Father Abbot is getting stricter and stricter all the time about correspondence and visits, the two things he is really strict about, and I just don't think it is possible that he will ever countenance visits of women who are not close relatives—or enormously wealthy benefactors. You are certainly a benefactor, but he doesn't look at it that way. You know how much I would enjoy talking over so many things: but as it is I am left in no doubt that he thinks I am way over my quota all the time, in these matters. . . .

. . . Dan Walsh wrote me that he had felt obliged to pan *Thoughts in Solitude* and was profusely apologetic about it, as he would be, but I never saw his review. That is a strange book. For a while I was dead against it myself. A lot of people say that they like it almost better than anything else I have done. Mystery. I still do not think it is particularly good: but I suppose it has something to say to a few special people whom God alone knows. . . .

. . . Have you heard of the new book of the Russian poet Pasternak? *Dr. Zhivago.* It is a tremendous thing and a lot of his poems are published in appendix. The book was not allowed to be published in Russia ("idealist deviation" and doubtless also "rootless cosmopolitanism"), but it actually has a very important basic content of religion and the poems (some of them) are the finest religious poems written *anywhere* in the 20th century. It is fabulous. I think this is one of the most significant events in literature in the whole 20th century and something we all ought to ponder. I'd like to write an article about him. In the refectory they are reading Newman's life by Louis Bouyer, a splendid book. . . . I think it is the wisest and most outspoken book about the problems of converts that I have ever seen—it has made me really understand and sympathize with Newman for the first time—and now I am sold on him, I think he was really a saint. . . .

I received wonderfully comforting words from Jacques Maritain about *Thoughts in Solitude.* Many people have not liked it, as I expected, and I do not mind the fact. The book does not say exactly what I wanted it to say. Nevertheless it is one of the books that really does come from the inner depths, where I most unequivocally mean everything in a very personal and definite way. It is a book in which I speak what is really on my mind, or what was on my mind in 1953. Now I would write quite a different one, because I have other things on my mind. . . .

APRIL 3, 1959

. . . Do pray for Nicaragua: the situation there is as bad as it was in Cuba, and one of my novices [Ernesto Cardenal] has relatives who have suffered much in prison, and been tortured. They want to throw out their own dictator someday soon and I hope they succeed. I only hope the stupidity of our State Department does not make it difficult for them. . . .

JULY 4, 1959

. . . At the moment, guess what, I am rewriting *What Is Contemplation?* It will be a patchy job. But I have been wanting to do it. I may revise other early material, too. It is all very unsatisfactory to me, in fact a lot of it disgusts me. I was much too superficial and too cerebral at the same time. I seem to have ignored the wholeness and integrity of life and concentrated on a kind of angelism in contemplation. That was when I was a rip-roaring Trappist, I guess. Now that I am a little less perfect I seem to have a saner perspective. . . .

SEPTEMBER 29, 1959

. . . I finished a book this summer called *The Inner Experience* which started out to be a simple revision of *What Is Contemplation?* but turned into something new, and just about full length. It has to be revised and has been sitting here on the desk, waiting for revision for some time, but I refuse to work around the house as they are blasting around on all sides with jackhammers and other machines and it is impossible to think. The novices have been making a good share of this noise, trying to put in a couple of new showers in our crowded cellar. . . .

MAY 30, 1960

. . . I have had a lot of difficulties and distracting cares. First of all with censors. You have no idea how absurd they have been. I wrote an article on solitude and anyone would think that it was an obscene novel, the way they landed on it. There is in the Order a kind of terror of any mention of the solitary life, no doubt because the tradition in this regard is unpalatable among us: we have decided that the cenobitic life is the *ne plus ultra* and we have to struggle by main force to keep ourselves convinced of this. Such absurdities arise from the arbitrary fantasies of institutional thought: thinking for the "outfit" rather than in accordance with truth and the full tradition of the Church. But I really got in trouble. I rewrote the thing three times. . . . Finally when I thought I had the whole thing simon pure, the censor declared that I was making "direct attacks on Superiors and the authority of the Church." This was for a sentence which ran something like: "Those who say interior solitude is sufficient do not realize what they are saying." This was interpreted to mean superiors, as if no one else would ever think of saying such a thing. In another sentence, where I said that the principal anguish of the solitary life was that the hermit did not have anyone to guide him and the will of God pressed upon him with immediacy or something like that. Overlooking the fact that I said this was a source of anguish, they picked that up and said I was preaching against authority and spiritual direction and saying that everyone should seek to be guided directly by the Holy Ghost. You never saw such a stupid mess. The Abbot General [Gabriel Sortais] picked this up and flew into one of his rages, which can be very stormy, and I was all but consigned to the nether regions as a contumacious heretic. . . .

The book in which these things are to appear is now in galleys. It is very appropriately called *Disputed Questions*. . . . I said some rather cutting things about conventional ideas of monasticism, things which were true and obvious, but one is not supposed to say them. . . .

DECEMBER 5, 1960

. . . I was happy about the presidential election, but certainly did not vote for Kennedy because of his religion, I assure you. I thought there was not too much to choose between them but that Kennedy is the better man, at least shows promise of much more development. . . .

I think I may do a rather thorough piece of revision on *Seeds of Contemplation,* a new edition is called for. I thought of this when I got a letter from a man in Pakistan [Abdul Aziz] who is an authority on Sufism and realized I couldn't send him the book because of an utterly stupid remark I had made about the Sufis. . . .

SEPTEMBER 19, 1961

. . . It seems that my time is more and more consumed, and there are reasons for it, as I am now seeing quite a lot of the various retreatants particularly Protestants still. Also a wonderful Rabbi from Winnipeg a Hasid [Zalman Schachter], an orthodox priest, a Negro working on fair labor practices for Negroes, and lots of others like that. They are wonderful people, and have so much. It is very encouraging, except that there does not seem to be much they can do with all the good that is in them. . . . I can still get mad at society all right. It is such a tragic thing that society as a whole should be so violent, corrupt, wasteful, and absurd. . . .

JUNE 15, 1962

Your book [a catalogue of her Merton "collection"], for it is really a book, really astonished me. It was quite an "experience" for me, too, and gave me much to reflect on. First of all, of course, the care and perspicacity with which you have handled all that material. What splendid use you have made of every little thing: and I was agreeably surprised to find that long forgotten bits of scraps and poems or even essays I had thought long ago destroyed or lost, all turn up there. . . .

JULY 17, 1962

. . . Today Victor Hammer, who has printed those various limited editions, is coming over. He has some more work to finish off the crucifix he did for our novitiate chapel. (I will try to dig up a photo of the chapel for you. It is nothing special as a chapel but this "rood" type crucifix is very fine.) And he has finished *Hagia Sophia.* I hope to send you a copy soon. He is a great craftsman and a wonderful person. I always enjoy his visits, and he has given talks to some of the young monks too, on art, work, etc.

SEPTEMBER 20, 1962

. . . Dan Berrigan's visit was most stimulating. He is a man full of fire, the right kind, and a real Jesuit, of which there are not too many perhaps. He wants to write about the real spirit of Ignatius and I think he would be capable of a good job. He is alive and full of spirit and truth. I think he will do much for the Church in America and so will his brother Phil, the only priest so far to have gone on a Freedom Ride. They will have a hard time, though, and will have to pay for every step forward with their blood.

There were other visits: a Rabbi friend [Zalman Schachter] from Manitoba, a Hasid. Apart from that I was busy with the *Reader,* and with the Peace book [*Peace in the Post-Christian Era*] that could not be published. Did I send you a copy? I think I did. I forget about it. I know you had the ["Cold War] Letters." *Breakthrough* [*to Peace*] is now out. The collection of essays . . . I think it is effective. I am sending that for your feast day also.

[Hans] Küng of course I read as soon as I could get my hands on him. I thought it a noble, straight and courageous book [*The Council, Reform and Reunion*]. The vigor and honesty of the message was tremendous. But such books raise vain hopes, perhaps. The Council cannot possibly measure up to all he suggested. Yet precisely for that reason we must doggedly hope that it will. . . .

DECEMBER 20, 1962

Here I come with a noise out of the woods, something to say for Christmas . . . the wise men are on the way, and the shepherds, and our own childhood. And it will be Christmas again, with all the invisible grace of His coming, His revolution. We do not understand that this business about the crib is the real revolution that once for all turned everything upside down so that nothing has ever been, or can ever be, the same again. But we try hard to sing the "old song" instead of the new one: the song of war, of money, of power, of success, of having a good time: when it is really all much simpler than that. Life is much more fun when you don't have to have a good time or force anybody to do anything or put anything across. . . .

The Council was tremendous, wasn't it? (Isn't it?) Really Pope John has been a great gift from God to all of us. What a superb Pope, and what a heart. The past few months have made me realize the greatness of the Church as

I had never realized it before, not the stuffed shirt pompous greatness that some of the Curia people evidently want it to be, but the charity and the real concern for all men, the *cura pastoralis*. This has been a tremendous experience, I think to all of us. And how providential. . . . And yet the Church is facing the same kind of critical juncture in thought that she faced with Galileo. . . . Much prayer is needed. . . .

FEBRUARY 19, 1963

. . . One of the things I did read was a manifesto by the Negro writer James Baldwin on the race situation. It is powerful and great. I even gave the publisher a blurb for it, which may get me hanged some day. But it is a tremendous and stirring document. Called *The Fire Next Time*. . . .

Jacques Maritain is so pleased that I translated a few of Raissa [Maritain]'s poems. He is deeply moved by any sign of response to her wonderful contemplative spirit—and his own. A wonderful person, to whom I feel very close these days. I have never got such letters. He wrote a wonderful one on "Hagia Sophia" too, which just came yesterday. He is spending all his time (besides teaching philosophy to the Little Brothers) editing Raissa's journal. I have seen a copy of it, and some of the material is really great. . . .

MAY 1, 1963

. . . I am being given an honorary LL.D. by the University of Kentucky. Of course it has to be *in absentia* and Victor Hammer has promised to get it for me. Also some kind of peace prize offered by an organization called New England Political Action for Peace. . . .

JUNE 30, 1963

. . . Pope John will, I think, be impossible to equal. No one can replace such a man. As time goes by we will see how extraordinary he really was. I have no doubt he was one of the great saints of our time. Am very happy to have a beautiful signed picture of him over the vesting table in the novitiate chapel. Pope Paul will, however, be good in a different way. Bright, energetic, experienced, and I think holy also. Maritain thought very highly of him years ago when he was in the Secretariat, and whatever slight contacts I have had with him have always impressed me favorably. . . .

JULY 12, 1964

. . . *Honest to God* is causing a bit of a stir in Protestant circles. He [author John A.T. Robinson] gives the impression when he is all over that there is no God left to be honest to. I think that is an exaggeration. He is just catching on to the truth that God cannot be expressed in adequate concepts. He is also strong on the new morality and such things. Good will, sincere, naïve I think, earnest about getting through to "the world." . . . I am currently reading Dietrich Bonhoeffer, Protestant [pastor] executed under Hitler: magnificent. . . .

SEPTEMBER 17, 1964

. . . I am now pushing fifty and realize more and more that every extra day is just a free gift, and so I relax and forget about past and future. The "I" that goes from day to day is not an important "I" and his future matters little. And the deeper "I" is in an eternal present. If a door should one day open from one realm to the other, then "I" (whoever that is) will be glad of it. I have no regrets except for sins that are forgiven in any case, and I forget the past, and don't get too excited about either the present or the future. . . .

JUNE 16, 1965

Thanks for sending the list to Naomi Burton [Stone]. This literary trusteeship is something that has become necessary. She and James Laughlin of New Directions have agreed to take care of everything, with a young Catholic lawyer [John J. Ford], and it ought to keep any number of problems from developing, as they tend to. But of course with such an awful lot of published and unpublished material around, it is a very complex job for them. I hope everything can be done to make it simple, and then they can handle it peacefully and easily. I suppose that the main thing is above all to keep track of unpublished material that is around in various collections or in the hands of friends or people I no longer know have it. The big job at the moment is for the trustees to get a good idea where everything is and *what* it is. You are the one who can be of most help in this, because you have the most complete collection and the one in which there are so many notes, sermons, unpublished pieces as well as original mss. . . .

My hermitage is dedicated to St. Mary of Carmel, and the time is getting close, (I hope) when I will be there permanently. I am semi-permanent there already. It is wonderful to live so close to birds etc. . . .

. . . I have been cleaning house, and this week I officially begin the hermit life (Saturday and Sunday, F. of the Immaculate Heart, will be so to speak the formal beginning). The Council voted favorably on it today, and the new novice master is all set to take over, and I am all set to go, except that it seems that I may go over the bumps a bit with my stomach taking everything too hard. But so what, I might as well pay my way, spiritually. But I can use your good prayers. It is quite a step, and something that has not been done this officially in the Order since the Lord knows when, way back in the Middle Ages, when we had a few hermit saints. . . .

I don't think I answered your last very interesting letter . . . Did I tell you that I had moved out to the woods? I came out over a month ago. Go down only once a day, for Mass and dinner, then come back. I get a little supper for myself and as I don't like to bother with cooking or washing dishes I try to keep it as simple as possible. It is really a wonderful life, a revelation, even much better than I expected. It is so good to get back to plain natural simplicity and the bare essentials, no monkeying around with artificialities and non-essentials. It really gives a wonderful new dimension to one's life. I didn't realize, until I got out here, how tense and frustrated I really was in community, though of course I love the monks. . . . I like being a hermit, and I do have real solitude. There is never anyone around in the woods except an occasional hunter, and we are trying to persuade them to go elsewhere. It is real solitude, and just perfect.

. . . The little book on Gandhi [*Gandhi on Non-Violence*] came out, at a curious time, now that India is swept with war fever. I am afraid that in the end we will have to admit that non-violence really failed in India, as Gandhi himself saw before he died. It asks very much of men: really, true non-violence cannot be carried out except by real saints. In this country there are indeed some really dedicated men in the non-violent civil rights movement, but a lot of them are anything but saints. This has its effect and as far as I can see the non-violent movement has been terribly set back by the violence this summer. . . .

FEBRUARY 16, 1966

. . . The cold spell . . . was quite an experience in the hermitage, and your prayers were answered: I had a lot of friendly birds around, and fed them with crackers. The deer are around too. It is fine and silent—and lonely. I have no questions about this being the kind of life for me, and it is certainly nothing to play with. It is hard. You really have to face yourself, and believe me that is quite grim. But at least it has one great consolation: it makes sense. I often had a very hard time convincing myself that the life down in the community did that. I always liked the other monks, but felt that the system itself was a bit artificial and unreal, and it seemed to be chewing so many of them up into hamburger, so to speak. I think of them a lot here and relate my own life to theirs. . . .

SEPTEMBER 5, 1967

It was good of you to send the little clipping about Ad Reinhardt [a fellow student of Merton's at Columbia]. I had known nothing about his death. It was a shock. . . . Tomorrow I shall offer Mass for Ad here in the hermitage, where I say Mass very quietly now by myself, early in the morning . . . after the preface I turn out the light and have nothing but the two candles shining on the ikons. Poor Ad. I had been thinking about him a lot lately, wanting to see him again. Had not seen him for about ten years I think. He was really a stupendous person. One of the very smartest and best, and there was a great deal packed into that painting of blacks on blacks. . . .

OCTOBER 13, 1967

Yes it was real!! I am probably as surprised as you are. I did not think I would be able to reach you, as I did not know the name of the convent, let alone the phone number. But somehow it got through. Hence, I recapitulate: the Bellarmine people are expecting you down in Louisville to give a talk— afternoon or evening of Nov. 4th. They will of course pay your expenses.

Mrs. O'Callaghan will take care of accommodations, and will bring you out to Gethsemani for a visit Tuesday. . . .

FEBRUARY 21, 1968

. . . I am having a little addition put on to the cottage: a chapel—and a replacement for the outhouse where I hope "that bastard" [the black snake] won't be able to get in. . . .

Our new Abbot [Flavian Burns] is very fine, and everyone likes him. It is not that he is wildly radical or progressive, just that he is frank and simple and you know where you stand. And he is willing to go along with anything fairly reasonable. And monastic. . . .

INDIA, NOVEMBER 21 [1968]

I have been a month in India—over a month—& most of it in the Himalayas. A great experience.

Your letter was forwarded from the monastery. Bro. Patrick [Hart] has been taking care of mail & all business. . . . I am going on to Ceylon & Indonesia & expect to see many more interesting people. God be with you.

On December 10, 1968, Sister Therese received a telegram, signed Abbot of Gethsemani, reading: "We regret to inform you of the death of Father Louis Merton in Bangkok."

PART 4

Speaking the Truth

Writing to Fellow Writers

"Basically our first duty today is to human truth in its existential reality. . . ."

—To Ernesto Cardenal, March 11, 1967

A writer himself, Merton felt deep kinship with other writers and poets with whom he could share his passion for writing. His letters contain expressions of admiration, encouragement, and support; discussions and critiques of their writing and his own; and reflections on the roles and responsibilities of writers and poets. Merton's letters reveal his affection for and solidarity with writers who had the courage to stand up to repressive and totalitarian regimes, even risking their lives to speak the truth. This sense of solidarity is especially evident in Merton's letters to Boris Pasternak and Czeslaw Milosz and in excerpts from Merton's letters to a number of Latin American writers. Merton's exchanges with writers and intellectuals also demonstrate the expansion of his idea of what it meant to be a monk and a contemplative. Writing to Pope John XXIII just months after the epiphany at Fourth and Walnut, which Merton reported in *Conjectures of a Guilty Bystander,* he characterizes his outreach as an "apostolate of friendship."

TO POPE JOHN XXIII   *Cardinal Angelo Giuseppe Roncalli was elected pope on October 28, 1958, taking the name of John XXIII. In January 1959, he announced that he was calling an ecumenical council, and on October 11, 1962, he convened the first session of the Second Vatican Council. Hailed as a watershed event, the Council initiated reforms that transformed the Catholic Church. Merton welcomed Pope John XXIII's encyclical on peace,* Pacem in Terris *(1963).*

NOVEMBER 10, 1958

. . . since my ordination nine years ago and through my experience as master of scholastics and then of novices, I have come to see more and more what abundant apostolic opportunities the contemplative life offers, without even going outside the monastic cloister.

It seems to me that, as a contemplative, I do not need to lock myself into solitude and lose all contact with the rest of the world; rather this poor world has a right to a place in my solitude. It is not enough for me to think of the apostolic value of prayer and penance; I have also to think in terms of a contemplative grasp of the political, intellectual, artistic and social movements in this world—by which I mean a sympathy for the honest aspirations of so many intellectuals everywhere in the world and the terrible problems they have to face. I have had the experience of seeing that this kind of understanding and friendly sympathy, on the part of a monk who really understands them, has produced striking effects among artists, writers, publishers, poets, etc., who have become my friends without my having to leave the cloister. I have even been in correspondence with the Russian writer who won the Nobel Prize in Literature, Boris Pasternak. This was before the tragic change in his situation. We got to understand one another very well. In short, with the approval of my Superiors, I have exercised an apostolate—small and limited though it be—within a circle of intellectuals from other parts of the world; and it has been quite simply an apostolate of friendship. . . .

TO BORIS PASTERNAK   *Although the exchange between Thomas Merton and Boris Pasternak (1890–1960) consists of only six letters—each wrote three times—the correspondence with the Russian writer was deeply significant to Merton and, it appears, to Pasternak as well. Pasternak was awarded the Nobel Prize for Literature in 1958. Even though he declined the award, he was expelled from the Soviet Writers' Union and labeled a traitor. Thomas Merton first wrote to Pasternak in August 1958, before reading* Dr. Zhivago, *and spoke of his deep kinship with the Russian: "It is as if we met on a deeper level of life on which individuals are not separate beings . . . it is as if we were known to one another in God." Pasternak responded to Merton in September with an enthusiasm that matched Merton's, confessing that he found Merton's letter "wonderfully filled with kindred thoughts." While Merton's letters to Pasternak reveal the deep regard with which Merton held the beleaguered writer, they also signal Merton's desire to enter into a dialogue with intellectuals all over the world. Merton's letters to Pasternak are reprinted below, together with excerpts from Merton's letter to Aleksei Surkov, the head of the Soviet Writers' Union, to whom Merton wrote to protest Pasternak's expulsion from the Union, as well as excerpts from Merton's letters to Helen Wolff, publisher of Pantheon Books, through whom Merton continued to receive news of Pasternak.*

Although we are separated by great distances and even greater barriers it gives me pleasure to speak to you as to one whom I feel to be a kindred mind. We are both poets—you a great one and I a very minor one. We share the same publisher in this country—New Directions. At least for our poetry; for your prose work is appearing under the Pantheon imprint and mine appears in another house.

I have not yet had the pleasure of reading your recent autobiography although I am familiar with the earlier one, *Safe Conduct*, by which I was profoundly impressed. It may surprise you when I say, in all sincerity, that I feel much more kinship with you, in your writing, than I do with most of the great modern writers in the West. That is to say that I feel that I can share your experience more deeply and with a greater intimacy and sureness, than that of writers like [James] Joyce whom I nevertheless so well like and understand. But when you write of your youth in the Urals, in Marburg, in Moscow, I feel as if it were my own experience, as if I were you. With other writers I can share ideas, but you seem to communicate something deeper. It is as if we met on a deeper level of life on which individuals are not separate beings. In the language familiar to me as a Catholic monk, it is as if we were known to one another in God. This is a very simple and to me obvious expression for something quite normal and ordinary, and I feel no need to apologize for it. I am convinced that you understand me perfectly. It is true that a person always remains a person and utterly separate and apart from every other person. But it is equally true that each person is destined to reach with others an understanding and a unity which transcend individuality, and Russian tradition describes this with a concept we do not fully possess in the West—*sobornost.*

It gives me pleasure to send you under separate cover a kind of prose poem or meditation on *Prometheus* [*Prometheus: A Meditation*] which has been privately printed near here recently. At least you will like the handsome printing. I hope the book reaches you. I am writing to you in your village home near Moscow—of which I happened to read in an English magazine. If you get this letter, and not the book, I hope you will let me know. I will try again.

It is my intention to begin learning Russian in order to try to get into Russian literature in the original. It is very hard to get much in the way of translations. I would much prefer to read you in Russian, though it will probably be a long time before I am able to do so. What I have read of modern Russian poets in translation is to me very stimulating. I have no difficulty in admitting a certain lassitude and decadence in much Western literature. I like [Vladimir] Mayakovsky and also I am very much interested in [Velimir] Khlebnikov (is that how you spell it?). What do you think of him? [Aleksandr] Blok of course I find very interesting. What about the new poets? Are there some good ones? Whom do you recommend? Do you know of the many very fine poets there have been in Latin America? I am particularly fond of a great Negro poet of Brazil, Jorge de Lima. [Pablo] Neruda, of Chile, is probably well known in the USSR and I presume you know him.

My dear Pasternak, it is a joy to write to you and to thank you for your fine poetry and your great prose. A voice like yours is of great importance for all mankind in our day—so too is a voice like that of [Dmitry] Shostakovich. The Russian leaders do not perhaps realize to the full how important and how great you are for Russia and for the world. Whatever may lie ahead for the world, I believe that men like yourself and I hope myself also may have the chance to enter upon a dialogue that will really lead to peace and to a fruitful age for man and his world. Such peace and fruitfulness are spiritual realities to which you already have access, though others do not.

These are the realities which are important. In the presence of these deeper things, and in witness of them, I clasp your hand in deep friendship and admiration. You are in my prayers and I beg God to bless you.

Pasternak replied on September 27, 1958, thanking Merton for the "congenial" letter, which seemed to him "wonderfully filled with kindred thoughts as having been written half by myself." On October 3, 1958, Pasternak wrote again to thank Merton for Prometheus.

What a great joy it was to receive your two letters. It has given me much food for thought, this bare fact of the communication between us: at a time when our two countries are unable to communicate with one another seriously and sincerely, but spend millions communicating with the moon. . . . No, the great business of our time is this: for one man to find himself in another one who is on the other side of the world. Only by such contacts can there be peace, can the sacredness of life be preserved and developed and the image of God manifest itself in the world.

Since my first letter to you I have obtained and read the book [*Dr. Zhivago*] published by Pantheon, and it has been a great and rewarding experience. First of all it has astounded me with the great number of sentences that I myself might have written, and in fact perhaps have written. Just one example at random: I am bringing out a book on sacred art in which one of the theses is practically this: "All genuine art resembles and continues the Revelation of St. John." This is to me so plain and so obvious that as a result I have seriously questioned the claim of the Renaissance to have produced much genuinely religious art. . . . But enough of the small details.

The book is a world in itself, a sophiological world, a paradise and a hell, in which the great mystical figures of Yurii and Lara stand out as Adam and Eve and though they walk in darkness walk with their hand in the hand of God. The earth they walk upon is sacred because of them. It is the sacred earth of Russia, with its magnificent destiny which remains hidden for it in the plans of God. To me the most overwhelmingly beautiful and moving passage is the short, tranquil section in the Siberian town where Yurii lying in the other room listens through the open door to the religious conversation of Lara and the other woman. This section is as it were the "eye" of a hurricane—that calm center of whirlwind, the emptiness in which is truth, spoken in all its fullness, in quiet voice, by lamplight. But it is hard to pick out any one passage. All through the book great waves of beauty break over the reader like waves of a newly discovered sea. Through you I have gained a great wondering love for the Urals (here I cannot accept your repudiation of the earlier books, where I first discovered this). The train journey to the east is magnificent. The exciting and rich part about the partisans is very interesting. Of course, I find in the book too little of Uncle Nikolai and his ideas—this is my only complaint and perhaps it is unjust, for his ideas speak in everything that happens.

Am I right in surmising that the ideas in this book run closely parallel to those in [Vladimir] Soloviev's *Meaning of Love*? There is a great similarity. Both works remind us to fight our way out of complacency and realize that all our work remains yet to be done, the work of transformation which is the work of love, and love alone. I need not tell you that I also am one who has tried to learn deeply from Dostoevsky's Grand Inquisitor, and I am passionately convinced that this is the most important of all lessons for our time. It is important here, and there. Equally important everywhere.

Shall I perhaps tell you how I know Lara, where I have met her? It is a simple enough story but obviously I do not tell it to people—you are the fourth who knows it, and there seems to be no point in a false discreetness that might restrain me from telling you since it is clear that we have so much in common.

One night I dreamt that I was sitting with a very young Jewish girl of fourteen or fifteen, and that she suddenly manifested a very deep and pure affection for me and embraced me so that I was moved to the depths of my soul. I learned that her name was "Proverb," which I thought very simple and beautiful. And also I thought: "She is of the race of Saint Anne." I spoke to her of her name, and she did not seem to be proud of it, because it seemed that the other young girls mocked her for it. But I told her that it was a very beautiful name, and there the dream ended. A few days later when I happened to be in a nearby city [Louisville], which is very rare for us, I was walking alone in the crowded street and suddenly saw that everybody was Proverb and that in all of them shone her extraordinary beauty and purity and shyness, even though they did not know who they were and were perhaps ashamed of their names—because they were mocked on account of them. And they did not know their real identity as the Child so dear to God who, from before the beginning, was playing in His sight all days, playing in the world.

Thus you are initiated into the scandalous secret of a monk who is in love with a girl, and a Jew at that! One cannot expect much from monks these days. The heroic asceticism of the past is no more.

I was so happy that you liked the best parts of *Prometheus*, and were able to tell me so. The other day I sent you a folder with some poems which I do not recommend as highly spiritual, but perhaps you might like them as poems. Yet I do not insist on this division between spirituality and art, for I think that even things that are not patently spiritual if they come from the heart of a spiritual person are spiritual. That is why I do not take you too seriously when you repudiate your earlier writings. True, they have not attained the stature of the latest great work, but they contain many seeds of it. I am deeply moved for instance by the florist's cellar in *Safe Conduct* which, like everything else in life, is symbolic. You yourself have said it!

I shall try to send you a book of mine, *The Sign of Jonas,* which is autobiographical and has things in it about the monastic life which might interest you. Perhaps New Directions can send you one or another book of my verse, but my poems are not very good.

So now I bring this letter to a close. It is a joy to write to you, and to hear from you. I continue to keep you in my prayers, and I remember you every day at Mass. Especially I shall say for you one of my Christmas Masses: on that day we have three Masses and one of them may be applied for our own intentions. Usually we have to say Mass for some stranger. But one of my Christmas Masses will be a special present for you. I was going to say a Mass on All Souls' Day (Nov. 2) for all your friends who had died especially in all the troubles recounted in the book. I was not able to arrange this, but I will do so some other time, I do not know when. I will try to drop you a line and let you know.

Meanwhile, then, with every blessing, I clasp your hand in warm friendship, my dear Pasternak. May the Most Holy Mother of God obtain for your soul light and peace and strength, and may her Holy Child be your joy and your protection at all times.

DECEMBER 15, 1958

For a long time I have been holding my breath in the midst of the turmoil of incomparable nonsense that has surrounded your name in every part of the world. It has been a tremendous relief to hear from you indirectly [through John Harris] and to learn that things are once again beginning to regain some semblance of sanity. You, like Job, have been surrounded not by three or four misguided comforters, but by a whole world of madmen, some of them reproaching you with reproaches that have been compliments, others complimenting you with compliments that have been reproaches, and seemingly very few of them have understood one word of what you have written. For what could be more blind and absurd than to make a political weapon, for one side or the other, out of a book that declares clearly the futility and malignity of tendencies on every side which seek to destroy man in his spiritual substance? Perhaps it is the destiny of every free man to bring out, like a poultice, the folly and the putrescence of our world: but such a vocation is not always pleasant.

One of the first things I did when I heard about the Nobel affair was to write a letter to [Aleksei] Surkov of the Writers' Union declaring that I spoke for all those who were fully aware that your book was not a political pamphlet and was not intended to be taken as such, and that it was a great work of art of which Soviet Russia should have the sense to be proud. I do not know if it did any good. Incidentally, since we have here no newspapers or radios, it was quite "accidental" or rather providential that I heard so much about the case so soon.

I do not know what the latest developments may be. If the question of making *Dr. Zh.* into a movie in America should arise and become an issue with you over there, I would strongly advise that you attach no importance to any movie but rather that you should, if the case arises to make a decision, rather *oppose* yourself to it. The movies here are quite bad, and I have always firmly resisted any attempt to use one of my books in a film. If a refusal on this point, by you, would aid your position with your government, then I would advise making such a refusal. Of course, remember I am perhaps not the wisest judge. But certainly a Hollywood production of *Dr. Zh.* would do more harm than good in every respect.

I have indeed been praying for you, and so have my young novices, young and pure souls, who know of you and who have been touched by your wonderful poem on Christ in the Garden of Gethsemani ["Garden of Gethsemane"]. We shall continue our prayers.

Do not let yourself be disturbed too much by either friends or enemies. I hope you will clear away every obstacle and continue with your writing on the great work that you surely have in store for us. May you find again within yourself the deep life-giving silence which is genuine truth and the source of truth: for it is a fountain of life and a window into the abyss of eternity and God. It is the wonderful silence of the winter night in which Yurii sat up in the sleeping house and wrote his poems while the wolves howled outside; but it is an inviolable house of peace, a fortress in the depths of our being, the virginity of our soul where, like the Blessed Mary, we give our brave and humble answer to life, the "Yes" which brings Christ into the world.

I cannot refrain from speaking to you of Abraham, and his laughter and prostration when he was told by God that he, a hundred years old, should be the father of a great nation and that from his body, almost dead, would come life to the whole world. The peak of liberty is in his laughter, which is a resurrection and a sacrament of the resurrection, the sweet and clean folly of the soul who has been liberated by God from his own nothingness. Here is what Philo of Alexandria has said about it:

"To convict us, so often proud and stiff-necked at the smallest cause, Abraham falls down (Genesis 17:17) and straightaway laughs with the laughter of the soul: mournfulness in his face but smiles in his mind where joy vast and unalloyed has made its lodging. For the sage who receives an inheritance of good beyond his hope, these two things were simultaneous, to fall and to laugh. He falls as a pledge that the proved nothingness of his mortal being keeps him from boasting. He laughs because God alone is good and the giver of great gifts that make strong his piety. Let created being fall with mourning in its face: it is only what nature demands, so feeble of footing, so sad of heart in itself. Then let it be raised up by God and laugh, for God alone is its support and joy."

I wish you this laughter in any sorrow that may touch your life.

Kurt W. [Wolff] has sent me the *Essai autobiographique* [written as the introduction to *A Sketch for an Autobiography* and published separately in 1958] and I am reading it with great pleasure. In my turn I am sending you a book of mine, also autobiographical in character, called *The Sign of Jonas*. It may take a little time to get there. New Directions may also send you a small volume of my poems, of which I am by no means proud.

I am learning Russian now, a little at a time, and later on I would be grateful if you would help me to get a few good simple books in Russian on which to practice—some good easy prose, and some poems. Is there a Russian book of saints? Someone has suggested that perhaps the legends of Sts. Evgraf, Lara, etc. might throw light on your characters. But anyway,

I know nothing of the Russian saints except of course for Seraphim of Sarov. I am very interested in the struggle between St. Nilus and Joseph of Volotsk—you can easily imagine why.

I hope this letter will reach you by Christmas, and it will bring you my blessings and my prayers and my deep affection, for the Holy Feast. My second Christmas Mass is for your intentions and for your family: and I will feast with you spiritually in the light of the Child of God Who comes shyly and silently into the midst of our darkness and transforms the winter night into Paradise for those who, like the Shepherds and the humble Kings, come to find Him where no one thinks of looking: in the obviousness and poverty of man's ordinary everyday life.

Pasternak last wrote to Merton on February 7, 1960, acknowledging Merton's gift of the privately printed Christmas book, Nativity Kerygma. *Merton published the letter in* Disputed Questions *as a "Postscript to 'The Pasternak Affair,'" noting that it reflected "the titanic inner struggle which the poet was waging to keep his head above water—no longer because of political pressure but because of the almost infinite complications of his life itself, as a result of his celebrity." Though Pasternak expressed deep frustration, he ended on a positive note: "I shall rise, you will see it. I finally will snatch myself and suddenly deserve and recover again your wonderful confidence. . . ." In a postscript, he urged Merton not to write to him: "The next turn to renew the correspondence will be mine."*

TO ALEKSEI SURKOV   *Following the announcement that Pasternak was to receive the Nobel Prize for Literature, Merton wrote to Aleksei Surkov, the head of the Soviet Writers' Union, to protest their expulsion of Pasternak.*

OCTOBER 29, 1958

I am writing this letter to you today as a sincere friend of literature wherever it may be found, including Russia. I write to you assuming that you are, as I am, interested in the future of man. I assume that we both attach supreme importance to basic human values, in spite of the diversity in the means which we take to protect them. . . .

...I am passionately opposed to every form of violent aggression in war, revolution or police terrorism, no matter who may exercise the aggression, and no matter for what "good" ends. I am a man dedicated entirely to peace and to justice, and to the rights of man whether as a citizen, a worker, or, in this case, as a *writer*.

I speak to you in the name of those innumerable Western intellectuals who have waited for years with keen hopeful sympathy to read some great work that might come out of Russia. I speak to you as one who has the most sincere admiration for the Russian literary heritage, in all its extreme richness. But I also speak to you as one who has been repeatedly disappointed by the failure of modern Russian writers to fulfill the tremendous expectations aroused by the great writers of the past.

It was therefore with great joy, and deep respect for Russia, that I and so many like me were able to hail the recent work of Boris Pasternak which burst upon us full of turbulent and irrepressible life, giving us a deeply moving picture of the heroic sufferings of the Russian nation and its struggles, sacrifices and achievements. That this work received the Nobel Prize certainly cannot have been a merely political trick. It is the expression of the sincere and unprejudiced admiration of the world for a Russian genius worthy to inherit the preeminence of the great Tolstoy. . . .

Pasternak indicates in this book that in the early days of the Revolution there was much senseless brutality. But if you silence Pasternak by violence *now*, are you not giving overwhelming evidence that what he attributed to the early days is still there today? I hardly see how you can avoid condemning yourselves in condemning Pasternak, because he obviously wrote this book with the conviction that tyranny and brutality had come to an end. If you condemn him, and prove him wrong, what does that mean?

If your government is strong and prosperous, what does it have to fear from anything said by Pasternak about the early days of the Revolution? If you silence him it will only be interpreted as a sign of insecurity and weakness. In 1956, the whole world hoped that at last freedom and prosperity would come to reward the long hard years of bitter sacrifice made by the supremely generous Russian nation under Stalin. *Dr. Zhivago* was written with nothing else but this hope in mind. That you condemn the book and its author means that this hope has proved to be a tragic illusion, and that the darkness is settling once again deeper than ever. In condemning Pasternak, you are condemning yourselves and are condemning Russia. If Pasternak suffers unjust and violent retribution for his well-intentioned work, the whole world will feel bitter sorrow for Russia. If Pasternak is punished unjustly when, in good faith, he simply followed the lead of the highest officials in the Party, and spoke out as they did, then it will be a proof that the Soviet system cannot survive where free speech is allowed, and consequently that the Soviet system is committed by its very nature to unrelieved despotism for as long as it may exist. . . .

I had asserted that this would not be a political letter, and yet I find that these last statements have a political nature. You will call them lies. *Please believe that I would be the first man in the world to rejoice if it were proven to me that these statements were false.* I beg you to give me some such proof. I will be delighted to embrace it and to proclaim it. But if Boris Pasternak is beaten down and persecuted for his work, I can never accept any "proof" you might wish to offer. The best proof will be if Pasternak is left free! . . .

TO HELEN WOLFF   *News of Pasternak continued to reach Merton through his friends John Harris, in England, and Helen Wolff, publisher at Pantheon Books, which brought out* Dr. Zhivago *in the United States. Even after Pasternak's death, Merton and Wolff continued to speak of the writer who was for them a paradigm of courage.*

APRIL 14, 1959

I owe you a whole variety of letters. And first of all I am grateful for all the news of Pasternak . . . Has anything materialized, to help him financially? . . .

Thank you also for *I Remember.* You have presented it very attractively, and I am delighted to find in it the notes on translating Shakespeare which are a very important addition. I have not been able to read them yet, I am saving them for a moment in which I can give them thought. With Pasternak one does not just read things in a rush. He puts himself so generously into everything, even and especially his letters—to strangers. I have not heard any more from him, but the quotes from his letters to Miriam Rogers etc. are most illuminating. I also received some news about him indirectly from a person to whom he writes in England [John Harris]—but this was before February 11th. . . .

Wolff invited Merton to submit an essay for a volume on Pasternak's Dr. Zhivago: *"No such book should appear without an essay by you. . . ." (Wolff to Merton, April 27, 1959).*

MAY 8, 1959

. . . I want my good wishes and this present to arrive with you in Zurich, and to assure you that I am with you in spirit and in affection, and follow you with my prayers. This article ["Boris Pasternak and the People with Watch Chains"] is not yet a full study of Pasternak's Christian symbolism by any means, it only prepares the ground. I have however added three pages that give it point. I intend to go much deeper into the question later when I have been through his book more carefully again. In the meantime, I do hope this will be satisfactory for the wonderful volume, and I am deeply touched that you have asked me. This is all censored so there are no more obstacles from our end. Please let me know if it is satisfactory. I look forward to the publication of the Volume with the greatest anticipation, and with my whole heart I join in this homage of friendship for a great man who has moved us all so deeply and helped us open our eyes with him and see the light of wisdom in our chaotic world. I hope someday he will see this article of mine and will feel that I have to some extent grasped his meaning and followed him.

Certainly I feel that the Christian poetry and literature of our time must abandon static and outworn concepts and utter their praise of Christ in intuitions that are dynamic and in full movement. Such is Pasternak's vision of reality, a reality which must be caught as it passes, reality which must carry us away with it. If we pause even for a moment to formulate abstractions we will have lost life as it goes by. *Timeo Jesum transeuntem et non revertentem* (I fear Jesus will go by and will not come back—as St. Augustine says). This is the very vision of reality we have in the *I Ching*. . . .

On June 5, 1959, Helen Wolff wrote that Pasternak did not want Pantheon to publish a volume of literary essays about Zhivago. Pasternak had been put off by the "Joycean symbol-hunting" in

Edmund Wilson's article in The Nation *and "evidently Pasternak did not want to enter posterity as the author of just one book." Wolff enclosed a copy of Pasternak's letter to his American and German publishers and said she would "copy those parts [of Merton's essay] that are not offensive to the censor" and send them to Pasternak.*

JUNE 22, 1959

. . . The letter from Pasternak was most refreshing. I was glad to hear that he repudiated the exaggerations of Edmund Wilson and Co. They were getting to be much too precisely pedantic. Though I can see that there is some foundation for the general view they take. But when it gets down to the etymological details of family names . . . I can well understand Pasternak's protests. I hope he doesn't feel I have taken too many liberties with his symbols myself. I am perhaps too eager to see them as religious: but I do not mean that they are religious in a narrow or institutional sense. I am not trying to claim him for a social group. I do believe he is very fundamentally Christian in the broad and prophetic sense that is vital today.

Certainly it seems wiser not to erect at once a monument to *Zhivago.* I am glad you sent him my article and hope he will have something good to say about it. The other one on the Pasternak Affair ["The Pasternak Affair in Perspective"] will have to be published later though I am no authority on that by any means. This one ["Boris Pasternak and the People with Watch Chains"] is in *Jubilee* for July and I will send you a copy when I have one. . . .

NOVEMBER 16, 1959

. . . I am distressed to hear that the article never got through to Pasternak. I should have been happy to think he had read it. Another, a rather more foolish one ["The Pasternak Affair in Perspective"], which is only an amplification of the first one I wrote last year, is coming out some time. I will send it but it has a lot of semi-political material and I suppose it would never get through to him. There would be no point in sending it through except perhaps to have him correct the errors. I am always glad of some little fragment of news about him, and think of him often. I pray for him every day at Mass, and hope later to send him my collected poems, or rather selected poems [*Selected Poems of Thomas Merton*], which New Directions is now busy with.

. . . This is an age of deep spiritual winter, in which everything is quite cold and the leaves and birds are all gone. We have ice to walk on instead of water, but that is the only advantage. And like you I believe we should never minimize suffering and try to explain it away, especially with seemingly religious rationalizations and clichés. . . .

JANUARY 4, 1960

. . . Your letter brought me the happy and satisfying news that my article had finally reached BP and that he was pleased with it. I am very glad. It is perfectly all right to go ahead and have it published in Germany and I hope you have not waited for my reply before going ahead and doing so. The other Pasternak article is on its way to you in two copies by sea mail. I still have not written to him, telling myself that he is swamped with mail. But I did send him the *Nativity Kerygma* which I think you received last year—in fact I remember that you liked it. I hope he received it. . . .

As soon as I get some copies of my *Selected Poems,* which New Directions has brought out, I will send one to you and one to Pasternak. . . .

FEBRUARY 19, 1960

. . . That brings me to great news—a fine letter from Pasternak himself arrived just the other day. But it tells the story of his struggles with an immense correspondence and his inability to get his work. I am not replying directly, it would only burden him. But as you must be always writing to him with solid reasons, I hope in one of the letters you will include a little word from me thanking him and saying how glad I was to hear from him. Though he does not want me to send him things, I think I will try to send him my *Selected Poems.* Did I send you these? Perhaps not. I can hardly remember when I send things out and when not. Do please let me know if you have not received them thus far. . . .

JUNE 9, 1960

Thank you for the thoughtful letter in which you wrote to me of Pasternak and of the end of his story on earth. Oddly this has come just at the moment when, in preparing for book publication [*Disputed Questions*] the two essays on him that I wrote, I have a chance to round out the whole story and pay some kind of definitive tribute to his greatness as a man and as a poet. I do not feel that I have begun to be capable of doing so, and the words I have written seem to me to be foolish and superficial. In the presence of such a story one feels helpless.

In our world where words have been multiplied without meaning, emptied of meaning, and in which gestures and actions are all to a great extent false, one is ashamed to try to speak of someone so genuine and so deeply honest. In the long run I think the simple, heartfelt expressions of his Russian friends, on the day of his funeral, convey what man can attempt to convey in such a situation. . . .

What stands out more and more, and what will continue to grow on us, is his sense of life: infinite life, eternal life. Hence his sense of resurrection. His sense of working actively and consciously, in a dedicated way, toward the accomplishment of the greatest mystery: the mystery so great that it must be a scandal to all. The impossible mystery of the resurrection, and the new creation. Of all the writers of our time, including all those who are most consciously and explicitly Christian, Pasternak is the one who had the deepest sense of this central Christian mystery. I would say that for the majority of conventional Christians what to him was a primary fact remained a scandal, something they had put out of their consciousness, in order to reduce their religion to ethical proprieties only.

Pasternak could approach this mystery with the confidence of the poet who is at home with symbols. His love gave the symbols great power and his vocation in the end was prophetic in a sense that has been granted to few religious men in our time. . . .

JULY 23, 1960

Today I have finally been able to squeeze some of the wonderful unpublished material about Pasternak into the book: only in the appendix, but better that way than not at all. Besides, it is a short appendix and perhaps more people will read it, after they have bogged down in the middle of the long article. I regret that the editors did not see fit to divide it up into numbered sections as I myself desired. It goes for fifty pages with barely a break. Most readers will have given up long before then: unless I can count on their exceptional devotion to B.P.

Really the pictures of the funeral floored me. They were tremendous, and a very moving witness to the love of the Russian people for the poet and prophet that has been given them—the only one in an age so dry of prophetic inspiration, and so full of the accents of false prophecy. It was just like Zhivago, except for the wonderful silent crowd filing through the trees and over the footbridge. Everywhere people are saying that they still feel Pasternak close to them. He is a great and eloquent witness of the resurrection and of immortality. We will never come to an end in wondering at these gifts and in loving his memory. . . .

In October 1967 Helen Wolff invited Merton to write an essay which she hoped to send out with advance copies of Pasternak's letters. It was fitting, she noted, that the essay be written "by a literary figure who would command respect and whom Pasternak would have wished to see associated with his work." Merton gladly accepted the invitation and wrote "Pasternak's Letters to Georgian Friends."

NOVEMBER 2, 1967

Many thanks for your letter and I am happy that you should think of me as someone appropriate to write the booklet you suggest about Pasternak. Although I have been saying no to the little side jobs lately, I certainly hope I can make an exception for him. I continue to admire him and revere him so much and never cease to feel close to him. I think it is terribly important today that we keep alive the sense and possibility of a strong communion of seemingly isolated individuals in various places and cultures: eventually the foundation of true human community is there and not in the big states or institutions. . . .

JANUARY 8, 1968

I have finished the piece on the Pasternak Letters and have enjoyed writing it. However it may take me a little time to have it typed up, but I hope to get it into your hands in a couple weeks. Very cold here now—Russian winter! I hope you are well. . . .

Here is my piece on the Pasternak letters. It is longer than we at
first planned but I assume that does not make much difference. I felt
it was worthwhile to develop some of the deep ideas that people might
not otherwise find in the letters. They are really quite remarkable. It is
always a joy to get in contact with a mind as rich and as free as was that
of Pasternak. . . .

*Merton's essay "Pasternak's Letters to Georgian Friends" was not pub-
lished until 1978, when it appeared in* The New Lazarus Review.

TO CZESLAW MILOSZ   *Polish poet and writer Czeslaw Milosz joined the
socialist resistance during World War II and wrote for the Polish underground.
After the war, he worked for the Polish diplomatic service in New York, Washington, and Paris. Milosz sought political asylum in France in 1951 and lived
there until 1960, when he took a position at the University of California at
Berkeley. In 1980, he was awarded the Nobel Prize for Literature. Merton first
wrote to Milosz after reading* The Captive Mind, *in which Milosz probed the
plight of Polish intellectuals in a repressive regime. Merton praised the book
and was eager to see more of Milosz's work, offering to assist the Polish writer
in any way he could, even suggesting that he might help Milosz translate his
poetry into English. From the first, admiration and honesty marked their
exchange on a wide array of topics: candid critiques of each other's work; suggestions for reading; and reflections on nature and history, on religion and the
Church, and on mass media and American society. They met together twice,
first in September 1964, when Milosz came to Gethsemani, and again in October 1968, when Merton met briefly with Milosz and his wife in California.
Merton wrote the letters excerpted below between 1958 and 1962. The two writers corresponded sporadically between 1963 and 1968.*

DECEMBER 6, 1958

Having read your remarkable book *The Captive Mind* I find it necessary
to write to you, as without your help I am unable to pursue certain lines of

thought which this book suggests. I would like to ask you a couple of questions and hope you will forgive this intrusion.

First of all I would like to say that I found your book to be one of the most intelligent and stimulating it has been my good fortune to read for a very long time. It is an important book, which makes most other books on the present state of man look abjectly foolish. I find it especially important for myself in my position as a monk, a priest and a writer. It is obvious that a Catholic writer in such a time as ours has an absolute duty to confine himself to reality and not waste his time in verbiage and empty rationalizations. Unfortunately, as I have no need to point out to you, most of us do this and much worse. The lamentable, pitiable emptiness of so much Catholic writing, including much of my own, is only too evident. Your book has come to me, then, as something I can call frankly "spiritual," that is to say, as the inspiration of much thought, meditation and prayer about my own obligations to the rest of the human race, and about the predicament of us all.

It seems to me that, as you point out, and as other writers like yourself say or imply (Koestler, Camus etc.), there *has to be* a third position, a position of integrity, which refuses subjection to the pressures of the two massive groups ranged against each other in the world. It is quite simply obvious that the future, in plain dialectical terms, rests with those of us who risk our heads and our necks and everything in the difficult, fantastic job of finding out the new position, the ever-changing and moving "line" that is no line at all because it cannot be traced out by political dogmatists. And that is the difficulty, and the challenge. I am the last in the world to pretend to know anything about it. One thing I do know, is that anyone who is interested in God Who is Truth, has to break out of the ready-made shells of the "captive" positions that offer their convenient escapes from freedom—one who loves freedom must go through the painful experience of seeking it, perhaps without success. And for my part, this letter represents a hearty peck at the inside of my own particular kind of shell, the nature and hardness of which I leave you to imagine. . . .

Is there anything I can do for you? It seems to me that the most obvious thing I can give you is the deep and friendly interest of a kindred mind and a will disposed for receptiveness and collaboration. And of course, my prayers. The address from which I write to you is that of a Cistercian monastery, where I have lived and worked for seventeen years as a monk and a priest. If you ever come by this way, I would be eager to have a talk with you and glad to welcome you to this house. I presume however you still live in France. You may reply to me in French or English, as you prefer.

FEBRUARY 28, 1959

Thanks for your splendid letter. It was delayed in reaching me by the inevitable monastic barriers and also by the annual retreat. And I have been thinking about it for a week or so. . . .

I am sorry that I did not think more deeply about the trouble of heart I might cause you in writing so bluntly and glibly about *The Captive Mind.* Obviously I should have realized the many problems that would be involved. Like all the people here, I have I suppose a sort of fantastic idea of the Iron Curtain—as if people on either side of it were simply dead to each other. The abyss between Abraham's bosom and Dives in hell. From what you write in the book, Alpha would certainly react as you have said. I have a great esteem for him and shall keep him in my prayers. And I can't say I am fond of Gamma. A real Stalinist type. Beta is perhaps something new to me, and Delta is familiar. I shall certainly get hold of *The Broken Mirror.* [Lionel] Trilling I generally take with a grain of salt (I knew him at Columbia where he was a professor).

Whatever you may feel about *The Captive Mind* (and I will not presume to try to make you feel otherwise), it is certainly a book that had to be written and evidently such a book could not be written at all, unless it were written with terrible shortcomings. All were necessary, perhaps. Good will come of the suffering involved for you and for others. It is an exceptional book, in my opinion. It is one of the very few books about the writer and Communism, or about Communism itself, that has any real value as far as I can see. The rest are often just compilations of magic formulas and exorcisms, or plain platitudes. I agree with you with all my heart in feeling revulsion at the standard, superficial attitude taken by "the West" on the common, political and social level, to Russia etc. Revulsion in fact at the hypocrisy on both sides. *No one* giving a thought to human values and persons, to man's spirit, to his real destiny, to his real obligation to rebuild his world from the ground up, on the ruins of what past generations have left him. I mean no one except those who are in the middle, and who realize that they are caught between the two millstones. All the others, just helping the stones to grind, for the sake of grinding. But precisely as you say, those who are ground are coming out as clean flour. . . .

. . . I am very happy whenever I hear of a Catholic review in Poland printing something of mine, but I feel that the things they have used are to a great extent beside the point, though that may not be true. In any case it is unbearable to me to feel that I may have let myself get too far away from the actual problems of my time in a kind of pious detachment that is an indefensible luxury. There are all sorts of complicated angles to this, though. . . .

Of my own work, I am sending you two packets; one of small things, *Prometheus, Monastic Peace,* and the *Tears of the Blind Lions.* Then a full-length book, *The Sign of Jonas,* and another less long, *Thoughts in Solitude,* though I fear perhaps the latter may seem to you esoteric and sterile. It is a book about which I am quite divided. It is based on notes about things to which I personally attach some importance, but these notes were revised and dressed up by me and became what I take to be a little commercial and hence false. I don't know if this is scrupulosity. The book in any case is by no means adequate. I should be interested to know very frankly if it bores you completely and seems to you to be completely alien, bourgeois etc. That would be worth knowing. The poems alas are not too good. If there is any other book of mine you hear of that you would like, I will gladly send it. Or anything I can get for you, I will send.

Milosz, life is on our side. The silence and the Cross of which we know are forces that cannot be defeated. In silence and suffering, in the heartbreaking effort to be honest in the midst of dishonesty (most of all our *own* dishonesty), in all these is victory. It is Christ in us who drives us through darkness to a light of which we have no conception and which can only be found by passing through apparent despair. Everything has to be tested. All relationships have to be tried. All loyalties have to pass through fire. Much has to be lost.

Much in us has to be killed, even much that is best in us. But Victory is certain. The Resurrection is the only light, and with that light there is no error.

FEBRUARY 28, 1959

I realize it might seem a great impertinence to offer this ["Letter to an Innocent Bystander"] as reading for people behind the Iron Curtain, and when I wrote to you about it in my last letter I had not considered that fact. However, if it is understood that it was written for other intellectuals on *this side* of the curtain, it might not seem so inappropriate. But I should never presume to speak up, in my safe corner of the world, and try to tell people in grave danger how to be "honest." God forbid. You can use your discretion in this matter and if it is simply useless, then please return it. And tell me if it is really a piece of presumptuous complacency. I have no way of getting a real perspective otherwise.

MAY 21, 1959

The only trouble with receiving letters as good and full as yours, is that it is a long time before one can answer worthily. I am grateful for your fine letter, which contains so much. . . .

First, your questions about the "Innocent Bystander"—I hope the fact of my not answering them has not mattered. I leave to you the choice of word for *Bystander,* and you have probably chosen satisfactorily. In English the special implication is that of one who stands by while a crime is being committed. I am glad you can use it in *Kultura,* but I feel ashamed of it, when I realize that it may be read by people who have a real problem. As for myself, I think the problem is still real enough for me to be able to write about it with feeling. I am more and more convinced every day that it is a religious as well as a civil obligation to be discontented with ready-made answers—no matter where they may come from. How much longer can the world subsist on institutional slogans?

Reading *The Broken Mirror,* I was moved by the sense of real kinship with most of the writers. Underneath the institutional shells which distinguish us, we have the same ardent desire for truth, for peace, for sanity in life, for reality, for sincerity. But the trouble is that our very efforts to attain these things tend to harden and make more rigid the institutional shell. And a turtle without a shell is not likely to lead a happy life, especially in a world like ours. But perhaps the trouble is that we imagine ourselves turtles. . . . I feel the greatest sympathy and sense of kinship with most of these writers, apart from the fact that their commitments are . . . quite alien to me. Be sure to send me Alpha's book. I think often of him, and admire him. I feel deeply for his predicament, and I pray for him. And for all the Polish writers.

Now about your own books. I suppose it is not strange that your younger earthy and cosmic self should be so sharply divided from the later political self. *Sur le bords de l'Issa* is admirably alive, rich in all kinds of archetypal material, with a deep vegetative substratum that gives it a great fertility of meanings. Your lyrical poem falls into the same category . . . this element in your being is very essential to you . . . you will not produce your greatest work without it. Its absence from *The Seizure of Power* is one of the things that makes the latter simply a routine job. Of course it is hard to see how ancient pagan naturalistic remnants from archaic Lithuanian peasant culture could be fitted into the tragic story of Warsaw. The fact is that *The Seizure of Power,* though very impressive in patches, did not seem to [hold] together well. You do not seem sure of yourself in it and your statement that you do not like the novel as a literary form by no means surprises me. Yet I think perhaps one day you may go over the same material and write a great novel. I think *The Seizure of Power* suffers from a lack of perspective, and from a natural inability to *assimilate* all the awful elements that had to go into it. One day when you have come to see it all in a unified way, it may turn out quite differently.

I am going to have to go into Simone Weil a little. My acquaintance with her is superficial. As for providence: certainly I think the glib clichés that are made about the will of God are enough to make anyone lose his faith. Such clichés are still possible in America but I don't see how they can still survive in Europe, at least for anyone who has seen a concentration camp. For my part, I have given up my compulsive need to answer such questions neatly. It is safer and cleaner to remain inarticulate, and does more honor to God. I think the reason why we cannot see Providence at work in our world is that it is much too simple. Our notions of Providence are too complicated and too human: a question of ends and means, and why this means to this end? God wills this *for* this purpose. . . . Whatever the mystery of Providence may be, I think it is more direct and more brutal in a way. But that is never evident as long as we think of God apart from the people in the concentration camp, "permitting them to be there for their own good" (time out while I vomit). Actually it is God Himself who is in the concentration camp. That is, of course, it is Christ. Not in the collective sense, but especially in the defilement and destruction of each individual soul, there is the renewal of the Crucifixion. This of course is familiar, I mean the words are familiar. People understand them to mean that a man in a concentration camp who remembers to renew his morning offering suffers like—and even, in some juridical sense, with—Christ. But the point is, whether he renews the morning offering or not, or whether he is a sinner, he *is* Christ. That this is not understood even by religious people: that it cannot be comprehended by the others, and that the last one to be able to understand it, so to speak, is "Christ" Himself. . . . Providence is not *for* this hidden Christ. He Himself is His own Providence. In us. Insofar as we are Christ, we are our own Providence. The thing is then not to struggle to work out the "laws" of a mysterious force alien to us and utterly outside us, but to come to terms with what is inmost in our own selves, the very depth of our own being. No matter what our "Providence" may have in store for us, on the surface of life (and this inner Providence is not really so directly concerned with the surface of life), what is within, inaccessible to the evil will of others, is always good unless we ourselves deliberately cut ourselves off from it. As for those who are too shattered to do anything about it one way or the other, they are lifted, in pieces, into heaven and find themselves together there with no sense of how it might have been possible.

When you talk about group action you say what most concerns me, because it is something I know nothing at all about. Even as a Catholic I am a complete lone wolf, and not as independent as I might seem to be, yet not integrated in anything else either. As you say, I represent my own life. But not as I ought to. I have still too much reflected the kind of person others may have assumed I ought to be. I am reaching a happy and dangerous age when I want to smash that image above all. But that is not the kind of thing that is likely to be viewed with favor. Nor do I have any idea of what way the road will take. But as far as solidarity with other people goes, I am committed to nothing except a very simple and elemental kind of solidarity, which is perhaps without significance politically, but which is I feel the only kind which works at all. That is to pick out the people whom I recognize in a crowd and hail them and rejoice with them for a moment that we speak the same language. Whether they be Communists or whatever else they may be. Whatever they may believe on the surface, whatever may be the formulas to which they are committed. I am less and less worried by what people say or think they say: and more and more concerned with what they and I are able to be. I am not convinced that anybody is really able to say what he means anymore, except insofar as he talks about himself. And even there it is very difficult. What do any of us "mean" when we talk politics?

And then Russia. I was very interested in what you said about the Russians. I am remote from all that. I have read a few books, I like Dostoevsky, and as you say there is a kind of craziness, a collective myth which strikes one as insincere. An uncharitable judgment: but perhaps there is an awful lot of old man Karamazov in all of the Russians—the barefaced liar who will accuse himself of everything and mean nothing. Who just wants to talk. Yet I am very taken with [Nikolai] Berdyaev. He is certainly too glib. His explanations and intuitions come up with a suspicious readiness, and he is always inexhaustible. But I find much less of the pseudomystic, or rather gnostic, in his later works. As time goes on he seems to me to get more and more solid. *The Meaning of Creation,* one of his earliest books, is one of the most fruitful, the most dangerous and the least reliable all at the same time. But a late one like *Solitude and Society* is, I think, almost perfect in its kind. As for Pasternak, of course what you say about *Zhivago* is true: he floats passively through the backwaters of history. But one does not hold it against him. . . .

About *Prometheus*—I wonder if you interpreted it correctly? I have nothing against fire. Certainly it is the fire of the spirit: my objection is that it does not have to be stolen, and that it cannot be successfully stolen. It has been already given, and Prometheus' climb, defeat and despair are all in his own imagination. That is the tragedy. He had the fire already.

Finally, I think it is eminently good that you, especially as a Pole, are not listed as a Catholic writer pure and simple. You can do much more good that way. Categories are of very little use, and often to be clearly labeled is equivalent to being silenced.

. . . The fact that you write for Poland is not too important. What you write for Poland will be read with interest everywhere. You do not have to change your mental image of your audience. The audience will take care of itself.

All you wrote about Valka [a refugee camp near Valka] seemed to me supremely important. These are things we have to think about and write about and do something about, otherwise we are not writers but innocent (?) bystanders. Especially shameful is this business of "using" these people for a cause, and if they cannot be used, then leaving them to rot. How clear it is that on both sides they are very much the same, and that the dividing lines are not where they appear to be.

God bless you and your family. You are wise even in your insecurity, for today insecurity and wisdom are inseparable. . . .

SEPTEMBER 12, 1959

. . . The only thing that is to be regretted without qualification is for a man to adapt perfectly to totalitarian society. Then he is indeed beyond hope. Hence we should all be sick in some way. We should all feel near to despair in some sense because this semi-despair is the normal form taken by hope in a time like ours. Hope without any sensible or tangible evidence on which to rest. Hope in spite of the sickness that fills us. Hope married to a firm refusal to accept any palliatives or anything that cheats hope by pretending to relieve apparent despair. And I would add, that for you especially hope must mean acceptance of limitations and imperfections and the deceitfulness of a nature that has been wounded and cheated of love and of security: this too we all feel and suffer. Thus we cannot enjoy the luxury of a hope based on our own integrity, our own honesty, our own purity of heart.

Yet on the other hand, our honesty consists in resisting the temptation to submerge our guilt in the collective deluge, and in refusing to be proud that our "hands are dirty" and making the fact a badge of adaptation and success in the totalitarian world. In the end, it comes to the old story that we are sinners, but that this is our hope because sinners are the ones who attract to themselves the infinite compassion of God. To be a sinner, to want to be pure, to remain in patient expectation of the divine mercy and above all to forgive and love others, as best we can, this is what makes us Christians. The great tragedy is that we feel so keenly that love has been twisted out of shape in us and beaten down and crippled. But Christ loves in us. . . .

Your piece in *Preuves* is very good reading, and promises that the book will be one of your very best. I am most eager to have it and to read it. The pages I have seen in the magazine are interesting and moving, and I was deeply impressed by the prophetic insights of Oscar Milosz, who seems to have been most remarkable. I too believe both in the coming destruction and in the coming resurrection of the Church and an age of worldwide Christianity. And I believe these things will happen very fast, and strangely, and without any apparent struggle on the part of men—I mean without any apparent struggle to bring about the good. Rather it will all take place against the concerted efforts of the whole human race to bring about evil and despair. The glory will belong not to man but to God.

I still do not share your scruples about writing, though lately I have been thinking of giving it up for a while, and seeking a more austere and solitary kind of existence (I go through that cycle frequently, as you have seen in *The Sign of Jonas,* but this time it is more serious). I will probably never give up writing definitively. I have just been finishing another book, *The Inner Experience* [not published until 2003]—a wider deeper view of the same thing, contemplation, with more reference to Oriental ideas. There is to me nothing but this that counts, but everything can enter into it. You are right to feel a certain shame about writing. I do too, but always too late—five years after a book has appeared I wish I had never been such a fool as to write it. But when I am writing it I think it is good. If we were not all fools we would never accomplish anything at all. As to people of good grain and bad grain, I do not have easy answers, but again I think a great deal depends on love, and that when people are loved they change. But what is happening in the world today is a wholesale collapse of man's capacity to love. He has been submerged under material concerns, and by the fantastic proliferation of men and things all around him, so that there are so many of everything that one lives in a state of constant bewilderment and fear. One cannot begin to commit himself to any definite love, because the whole game is too complex and too hazardous and one has lost all focus. So we are carried away by the whirlwind, and our children are even more helpless than we ourselves. It is the basic *helplessness* of man coming out at the moment of his greatest power over things other than himself, that has precipitated this moral crisis. But there have always been this fear of helplessness, this impatience and panic which makes a man want to assure himself of his power before he relaxes and allows himself to love. And so he gets carried away with his projects to remind himself that he exists, and can never allow himself to love fully—to get away from himself. Who is to blame? Everyone. The answer—the only answer I know—is that of Staretz Zossima in *The Brothers Karamazov*—to be responsible to everybody, to take upon oneself *all* the guilt—but I don't know what that means. It is romantic, and I believe it is true. But what is it? Behind it all is the secret that love has an infinite power, and its power, once released, can in an instant destroy and swallow up all hatred, all evil, all injustice, all that is diabolical. That is the meaning of Calvary. . . .

In his letter of February 28, 1960, Milosz challenged Merton's view of nature as expressed in The Sign of Jonas: *"Every time you speak of Nature, it appears to you as soothing, rich in symbols, as a veil or a curtain. You do not pay much attention to torture and suffering in Nature. . . . I am far from wishing to convert you to Manichaeism. Only it is so that the palate of your readers is used to very strong sauces and* le Prince de ce monde *is a constant subject of their reflections. That ruler of Nature and of History . . . does not annoy you enough in your writings."*

MAY 6, 1960

It is a shame to make so fine a letter as your last one wait so long for an answer, and yet it is precisely the good letters that take time to answer. Yours required much thought, and I still haven't come through with anything intelligent or worthy of your wise observations.

Not that there is not plenty of resentment in me: but it is not resentment against nature, only against people, institutions and myself. I suppose this is a real defect, or rather a limitation: but actually what it amounts to is that I am in complete and deep complicity with nature, or imagine I am: that nature and I are very good friends, and console one another for the stupidity and the infamy of the human race and its civilization. We at least get along, I say to the trees, and though I am perfectly aware that the spider eats the fly, that the singing of the birds may perhaps have something to do with hatred or pain of which I know nothing, still I can't make much of it. Spiders have always eaten flies and I can shut it out of my consciousness without guilt. It is the spider, not I, that kills and eats the fly. As for snakes, I do not like them much, but I can be neutral and respectful towards them, and find them very beautiful in fact, though this is a recent development. They used to strike me with terror. But they are not evil. I don't find it in myself to generate any horror for nature or a feeling of evil in it. Or myself. There, of course, there is more guilt, and shame. I do not find it at all hard to hate myself, and I am certainly not always charitable about other people; I like to flay them in words, and probably I should feel more guilty about it than I do, because here I sin, and keep on sinning.

At the same time I enjoy and respect Camus, and think I understand him. What you said about *La Chute* struck me very forcibly when I read it: it is a fine piece of Manichaean theology and very applicable to this Trappist kind of life. In fact I was able to use it to good effect, perhaps cruelly, in the spiritual direction of a narcissistic novice. But the thing of Camus that really "sends" me is the marvelous short story about the missionary who ends up as a prisoner in the city of salt. There, in a few words, you have a superb *ricanement,* in theology! . . .

Of course, the funny thing is that I am very frequently accused, here in America and also in England, of being too Manichaean. Perhaps that is why I have obediently tried to mute the rancor that is quite often an undertone in my writing, but perhaps too it is so much of an undertone that I am the only one left who can hear it. And in the end, everyone envies me for being so happy. I do not have the impression of being especially happy, and I am in definite reaction against my surroundings: for a "happy monk," I must admit that I certainly protest a great deal against the monastic Order, and the Order itself thinks I protest a great deal too much. But of course, it must be understood that in an institution like ours even the slightest hint of protest is already too much.

I am willing to admit that in the sight of God I do not protest enough, and that the protests I generally make are always beside the target. I have the impression that when I am indignant in print, I am always indignant about something vague and abstract, and not about something more concrete which I really hate and which I cannot recognize. It is absurd to rave vaguely about "the world," the "modern age," the "times." I suppose I will gradually get over that.

What I get back to, and here you can tell me if my examination of conscience is correct, is that in actual fact my real guilt is for being a bourgeois. I am after all the prisoner of my class, and I tell myself that I don't care if I am. One has to be prisoner of some class or other, and I might as well be what I am instead of going through the ridiculous and pharisaical pretense of being the avant-garde of a classless world. But the fact remains that I hate being a bourgeois, and hate the fact that my reaction against it is not a success: simply the bohemian reaction, I suppose, with a new twist, a religious modality.

When all this is said, I find it difficult to be sincerely bitter in the way that you describe, but also the real *ricanement* people bore me to death. I do not have much interest in Sartre, he puts me to sleep, as if he were deliberately dull: *assommant* is a much better word. He shaves me, as the French say. He beats me over the head with his dullness though *Huis Clos* strikes me as a good and somewhat puritanical play. The other thing of his I have tried to read, *La Nausée,* is drab and stupid.

All that you have said remains unchallenged by these evasive explanations. It is quite true that I ought to speak more with the accents of my time. They are serious, they are not just a pose, the bitterness of people is not just something to be dismissed. I detest the fake optimism that is current in America, including the American religion. I shall continue to think about these things. The books of mine you have read belong however to a sort of Edenic period in my life, and what is later is more sardonic. I think the last poems will prove that statement, including the "Elegy for the Five Old Ladies.". . .

Whether or not you should come to America depends on a lot of things, but the atmosphere of this country is singularly unstimulating. Why live among lotus-eaters and conformists, and such conformists. Never was there a place where freedom was so much an illusion. But if you do come, then I would have the pleasure of talking to you down here, I hope. For that reason I hope you will come. But for the rest you will find here no imagination, nothing but people counting, counting and counting, whether with giant machines, or on their stupid fingers. All they know how to do is count. I wish you could see one good book, though, that is unknown, by my friend Robert Lax— *The Circus of the Sun.* I'll ask him to send you a review copy for *Kultura.* It is an expensive limited edition, beautifully done. Lax you would like. I have read the [P. Louis] Bouyer book, or part of it, and it is very fine. I am interested in Protestantism now, am having some meetings with Protestant theologians, pleasant, honest and earnest men: but how serious are they I wonder. No more than Catholic theologians of the same temper and background.

What I am going to do now is send you a manuscript of a recent thing of mine, which might interest you: Notes on a "Philosophy of Solitude" ["Notes for a Philosophy of Solitude" in *Disputed Questions*]. I do not say it represents anything much but it is my own authentic voice of the moment and it has had a hard time with the censors of the Order. And here is a poem too: optimistic I suppose, but it is an optimistic-*néant.* But you see, for me emptiness is fullness, not mere vacuum. But in tribute to the seriousness of this happy void I ought to make it more empty and not be so quick to say positive things about it. This I agree. . . .

NOVEMBER 9, 1960

. . . Certainly there are enormous problems and difficulties about the life of an intellectual in America. There is the awful shame and revolt at being in this continual milkshake, of being a passive, inert captive of Calypso's Island where no one is ever tempted to think and where one just eats and exists and supports the supermarket and the drugstore and General Motors and the TV. Above all, there is the shame, the weakness which makes us hesitate to associate ourselves with what has become the object of universal scorn and hate on the part of the intellectuals in Europe. But since courage is the first thing, maybe we need courage to dissociate ourselves from our own tribe and its conventions, which are just a little more subtle, a little differently poisonous, from the obvious depravation of the lotus-eaters. In reality I think you will find here many healthy unexploited possibili-ties. There are fine and honest people who really do seek honest answers and ask to be *led* by someone. God knows, no one with any sense wants to command an army of intellectual lotus-eaters. And in the end one gets the feeling that as soon as anything gets serious they will drop off and vanish into the undergrowth. One feels these people coming at one with childlike good will, sincere curiosity, and no depth, no earnestness except in pretense. They *seem* to want something, in fact to want everything. But to want everything is in fact to want nothing. One has to specify, otherwise choices are of no significance: they are not choices.

Then in the background are the army high command and the captains of industry. These are the serious birds, and theirs is another kind of seriousness altogether, because they are definitely not fooling. The intellectuals, perhaps, are. The brass hats don't know exactly what they want, but they almost know: and it is negative. They are getting tired of being hated and want to give the world a genuine reason for hating them. No doubt they will. Theirs is a pragmatic, unspoken pride which is all the deeper and more incurable for being unspoken. It speaks with its effects, for which no one claims either honor or responsibility, but they are devastating and inescapable.

So I am tempted to wonder whether you and I do not after all have some kind of responsibility toward these people who are certainly, up to a point, waiting for anything we say, and quite ready to accept it. I fear being deluded and deceived by them. Perhaps I fear it too much and this may have a lot to do with my solitude, which always anticipates defeat and frustration. But after all if we have a hearing, we ought to humbly and courageously say what we have to say, clearly, forcefully, insistently and for the glory of God's truth, not for any self-interest. And of course this means that we will *not* be pure, either. But knowing we will partly fail, we can at least try to be, and accept the consequences. . . .

You gave me some very good suggestions in the other letter. Especially about the oblique approach, through literary criticism. I might do that, or better go at it through creative writing. I am also doing some abstract drawings at the moment. Other avenues will open up to me I am sure. Pious literature is not going to go very far, but more reflective and more fundamental things can be expressed in a variety of ways. . . .

It is a terribly long time since your last letter. And it was a good one too. The better they are, the longer I wait to answer them, because I am always hoping for a chance to really think about everything you say and really answer it. Because it is true that what you say affects me deeply, seeing that we are in many respects very much alike. Consequently any answer must involve the deepest in me, and that is not easy. We always seek to evade the expression of what is most important to us, in fact we are usually not able even to confront it. Haste gives us the opportunity to substitute something else for the deepest statements.

I am very glad you came to America, and have seen everything close at hand. You are all too right about the sickness of this society. It is terrible and seems to get worse. I feel nothing but helplessness in my situation: I should, ideally speaking, have a wonderful perspective from which to see things in a different—a Heraclitean—light. . . . You are perfectly right about the "spell-bound dance of paralytics." You are right too that they anesthetize themselves with the double-talk of lotus-eaters, the psychological talk: all this talk about responsibility and personalism and organization men and whatnot tends to be a part of the spell and of the dance. What is behind it? The obsession with concepts, with knowledge, with techniques, as if we were supposed to be able to manipulate everything. We have got ourselves into a complete fog of concepts and "answers." Illusory answers to illusory problems and never facing the real problem: that we have all become zombies.

This works on several levels, of course. It is quite obvious on the level of the race fanatics, but on the intellectual level it persists too. I think the Marxist psychology of bourgeois individualism is not too far wrong when it condemns the perpetual turning around and around in circles of guilt and self-analysis: as if this were capable of doing something, or exorcizing the real guilt. . . . But they are in the same boat themselves, only a few stages farther back. They haven't yet got to the stage of idleness and surfeiting that will permit them to do the same thing. The poison is exactly the alienation you speak of, and it is not the individual, not society, but what comes of being an individual helpless to liberate himself from the images that society fills him with. It is a very fine picture of hell sometimes. When I see advertisements I want to curse they make me so sick, and I do curse them. I have never seen TV, that is, never watched it. Once when I did happen to pass in front of a set I saw the commercial that was on: two little figures were dancing around worshipping a roll of toilet paper, chanting a hymn in its honor. I think this is symbolic enough isn't it? We have simply lost the ability to see what is right in front of us: things like this need no comment. . . .

Speaking in monastic terms, of fidelity to the truth, to the light that is in us from God, that is the horror: everyone has been more or less unfaithful, and those who have seemed to be faithful have been so partially, in a way that sanctified greater evasions (the Grand Inquisitor). Perhaps the great reality of our time is this, that no one is capable of this fidelity, and all have failed in it, and that there is no hope to be looked for in any one of us. But God is faithful. It is what the Holy Week liturgy tells of His "treading the winepress by Himself." This, I think, is the central reality.

Turning back from this perspective, and looking again at the possibility of my doing something to heal the country: I don't trust myself to even begin it. There are too many ambiguities, too many hatreds, that would have to be sweated out first. I do not know if these are ever going to be sweated out in this present life. There is so much nonsense to struggle with at all times. In myself. At present I am beginning to accept this fact not with indifference but with peace and happiness because it is not as important as it seems. This, I imagine, is at least a beginning. . . .

MARCH 28, 1961

This is just an added note to the longer letter I mailed this morning. Don't be perturbed about *The Captive Mind*. It was something that had to be written & apart from the circumstances, it stands as a very valid statement by itself, irrespective of how it may be read & how it may be used. In any case no matter what a writer does these days it can be "used" for the cold war or for other purposes. Our very existence can be "used" by somebody or other to "prove" something that suits him. Such things are largely meaningless & we are wrong to be too affected by them. . . .

We have to get used to our total moral isolation. It is going to get worse. We have to regain our sense of *being*, our confidence in reality, not in words. You are what you are, & what happened to the Paris writers you recorded truthfully. It happened and it has to be said. Now go on to other things, for that is already ancient history & you cannot, & need not, change it.

Bear your solitude. It is a great pain for you & there is great strength in it if you can continue to find & accept it, which you do. The torment of doubt & self-recrimination is inevitable: only do nothing to make it worse!

JUNE 5, 1961

Your letter is very meaningful to me. Without having anything specific to say either, I respond to it. I think we are both grasping something very important, that cannot be affirmed. I have made too many affirmations, and while I hold to them, they do not affirm what I have intended, and they cannot. I think that I have never fully reached my final choice or stated it, and that when it comes to be stated I will end up on your side, in the metaphysical torment. I have *not* coped with the basic theological questions. It only looks that way. In the depths I have more of [Charles] Péguy in me, more of Simone Weil than even I have realized, and certainly I have not let it be apparent to anyone else. There are times when I feel spiritually excommunicated. And that it is right and honest for me to be so. It is certain that my writing is not adequate and I am oppressed by the people who think that it is and who admire it as if it really answered questions. I have given the impression I had answers.

There is something wrong with the questions that are supposed to be disposed of by answers. That is the trouble with the squares. They think that when you have answers you no longer have questions. And they want the greatest possible number of answers, the smallest number of questions. The ideal is to have no more questions. Then when you have no questions you have "peace." On the other hand, the more you simply stand with the questions all sticking in your throat at once, the more you unsettle the "peace" of those who think they have swallowed all the answers. The questions cause one to be nauseated by answers. This is a healthy state, but it is not acceptable. Hence I am nauseated by answers and nauseated by optimism. There is an optimism which cheapens Christianity and makes it absurd, empties it. It is a silly, petty optimism which consists in being secure because one knows the right answers.

Sometimes the answers are beautiful and obviously right. That is the great trouble, really, not that we are stopped by answers that are inadequate.

The answers are in every way apparently adequate. To grasp them and hold them is to appear to be with saints and fully embodied in the community of the saints. Yet one is nauseated by them, and cast out. One is left without answers, without comfort, without companionship, without a community. That is the thing that has finally hit me. My darkness was very tolerable when it was only dark night, something spiritually approved. But it is rapidly becoming "exterior" darkness. A nothingness in oneself into which one is pressed down further and further, until one is inferior to the entire human race and hates the inferiority. Yet clings to it as the only thing one has. Then the problem is that perhaps here in this nothingness is infinite preciousness, the presence of the God Who is not an answer, the God of Job, to Whom we must be faithful above all, beyond all. But the terrible thing is that He is *not known to others,* is incommunicable. . . .

Merton's writings on war and peace did not sit well with Milosz: "I am completely puzzled by your papers on duties of a Christian and on war. Perhaps I am wrong. My reaction is emotional: no. Reasons: 1) My deep skepticism as to moral action which seems to be utopian. 2) My distrust of any peace movements, a distrust shared probably by all the Poles, as we experienced to what use various peace movements served. . . . 3) Noble-sounding words turning around the obvious because nobody would deny that the atomic war is one of the greatest evils. . . . Any peace action should take into account its probable effects and not only moral duty. It is possible that every peace manifesto for every 1 person converted, throws 5 persons to the extreme right by a reaction against 'defeatism'" (Milosz's letter to Merton is undated but it was written after January 18, 1962). Later Milosz worried that he had offended Merton: "I should not have used in a hurry so harsh words speaking of your writings for peace. . . . I got so used to treat any talk on peace as a part of the ritual in the Soviet bloc, as a smoke screen spread by the officialdom at celebrations, meetings etc. that my reaction is just a reflex, an emotional outburst." Milosz also questioned Merton's motivation: "I ask myself why you feel such an itch for activity? Is that so that you are unsatisfied with your having plunged too deep into contemplation and now you wish to compensate through growing another wing, so to say? And peace provides you with the only link with American young intellectuals outside? Yet activity to which you are called is perhaps different? Should you become a belated rebel, out of solidarity with rebels without a cause?" (March 14, 1962).

[COLD WAR LETTER 56] MARCH 1962

There are few people whose advice I respect as much as I do yours, and whatever you say I take seriously. Hence I do not feel at all disturbed or unsettled by what you say concerning my articles about peace, because I can see the wisdom of your statements and I agree with them to a great extent.

This is one of those phases one goes through. I certainly do not consider myself permanently dedicated to a crusade for peace and I am beginning to see the uselessness and absurdity of getting too involved in a "peace movement." The chief reason why I have spoken out was that I felt I owed it to my conscience to do so. There are certain things that have to be clearly stated. I had in mind particularly the danger arising from the fact that some of the most belligerent people in this country are Christians, on the one hand fundamentalist Protestants and on the other certain Catholics. They both tend to appeal to the bomb to do a "holy" work of destruction in the name of Christ and Christian truth. This is completely intolerable and the truth has to be stated. I cannot in conscience remain indifferent. Perhaps this sounds priggish, and perhaps I am yielding to subtle temptations of self-righteousness. Perhaps too there is a great deal of bourgeois self-justification in all this. Perhaps I am just trying to make myself feel that I am still in continuous contact with the tradition of my fathers, in English history, fighting for rights and truth and so on. And so on. In other words there is a large element of myth in it all. And yet one cannot know everything and analyze everything. It seems that there may be some point in saying what I have said, and so I have said it.

You are right about the temptation to get lined up with rebels without a cause. There is something attractive and comforting about the young kids that are going off into non-violent resistance with the same kind of enthusiasm I used to have myself in the thirties for left-wing action. But this too may be a great illusion. I trust your experience.

As far as I am concerned I have just about said what I have to say. I have written four or five articles, which are gradually getting published, hailed, attacked, and causing a small stir. I may revise them all and put them together into a small book. . . .

In a word, I have many doubts myself about all this. It seems to be largely self-deception. Yet to the best of my ability to judge, I feel that what I have done so far was necessary. Perhaps it was not done well. Perhaps it was naïve. Undoubtedly I have not said the last word, nor has all that I have said been perfectly objective and well balanced. . . .

Meanwhile, I enjoy the spring rains (and there have been a lot of them) and am getting ready to do my usual planting of tree seedlings for reforestation.

Keep well, and thanks for all your advice and for your understanding. I repeat that I value both.

TO LATIN AMERICAN WRITERS

Thomas Merton's letters to Latin American writers express an interest that his correspondence nurtured. His early fascination with Latin American life and culture—so vividly documented in *The Seven Storey Mountain* and *Secular Journal*—developed into a strong sense of solidarity with Latin Americans as they struggled against oppression, tyranny, and poverty. As Merton came to learn more about the political and social situation in Latin America, first from Ernesto Cardenal, who was a novice under Merton in the late fifties, and later by corresponding with many Latin American writers, publishers, and poets, Merton identified himself with their struggle for freedom and justice and recognized the critical role writers could play in that struggle. Merton conceived of his collaboration with Latin American writers as nothing less than a vocation to unite Americans—of the northern and southern hemispheres: "We have a tremendous and marvelous vocation, the vocation of being Americans, that is to say, of being and of forming the true America that is the Christ of the Americas. . . ."

TO PABLO ANTONIO CUADRA   *Nicaraguan intellectual, poet, and journalist Pablo Antonio Cuadra edited* La Prensa—*a "new revolutionary newspaper . . . a voice of the people"—which resisted the censorship and brutality of the Samoza regime. Cuadra studied the history and folklore of Nicaragua and the culture and language of the indigenous peoples. Merton was excited by the "indigenous" quality of Cuadra's poetry and wrote an introduction to Cuadra's collection of poems* The Jaguar and the Moon. *In 1961, Merton wrote an article denouncing both the Soviet Union and the United States. The article, titled "Letter to Pablo Antonio Cuadra Concerning Giants," was published in Nicaragua, Argentina, El Salvador, and the United States.*

OCTOBER 13, 1958

I would . . . like to write an introduction explaining the original idea of your poems "to be inscribed on ceramics"—and we could include one of the drawings as an example, in the case of the publication in *World Poets*. Do you want to send me an explanation of your idea? Also, explain to me your admirable poem about Acahualinca. Fr. Lawrence [Ernesto Cardenal] has already told me a little about the history (behind the poem). It is a magnificent poem, and an admirable example of the current political situation with its Indian themes! I really like that prophetic fusion of the past and the present, giving the poem an eternal character, a very religious and solemn aspect! Today, we all have a great deal to do facing the terrible reality of the volcano. . . .

I spent some very pleasant afternoons under the silent trees translating your poems—a labor that is, like all monastic work, consecrated, something that the profound seriousness of the poems deserves. I am overjoyed at their originality and spiritual independence in taking and using the Indian religious tradition as our Christian property. We have an enormous debt to repay to the Indians, and we should at least begin by recognizing the spiritual richness of the Indian religious genius. I have read English translations of Maya and Aztec poems in several books, and if a collection of Indian poems in Spanish exists, I would very much like to have it. . . .

DECEMBER 4, 1958

. . . How can I tell you, dear Pablo Antonio, what our collaboration means to me . . . ? Man, image of God, should be a creator, but not only as an individual person, but as a brother of other creators. Let us continue creating and struggling for the truth and the kingdom of God. We have a tremendous and marvelous vocation, the vocation of being *Americans,* that is to say, of being and of forming the true America that is the Christ of the Americas: the Christ that was born among the Indians already many centuries ago, who manifested himself in the Indian culture, before the coming of official Christianity: the Christ that has been crucified for centuries on this great cross of our double continent; the Christ that is agonizing on this same cross; when will the hour of the Resurrection of our Christ of the Americas come?, the Christ of the united, free America, (the America) emancipated from "the liturgy of the lie and of the pontificate of the infallible ignorance" which is modern politics; many years will pass, and we will not see the true America that still has not been born. We can and should be prophets of its advent—just as Pasternak in Russia is a prophet of a new age. . . .

JANUARY 8, 1959

. . . Let us continue searching in the secret of our hearts for the purity and integrity of the spirit—that "spiritus" that is the result of the union of the soul with God in a new and pure being, full of truth, humble instrument of God in the world.

JUNE 13, 1959

We are both very relieved to hear that you are safe in Costa Rica. The news of the revolution [an attempt to overthrow the Somoza government] has reached us, but the last information that I got was not favorable: it was largely a propaganda announcement of the Somoza government, to the effect that the guerrillas had been largely wiped out. I hope this is not true. I also hope that the United States will not intervene on behalf of Somoza's tyranny. Is there anything I can do? Can I write to the O.A.S.? . . .

. . . The tyrannies and compulsions under which we live in these days are a moral affront to man, the image of God. And it is becoming more and more clear that our fundamental moral obligation is to resist complicity and submission to every form of abusive power, whether physical or moral or spiritual. And this is both complicated and perilous. Mistakes will be made, and violence is hard to check. It is sometimes necessary to meet force with force, and then one can only hope that the violence that follows will not go too far beyond reasonable limits. In the great international problems of the world, this hope no longer clearly exists. In local situations such things are still possible. May freedom and justice come to Nicaragua, and to all the Latin American states. And may a greater comprehension exist everywhere on our continent. I regret that the United States takes such a short-sighted and materially interested view of everything. We live in very bad times, and our vocation to redeem them is something almost beyond bearing. It must be so. We can do nothing without the hidden power of God, and in our time more than any other, God seems absent. It is in this apparent "absence" of God that we must go forward with faith, in the perilous exercise of our freedom. . . .

On July 4, Merton wrote to President Luis Somoza and to the Organization of American States, interceding on behalf of those who had been imprisoned as a result of an attempt to overthrow the Somoza government in Nicaragua. Merton begged Somoza to remember his responsibility to protect those arrested "from injustice and coercion and to see that they are given a fair trial without undue or illegal pressures being brought to bear on them." In both letters, Merton interceded for leaders of the insurrection, particularly for La Prensa's Pedro Joaquin Chamorro, who had previously suffered imprisonment and torture. Though more than a hundred insurgents were tried, convicted, and sentenced to prison, within a year they were granted amnesty by President Somoza. Chamorro was assassinated on January 10, 1978.

JANUARY 4, 1960

. . . I pray often for all of Latin America, and think of all my friends there. No matter what happens, I feel myself more and more closely united with those who, everywhere, devote themselves to the glory of God's truth, to the search for divine values hidden among the poor and the outcast, to the love of that cultural heritage without which man cannot be healthy. The air of the world is foul with lies, hypocrisy, falsity, and life is short, death approaches. We must devote ourselves with generosity and integrity to the real values: there is no time for falsity and compromise. But on the other hand we do not have to be greatly successful or even well known. It is enough for our integrity to be known to God. What we do that is pure in His sight will avail for the liberty, the enlightenment, and the salvation of His children everywhere.

SEPTEMBER 16, 1961

It is time that I write to you, and as a matter of fact I have really written you a long letter which is now being typed out and which can serve for publication in *El Pez y la Serpiente* if you want it. What I had to say took the form of a letter because I felt I could say it better if I knew the person I was addressing. Hence in speaking to you first of all I have said what I thought needed to be said to everyone else, especially in Latin America. The piece is really an article, entitled "Letter to Pablo Antonio Cuadra concerning Giants" and the giants in question are of course the big power blocs that are beginning to enter the final states of the death struggle in which they will tear each other to pieces. Though the moment of supreme crisis may come quite suddenly and probably will, I do not think it is immediately near. But I think it is inevitable, unless there is some very remarkable intervention of Providence. Since I trust such intervention may take place, I see no reason for becoming desperate or even excited. However the sober facts seem to point to a nuclear war in the near future. Since there is at least a serious possibility of this, I felt that my position called for some kind of a statement of where I stand, morally, as a Christian writer. That statement has been made in the letter to you. . . .

AUGUST 1, 1963

But the general lack of understanding, the incapacity to break away from the obsession with technics and with results, the madness of space flights and shooting at the moon, shows that the human spirit is being overwhelmed by the riot of its own richness, which in the end is the worst kind of poverty. The poor man who can be himself is at least a man and a person and is richer than the rich man who is carried away by the forces to which he has sold himself. This elementary truth no one bothers to recognize. It may ruin us. Yet still the grinding poverty of Latin America has to be relieved, but it must not be the moon lit by the North American sun. It must relieve itself from within its own resources, which must be spiritual and human and creative. . . .

So we continue to live and try to seek truth. Each must do so with courage and indefatigable patience, constantly discerning it from the obsessive fictions of the establishment everywhere. . . .

TO NAPOLEON CHOW *Nicaraguan poet Napoleon Chow belonged to a circle of poets who together made up a new literary movement that Merton admired and of which he considered himself a part.*

DECEMBER 26, 1962

. . . You know from Ernesto and Pablo Antonio Cuadra, how sympathetic I am to the literary movement in Nicaragua. It is to me a joy, through these friends, to find myself close to the movement and in a certain sense part of it. As a matter of fact, it seems to me that I fit more naturally into Latin American culture than into that of North America; I certainly find no "movement" or group in this country with which I can begin to consider myself affiliated. On the contrary, I am here something of a solitary figure, both among Catholics and among writers. I have the impression that though quite a few people read me, not all are comfortable with me and most do not quite know where to place me. This is as it should be, because one does not want to fit into a neat category, especially in this land of commerce and commercial methods, of public relations, and statistics drawn up with a view to manipulating the consumer-public. I am definitely not a harmonious part of this society: but the fact that I can be considered a part of it at all is testimony to the fact that there does still remain at least a minimum of freedom and the power to speak one's own mind, even though what one says is not always acceptable.

This, it seems to me, is likely to be the place of the Christian writer and intellectual everywhere in the world. I think we have to be very careful of our honesty and our refusal to be swept away by large groups, into monolithic systems. We have to guard and defend our eccentricity, even when we are reminded that it is an expendable luxury, a self-indulgence. It is not, and those who try to make us yield our right to think as we see fit, secretly suffer and are ashamed when we yield to their enticements or to their pressures. Even though they have no other way of praising us than by taking us so seriously that they silence us, this itself is the witness we have to bear to truth. . . .

I wish, then, through you to send a message of solidarity and friendship to the young writers of Nicaragua, and to encourage them in their creative work. I am not for my part discouraged by the necessary and inevitable divisions, or by the need for dialogue which these divisions create. On the other hand I am not overoptimistic about the possibilities of achievement through exchanges of ideas with groups that are dedicated to one fixed idea and which really have no intention of "exchanging" ideas. Yet I think we must cling to a higher wisdom which sees possibilities of communication even where this is explicitly rejected and denied. This will be possible if we do not attach too much importance to our own "power" to convince others or to make them agree with us. What is important is that all should agree with the truth, or at least that all should admit the existence of a truth which is not the exclusive property of a political party. . . .

TO MARGARET RANDALL   JANUARY 15, 1963

. . . I am personally convinced that the best American poetry is written in Latin America. Besides Octavio Paz and a host of other Mexican and Central American poets I can think of, there are the great ones of a genera-tion past, like César Vallejo, who is to me, I think, the poet of our century who seems to have the most to say. And all the new ones who are, or will be, coming up. One feels that in Latin America the voice of the poet has significance because it has something to do with life. Doubtless I am not in a position to give a sweeping critical judgment of the poets of the United States at the present moment as I do not get to read them, except for a few. Some have an unquestionable maturity and excellence, but few really say anything. In the midst of technological and scientific virtuosity we find ourselves (many of us anyway) in a spiritual stupor. My own work is, in its way, a protest against this. It is also an expression of something else again, of a dimension of life and experience in which the North American mind is not really interested. . . .

Born in Havana, Cuba, Cintio Vitier was mentored by Spanish Nobel laureate Juan Ramón Jiménez. Merton very much liked Vitier's Canto llano. *Merton included the letter to Vitier excerpted below in* Seeds of Destruction, *titling it "To a Cuban Poet."*

Yes, your letter reached me, and I have been thinking about it deeply, as also about your poem about Christ and the Robbers. I have been thinking about these things in silence, at a long distance from the noise of official answers and declamations.

I am alone with the bronze hills and a vast sky and shadows of pine trees. Sometimes the shadows are alive with golden butterflies. Everywhere is the inscrutable and gentle and very silent face of truth. Nothing is said. In this silence and in this presence I have been reading your poems, and those of Fina [García Marruz], and Eliseo [Diego], and Octavio [Smith]. And I have not been able to find those of Roberto [Friol]. He should send me some more, and all of you please send me new poems. It may take time for me to get them in the silence like this, but I will do so. The time is come when the publication of poems is to be like that of pale and very light airborne seeds flowing in the current of forest air through the blue shadows, and falling on the grass where God says [Merton changed "says" to "decrees" in the letter published in *Seeds of Destruction*]. I am convinced that we are now already in the time where the printed word is not read, but the paper passed from hand to hand is read eagerly. A time of small letters, hesitant, but serious and personal, and out of the meaningless dimension of the huge, the monstrous and the cruel. . . .

Really, the reading of your poems in this silence has been very meaningful and serious: much more serious than the publication of new magazines with poetic manifestos. I have written something for Miguel Grinberg in the Argentine on "the poet and freedom" ["Answers on Art and Freedom"], but I wonder sometimes whether such declarations have a meaning. I am sad at the different kinds of programmatic affirmations made by poets, and the outcry about freedom from poets who have no concept of what it is all about, who are so absurd as to think it means freedom to knock themselves out with dope or something of the sort. Sick. Absurd. What waste of the opportunities: their freedom is pure aimlessness and in the end it collapses in the worst kind of unfreedom and arbitrariness. . . .

TO JOSÉ CORONEL URTECHO   *Born in Nicaragua, José Coronel Urtecho studied in the United States and, when he returned home, introduced his fellow writers to the work of North American poets. As a poet and founder of the Vanguard movement, he influenced future generations of Nicaraguan poets, including his nephew, Ernesto Cardenal.*

MARCH 15, 1964

Ernesto [Cardenal] in one of his fine letters spoke to me of your project [a reader of Merton's work], and I have written to him about it. It is a joy to me because it brings me more in contact with you both, for what is important is not the project but the communion of which the project is an expression. For it would be of little profit to me to be simply here in a monastery if being here did not enable me to be everywhere. And I am often with you in thought in the solitudes of the Rio San Juan. Also I think much of all Latin America for in some strange way Latin America has a great deal to do with my vocation: not that I have anything to tell LA but that I have much to learn from it, and it is our vocation to learn from one another, and to find the great mercy of God hidden in a distant jungle, as well as near at hand. For the voice of God must always come to us at every moment both from near and far and from the point that is nowhere and everywhere, from the O of admiration which is a boundless circle, and from the humility of love that breaks through limits set by national pride and the arrogance of wealth and power. Let us then live in a communion which undermines the power and arrogance of the great of this world, which seeks to separate men in the power struggle. . . .

. . . I feel much more close to the poets of Latin and South America than to many of this country where I am in so many ways an alien. But one must necessarily be an alien everywhere, to help the world become one, and deliver it from its obsession with small definitions and limited boundaries.

Last Sunday Miguel Grinberg of Argentina was here, and had encouraging things to say about the great movement that is stirring, the awakening of poets, and from this there is much to be hoped, for the poets remain almost the only ones who have anything to say. All the rest are turning out absurd and lifeless pronouncements and empty slogans. But the poets have the humility to seek truth from the springs of life which are first of all silent. They have the courage to disbelieve what is shouted with the greatest amount of noise from every loudspeaker, and it is this courage that is most of all necessary today. A courage not to rebel, for rebellion itself tends to substitute another and louder noise from the noise that already deafens everyone, but an independence, a personal and spiritual liberty which is above noise and outside it and which can unite men in a solidarity which noise and terror cannot penetrate. This solidarity in Christ and in His Spirit, where the only liberty is found.

I think Ernesto's work with the Indian culture and so on is really magnificent and I pray that he may become another Bartolomé de Las Cases [sixteenth-century Spanish missionary who exposed the oppression of the Indians by European colonizers], but in the spirit of our times, which is vastly different. It is quite possible that there is great hope for the world in the spiritual emancipation of the Indians, if this be possible, as there is also hope in Africa. From the old so-called civilization I have not much hope, and from the peculiar ferment which is the United States I look for nothing but violence and perplexity unless there is a capacity to become humble and learn. This is not apparent at the moment. There is of course a peculiar and confused good will, which may mean anything or nothing. The phenomena we face are all new ones, and without precedent. Or else they are apocalyptic. . . .

APRIL 17, 1964

The other day a copy of the [*Thomas Merton*] *Reader* went off to you by air mail and I also enclosed *The Behavior of the Titans.* At the same time I spoke to New Directions about your project. In the *Reader* I hastily marked some passages that might be of interest, but I think that there are better ones that exist in mimeograph or in articles which I could send. I am not sure I will be able to find all the copies, but here are some of the things that ought to be in the book rather than much that is in the big *Reader.*

- Preface to Japanese Edition of *Seven Storey Mountain*
- "To Each His Darkness" (about Julien Green, Ernesto may have this)

- "The Jesuits in China"
- "Classic Chinese Thought"
- "Message to Poets" (I think you have this)
- "[Answers] On Art and Freedom" (This is being published in a magazine in Argentina [*Eco Contemporáneo*] by M. Grinberg.)
- "Legend of Tucker Caliban" (On the Race Question)
- "Meditation on [Adolf] Eichmann"

and of course things like the "Letter to Pablo Antonio [Concerning Giants].". . . . Besides this there is material in some books which were not used for the *Reader*. For instance in *Disputed Questions* there is an article on Pasternak ["The Pasternak Affair"], as well as an article on Love ["The Power and Meaning of Love"] which is important, and especially Notes on a "Philosophy of Solitude" ["Notes for a Philosophy of Solitude"]. I will have *Disputed Questions* sent.

This ought to be enough, and I don't want to make everything too complicated. . . .

TO CINTIO VITIER   MAY 26, 1964

It is a long time since I have written. Did you get the "Message to Poets" which I sent last winter? I hope so. Meanwhile I have followed up your allusion to Vallejo. . . . I think that an understanding and love of Vallejo, this Inca and Prophet, is the key to the deep realization of the problems and predicaments of the two Americas today. First of all because Latin American poetry, which tends to be more personal and more prophetic than that of the U.S. while at the same time speaking for "the people" more than the individualist and sometimes hermetic subjectivism of the U.S. poets, is all gathered around Vallejo as around its deepest center and as a kind of source of life. . . .

TO MIGUEL GRINBERG   *An Argentinean poet and editor of* Eco Contemporáneo, *begun in 1961, Miguel Grinberg published Merton's writings in Buenos Aires. In 1963, Grinberg sent Merton nine questions. In response, Merton wrote "Answers on Art and Freedom." In 1964, Grinberg invited Merton to attend a meeting of poets in Mexico City. Unable to attend, Merton sent "Message to Poets," expressing his solidarity with the young poets meeting in "a spontaneous explosion of hope."*

JULY 12, 1964

I sent Henry Miller a picture of the two of us in the front garden of the monastery and amid cold winds, snow, fallout, sleet, darkness, chaos and night. He thought he was able to discern in me a likeness to himself, and I agree as I had already thought of that too. Maybe I said it in a letter. He thinks I look like him and like Genet and like an ex-convict. He thinks you look like a pugilist and a vagabond. In all these things he is undoubtedly partly right, for only ex-convicts and vagabonds have any right to be moving about and breathing the air of night which is our ordinary climate. . . .

Should you change *Eco C[ontemporáneo]*? It is very good that way, should it become pseudo-sociological? What is the good of sociology? Maybe a little of it is all right. There has to be more poetry. For *exploración*. The exploration by poetry is the kind most needed now. Drama too, art, music, dancing, seminars, silence. Someone has got to listen to the immense silence of South America which is full of living vegetables and plants; all the other silences have become full of wrecked cars, busted stoves and sewing machines, junk lying around unable to speak. . . .

TO ALEJANDRO VIGNATI   *In 1960, Argentinean Alejandro Vignati published his first books of poetry:* Volcado luna *and* El cielo no arde.

NOVEMBER 1, 1964

. . . Thank you for your own poems. The voices that come up to me from the South, from beyond the Caribbean and the equator, move me very much. They are strong, sometimes angry, full of clear intuitions, free from the involvement, the desperation and self-frustration of some of the voices here, so many of the voices here. Your own poem presented by Miguel [Grinberg] in the latest *Americas* speaks to me very directly of the age-old aspiration to the paradise and innocence of true liberty, of which the flying bird is the silent witness.

You are in Rio, you see other skies than I and hear different harmonies and rhythms, but we seek the same innocence. It has its price, and we must seek it without turning back and without listening too strongly to the voices full of dust that speak only words of cotton. Such words are smothering everything, but the poets must let in air to the whole world. This demands innocence and insistence. And the childlikeness that is not understood by potentates. Peace, then, and may you have joy and light to continue to sing.

TO LUDOVICO SILVA   *Ludovico Silva, Venezuelan author of books, poetry, essays, and literary criticism, invited Merton to write "Day of a Stranger," an autobiographical essay in which Merton described a "typical day" in the hermitage. The essay first appeared in* Papales, *a literary magazine published in Caracas.*

MARCH 13, 1965

. . . I wish my life were nothing but silences and spaces, but there is also action and responsibility, much of which turns out to be illusion. However, as time goes on perhaps I will be able to get rid of the useless motions and think only thoughts that will enable me to write sooner and more intelligibly to poets. It is to me a great joy and encouragement to hear voices like yours from South America. Here in this country all is sickness and confusion, the poetry itself (some of it good) is drab and bitter. Under the mask of power in this land is a great hopelessness. I think it is due in part to the fact that anyone with any sensitivity is overwhelmed with a diffuse and inexpiable shame.

May you have peace and joy and insight.

TO NICANOR PARRA   *Chilean physicist and poet Nicanor Parra's* Poemas y Antipoemas *(1953) and* Versos de salon *(1962) appealed to Merton, who translated some of Parra's poems. Parra visited Merton at Gethsemani in May 1966.*

MARCH 20, 1965

. . . I find that I agree with your dissonances, and find them to be in fact very monastic. In fact, today the poets and other artists tend to fulfill many of the functions that were once the monopoly of monks—and which of course the monks have made haste to abandon, in order to center themselves firmly in the midst of a square society. . . .

TO ALFONSO CORTÉS   *Alfonso Cortés, who despite decades of mental illness wrote and published many volumes of poetry, was regarded as one of Nicaragua's most outstanding poets. Merton's poem "To Alfonso Cortés" and Merton's translations of some poems by Cortés appear in* Emblems of a Season of Fury.

APRIL 20, 1965

I am very happy to have in hand your new book, *Las rimas universales,* in which I read with admiration of new poetry and where I come to know you even better. You know with what esteem I had read and even tried to translate some of your very great poems, so profound and so penetrating. You are as a matter of fact a poet to whom God has given a very original intuition, even in a prophetic sense. You have suffered much, but in you the power of the artist and of the contemplative has made you master the suffering. It has been very fertile in your life, and you have not regretted a malady to which so many others, less endowed than you, would certainly have succumbed.

Continue then, dear Master, to give us your truly universal songs, for you are, to speak the truth, one of the only truly universal voices in this world turned upside down and divided by the hate and the ambiguities of the men of power. I greet you with the most respectful friendship.

TO NICANOR PARRA   JUNE 12, 1965

. . . I am happy that you are thinking about maybe translating some poems of mine: you will find that before knowing your work I had written some antipoems, for example "Chant to Be Used in Processions. . . ." In truth this poem is composed almost in its entirety from the very words of the commanders of Auschwitz. It would be impossible to invent something more terrifying than the truth itself. In any event it is a somewhat difficult poem to translate. They have attempted it in Russian, without success I believe. But when they publish something in Russian it is hard to know. I think that you could do something with this poem, changing just a little bit the insinuations according to your own judgment and the spirit of your language. What do you think? Another antipoem is the one about the flight in space ["Why Some Look Up to Planets and Heroes"], and another is

about a Chinese girl, Lee Ying ["A Picture of Lee Ying"], etc. But maybe you
like the others better. . . .

TO JOSÉ CORONEL URTECHO   JUNE 30, 1965

. . . The thing that impresses me most and gives me most hope is that
this is a genuinely human level of communication. With you and Ernesto
and Pablo Antonio and the gradually widening circle of my good friends
in Latin America, there is a real exchange on a deep level. Ernesto's new
book of poems strikes me as very powerful in its simplicity. He has an
unequaled gift of getting poetry out of the confusion and pathos of the
modern world, without being bitter about it. And your work, and that of
Pablo Antonio, strikes me as so much more alive than what is nearer to
me here, geographically.

Ludovico Silva in Caracas is translating a short piece ["Day of a
Stranger"] I sent him: he might send you a copy of his translation for the
book, if you like . . . I will put a bunch of new things in an envelope for you,
and enclose here a poem on "Origen." I have been quite busy this summer,
and am starting on an article on existentialism which I hope to send soon.
I have been living more and more in the little house I have in the woods.
I often think of the silence and solitude you enjoy on the Rio San Juan.
Ernesto's project [the monastic community at Solentiname] sounds magnificent, and I understand it is quite near you. I wish I could see it some day.
Tell me more about those Islands.

I have just finished a book of poems [*The Way of Chuang Tzu*] based
on the Chinese writer Chuang Tzu. What I send, of him, is only a sample.
There is much more, but I do not yet have copies. . . .

I return to the original idea of this letter: the joy of being able to communicate with friends, in a world where there is so much noise and very
little contact. We cannot realize the extent of our trouble and our risk, and
yet we do not know what to do—except to go on being human. This in itself
is already an achievement. And we hope that since God became man, there
is nothing greater for us than simply to be men ourselves, and persons in
His image, and accept the risks and torments of a confused age. And though

the age is confused, it is no sin for us to be nevertheless happy and to have hopes, provided they are not the vain and empty hopes of a world that is merely affluent....

TO ALEJANDRO VIGNATI   JULY 23, 1965

... I agree with what you say about the religious values of the Indians. You are right a thousand times over. The history of the conquest was tragic, but not as tragic as that of this continent here in the North, where almost all of the Indians were exterminated. Some remain, in silence, as an accusation, and each year the white people try to steal from them another piece of the reservation that remains theirs. I would very much like to see those ancient cities of the Incas and the Mayas, but I think I will never be able to. Well, I do not like being a tourist, and I am not a "missionary," I am not a scholar, I am a hermit and nothing else. That is not wrong: it is a simple fact, and I am happy about it all.

I like the young Peruvian poets very much....

Beautiful poems of Rio: to the South of the sun. I have walked with you the brilliant and dark streets of the city. Here right now, it is as hot as in Rio.

TO ALFONSO CORTÉS   SEPTEMBER 3, 1965

... I am very moved to know that you are writing a book "for the humble." In fact only the humble, the poor and especially the disinherited are the ones who before all else deserve our attention and our compassion in the world. But even among the intellectuals there are many humble and poor persons. In any event, in this world where money and power threaten to destroy everything, it is necessary to unite oneself with the innocent and the poor sinners which we all are, it is necessary to know how to be nothing more because the Saviour lives and suffers in those who are left to depend on their self to live in others and in God. So it is that by suffering you speak even for those who must read your books in the generations to come: because they will read you as one of the mysterious and prophetic poets of America: but as a poet whom all will understand....

TO LUDOVICO SILVA   JANUARY 17, 1966

You are right about the North American poets. The more I think about
it, though, the more I see that the whole question of American poetry, North
and South, is a very big question. It is something so big that I for one never
face it, and I do not think anyone has. But anyway, I do not even read most
of the North Americans. I do not even know who most of them are. Once in
a while I come across someone I think is good, then I even forget his name.
George Oppen is an unknown who I think is pretty good. I don't know
what [Robert] Lowell means to you in South America; probably nothing. I
think he is a good poet for the U.S. but I don't know what he could mean
to the rest of the world (except England). Perhaps one of the few American
U.S. poets that has something to say for everybody is [Allen] Ginsberg. Do
you know him? I [will] send a volume of his stuff. Do I like him? That is not
the question. When I read Ginsberg I do not feel at home with him or like
him as I like [César] Vallejo or Nicanor Parra, but it is a curious experience
of recognizing an authentic interpretation of a society in which I live and
from which I am in many ways alien. Ginsberg speaks a language I know
because I hear it every day, and yet he is remote also. He talks about a country of which I happen to be a citizen, and yet it is not "mine." As a matter
of fact, in many ways I have no country at all. The country in which I live is
incomprehensible. I think all the clichés about it are crazy, but I do not want
to invent others. I do not know whether it is all headed for ruin, or what.
A North American poet has to say something of this, and I think the merit
of Ginsberg is that he is authentic and does not judge. On the other hand I
think it is a pity that it all has to be done with drugs. . . .

                                               SEPTEMBER 13, 1966

. . . I am as always living my days of a stranger. I think that in my last letter (of May?) I spoke to you of my experience in the hospital. Maybe I sent
you the poem that I wrote then ["With the World in My Bloodstream"]. In
any case, here is another copy. I am reading poetry, especially René Char, I
am writing poetry as well. I realize that for me to write theology is to waste
time, given that I am in no way a theologian: I am more a philosopher and
poet, an existentialist, a rebel and a general problem. . . .

TO MIGUEL GRINBERG   OCTOBER 28, 1966

Sun rises in mist with thousands of very soft explosions and I am entirely splashed with designs coming through the holes in the lace wall of trees. Everything in the world is transparent. The ferocities of mankind mean nothing to the hope of light. You are right, preserve your hopes. For this one must keep eyes open always and see. The new consciousness will keep awakening. I know it. Poets, designers, musicians, singers. Do you know Bob Dylan's songs? Wonderful poet . . . I am writing about Camus. I am writing five million poems. . . .

New consciousness. There has to be clean water in the mind for the spirit to drink.

Courage and joy. Big *abrazo* for everybody.

TO VICTORIA OCAMPO   *A prolific writer herself, in 1931 Argentinean Victoria Ocampo founded a literary review,* Sur, *which she edited for more than forty years, publishing the work of Thomas Mann, Jacques Maritain, Henry Miller, T. S. Eliot, Simone Weil, Albert Camus, and Thomas Merton among others. The publishing house, also named* Sur, *brought out, in translation, works by writers such as C. J. Jung, Virginia Woolf, D. H. Lawrence, and William Faulkner. Merton considered Victoria Ocampo as "one of those wonderful people who includes in herself all the grace and wisdom of a universal culture."*

JANUARY 20, 1967

Thank you for your kind letter rising up out of solitude. I try to imagine myself down there by the sea listening to its winds. . . . Yes, I do understand you. Solitude is difficult, especially when the conduct of our friends ends up pushing us into it ever more deeply. We are truly pilgrims and exiles. It is necessary to know it and to "digest" it as you say so well. And we shouldn't let it poison us. For this it is necessary to have a little patience, because there will be days that, in spite of ourselves, will be full of this terrible venom. Yet it purifies, if one knows how to make use of it: if one absolutely refuses to be mean and to search for ways to enjoy one's resentment. And for "intellectuals" the means are always there: we know so well how to tear each other apart. It seems that it is for this that the "literary world" sometimes exists. Therefore it would be better to do as you do and to digest this bitterness in your solitude, let it be blown away by the winds of the sea. And then all is right.

But in short, psychology does not suffice. There is that mysterious "grace" of which the theologians speak not knowing of what they are speaking and of which clerics sometimes preach in a way that makes it suspect and odious to us. There is always this grace of God for which it suffices to seek, to ask for deep in one's heart. . . .

Dear Victoria, you can count on my prayers and on my friendship— from afar. Right now I live alone in the woods. I am a hermit, by desire and by fact. It is very good. I do my work. I pray. I meditate. I study Zen. I write quite a few articles on Buddhism. And I am "present" to my friends in all parts of the world. My life as a hermit is much more "open" than that which I was living in the monastery. (I am still a member of the community, and I love living on the monastery property, where I take my meals to avoid my own cooking!) Keep well. Stay in peace. Have confidence. God bless you.

TO LUDOVICO SILVA   APRIL 27, 1967

. . . The future of poetry: my reaction is totally positive. The poets have much to say and do: they have the same mission as the prophets in the technical world. They have to be the consciousness of the revolutionary man because they have the keys of the subconscious and of the great secrets of real life. But the governments are full of poet-killers and of anti-poets with machines to fabricate only death and nothing more. Then, the future of the poets depends upon their freedom, the freedom of conscience and of creation. The future of poetry is also the future of the world. For one cannot truly believe in God if one does not believe in mankind as well: the poets will triumph. We will triumph. God is with the poets. That is why I am especially happy to know that *Boom* has some success with those who know how to read. . . .

TO MARGARET RANDALL   APRIL 30, 1967

. . . It is spooky living in this country which is totally blind and with all instruments for seeing everything but the obvious. Poets see but what they say is not heard. All instruments for hearing everything except poets, prophets, etc. Or people. Only poems by cardinals and mandarins in an unknown language are scrupulously recorded and sung by the Republican and Democratic tenors in chorus. The fine smelling castrati laying scientific and literary eggs. Death is said to be very clean. Gradually this belief permeates the entire world.

I liked your Cuban poems. I envy you. I love Cuba, Cuban people. Not permitted in this country even to think of Cuba, still less of going to Cuba. Of course the thing is that when people are able to do something about deciding their own destiny they are relatively happy because they begin to become themselves. But also when a big fat people starts deciding everybody else's destiny then it becomes alienated by its own abuse of power, ceases to be anything but its own image of itself. A bad thing to have happen: death sits under the helmet, so sincere. Nothing else seems to exist. Communication is reduced to the algebra of death: equations from the Rand Corp. Apocalypse. . . .

JULY 6, 1967

. . . It seems to me that we all have an enormous amount to do just looking for what is real: and of course that has to go on all the time because you never definitively find anything that stays real in the same way the next day (except in its metaphysical ground, and that can't be "possessed" by an individual as his "own"). We have our life's work cut out for us just keeping real. The tragedy is to suppose that a society, an institution, a cause, or even a Church, will do the job for us. And it is rough to have to recognize that what we have been trying to build has to be taken apart and put back together in a better way—and with a lot of trouble. Yet there is always something very good about starting out all over again. I seem to be getting along toward something like that, as I suggested: finding new dimensions and directions. The best ones are those that do not appear to be anything much and cannot be explained. . . .

DECEMBER 13, 1967

. . . This is just a real quick letter to say I have decided to edit a tempo-
rary magazine [*Monks Pond*], four issues only, four collections, offset, can
be done without trouble here so might as well do it. Need poems, prose,
ideas, anything, so long as it doesn't get me burned by the monks. If it is
something they don't figure out ok. Can you send me a poem or something?
And Sergio? How about something on yoga? On meditation? Or what is
wrong with monks? Or about anything that makes life have meaning. Ideas.
Visions. Or just what the sun shines like. Anyone you know who is interested. Tell. It will be only four collections (4). No money either way, all given
away.

PART 5

Seeking God in the Ordinariness of Life

Merton's Contemplative Spirituality

"God loves us irrespective of our merits and whatever is good in us comes from his love, not from our own doing."

—To Dom Francis Decroix, August 21, 1967

While Merton's many writings on spirituality were grounded in his own life of contemplative prayer, they were also informed by his in-depth knowledge of Christian mysticism. As a result, Merton became "an explorer" for others, mapping the inner terrain of the human heart, and speaking of "the inner experience" in ways that invited his readers to the life of contemplative spirituality, not apart from but in the very midst of the world. These letters reveal something of his own way of prayer and his understanding of what the contemplative has to share with others, as well as his efforts to translate the language of the tradition into a contemporary idiom. This section opens with Merton's contribution to Pope Paul VI's request for a "message of contemplatives to the world," continues with selections from Merton's extensive correspondence with Etta Gullick, and concludes with excerpts from letters spanning almost two decades.

A "MESSAGE OF CONTEMPLATIVES TO THE WORLD"

TO DOM FRANCIS DECROIX *Dom Francis Decroix, abbot of the Cistercian monastery of Frattocchie near Rome, received in 1967 a request from Paul VI for a "message of contemplatives to the world." The pope suggested that Thomas Merton might be one of the monks asked to compose such a message. Accordingly, Dom Francis in a letter of August 14 requested a statement by the end of the month. Merton wrote his statement on August 21, the very day he received the abbot's letter. He mailed it the following day with an additional statement.*

AUGUST 21, 1967

This morning I received your letter of August 14th and I realize I must answer it immediately in order to get the reply to you before the end of the month. This does not leave me time to plan and think, and hence I must write rapidly and spontaneously. I must also write directly and simply, saying precisely what I think, and not pretending to announce a magnificent message which is really not mine. I will say what I can. It is not much. . . .

On the other hand I must begin by saying that I was acutely embarrassed by the Holy Father's request. It puts us all in a difficult position.

We are not experts in anything. There are few real contemplatives in our monasteries. We know nothing whatever of spiritual aviation and it would be the first duty of honesty to admit that fact frankly, and to add that we do not speak the language of modern man. There is considerable danger that in our haste to comply with the Holy Father's generous request, based on an even more generous estimate of us, we may come out with one more solemn pronouncement which will end not by giving modern man hope but by driving him further into despair, simply by convincing him that we belong to an entirely different world, in which we have managed, by dint of strong will and dogged refusals, to remain in a past era. I plead with you: we must at all costs avoid this error and act of uncharity. We must, before all else, whatever else we do, speak to modern man as his brothers, as people who are in very much the same difficulties as he is, as people who suffer much of what he suffers, though we are immensely privileged to be exempt from so many, so very many, of his responsibilities and sufferings. And we must not arrogate to ourselves the right to talk down to modern man, to dictate to him from a position of supposed eminence, when perhaps he suspects that our cloister walls have not done anything except confirm us in unreality. I must say these things frankly. I have seen over a thousand young men of our time, or rather nearly two thousand, enter and leave this monastery, coming with a hunger for God and leaving in a state of confusion, disarray, uncomprehending frustration and often deep bitterness: because they could not feel that our claims here could be real for them. The problem of the contemplative Orders at present, in the presence of modern man, is a problem of great ambiguity. People look at us, recognize we are sincere, recognize that we have indeed found a certain peace, and see that there may after all be some worth to it: but can we convince them that this means anything *to them*? I mean, can we convince them professionally and collectively, as "the contemplatives" in our walled institution, that what our institutional life represents has any meaning for them? If I were absolutely confident in answering yes to this, then it would be simple to draft the message we are asked to draw up. But to me, at least, it is not that simple. And for that reason I am perhaps disqualified from participating in this at all. In fact, this preface is in part a plea to be left out, to be exempted from a task to which I do not in the least recognize myself equal. However, as I said before, I will attempt to say in my own words what I personally, as an individual, have to say and usually do say to my brother who is in the world and who more and more often comes to me with his wounds which turn out to be also my own. The Holy Father, he can be a good Samaritan, but myself and my brothers in the world we are just two men who have fallen among thieves and we do our best to get each other out of the ditch.

Hence what I write here I write only as a sinner to another sinner, and in no sense do I speak officially for "the monastic Order" with all its advantages and its prestige and its tradition.

Let us suppose the message of a so-called contemplative to a so-called man of the world to be something like this:

My dear brother, first of all, I apologize for addressing you when you have not addressed me and have not really asked me anything. And I apologize for being behind a high wall which you do not understand. This high wall is to you a problem, and perhaps it is also a problem to me, O my brother. Perhaps you ask me why I stay behind it out of obedience? Perhaps you are no longer satisfied with the reply that if I stay behind this wall I have quiet, recollection, tranquility of heart. Perhaps you ask me what right I have to all this peace and tranquility when some sociologists have estimated that within the lifetime of our younger generations a private room will become an unheard-of luxury. I do not have a satisfactory answer: it is true, as an Islamic proverb says, "The hen does not lay eggs in the marketplace." It is true that when I came to this monastery where I am, I came in revolt against the meaningless confusion of a life in which there was so much activity, so much movement, so much useless talk, so much superficial and needless stimulation, that I could not remember who I was. But the fact remains that my flight from the world is not a reproach to you who remain in the world, and I have no right to repudiate the world in a purely negative fashion, because if I do that my flight will have taken me not to truth and to God but to a private, though doubtless pious, illusion.

Can I tell you that I have found answers to the questions that torment the man of our time? I do not know if I have found answers. When I first became a monk, yes, I was more sure of "answers." But as I grow old in the monastic life and advance further into solitude, I become aware that I have only begun to seek the questions. And what are the questions? Can man make sense out of his existence? Can man honestly give his life meaning merely by adopting a certain set of explanations which pretend to tell him why the world began and where it will end, why there is evil and what is necessary for a good life? My brother, perhaps in my solitude I have become as it were an explorer for you, a searcher in realms which you are not able to visit—except perhaps in the company of your psychiatrist. I have been summoned to explore a desert area of man's heart in which explanations no longer suffice, and in which one learns that only experience counts. An arid, rocky, dark land of the soul, sometimes illuminated by strange fires which men fear and peopled by specters which men studiously avoid except in their nightmares. And in this area I have learned that one cannot truly know hope unless he has found out how like despair hope is. The language of Christianity has said this for centuries in other less naked terms. But the language of Christianity has been so used and so misused that sometimes you distrust it: you do not know whether or not behind the word "Cross" there stands the experience of mercy and salvation, or only the threat of punishment. If my word means anything to you, I can say to you that I have experienced the Cross to mean mercy and not cruelty, truth and not deception: that the news of the truth and love of Jesus is indeed the true good news, but in our time it speaks out in strange places. And perhaps it speaks out in you more than it does in me: perhaps Christ is nearer to you than He is to me: this I say without shame or guilt because I have learned to rejoice that Jesus is in the world in people who know Him not, that He is at work in them when they think themselves far from Him, and it is my joy to tell you to hope though you think that for you of all men hope is impossible. Hope not because you think you can be good, but because God loves us irrespective of our merits and whatever is good in us comes from His love, not from our own doing. Hope because Jesus is with those who are poor and outcasts and perhaps despised even by those who should seek them and care for them most lovingly because they act in God's name. . . . No one on earth has reason to despair of Jesus because Jesus loves man, loves him in his sin, and we too must love man in his sin.

God is not a "problem" and we who live the contemplative life have learned by experience that one cannot know God as long as one seeks to solve "the problem of God." To seek to solve the problem of God is to seek to see one's own eyes. One cannot see his own eyes because they are that with which he sees and God is the light by which we see—by which we see not a clearly defined "object" called God, but everything else in the invisible One. God is then the Seer and the Seeing, but on earth He is not seen. In heaven, He is the Seer, the Seeing and the Seen. God seeks Himself in us, and the aridity and sorrow of our heart is the sorrow of God who is not known in us, who cannot find Himself in us because we do not dare to believe or trust the incredible truth that He could live in us, and live there out of choice, out of preference. But indeed we exist solely for this, to be the place He has chosen for His presence, His manifestation in the world, His epiphany. But we make all this dark and inglorious because we fail to believe it, we refuse to believe it. It is not that we hate God, rather that we hate ourselves, despair of ourselves: if we once began to recognize, humbly but truly, the real value of our own self, we would see that this value was the sign of God in our being, the signature of God upon our being. Fortunately, the love of our fellow man is given us as the way of realizing this. For the love of our brother, our sister, our beloved, our wife, our child, is there to see with the clarity of God Himself that we are good. It is the love of my lover, my brothers or my child that sees God in me, makes God credible to myself in me. And it is my love for my lover, my child, my brother, that enables me to show God to him or her in himself or herself. Love is the epiphany of God in our poverty. The contemplative life is then the search for peace not in an abstract exclusion of all outside reality, not in a barren negative closing of the senses upon the world, but in the openness of love. It begins with the acceptance of my own self in my poverty and my nearness to despair in order to recognize that where God is there can be no despair, and God is in me even if I despair. That nothing can change God's love for me, since my very existence is the sign that God loves me and the presence of His love creates and sustains me. Nor is there any need to understand how this can be or to explain it or to solve the problems it seems to raise. For there is in our hearts and in the very ground of our being a natural certainty which is co-extensive with our very existence: a certainty that says that insofar as we exist we are penetrated through and through with the sense and reality of God even though we may be utterly unable to believe or experience this in philosophic or even religious terms.

O my brother, the contemplative is the man not who has fiery visions of the cherubim carrying God on their imagined chariot, but simply he who has risked his mind in the desert beyond language and beyond ideas where God is encountered in the nakedness of pure trust, that is to say in the surrender of our poverty and incompleteness in order no longer to clench our minds in a cramp upon themselves, as if thinking made us exist. The message of hope the contemplative offers you, then, brother, is not that you need to find your way through the jungle of language and problems that today surround God: but that whether you understand or not, God loves you, is present in you, lives in you, dwells in you, calls you, saves you, and offers you an understanding and light which are like nothing you ever found in books or heard in sermons. The contemplative has nothing to tell you except to reassure you and say that if you dare to penetrate your own silence and risk the sharing of that solitude with the lonely other who seeks God through you, then you will truly recover the light and the capacity to understand what is beyond words and beyond explanations because it is too close to be explained: it is the intimate union in the depths of your own heart, of God's spirit and your own secret inmost self, so that you and He are in all truth One Spirit. I love you, in Christ.

AUGUST 22, 1967

Since the letter I wrote yesterday was too late for yesterday's mail, I am sending this one which may perhaps be more succinct and more useful. I thought of destroying yesterday's letter or entirely rewriting it, but I send it as it is, in the hope that there may still be some point in it.

First of all, I want to say how touched and grateful I am that the Holy Father should remember me, and I will write to him myself to express my gratitude and devotion.

About the message he asks of us: I should say first of all that it is not our place to write anything apologetic. Thus I am sure we all agree that it is not for us to spell out proofs for the existence of God, but merely to bear witness in our simplicity to His universal love for all men and His message of salvation, but above all to His presence in the hearts of all men, including sinners, including those who hate Him. Without going into technical distinctions of natural, supernatural, and so on, though emphasizing grace later on.

The important thing in our message should, it seems to me, be prayer and contemplation. But we must be careful not to present prayer as a mere formal duty or to emphasize prayer of petition. We should bear in mind that Marx taught an interesting doctrine about religious alienation, which is a consequence of regarding God as distant and purely transcendent and putting all our hope for every good in the future life, not realizing God's presence to us in this life, and not realizing that prayer means contact with the deepest reality of life, our own truth in Him. Also we should perhaps point out that prayer is the truest guarantee of personal freedom. That we are most truly free in the free encounter of our hearts with God in His word and in receiving His Spirit which is the Spirit of sonship, truth and freedom. The Truth that makes us free is not merely a matter of information about God but the presence in us of a divine person by love and grace, bringing us into the intimate personal life of God as His Sons by adoption. This is the basis of all prayer and all prayer should be oriented to this mystery of sonship in which the Spirit in us recognizes the Father. The cry of the Spirit in us, the cry of recognition that we are Sons in the Son, is the heart of our prayer and the great motive of prayer. Hence recollection is not the exclusion of material things but attentiveness to the Spirit in our inmost heart. The contemplative life should not be regarded as the exclusive prerogative of those who dwell in monastic walls. All men can seek and find this intimate awareness and awakening which is a gift of love and a vivifying touch of creative and redemptive power, that power which raised Christ from the dead and cleanses us from dead works to serve the living God. Which should remind us also that the monastery must not be a place of mere "dead works" and that faith is the most important thing in our lives, not the empty formalities and rites which are mere routines not vivified by the living presence of God and by His love which is beyond all legalism. It should certainly be emphasized today that prayer is a real source of personal freedom in the midst of a world in which men are dominated by massive organizations and rigid institutions which seek only to exploit them for money and power. Far from being the cause of alienation, true religion in spirit is a liberating force that helps man to find himself in God.

I regret that time does not permit me to write more on this. I feel it is useless to try to convey these ideas on paper when it would be much more worthwhile to be able to discuss them with you in living words and work out with you and other Fathers just what ought to be said. I will in any case pray that you may arrive at something corresponding to what the Holy Father really wants.

TO ETTA GULLICK   *In 1965 Etta Gullick began teaching at St. Stephen's, an Anglican theological college at Oxford. Her spiritual director, Christopher Butler, abbot of Downside, recommended that she study a manuscript by the Capuchin Benet of Canfield. She began preparing an edition of a section of his work that had not yet been translated into English. She contacted Merton, hoping he would read her translation and write a preface for it. Though Etta never finished her edition and Merton never got to write a preface, there are scattered references to Benet throughout their lengthy correspondence. But their interest branched off to other spiritual writers, problems of prayer, and the pains and joys of a dedicated spiritual life, as well as issues of war and peace.*

MARCH 5, 1961

I am reading Part III of Benet with the very greatest interest. It is true that he has a welter of divisions and subdivisions which I rather regret, but in between there are some marvelous passages. I find him very like Eckhart. We do have to open our hearts and "flow with God" with self-forgetfulness and the renunciation of mental objects, even the highest forms. In this of course we must always be called and led. He makes it clear. We are too rational. We do not permit anything to remain unconscious. Yet all that is best is unconscious or superconscious. . . .

JUNE 10, 1961

. . . We did not begin taking the *Downside Review* until just recently, and so I have not read the articles on Eckhart. I like him, but now and again he leaves one with a sense of being let down, when he goes beyond all bounds. He is more brilliant than all the other Rhenish mystics and really more interesting. Yet I like [fourteenth-century German Dominican mystic John] Tauler for a more steady diet. . . .

. . . I like the fourteenth-century English mystics more and more. I am reading [Walter Hilton's] *The Scale [of Perfection]*, which has such a great deal in it. And you are of course right about Eckhart. He is more and more wonderful, and when properly interpreted, becomes less "way out" as our beats say. There is more in one sermon of Eckhart than in volumes of other people. There is so much packed in between the lines. . . .

. . . Today came the [Vladimir] Lossky book on Eckhart. It is fabulously good, and not only that but it is for me personally a book of enormous and providential importance, because I can see right away in the first chapter that I am right in the middle of the most fundamental intuition of unknowing which was the first source of my faith and has ever since been my whole life . . . I cannot thank you enough.

Your last letter was very interesting and good to have. I am so happy now to "see" you, in the England that has always meant so much to me. . . .

. . . I envy you seeing all those wonderful places [in France] that I have not seen for so long. And you really seem to have living connections with them, in all sorts of various ways. I shall never forget the lycée: its grimness is in my bones. As for the mysterious redness and dustiness of Montauban, that too is an indescribable part of me. I remember all the walks we used to take on Thursdays, two by two. . . . I loved St. Antonin. I don't think I ever liked a place so much, until the hermitage which has been built and to which I have access in the woods here. Did you see the house we built there? . . .

I do not think strictly that contemplation should be the goal of "all devout souls," though I may have said this earlier on. In reality, I think a lot of them should be very good and forget themselves in virtuous action and love and let the contemplation come in the window unheeded, so to speak. They will be contemplatives without ever really knowing it. I feel that in the monastery here those who are too keen on being contemplatives with the capital C make of contemplation an "object" from which they are eternally separated, because they are always holding it at arms' length in order to see if it is there. As for the call to solitude it is in some respects unavoidable, and imperative, and even if you are prevented by circumstances (e.g., marriage!) from doing anything about it, solitude will come and find you anyway, and this is not always the easiest thing in life either. . . . In any case the right result should be a great purity of heart and selflessness and detachment.

I know what you are trying to say about loving God more than anything that exists but at the same time this is a measure of self-preservation. Beyond all is a love of God in and through all that exists. We must not hold them apart one from the other. But He must be One in all and Is. There comes a time when one loses everything, even love. Apparently. Even oneself, above all oneself. . . .

[COLD WAR LETTER 1] OCTOBER 25, 1961

. . . I was very interested in your marvelous trip through the Balkans, your visit to the Patriarch at Istanbul. It must have been most impressive. I hear he is wonderful. A friend of mine in New York has written back and forth and published magazine articles on him. He is very cordial. . . .

Thanks especially for the *Downside Reviews* with C. F. Kelley's excellent articles. These are very fine and I like them a lot. But do you realize that in sending me his address you did not give the name of any town? California is a big place, you know! . . .

. . . I am now perfectly convinced that there is one task for me that takes precedence over everything else: working with such means as I have at my disposal for the abolition of war. This is like going into the prize ring blindfolded and with hands tied, since I am cloistered and subject to the most discouragingly long and frustrating kinds of censorship on top of it. I must do what I can. Prayer of course remains my chief means, but it is also an obligation on my part to speak out insofar as I am able, and to speak as clearly, as forthrightly and as uncompromisingly as I can. A lot of people are not going to like this and it may mean my head, so do please pray for me in a very special way, because I cannot in conscience willingly betray the truth or let it be betrayed. The issue is too serious. . . . Of course there is in it all the great mercy of God Whose Word descends like the rain and snow from heaven and cannot return to Him empty: but the demonic power at work in history is appalling, especially in these last months. We are reaching a moment of great crisis, through the blindness and stupidity of our leaders and all who believe in them and in the society we have set up for ourselves, and which is falling apart. . . .

[COLD WAR LETTER 14] DECEMBER 22, 1961

. . . The question of peace is important, it seems to me, and so important that I do not believe anyone who takes his Christian faith seriously can afford to neglect it. I do not mean to say that you have to swim out to Polaris submarines carrying a banner between your teeth, but it is absolutely necessary to take a serious and articulate stand on the question of nuclear war. And I mean against nuclear war. The passivity, the apparent indifference, the incoherence of so many Christians on this issue, and worse still the active belligerency of some religious spokesmen, especially in this country, is rapidly becoming one of the most frightful scandals in the history of Christendom. I do not mean these words to be in any sense a hyperbole. The issue is very grave.

It is also, of course, very complex. Certainly I do not say that to be a Christian one must be a pacifist. And indeed there is the awful obstacle that in some schools of thought a Catholic "cannot be a conscientious objector." This is still open to debate even on the theoretical plane. In practice, since there is every reason to doubt the justice of nuclear war and since a Christian is not only allowed but obliged to refuse participation in an unjust war, there is certainly every reason why a person may on the grounds of conscience refuse to support any measure that leads to nuclear war, or even to a policy of deterrence. . . .

One could certainly wish that the Catholic position on nuclear war was half as strict as the Catholic position on birth control. It seems a little strange that we are so wildly exercised about the "murder" (and the word is of course correct) of an unborn infant by abortion, or even the prevention of conception which is hardly murder, and yet accept without a qualm the extermination of millions of helpless and innocent adults, some of whom may be Christians and even our friends rather than our enemies. I submit that we ought to fulfill the one without omitting the other. . . .

JANUARY 29, 1962

. . . Your intuition that Christ suffers in us in the Dark Night of the Soul seems to me to be especially apt and true. In the Night of Sense it is we who suffer in our own emptiness; in the Night of the Spirit he is emptiness in us, *exinanivit semetipsum* (He emptied himself). The special awfulness of that seeming void can certainly be taken as a personal presence, but without duality, without too much of the subject-object relationship. But above that.

Everybody is suffering emptiness. All that is familiar to us is being threatened and taken away . . . there may be little or nothing left and we may all have evaporated. Surely one cannot feel comfortable or at ease in such a world. We are under sentence of death, an extinction without remembrance or memorial, and we cling to life and to the present. This causes bitterness and anguish. Christ will cure us of this clinging and then we will be free and joyful, even in the night.

MARCH 30, 1962

. . . Did you ever get anywhere with Julian of Norwich? Though it might not seem so at first sight, I think there is much in her that is relevant to the Dark Night. At least theologically, if not exactly in the order of the classic experience. But certainly the great thing is passing with Christ through death out of this world to the Father, and one does not reduce this to a "classic experience." It must remain incomprehensible to a great extent. . . .

Am I unpopular because of the writing on peace? You ask this. The answer is yes and no. Unpopular with some bishops, yes. Probably get hit over the head. Yes. Certainly criticized vigorously and unfairly. I get the impression that people have not the time to really think about this issue. They have the wind up and are moved to vehement malevolence whenever someone suggests that the bomb might not be the solution to all their problems, and might not be a fully ethical solution to any problem. . . .

To return to the question of peace, I am interested in E. I. Watkin's book against nuclear war and am doing one myself. I like everyone that is mixed up with Pax in England. I think they make sense. We are starting a Pax over here, but of course too late to mean anything. . . .

. . . Instead of fourteenth- and fifteenth-century mystics, I have been back with the early Fathers. Tertullian, whom I have read for the first time. He is a great writer, but in many ways an awful person. His Latin is fascinating. . . .

You can guess that what occupied me most for the first four or five months of this year was the war business. A lot of people have wondered why I got involved in this, and have complained about it, to such good effect that my Superiors have now asked me to stop publishing on that altogether. Which I expected. But no matter what people may think about it, this was absolutely necessary. There was not a single Catholic voice raised in this country, except for Dorothy Day at the *Catholic Worker,* and who listens to her? The moral climate was absolutely oppressive and vile. Total unquestioning acceptance of the bomb without distinctions made, without serious thought of the meaning of annihilation bombing. I would not have considered myself a monk, a contemplative or a Christian at all if in the face of that I did not say something. . . .

JULY 14, 1962

. . . Your letters are always most welcome, and as a matter of fact I can hardly think of letters I enjoy more. You are, for one thing, my most real contact with England. I have lots of friends in England, but they never write much about England, just about this or that ax we happen to be grinding. But you write about the university and about people, and one gets echoes of Downside (which of course I never knew anyway), but it is really almost as if I had a sister still living there (in England). I never had a sister, and really I have felt this as a kind of lack. So really you must never feel diffident about your letters being "chatty." I am so glad that they are. I do get lots of letters that are awful penance and it is real work to plow through them out of sheer charity. Not so yours at all. . . .

. . . I wonder if the best thing in the world to read in a period of night is [John of] Ruysbroeck? Personally I rather doubt it. I think that he will only make you feel worse. Have you ever tried reading Sophocles or Aeschylus at such a time? In the first place they have the immense advantage of being people you at no time have to agree with. The whole notion of one's "spiritual state" is not called into question, and therefore they can get in under your guard, so to speak, and I find that the *Antigone* or *Oedipus at Colonus* is most helpful in a shattering sort of way. . . .

AUGUST 31, 1962

. . . Do send me a card from Arles, I have been studying Evagrius and all the people from Lerins (Honoratus, etc.). Much joy and blessing on your trip to France.

[COLD WAR LETTER 108] OCTOBER 29, 1962

. . . I thought the opening of the Council was tremendous. . . .

Apparently they are on the liturgy now. I don't know what will come, but the whole thing seems to be making sense. Probably it is bound to bog down a bit somewhere, but it is going better than expected. . . .

JANUARY 18, 1963

. . . I think Western mysticism, and particularly the Dionysians in the West, tend to get departmentalized. Except the really great ones like Eckhart. I think more and more of him. He towers over all his century. . . .

As for spiritual life: what I object to about "the Spiritual Life" is the fact that it is a part, a section, set off as if it were a whole. It is an aberration to set off our "prayer" etc. from the rest of our existence, as if we were sometimes spiritual, sometimes not. As if we had to resign ourselves to feeling that the unspiritual moments were a dead loss. That is not right at all, and because it is an aberration, it causes an enormous amount of useless suffering.

Our "life in the Spirit" is all-embracing, or should be. First it is the response of faith receiving the word of God not only as a truth to be believed but as a gift of life to be lived in total submission and pure confidence. Then this implies fidelity and obedience, but a total fidelity and a total obedience. From the moment that I obey God in everything, where is my "spiritual life"? It is gone out the window, there is no spiritual life, only God and His word and my total response. . . .

This is where you and I have to suffer much. In actual fact, if we could really let go of everything and follow the Spirit where He leads, who knows where we would be? But besides the interior exigencies of the Spirit there are also hard external facts, and they too are "God's will," but nevertheless they may mean that one is bound to a certain mediocrity and futility: that there is waste, and ineffective use of grace (bad way to talk, but you understand). The comfortable and respectable existence that you and I lead is in fact to a great degree *opposed* to the real demands of the Spirit in our lives. Yet paradoxically we are restricted and limited to this. Our acceptance of these restrictions cannot purely and simply be regarded as the ultimate obedience that is demanded of us. We cannot say that our bourgeois existence is purely and simply the "will of God." It both is and is not. Hence the burning and the darkness and the desperation we feel. The sense of untruth, of infidelity, even though we try as best we can to be faithful. . . . But we are *held back* from the deep and total gift which is not altogether possible to make in a conventional and tame setting where we do not suffer the things that the poor and disinherited and the outcast must suffer. The crosses we may find or fabricate in this life of ours, may serve to salve our conscience a little, and legitimately so: but we are not in the fullest sense Christians because we have not fully and completely obeyed the Spirit of Christ. . . .

MARCH 24, 1963

. . . What you say about the fact that you (and all of us) are unbelieving and that it is God in you who believes, is quite true. We do not realize how little faith we have, and the more people talk about "my" faith, the more I wonder if they have it. It can easily be simply a matter of subscribing to what other people, like oneself, think is proper to believe. But as to you being a heretic, I suppose in some theoretic sense you may be so to one on my side of the fence, but personally I have long since given up attaching importance to that sort of thing, because I have no idea what you may be in the eyes of God, and that is what counts. I do think, though, that you and I are one in Christ, and hence the presence of some material heresy (according to my side of the fence) does not make that much difference. . . .

APRIL 29, 1963

. . . The school [Oakham] where I went was just right. I wonder if you ever get any boys from there? They used to all go to Cambridge, where we had closed scholarships. . . .

. . . The other day a good distinction came to mind: but there is all the difference in the world between theology as *experienced* (which is basically identical in all who know and love Christ, at least in its root) and theology as *formulated* in which there can be great differences. In the former, it is the One Spirit who teaches and enlightens us. In the second it is the Church, and in this of course I believe that the Roman Church is the only one that can claim to say the last word. But I do not think it makes sense to be narrowly Roman in a sort of curial-party sense, and I am also very attracted to the orthodox *sobornost* idea. And of course I think in reality Pope John has been quietly moving in that direction, and he has been perfectly right in so doing, without affecting his own primacy and so on. As I look back on the sentences above, I can see that what I said is misleading too: I do not of course intend a hard-and-fast distinction between the Spirit on one hand teaching the individual and the Church teaching him: this would be erroneous. But I mean the Spirit teaching us all interiorly, and also exteriorly through the magisterium. In either case it is the Spirit of the Church, and the Church, living and speaking. But in exterior doctrinal formulations, where there are different groups, there are various confusions and differences. And so on. I am not a very sharp technical theologian, as you can see. . . .

JULY 28, 1963

. . . I have been reading a very fine book of R. W. Southern on St. Anselm. I suppose you must know Southern. I think he did a very good job. I took this occasion to get into St. Anselm a little, too. I had always been put off him by the standard philosophy textbooks, but I find him fascinating. And am reading Erasmus too, since we have his collected works in one of those photo-offset editions of the old folios. . . .

. . . I think some active charitable work is good for the contemplative life, provided that we don't get into it purely out of restlessness and aimlessness. In everything, however, the great thing is God's will. A contemplative is one who has God's will bearing right down upon him, often in the most incomprehensible way. One feels that if one could only *see* clearly *how* it was God's Will, the whole thing would be less painful. But it just is and there is no explanation. . . .

. . . About confession: it is not usually linked with direction, probably because of the shortage of time, with us. I mean with the RC's. Here in the monastery in practice we have confession and direction together. Mine is never more than ten or fifteen minutes, and actually I get very little direction. Not that I don't need it, but I just have nowhere to turn for it. In a way that is all right. It forces one to rely on the Holy Spirit, and to do so in stress and I hope with humility and the "dread" these existentialist lads are always talking about. Very salutary. It would be all too easy to get embedded in an institutional routine.

. . . I do not think contemplation can be taught, but certainly an aptitude for it can be awakened. It is an aptitude which quite a lot of people might have, in seminaries and monasteries at least, as well as in any walk of life. The important thing is that this be made real and credible by someone who knows by experience what it is, and who can make it real to those in whom it begins to awaken. In a word it is a question of showing them in a mysterious way by example how to proceed. Not by the example of doing, but the example of being, and by one's attitude toward life and things.

Certainly you have some sort of vocation in this regard, but you do not have to be too aware of it. Simply be content to let God use you in whatever way He wills, and be sure you do not get in His way with misplaced initiatives. . . .

. . . Your letters all sound good. I am glad you are in contact with so many people who are following a good and simple path. I have greater and greater confidence in the reality of the path that is no path at all, and to see people follow it in spite of everything is comforting. . . .

. . . I must say though that there is a good proportion of contemplative prayer in the novitiate. I don't use special methods. I try to make them love the freedom and peace of being with God alone in faith and simplicity, to abolish all divisiveness and diminish all useless strain and concentration on one's own efforts and all formalism: all the nonsense of taking seriously the apparatus of an official prayer life, in the wrong way (but to love liturgy in simple faith as the place of Christ's sanctifying presence in the community). . . .

JANUARY 25, 1965

. . . What you say about the Trinity in your life of prayer is of course the most traditional thing. It is good to understand the theology of it, because when it is put into words one gets the impression that the talk is about "three objects" which one is experiencing. The ancient way of looking at it, "to the Father in the Son by the Holy Spirit," reminds us of the *unity* and the un-objective character of it. And yet they are Three, or we are in their Three and One in the Three. The authenticity of the experience depends on the dissolution of the apparent "I" that can seem to stand outside all this as subject and observe it from somewhere else. . . .

MAY 5, 1965

. . . Things are rather gloomy here. The war in Vietnam is being pushed, against the protests and desires of most of the people. The country is not behind it, and yet Johnson insists on going on. I think he is very stupid and that he, and everyone else, will have cause to regret it. It may become quite serious, though it seems they are playing a daring political game rather than trying to start a nuclear war. But it might come to that, they are such fools. . . .

JUNE 9, 1965

. . . The more I see of it, the more I realize the absolute primacy and necessity of silent, hidden, poor, apparently fruitless prayer. . . .

NOVEMBER 1, 1965

. . . Do please above all tell the Abbot of Downside how happy I was with his intervention in the Council on conscientious objection. I thought it was most important. From what I know of the discussion of peace and war there, it went well. There is a lot of fuss about that in this country now, since there is, quite rightly, a great deal of protest against this absurd business in Vietnam, which in the end cannot be anything but ruinous for the U.S. But also from the moral point of view it is a very dubious "just war." Feelings are running high, however. I don't know what will become of this country, but I still have hope in unsuspected moral resources somewhere. . . .

. . . You say you do not think you love God, and that is probably perfectly true. But what matters is that God loves you, isn't it? If we had to rely on *our* love where would we be?

If I don't have much to say for myself for another month or two, don't be surprised. I have to go to the hospital for a back operation. I hope it comes out all right, because my ability to chop wood next winter will very much depend on it. . . .

. . . The operation went well—two very skillful surgeons. First week of recovery was a bit hard but I am all right now and they will let me get back to the monastery for Easter.

In the hospital I have read a lot of Eckhart and am more and more convinced of his greatness. . . .

. . . Progress in Prayer: all right, if you like, I will think about writing something on it, but it is a ticklish subject because the chief obstacle to progress is too much self-awareness and to talk about "how to make progress" is a good way to make people too aware of themselves. In the long run I think progress in prayer comes from the Cross and humiliation and whatever makes us really experience our total poverty and nothingness, and also gets our mind off ourselves. . . .

Incidentally, while I was writing this, a huge SAC plane flew directly over the hermitage: this letter has been under the H-bomb. . . .

. . . Of course I can understand your being a bit anguished about the obvious fact that there can be little hope of institutional or sacramental union as yet between Anglicans and Romans. Perhaps on the other hand I am too stoical about it all, but I frankly am not terribly anguished. I am not able to get too involved in the institutional side of any of the efforts now being made as I think, for very many reasons, they are bound to be illusory in large measure. And this kind of thing is for others who know more about it. To me it is enough to be united with people in love and in the Holy Spirit, as I am sure I am, and they are, in spite of the sometimes momentous institutional and doctrinal differences. But where there is a sincere desire for truth and real good will and genuine love, there God Himself will take care of the differences far better than any human or political ingenuity can. . . .

APRIL 26, 1968

. . . I will not go into a long discourse on the state of things here. The atmosphere is bad, in the country as a whole. . . . No one really trusts Johnson and it is evident that even the most seemingly honest gestures he makes, like his recent renunciation of candidacy and "the bombing pause," are ninety percent hoax.

Never was a deeply honest and simple life of prayer more necessary. It is about all there is left. But people don't trust God either.

As to your own desolation and loneliness: what can anyone say? It is the desolation of all of us in the presence of death and nothingness, but Christ in us bears it for us: without our being consoled. To accept non-consolation is to mysteriously help others who have more than they can bear.

ADDITIONAL LETTERS SPANNING TWO DECADES

TO SISTER THERESE LENTFOEHR   AUGUST 28, 1949

About prayer: have you a garden or somewhere that you can walk in, by yourself? Take half an hour, or fifteen minutes a day and just walk up and down among the flowerbeds with the intention of offering this walk up as a meditation and a prayer to Our Lord. Do not try to think about anything in particular and when thoughts about work, etc., come to you, do not try to push them out by main force, but see if you can't drop them just by relaxing your mind. Do this because you "are praying" and because Our Lord is with you. But if thoughts about work will not go away, accept them idly and without too much eagerness with the intention of letting Our Lord reveal His will to you through these thoughts.

TO VICTOR HAMMER   *An artist born in Vienna in 1882, Victor Hammer at age sixteen entered the Academy of Fine Arts in Vienna, where he later became a professor of art. With Hitler's rise to power, he came to the United States. He taught in Aurora, New York, and later in Lexington, Kentucky, where his acquaintance with Thomas Merton began. On one of Merton's visits to his home, he asked him to identify a painting he had done of a woman with a young boy standing before her, on whom she is placing a crown. He said he had intended a madonna and child, but he no longer knew who she was. Merton said: "I know who she is. I have always known her. She is Hagia Sophia." Later Hammer asked Merton to put in writing what he had said. He did so in the following letter.*

MAY 14, 1959

I have not rushed to reply to your letter—first, because I have been a little busy, and second, because it is most difficult to write anything that really makes sense about this most mysterious reality in the mystery of God—Hagia Sophia [Holy Wisdom].

The first thing to be said, of course, is that Hagia Sophia is God Himself. God is not only a Father but a Mother. He is both at the same time, and it is the "feminine aspect" or "feminine principle" in the divinity that is the Hagia Sophia. But of course as soon as you say this the whole thing becomes misleading: a division of an "abstract" divinity into two abstract principles. Nevertheless, to ignore this distinction is to lose touch with the fullness of God. This is a very ancient intuition of reality which goes back to the oldest Oriental thought. . . . For the "masculine-feminine" relationship is basic in *all* reality—simply because all reality mirrors the reality of God.

In its most primitive aspect, Hagia Sophia is the dark, nameless *Ousia* [Being] of the Father, the Son and the Holy Ghost, the incomprehensible, "primordial" darkness which is infinite light. The Three Divine Persons, each at the same time, are Sophia and manifest her. But where the Sophia of your picture comes in is this: the wisdom of God, "reaching from end to end mightily" is also the Tao, the nameless pivot of all being and nature, the center and meaning of all, that which is the smallest and poorest and most humble in all: the "feminine child" playing before God the Creator in His universe, "playing before Him at all times, playing in the world" (Proverbs 8). . . . This feminine principle in the universe is the inexhaustible source of creative realizations of the Father's glory in the world and is in fact the manifestation of His glory. Pushing it further, Sophia in ourselves is the *mercy* of God, the tenderness which by the infinitely mysterious power of pardon turns the darkness of our sins into the light of God's love.

Hence, Sophia is the feminine, dark, yielding, tender counterpart of the power, justice, creative dynamism of the Father.

Now the Blessed Virgin is the one created being who in herself realizes perfectly all that is hidden in Sophia. She is a kind of personal manifestation of Sophia. She crowns the Second Person of the Trinity with His human nature (with what is weak, able to suffer, able to be defeated) and sends Him forth with His mission of inexpressible mercy, to die for man on the cross, and this death, followed by the Resurrection, is the greatest expression of the "manifold wisdom of God" which unites us all in the mystery of Christ—the Church. Finally, it is the Church herself, properly understood as the great manifestation of the mercy of God, who is the revelation of Sophia in the sight of the angels.

The key to the whole thing is, of course, *mercy and love.* In the sense that God is Love, is Mercy, is Humility, is Hiddenness, He shows Himself to us within ourselves as our own poverty, our own nothingness (which Christ took upon Himself, ordained for this by the Incarnation in the womb of the Virgin) (the crowning in your picture), and if we receive the humility of God into our hearts, we become able to accept and embrace and love this very poverty, which is Himself and His Sophia. And then the darkness of Wisdom becomes to us inexpressible light. We pass thorough the center of our own nothingness into the light of God. . . .

The beauty of all creation is a reflection of Sophia living and hidden in creation. But it is only our reflection. And the misleading thing about beauty, created beauty, is that we expect Sophia to be simply a more intense and more perfect and more brilliant; unspoiled, spiritual revelation of the same beauty. Whereas to arrive at her beauty we must pass through an apparent negation of created beauty, and to reach her light we must realize that in comparison with created light it is a darkness. But this is only because created beauty and light are ugliness and darkness compared with her. Again the whole thing is in the question of mercy, which cuts across the divisions and passes beyond every philosophical and religious ideal. For Sophia is not an ideal, not an abstraction, but the highest reality, and the highest reality must manifest herself to us not only in power but also in poverty, otherwise we never see it. Sophia is the Lady Poverty to whom St. Francis was married. And of course she dwelt with the Desert Fathers in their solitude, for it was she who brought them there and she whom they knew there. It was with her that they conversed all the time in their silence. . . .

TO PABLO ANTONIO CUADRA   AUGUST 22, 1959

. . . In any case, let us pray for one another that we may make creative use of the mysterious difficulties of life and shape our courses in "new directions" if that be the will of God. I fear nothing so much as conventionalism and inertia, which for me is fatal. Yet there is that all-important stillness, and listening to God, which seems to be inertia, and yet is the highest action. One must always be awake to tell the difference between action and inaction, when appearances are so often deceiving. . . .

TO JOSEPH TJO TCHEL-OUNG   *Daniel Bouchez, a professor at Holy Ghost College, a seminary in Seoul, Korea, wrote to Merton of the publication of the Korean translation of* Seeds of Contemplation (Myung sand eui ssee). *The translation has been done by Joseph Tjo Tchel-oung (also Romanized as Jo Chuloong), a seminarian at Holy Ghost.*

APRIL 28, 1961

. . . Even before I became a Christian myself I took a deep interest in Oriental philosophy, and I believe that interest certainly helped to prepare me to understand Christianity which is in many ways alien to the aggressive, materialistic and pragmatic world of the west. We must never forget that Christianity came to the west from the Orient. It is not purely and simply the "religion of the west." The specifically western elements which have come to be identified with Christianity are rather cultural and social elements, the outer garments of the religion, not the religion itself. Christianity, as Dr. John C. H. Wu, of China, has so well observed, is "beyond East and West." Christ is the fulfillment of the latent desires and aspirations of all religions and all philosophies. One must transcend them all to come to Him: yet in Him one finds all that was good and true in every other religion.

Ordinarily the Christian religion presents only its active, apostolic face to the East: the Christian comes as a builder of schools, churches and hospitals, with a message of mercy and of spiritual development. But the active side of Christianity is nothing without the hidden, passive and contemplative aspect. Indeed, without the secret, interior, lowly, obscure knowledge of God in contemplation, the activity of the apostle is empty and fruitless. Indeed, it is perhaps because the contemplative aspect of Christianity has been to a great extent ignored by so many in the west, that Christianity has been less fruitful than it might have been in the east. It is the union with God in a darkness where nothing is seen or understood, that is the source of the mysterious love which is the life blood of Christianity. It is in the darkness of faith that the soul is united to Christ, and in this darkness the Holy Spirit, like an inexhaustible spring of living water, irrigates the dry wastes of the soul that is exhausted by attachment to the things of sense. This living water revives the soul and makes it capable of a love and compassion which are the most powerful of all spiritual forces because they are the power of God Himself in us: and God is Love.

TO JEANNE BURDICK   *Jeanne Burdick had asked Merton to explain what he meant in* The Seven Storey Mountain *by "disinterested love." Merton became something of a spiritual director for her through the letters they exchanged.*

DECEMBER 26, 1961

. . . [We need to realize] that in the eyes of God . . . "we are His joy" and He delights to be loved by us with perfect confidence in Him because He is love itself. This is of course not capable of being put in scientific language, it is a religious symbol. . . . I think you will find it is the most fundamental symbol and the deepest truth. . . . It is not that we have to sweat and groan to placate an austere Father God in our own imagination, but rather to realize, with liberation and joy, that *He is not that at all.* That in fact He is none of our idols, none of our figments, nothing that we can imagine anyway, but that He is Love Itself. And if we realize this and love Him simply and purely in order "to please Him," we become as it were His "crown" and His "delight" and life itself is transformed in this light which is disinterested love. . . .

TO RIPU DAMAN LAMA   *Ripu Daman Lama was an Indian student who came to Cracow, Poland, to work for a doctor of science degree in mining engineering at the mining academy in that city. In a letter written on June 13, 1964, he says that Merton's name was frequently on the lips of the students with whom he discussed problems of philosophy and especially the problem of the growing atheism in the world.*

AUGUST 16, 1964

. . . The phenomenon of atheism today is quite ambiguous. In one sense, it remains the naïve atheism of nineteenth-century scientism. The scientists of today have themselves traveled far beyond this point and it must be realized that nineteenth-century materialism created a scientific myth which endeavored to replace the religious myth. In effect, the communist countries are dealing in pseudo-scientific mythology today, when it comes to religion and to the basic philosophic truths. At the same time they take the true and deep concept of God and regard it in a light in which it is false and debased. They think that religious people believe in a God who is simply "a being" among other beings, part of a series of beings, an "object" which can be discovered and demonstrated. This of course is a false notion of God, the Absolute, the source and origin of all Being, beyond all beings and transcending them all and hence not to be sought as one among them. It is not hard to disprove that God "exists" as a being among beings, and this is no menace to religion. On the contrary. However, religious people make the mistake of replying to this argument as if it had some relevance, instead of trying to clarify the real meaning of God. In any case, the level on which atheist argumentation is carried out has not the remotest relation to true religion or metaphysics. . . .

TO ROSITA AND LUDOVICO SILVA   APRIL 10, 1965

. . . The religion of our time, to be authentic, needs to be the kind that escapes practically all religious definition. Because there has been endless definition, endless verbalizing, and words have become gods. There are so many words that one cannot get to God as long as He is thought to be on the other side of the words. . . . One's whole being must be an act for which there can be found no word. This is the primary meaning of faith. On this basis, other dimensions of belief can be made credible. Otherwise not. My whole being must be a yes and an amen and an exclamation that is not heard. . . .

That is where the silence of the woods comes in. Not that there is something new to be thought and discovered in the woods, but only that the trees are all sufficient exclamations of silence, and one works there, cutting wood, clearing ground, cutting grass, cooking soup, drinking fruit juice, sweating, washing, making fire, smelling smoke, sweeping, etc. This is religion. The further one gets away from this, the more one sinks in the mud of words and gestures. The flies gather. . . .

TO LUDOVICO SILVA   JUNE 30, 1965

. . . The important thing in thoughts about God is not to reduce the idea of God to that of an *object*. Unfortunately, this is what most talk about Him implicitly does, and that is why you instinctively . . . are seeking to over-leap the subject-object division. . . . The best approach is existentialist, and the existentialist approach, in theology, is not through abstract dogmas but through direct personal confrontation, not of a subject with an object but of a person with an inner demand. . . .

To Abdul Aziz   *(For biographical note, see Part 9, Seeking Unity Beyond Difference.)*

... Now you ask about my method of meditation. Strictly speaking I have a very simple way of prayer. It is centered entirely on attention to the presence of God and to His will and His love. That is to say that it is centered on *faith* by which alone we can know the presence of God. One might say this gives my meditation the character described by the Prophet as "being before God as if you saw Him." Yet it does not mean imagining anything or conceiving a precise image of God, for to my mind this would be a kind of idolatry. On the contrary, it is a matter of adoring Him as invisible and infinitely beyond our comprehension, and realizing Him as all. My prayer tends very much toward what you call *fana*. There is in my heart this great thirst to recognize totally the nothingness of all that is not God. My prayer is then a kind of praise rising up out of the center of Nothing and Silence. If I am still present "myself" this I recognize as an obstacle about which I can do nothing unless He Himself removes the obstacle. If He wills He can then make the Nothingness into a total clarity. If He does not will, then the Nothingness seems to itself to be an object and remains an obstacle. Such is my ordinary way of prayer, or meditation. It is not "thinking about" anything, but a direct seeking of the Face of the Invisible. ...

to John Hunt   *John Hunt was senior editor of the* Saturday Evening Post. *In December 1966 he invited Merton to write an article on monasticism for the "Speaking Out" column. As the following letter indicates, Merton had other ideas. The article was never written.*

Thanks for your letter of the 13th. All right, I am still open to all kinds of suggestions and even have one of my own. ... Let's see how I can put it in a few words.

Say an article "Speaking Out for the Inside." An attempt to make people realize that life can have an interior dimension of depth and awareness which is systematically blocked by our habitual way of life, all concentrated on externals. The poverty of a life fragmented and dispersed in "things" and built on a superficial idea of the self and its relation to what is outside and around it. Importance of freedom from the routines and illusions which keep us subject to things, dependent on what is outside us. The need to open up an inner freedom and vision, which is found in relatedness to something in us which we *don't really know.* This is not just the psychological unconscious. It is much more than that. Tillich called it the ground of our being. Traditionally it is called "God," but images and ideas of the deity do not comprehend it. What is it?

The real inner life and freedom of man begin when this inner dimension opens up and man lives in communion with the unknown within him. On the basis of this he can also be in communion with the same unknown in others. How to describe it? Impossible to describe it. Is it real? People like William James "scientifically" verified its reality at least as a fact of experience in many lives. The appetite for Zen, etc., reflects a need for this. What is Zen? What about LSD? What can one do? And with some observations on the tragic effects of *neglect* on this: possibly our society will be wrecked because it is completely taken up with externals and has no grasp on this inner dimension of life.

That is rather tough, and it will demand a lot of your readers. My suggestion is: frankly admit the toughness and unpalatableness of the subject and treat it as it is. Some may be hit hard, most will remain indifferent.

TO FRIENDS   *In "A Christmas Letter—1965," Merton explained: "I hate to resort to mimeographed letters, but it has now become completely impossible for me to answer most of my mail personally." Between 1966 and 1968, Merton wrote sixteen "circular letters," which he sent "To Friends."*

CHRISTMAS MORNING 1966

. . . The heart of man can be full of so much pain, even when things are exteriorly "all right." It becomes all the more difficult because today we are used to thinking that there are explanations for everything. But there is no explanation for most of what goes on in our own hearts, and we cannot account for it all. No use resorting to the kind of mental tranquilizers that even religious explanations sometimes offer. Faith must be deeper than that, rooted in the unknown and in the abyss of darkness that is the ground of our being. No use teasing the darkness to try to make answers grow out of it. But if we learn how to have a deep inner patience things solve themselves, or God solves them if you prefer: but do not expect to see how. Just learn to wait, and do what you can and help other people. Often in helping someone else we find the best way to bear with our own trouble. . . .

TO MARIE BYLES　*A scholar in Japanese religions, Marie Byles wrote to Merton from Cheltenham, New South Wales, Australia.*

JANUARY 9, 1967

Your kind letter of October 20th took a good long time to reach me via India, and I only got it a couple of days ago. Thanks for your favorable remarks about my Gandhi book. . . .

You ask about the Catholic idea of holy obedience. What you are really interested in is evidently the ancient ascetic idea of obedience which goes back to the Gospels, the Sermon on the Mount, and so on, is exemplified by the saints, and is analogous to the perfect obedience, docility, and so forth found in other religious ideals. The idea is fundamentally the same: to become free from the need to assert one's ego, to be liberated from the desire to dominate others, to renounce selfish demands, and so on. Ultimately the idea is that if you renounce your own will you will be guided directly by God and moved by Him in everything. Hence in the Rule of St. Benedict it is said that the monk will obey not only his Abbot but also all his brethren insofar as this does not conflict with obedience to the Abbot and to God. The real purpose of obedience is to obey God and give one's will to Him.

This idea of obedience is somewhat ambiguous in the later legalistic context that it got into, when the religious Orders got highly organized and became big impersonal structures run by bureaucracies. The ascetic idea was pressed into the service of a different kind of ideal, and "blind obedience" was stressed as an ideal since it meant the subject simply submitted to authority and became a cog in a machine. This of course has led to a perverse idea of obedience (ultimately Eichmann is the Exemplification of all that it can lead to) and in fact has brought great discredit upon the authentic notion of obedience. So at present people are confused, struggling with these ambiguities. I think that what is needed is certainly a return to the pure Gospel idea, as far as possible, in a new context. How far this can be done is another matter. The confusions remain our big problem in the Catholic Church today, I am afraid. As long as the notion of obedience is implicated in an impersonal power system it will be corrupted by the very things it is supposed to liberate us from—worldliness, selfishness, ambition, and so on. . . .

EASTER 1967

. . . Easter celebrates the victory of love over everything. *Amor vincit omnia.* If we believe it we still understand it, because belief is what opens the door to love. But to believe only in systems and *statements* and not in *people* is an evasion, a betrayal of love. When we really believe as Christians, we find ourselves trusting and accepting *people* as well as dogmas. Woe to us when we are merely orthodox, and reject human beings, flesh and blood, the aspirations, joys and needs of men. Yet there is no fruit, either, in merely sentimental gestures of communion that mean little, and seek only to flatter or placate. Love can also be tough and uncompromising in its fidelity to its own highest principles. Let us be united in joy, peace and prayer this Easter and always. "Fear not," says Jesus. "It is I. I am with you all days!"

PENTECOST 1967

. . . The idea that "the Church does all your thinking, feeling, willing, and experiencing for you" is, to my mind, carried too far. It leads to alienation. After all, the Church is made up of living and loving human beings: if they all act and feel like robots, the church can't experience and love in their behalf. The whole thing becomes an abstraction. . . . But we need a real deepening of life in every area, and that is why it is proper that laypeople and others who have been kept in subordinate positions are now claiming the right to make decisions in what concerns their own lives. This is also true in religious orders. As long as everything is decided at the top, and received passively by those at the bottom, the vocation crisis will continue. There is no longer any place in our life for a passive and inert religiosity in which one simply takes orders and lets someone else do all the thinking. Those who fail to accept such a situation are not rebels, most of the time, they are sensitive and intelligent human beings who protest against a real disorder and who have a right to be heard. . . .

TO WILLIAM JOHNSTON   *An Irish Jesuit who has lived in Japan since 1961, William Johnston received a doctorate in mystical theology from the University of Tokyo. He has written a number of books on mysticism. He invited Merton to write a preface for his first book,* The Mysticism of the Cloud of Unknowing. *Merton wrote the preface, and Johnston was preparing for Merton's visit when word came of his sudden and tragic death.*

JULY 5, 1967

. . . I will give an opinion that may have some general bearing on the question: I hope it may. I suppose first of all that the Japanese Zen people have their own rather schematic idea of what it means to "believe in God." Obviously, if it implies essentially a sort of subject-object relationship, then it means a "dualism" which categorically excludes *satori*. They probably have never investigated the witness of mystics like Eckhart for whom it is possible to be "so poor" that one does not even "have a God." This does not mean "Christian atheism" or "God-is-dead theology." It is simply a fact of a certain area of apophatic experience. Also the Japanese Zen people probably think of Christian mysticism in terms of "bridal mysticism," the gift of mystical rings, embraces, ecstasies and all that. Well, OK, no *satori* along those lines.

On the other hand, to look at it more subtly: I wonder if someone in Fr. [Enomiye] Lasalle's position [a professor at Sophia University in Tokyo], wanting as a Christian to attain *satori,* does not inevitably get into a psychological position which makes *satori* difficult if not impossible. Because for there to be a real *satori* the idea of "a Christian who can attain *satori*" has to go out the window as utterly irrelevant. Hence, perhaps that is what the Zen people intuitively feel about your group as such.

Personally I do not think *satori* is impossible for a Christian any more than it is for a Buddhist. In either case, one goes in a certain sense beyond all categories, religious or otherwise. But perhaps our very attitude toward

Christianity makes this harder for us. I do think it is probably best to simply take what Zen can offer us in the way of inner purification and freedom from systems and concepts, and not worry too much about precisely where we get. But I am all for Fr. Lasalle getting there if that is what he should do. I'm rooting for him! I'd be very interested to hear more about all this. . . .

PART 6

Reading the Signs of the Times

Merton's Critique of Culture

"The fact is that each new situation in life has its own mysterious logos. . . . We must always pray to be attentive to the language of events, and shape our actions accordingly."

—To Pablo Antonio Cuadra, August 22, 1959

With astounding clarity and uncanny insight, Thomas Merton was able, in the words of the Second Vatican Council, to read "the signs of the times," aware of the claim that they made on him. Merton put it this way in an essay entitled "Is the World a Problem?": "That I should have been born in 1915, that I should be the contemporary of Auschwitz, Hiroshima, Viet Nam and the Watts riots, are things about which I was not first consulted. Yet they are also events in which, whether I like it or not, I am deeply and personally involved." This sense of personal involvement and responsibility, informed by Christian faith and monastic practice, enabled Merton to see through the myths and fictions that obscure truth. He recognized how the power of the "the illusion of America as the earthly paradise" and the pervasiveness of "the myth of technology" are at the root of "the absolute use of power" and contribute to the "the debasement" of humanity.

The letters excerpted below represent Merton's efforts to name and address the cycle of violence and the mounting ecological crisis as well as the insidiousness of racism. Merton's concern with these "signs of darkness," evident throughout Merton's correspondence, is especially prominent in the letters reprinted below, as is his conviction that these social and political ills mirror a deep spiritual and moral crisis. But Merton also points to some "signs of hope" in efforts at genuine communication, a new humanism, a recovery of wisdom, an emerging "ecological consciousness," the courage of those who speak out, and the unbounded mercy of God. Merton gives expression to the hope that lives in us "in spite of what we may be thinking." Such hope is evident in the vision of the Shakers and is embodied by the people of Hiroshima, who serve as "a symbol of the hopes of humanity."

This section is divided into two parts, each organized chronologically: the first part is titled "Signs of Destruction, Signs of Hope"; the second, "The Race Question." The section opens with an excerpt from a letter that Merton himself selected as the first in the mimeographed collection that he called "Cold War Letters." Written in October 1961, the letter expresses, in unequivocal terms, Merton's conviction that war is the most urgent issue of the day and the most dangerous "sign of the time."

SIGNS OF DESTRUCTION, SIGNS OF HOPE

TO ETTA GULLICK [COLD WAR LETTER 1]   OCTOBER 25, 1961

. . . One thing that has kept me very busy in the last few weeks is the international crisis. It is not really my business to speak out about it but since there is such frightful apathy and passivity everywhere, with people simply unable to face the issue squarely, and with only a stray voice raised tentatively here and there, it has become an urgent obligation. This has kept me occupied and will keep me even more occupied, because I am now perfectly convinced that there is one task for me that takes precedence over everything else: working with such means as I have at my disposal for the abolition of war. This is like going into the prize ring blindfolded and with hands tied, since I am cloistered and subject to the most discouragingly long and frustrating kinds of censorship on top of it. I must do what I can. Prayer of course remains my chief means, but it is also an obligation on my part to speak out in so far as I am able, and to speak as clearly, as forthrightly, and as uncompromisingly as I can. A lot of people are not going to like this and it may mean my head, so do please pray for me in a very special way, because I cannot in conscience willingly betray the truth or let it be betrayed. The issue is too serious. This is purely and simply the crucifixion over again. Those who think there can be a just cause for measures that gravely risk leading to the destruction of the entire human race are in the most dangerous illusion, and if they are Christian they are purely and simply arming themselves with hammer and nails, without realizing it, to crucify and deny Christ. The extent of our spiritual obtuseness is reaching a frightful scale. Of course there is in it all a great mercy of God Whose Word descends like the rain and snow from heaven and cannot return to Him empty: but the demonic power at work in history is appalling, especially in these last months. We are reaching a moment of greatest crisis, through the blindness and stupidity of our leaders and all who believe in them and in the society we have set up for ourselves, and which is falling apart. . . .

TO CZESLAW MILOSZ   SEPTEMBER 16, 1961

. . . There is no question in my mind that there is a need to integrate new questions and answers in a human universe: when I said I was fed up with the answers, I meant square answers, ready-made answers, answers that ignore the question. All clear answers tend to be of this nature today, because we are so deep in confusion and grab desperately at five thousand glimmers of seeming clarity. It is better to start with a good acceptance of the dark. That in itself contains many answers in a form that is not yet worked out: one has the answers, but not the full meaning. . . .

TO ALCEU AMOROSO LIMA   *Brazilian scholar and prolific writer Alceu Amoroso Lima helped make Merton's work known in Brazil. He wrote introductions to Portuguese translations of Merton's books and himself translated many of those books.*

[COLD WAR LETTER 3] NOVEMBER 1961

. . . This is a crucial and perhaps calamitous moment in history, a moment in which reason and understanding threaten to be swallowed up, even if man himself manages to survive. It is certainly an age in which Christianity is vanishing into an area of shadows and uncertainty, from the human point of view. It is all very well for me to meditate on these things in the shelter of the monastery: but there are times when this shelter itself is deceptive. Everything is deceptive today. And grains of error planted innocently in a well-kept greenhouse can become giant poisonous trees.

Everything healthy, everything certain, everything holy, if we can find such things, they all need to be emphasized and articulated. For this it is necessary that there be communication between the hearts and minds of men, communication and not the noise of slogans or the repetition of clichés. Communication is becoming more and more difficult, and when speech is in danger of perishing or being perverted in the amplified noises of beasts, perhaps it becomes obligatory for a monk to try to speak. There is therefore it seems to me every reason why we should attempt to cry out to one another and comfort one another, insofar as this may be possible, with the truth of Christ and also with the truth of humanism and reason.

For faith cannot be preserved if reason goes under, and the Church cannot survive if man is destroyed; that is to say if his humanity is utterly debased and mechanized, while he himself remains on earth as the instrument of enormous and unidentified forces like those which press us inexorably to the brink of cataclysmic war. . . .

. . . We are all nearing the end of our work. The night is falling upon us, and we find ourselves without the serenity and fulfillment that were the lot of our fathers. I do not think this is necessarily a sign that anything is lacking, but rather is to be taken as a greater incentive to trust more fully in the mercy of God, and to advance further into His mystery. Our faith can no longer serve merely as a happiness pill. It has to be the Cross and the Resurrection of Christ. And this it will be, for all of us who so desire.

TO BRUNO P. SCHLESINGER   *As professor and director of the Christian Culture Program at St. Mary's College, Notre Dame, Indiana, Bruno P. Schlesinger wrote to Merton (and to others as well) inviting comments on the program. Merton took the opportunity to express "a few thoughts" about Christian humanism, "the Christian notion of man," and religion. Christian culture, Merton wrote, is "a matter of wisdom."*

[COLD WAR LETTER 8] DECEMBER 13, 1961

I have taken a little time to get around to your letter of November 10th about the program for Christian Culture at St. Mary's. This is a very important question and I am afraid I will not entirely do justice to it, but at least I can set down a few thoughts that occur to me, and hope for the best.

First of all, the urgent need for Christian humanism. I stress the word "humanism," perhaps running the risk of creating wrong impressions. What is important is the fully Christian notion of man: a notion radically modified by the mystery of the Incarnation. This I think is the very heart of the matter. And therefore it seems to me that a program of Christian culture needs to be rooted in the biblical notions of man as the object of divine mercy, and of special concern on the part of God, as the spouse of God, as, in some mysterious sense, an epiphany of the divine wisdom. Man in Christ. The New Adam, presupposing the Old Adam, presupposing the old paradise and the new paradise, the creation and the new creation.

At the present time man has ceased entirely to be seen as any of these. The whole Christian notion of man has been turned inside out; instead of paradise we have Auschwitz. But note that the men who went into the ovens at Auschwitz were still the same elect race, the object of the divine predilection. . . . These perspectives are shattering, and they are vital for Christian culture. For then in the study of Europe and European Christianity, Latin Christianity, we come up against a dialectic of fidelity and betrayal, understanding and blindness. That we have come to a certain kind of "end" of the development of western Christianity is no accident, nor yet is it the responsibility of Christian culture, for Christian culture has precisely saved all that could be saved. Yet was this enough? These are terrible problems and I am sure no one can answer. In a word, perhaps we might profitably run the risk, at least those who are thinking about the course behind the scenes, not just of assuming that Christian culture is a body of perfections to be salvaged but of asking where there was infidelity and imperfection. And yet at the same time stressing above all the value and the supreme importance of our Western Christian cultural heritage. For it is the survival of religion apart from man and almost in some sense apart from God Himself (God figuring only as a Lawgiver and not as a Savior), religion without any human epiphany in art, in work, in social forms: this is what is killing religion in our midst today, not the atheists. So that one who seeks God without culture and without humanism tends inevitably to promote a religion that is irreligious and even unconsciously atheistic.

It would seem that the a-cultural philistinism of our society were the preferred instrument of demonic forces to finally eviscerate all that is left of Christian humanism. I am thinking of an appalling item read in our refectory yesterday in which we were informed that at last religion was going to be put on the map in America by the "advertising industry." (sic) Here with a sublimely cynical complacency we were informed that now everybody would be urged in the most shallow, importunate, tasteless, and meaningless ways, that they had to go to some church or synagogue or conventicle of some sect. Just get into the nearest damn conventicle as fast as your legs can carry you, brother, and get on your knees and *worship;* we don't give a hoot how you do it or why you do it, but you got to get in there and worship, brother, because the advertising industry says so and it is written right here on the napkin in the place where you eat your fallout lettuce sand-wich. Sorry if I sound like a beatnik, but this is what is driving intelligent people as far from Christianity as they can travel. Hence in one word a pretended Christianity without the human and cultural dimensions which *nature* herself has provided, in history, in social tradition, etc., our religion becomes a lunar landscape of meaningless gestures and observances. A false supernaturalism which theoretically admits that grace builds on nature and then proceeds to eliminate everything natural; there you have the result of forgetting our cultural and humanistic tradition.

To my mind it is very important that this experiment is being conducted in a Catholic women's college. This is to me a hopeful sign. I think women are perhaps capable of salvaging something of humanity in our world today. . . .

But the whole question of Christian culture is a matter of wisdom more than of culture. For wisdom is the full epiphany of God the Logos, or Tao, in man and the world of which man is a little exemplar. Wisdom does not reveal herself until man is seen as microcosm, and the whole world is seen in relation to the measure of man. It is this measure which is essential to Christian culture, and whatever we say or read it must always be remem-bered. I could develop this more, but have no time. I could refer you to a booklet that is being printed in a limited edition by Victor Hammer on this. . . . The booklet is my *Hagia Sophia,* which might or might not have something to say that would be relevant. I hope I don't sound commercial, but probably do, alas.

. . . Mark Van Doren was here talking about liberal education recently. He would be a good man to consult. He stresses the point that liberal education is that which frees an (adult) mind from the automatisms and compulsions of a sensual outlook. Here again we rejoin the Alexandrians and Greeks. The purpose of the Christian humanism should be to liberate man from the mere status of *animalis homo (sarkikos)* to at least the level of *rationalis (psuchicos)* and better still, spiritual, Gnostic or pneumatic. . . .

TO ETHEL KENNEDY   *When he wrote to Ethel Kennedy in September 1961 to express his "very strong objection to the resumption of testing nuclear weap-ons," Merton was mindful that Ethel Kennedy was "so close" to President John F.*

Kennedy. *Ethel Kennedy's family—the Skakels—were longtime benefactors of Gethsemani.*

[COLD WAR LETTER 10] DECEMBER 1961

... Why is war such a problem to us? I do not pretend to be able to give a reason for everything under the sun, but if I am to be consistent with my own experience and my religious beliefs, as well as with the crying evidence that is all around us, one main reason is our moral decline. As a nation we have begun to float off into a moral void and all the sermons of all the priests in the country (if they preach at all) are not going to help much. ...

... It seems to me that there are dangerous ambiguities about our democracy in its actual present condition. I wonder to what extent our ideals are now a front for organized selfishness and systematic irresponsibility. ... We cannot go on living every man for himself. The most actual danger of all is that we may someday float without realizing it into a nice tight fascist society in which all the resentments and all the guilt in all the messed-up teenagers (and older ones) will be channeled in a destructive groove. ...

Anyway, these are not easy times to live in, and there are no easy answers. I think that the fact that the president works overtime at trying to get people to face the situation as it really is may be the greatest thing he is doing. Certainly our basic need is for truth, and not for "images" and slogans that "engineer consent." We are living in a dream world. We do not know ourselves or our adversaries. We are myths to ourselves and they are myths to us. And we are secretly persuaded that we can shoot it out like the sheriffs on TV. This is not reality. ...

TO MARY CHILDS BLACK *Mary Childs Black was director of the Abby Aldrich Rockefeller Folk Art Museum in Williamsburg, Virginia.*

[COLD WAR LETTER 24] [CA. JANUARY 24, 1962]

I need not tell you how I would love to be there on February 2nd. There are few earthly desires I cherish more than the desire to see the Shaker spiritual drawings in the original. I am still hoping that the collection may find its way out here. ...

Recently, though, I did have the happiness to get to the old Pleasant Hill Shaker Community near here, and even took some photographs which came out quite well and I hope I will be able to use them in a little photo essay on the place and on the Shakers. The ideas have not crystallized out yet, and one must give them time. I know Edward [Deming] Andrews [an authority on the Shakers] will be interested, though.

This much I can do: share with you all a few thoughts that are at work in my mind about the Shakers and their deep significance, which manifests itself in a hidden and archetypal way in their art, craftsmanship and in all their works. Their spirit is perhaps the most authentic expression of the primitive American "mystery" or "myth": the paradise myth. The New World, the world of renewal, of return to simplicity, to the innocence of Adam, the recovery of the primeval cosmic simplicity, the reduction of divisions, the restoration of unity. But not just a return to the beginning, it is also an anticipation of the end. The anticipation of eschatological fulfillment, of completion, the New World was an earnest and a type of the New Spiritual Creation.

In the secular realm this consciousness was of course very pronounced, the consciousness of the pioneer and later of the businessman who thought that America could literally be the earthly paradise. The belief that there was nothing impossible, that all goodness and all happiness was there for the asking. And in the poor of other lands, America existed as the place where they thought gold could be picked up on the streets.

For the Shakers, it was a different consciousness, for at the same time they saw the deceptiveness of the secular hope, and their eyes were open, in childlike innocence, to the evil, the violence, the unscrupulousness that too often underlay the secular vision of the earthly paradise. It was a paradise in which the Indian had been slaughtered and the Negro was enslaved. In which the immigrant was treated as an inferior being, and in which he had to work very hard for the "gold" that was to be "picked up in the streets."

The Shakers realized that to enter into a genuine contact with the reality of the "paradise spirit" which existed in the wonderful new world, they had to undergo a special kind of conversion. And their conversion had this special, unique, wonderful quality in that it, more than any other "spirit," grasped the unique substance of the American paradise myth, and embodied it in a wonderful expression. For myths are realities, and they themselves open into deeper realms. The Shakers apprehended something totally origi-

nal about the spirit and the vocation of America. This has remained hidden
to everyone else. The sobering thing is that their vision was eschatological!
And they themselves ended.

TO HENRY MILLER   AUGUST 7, 1962

. . . In the whole question of religion today: all I can say is I wish I could
really see what is there to see. Nobody can see the full dimension of the
problem, which is more than a problem, it is one of those things you read
about in the Apocalypse. There are no problems in the Apocalypse, just
monsters. This one is a monster.

The religion of religious people tends at times to poke out a monster head
just when you are beginning to calm down and get reassured. The religion of
half-religious people doesn't tend: it bristles with heads. The horns, the horns
with eyes on the end of them, the teeth, the teeth with eyes in them, the eyes
as sharp as horns, the dull eyes, the ears that now listen to all the stars and
decode their message into something about business upswing. . . .

The religion of non-religious people tends to be clear of religious idols
and is in many ways much less pseudo. But on the other hand, they often
have no defense against the totalitarian kind, which end up being bigger
and worse.

I frankly don't have an answer. As a priest I ought, of course, to be able
to give Christ's answer. But unfortunately . . . it is no longer a matter of
answers. It is a time perhaps of great spiritual silence. . . .

TO LESLIE DEWART   *Leslie Dewart, professor of religion and philosophy at
St. Michael's College at the University of Toronto, sent Merton the manuscript
of* Christianity and Revolution: The Lesson of Cuba, *published in 1963. The
two writers discussed the manuscript as well as the political and social realities
facing the Catholic Church. In his first letter to Dewart, Merton reflects on the
American "illusion of innocence."*

[COLD WAR LETTER 103] SEPTEMBER 1962

. . . The whole issue today depends, in great measure, in the last resort,
on the American mentality. And that mentality is involved in deep illusions,

most of all about itself. These illusions are nevertheless part and parcel of its goodness. It seems to be an immensely complex problem. The problem of Christian hopes, after centuries of frustration and deviation, suddenly finding an unexpected, secular fulfillment and a new, seemingly secular direction. The illusion of America as the earthly paradise, in which everyone recovers original goodness: which becomes in fact a curious idea that prosperity itself justifies everything, is a sign of goodness, is a carte blanche to continue to be prosperous in any way feasible: and this leads to the horror that we now see: because we are prosperous, because we are successful, because we have all this amazing "know-how" (without real intelligence or moral wisdom, without even a really deep scientific spirit), we are entitled to defend ourselves by any means whatever, without any limitation, and all the more so because what we are defending is our illusion of innocence. . . .

TO THE HON. SHINZO HAMAI   *Shinzo Hamai was elected mayor of Hiroshima, Japan, in 1947. He served as Hiroshima's mayor until 1955 and, in 1959, was reelected mayor and served until 1967. Merton admired the courage of the mayor's witness and saw the people of Hiroshima "as a symbol of the hopes of humanity."*

[COLD WAR LETTER 98] AUGUST 9, 1962

In a solemn and grave hour for humanity I address this letter to you and to your people. I thank you for the sincerity and courage with which you are, at this time, giving witness for peace and sanity. I wish to join my own thoughts, efforts and prayers to yours. There is no hope for mankind unless the truth prevails in us. We must purify our hearts and open them to the light of truth and mercy. You are giving us the example. May we follow. . . .

Man should use political instruments in behalf of truth, sanity, and international Order. Unfortunately the blindness and madness of a society that is shaken to its very roots by the storms of passion and greed for power make the fully effective use of political negotiation impossible. Men want to negotiate for peace, and strive to do so, but their fear is greater than their good will. They do not dare to take serious and bold initiatives for peace. Fear of losing face, fear of the propaganda consequences of apparent "weakness," make it impossible for them to do what is really courageous:

to take firm steps toward world peace. When they take one step forward they immediately tell the whole world about it and then take four steps backward. We are all walking backward toward a precipice. We know the precipice is there, but we assert that we are all the while going forward. This is because the world in its madness is guided by military men, who are the blindest of the blind.

It is my conviction that the people of Hiroshima stand today as a symbol of the hopes of humanity. It is good that such a symbol should exist. The events of August 6, 1945, give you the most solemn right to be heard and respected by the whole world. But the world only pretends to respect your witness. In reality it cannot face the truth which you represent. But I wish to say on my own behalf and on behalf of my fellow monks and those who are like-minded, that I never cease to face the truth which is symbolized in the names Hiroshima, Nagasaki. Each day I pray humbly and with love for the victims of the atomic bombardments which took place there. All the holy spirits of those who lost their lives then, I regard as my dear and real friends. I express my fraternal and humble love for all the citizens of Hiroshima and Nagasaki.

TO RACHEL CARSON   *Biologist, ecologist, and writer Rachel Carson is best known for* Silent Spring, *published in 1962. Merton wrote to Carson after reading the book. Merton praised* Silent Spring *as "fine, exact and persuasive" and also "timely."*

JANUARY 12, 1963

Anne Ford very kindly sent me your latest book, *Silent Spring,* which I am reading carefully and with great concern. I want to tell you first of all that I compliment you on the fine, exact, and persuasive book you have written, and secondly that it is perhaps much more timely even than you or I realize. Though you are treating just one aspect, and a rather detailed aspect, of our technological civilization, you are, perhaps without altogether realizing, contributing a most valuable and essential piece of evidence for the diagnosis of the ills of our civilization.

The awful irresponsibility with which we scorn the smallest values is part of the same portentous irresponsibility with which we dare to use our titanic power in a way that threatens not only civilization but life itself. The same mental processing—I almost said mental illness—seems to be at work in both cases, and your book makes it clear to me that there is a *consistent pattern* running through everything that we do, through every aspect of our culture, our thought, our economy, our whole way of life. What this pattern is I cannot say clearly, but I believe it is now the most vitally important thing for all of us, however we may be concerned with our society, to try to arrive at a clear, cogent statement of our ills, so that we may begin to correct them. Otherwise, our efforts will be directed to purely superficial symptoms only, and perhaps not even at things related directly to the illness. On the contrary, it seems that our remedies are instinctively those which aggravate the sickness: *the remedies are expressions of the sickness itself.*

I would almost dare to say that the sickness is perhaps a very real and very dreadful hatred of life as such, of course subconscious, buried under our pitiful and superficial optimism about ourselves and our affluent society. But I think that the very thought processes of materialistic affluence (and here the same things are found in all the different economic systems that seek affluence for its own sake) are ultimately self-defeating. They contain so many built-in frustrations that they inevitably lead us to despair in the midst of "plenty" and "happiness" and the awful fruit of this despair is indiscriminate, irresponsible destructiveness, hatred of life, carried on in the name of life itself. In order to "survive" we instinctively destroy that on which our survival depends.

Another thought that has struck me with powerful impact on reading your book: together with my friends Erich Fromm and D. T. Suzuki, I have been absorbed in the ideas of the mythical and poetic expression of the doctrine of the "fall" of man and original sin. The pattern in the Genesis account is very instructive. It seems to indicate that the meaning of original sin, whatever may be one's dogmatic convictions about it, is that man has built into himself a tendency to destroy and negate himself when everything is at its best, and that it is just when things are paradisiacal that he uses this power. The whole world itself, to religious thinkers, has always appeared as a transparent manifestation of the love of God, as a "paradise" of His wisdom, manifested in all His creatures, down to the tiniest, and in the most wonderful interrelationship between them.

Man's vocation was to be in this cosmic creation, so to speak, as the eye in the body. What I say now is a religious, not a scientific statement. That is to say, man is at once a part of nature and he transcends it. In maintaining this delicate balance, he must make use of nature wisely, and understand his position, ultimately relating both himself and visible nature to the invisible—in my terms, to the Creator, in any case, to the source and exemplar of all being and all life.

But man has lost his "sight" and is blundering around aimlessly in the midst of the wonderful works of God. It is in thinking that he sees, in gaining power and technical know-how, that he has lost his wisdom and his cosmic perspective. I see this clearly, too, in books like those of Laurens van der Post about the South African Bushmen. I am sure you must have read some of them.

Technics and wisdom are not by any means opposed. On the contrary, the duty of our age, the "vocation" of modern man is to unite them in a supreme humility which will result in a totally self-forgetful creativity and service. Can we do this? Certainly we are not going in the right direction. But a book like yours is a most salutary and important warning. I desperately hope that everyone who has a chance to help form public opinion on these vital practical matters may read your book. I hope also that lawmakers will be able to see the connection between what you say and the vastly more important problem of nuclear war: the relationship is so terribly close. It is exactly the same kind of "logic." We don't like the looks of a Japanese beetle. We let ourselves be convinced by a salesman that the beetle is a dire threat. It then becomes obvious that the thing to do is exterminate the beetle by any means whatever even if it means the extermination of many other beings which have not harmed us and which even bring joy into our lives: worse still, we will exterminate the beetle even it if means danger to our children and to our very selves. To make this seem "reasonable" we go to some lengths to produce arguments that our steps are really "harmless." I am afraid I do not relish the safety of the atomic age, but I hope I can use it to attain to a salutary detachment from life and from temporal things so that I can dedicate myself entirely and freely to truth and to my fellow man. A dangerous situation after all has certain spiritual advantages. Let us hope that we may be guided effectively in the right directions.

I want to conclude by sending you my very best wishes and every expression of personal esteem. I love your books, and I love the nature that is all around me here. And I regret my own follies with DDT, which I have not totally renounced.

P.S.: Sometime I would like to write to you about some of our problems here. Cedar trees dying out unaccountably, an awful plague of bagworms, etc., etc.

TO MIGUEL GRINBERG   JUNE 21, 1963

. . . The whole question of inter-American contacts and exchange is of the greatest importance. It is important for Latin America but it is even more important for North America, because unless the United States finally gets in touch with the reality of American life in its broadest and most relevant sense, there is going to be a lot of trouble for everybody. It is of the greatest importance, then, that the cultural vitality of the Latin American countries should be known and recognized here. It is a great misfortune that the technological blindness of the "advanced" countries should gradually be spreading everywhere, without necessarily bringing any real benefits, and communicating mostly the severe disadvantages of our state. The world is falling into a state of confusion and barbarism, for which the responsibility lies, perhaps, with those who think themselves the most enlightened. . . .

Henry Miller is a good friend of mine and I think he has very good insight into this problem. He has said many really urgent things about the question of our modern world and where it is going. The problem is the dehumanization of man, the alienation of man. The Marxists could have developed this concept, which is found in Marx, but they have not been able to. On the contrary, the world today seems to be in a maniacal competition between giant powers, each one striving to show it can do more than the others in brutalizing, stupefying and dehumanizing man, in the name of humanism, freedom and progress. Indeed, the frankness with which the Nazis built their extermination camps is to some extent the index of what is more secretly going on everywhere. Yet the West is not beyond redemption: there are faint and confused stirrings of human hope, as also in the East with some of the revisionists. I think Pope John [XXIII] was one of those who intuitively sized up the situation and reached out for the elements of positive hope that he was still able to see. I hope the new Pope [Paul VI], who has great potentialities, will be able to continue Pope John's work.

. . . I have many friends all over the hemisphere in whom I think there is great hope of awakening and of life. I wish I had more time and more leisure to communicate with everyone, but the limitations of my vocation do impose restraints which I cannot always ignore! However, do believe me in deep union and agreement with the forces of life and hope that are struggling for the renewal of the true cultural and spiritual vitality of the "new work" which is sometimes so tired, so old and so shabby. It is what pretends to be most "new" that is often the oldest and weariest thing of all. But the forces of life must win. And Christians must rediscover the truth that the Cross is the sign of life, renewal, affirmation and joy, not of death, repression, negation and the refusal of life. We must not refuse the providential opportunities that come to us in the midst of darkness.

TO ETHEL KENNEDY NOVEMBER 23, 1963 [THE DAY AFTER PRESIDENT JOHN F. KENNEDY WAS ASSASSINATED]

. . . We are all offering many prayers for him and for all the family. A Solemn High Mass will be sung today, and I will offer my Masses for him tomorrow and Monday also.

Please offer my very special message of sympathy to Jackie. I feel for her most deeply. In a way she is perhaps the one who has had most to suffer from this cruel and senseless thing. I keep her most especially in my prayers along with all of you. . . .

It is easy enough to say that this is the will of God. The question arises, precisely what is the will of God in this mysterious situation. It would be tautology to say that it was the will of God just because it happened. But to me the whole thing is so uncanny and so strange that I think we must see it as a warning once again to the whole country: it is in some sense a reminder that our moral condition is very hazardous, when the rights of a whole race are flagrantly violated, when those who attempt to do right and uphold justice are menaced and even killed. It means we must certainly pray and work hard for this country, to try and bring it through the critical times that do not seem to become any less tense as time goes on. I suppose we must resign ourselves to the task of living under special difficulties. May we be generous in doing so. . . .

TO JACQUELINE KENNEDY   *Jacqueline Kennedy was beside President John F. Kennedy when he was assassinated in Dallas, Texas.*

NOVEMBER 27, 1963

. . . The awful events of the past week have certainly been a kind of spiritual crisis for the whole nation, and a tragic, momentous, utterly mysterious expression of something hidden in the whole world, that had to express itself as it has done, in evil and in good. I think it is beginning to be clear that God allowed this that He might bring great good out of it. You know what help He has given you, and given us all. You can surely hope that from this tragic and cruel explosion of irrationality and violence, clarity and reason can emerge.

There can be no doubt now that the greatness of President Kennedy has been made dazzlingly clear to everyone, and that the scope and integrity of his work have established themselves beyond all question. It is now that people will perhaps be able to understand the necessity of the reforms he proposed and lend their willing cooperation which, if he still lived, they might have continued to refuse.

There can be no doubt too that your contribution to this has been enormous. Merely by being there, and by being you, you have impressed upon the entire world the meaning and validity of all those things President Kennedy stood for. I would like therefore to thank you simply for existing and for being you, and say how much your bravery has meant to us all here, as a manifestation of Christian strength, not the strength of natural heroism but the strength that comes from accepting the love of God in its most inscrutable form. Such praise as has been given you, you must accept humbly, because it is not for you alone. It is for Him who lives in you. It is for your husband, who obeyed God and served his country most loyally. And it is for your children. May they grow in Christ.

I know how sick you must feel of noise and confusion, and all the rest. Perhaps, too, when this passes, you will be left slack and empty, and depressed. That too is part of the bitter gift that has been given you, and God will grant you to see the meaning of it, I am sure. Our faith demands of us that we find meaning in meaninglessness these days. It is not a source of unending comfort all the time. Those who claim that it is only tempt us against it. . . .

TO MIGUEL GRINBERG   MAY 11, 1964

. . . What you say in your letter is right. *Fluencia* is the right way. What stops *fluencia* is the wrong kind of ignorance and the wrong kind of ignorance is the conviction that we can know exactly what is going on. Those who have too many programs and answers are absolutely blind and their ignorance leads them to destruction. Those who know that they do not know, are able at least to see something of what is in front of their nose. They can see a shadow of it, anyway. And they can move with the light and the shadow and keep from getting immediate sunstroke. So we must all move, even with motionless movement, even if we do not see clearly. A few little flames, yes. You can't grasp them, but anyway look at them obliquely. To look too directly at anything is to see something else because we force it to submit to the impertinence of our preconceptions. After a while though everything will speak to us if we let it and do not demand that it say what we dictate. . . .

TO BERNARD HÄRING   *Bernard Häring, a Redemptorist priest who taught moral theology at the Academia Alfonsiana of the Lateran University in Rome and published more than a hundred books, died in 1998. He served on the Preparatory Commission of the Second Vatican Council and is regarded as a leading Roman Catholic moral theologian of the twentieth century.*

DECEMBER 26, 1964

. . . The whole massive complex of technology, which reaches into every aspect of social life today, implies a huge organization of which no one is really in control, and which dictates its own solutions irrespective of human needs or even of reason. Technology now has reasons entirely its own which do not necessarily take into account the needs of man, and this huge inhuman mechanism, which the whole human race is now serving rather than commanding, seems quite probably geared for the systematic destruction of the natural world, quite apart from the question of the "bomb" which, in fact, is only one rather acute symptom of the whole disease. I am not of course saying that technology is "bad," and that progress is something to be feared. But I am saying that behind the cloak of specious myths about technology and progress, there seems to be at work a vast uncontrolled power which is leading man where he does not want to go in spite of himself and in which the Church, it seems to me, ought to be somewhat aware of the intervention of the "principalities and powers" of which St. Paul speaks. I know this kind of language is not very popular today, but I think it is so important that it cannot be left out of account. For instance I think that the monumental work of Jacques Ellul on *La Technique* is something that cannot be ignored by the Council Fathers if they wish to see all the aspects of the crucial question of the Church and the world.

TO ANGEL MARTÍNEZ BAIGGORI, S.J.   *Angel Martínez Baiggori, S.J., was a Nicaraguan priest and poet.*

JUNE 2, 1965

. . . Life in the United States poses more and more problems and fills one with confusion. The massive drift toward war, the unquestioned suppositions about the absolute use of power anywhere and everywhere, telling other countries how to arrange their own business, and doing this when we do not manage our own business in too edifying a manner. . . . All this raises perpetual questions. Yet one of the most serious questions is that the questions themselves are not even seen except by a few. Pray for us. There are some of us who try to resist the drift. . . .

Fifty years in our time takes one through many changes. I think I have seen too much history already, but there is probably more. Let us hope that what we will see in the next few years will surprise us by being less bad than we fear, and that God may show His Face and His truth in our history, in spite of the pride of men. And that we may reach a period of peaceful development, if it be possible.

TO NICANOR PARRA   JUNE 12, 1965

... We are in a time of the worst barbarity, much worse than in the time of the fall of the Roman empire. It is sufficient to look at what is happening in Vietnam and everywhere, most of all here. Sermons are worth nothing in this situation. It is necessary to state, without judgment, the truth of things. . . .

TO MADAME CAMILLE DREVET   *Camille Drevet lived in Paris and belonged to Les Amis de Gandhi (Friends of Gandhi), an organization founded by Louis Massignon.*

JULY 1, 1965

... I think the most dangerous thing in the world is the stupidity and moral blindness of the American leaders today. They are blindly and absurdly convinced of their moral rightness, and they think that anything they do is in some way perfectly justified merely because they feel that they have good intentions. They will maintain against the whole world, and against all intelligent and objective criticism, that they alone understand what they are doing. The basis of this superstition is twofold: first the inane confidence that a superior technology and more elaborate cybernetics are a sign of moral infallibility and superior wisdom. And second there is the ancient American myth of rejuvenation, justification, and a totally new start. By definition this is the land not only of "liberty" but also of primeval innocence and indeed complete impeccability. The evidence, unfortunately, is all to the contrary, and one cannot evade the guilt which the evidence produces. Nevertheless, the greater the guilt, the more frenzied and complacent are the arguments that the U.S. cannot possibly be culpable in anything and that in the long run all is to be blamed on the enemy. . . .

TO MIGUEL GRINBERG   OCTOBER 8, 1966

... What is in this country? If you want to know what is inside this country, look at Vietnam because that is where it all comes out into the open. A big bucket of sickness. But everything here goes on in a dazed tranquility.

The patient is etherized upon the table. He makes no remarks and does not complain. The beasts chew on his flesh but he observes nothing.

I have lost the art of making reassuring noises. But we are nevertheless ourselves the body of hope and hope lives in spite of what we may be thinking: it does not need to be pushed any more than the grass does. But I am afraid there is going to be a very big war indeed. In the presence of which it would be foolish to make statements. Perhaps however we will be lucky, and it will not happen, and small statements will once again be possible. . . .

OCTOBER 28, 1966

Sun rises in mist with thousands of very soft explosions and I am entirely splashed with designs coming through the holes in the lace wall of trees. Everything in the world is transparent. The ferocities of mankind mean nothing to the hope of light. You are right, preserve your hopes. For this one must keep eyes open always and see. The new consciousness will keep awakening. I know it. Poets, designers, musicians, singers. Do you know Bob Dylan's songs? Wonderful poet. . . .

New consciousness. There has to be clean water in the mind for the spirit to drink.

Courage and joy. Big *abrazo* for everybody.

TO FRIENDS   LENT 1967

. . . I got a letter from a Holy Cross Brother in Brazil taking me to task, as many critics have done, for what seems to be a negative attitude on technology in *Conjectures* [*of a Guilty Bystander*]. It might be well to try to dot the i's and cross the t's on this point. Am I "against technology"?

Obviously I am not maintaining that we ought to get rid of matches and go back to making fires by rubbing sticks together (thought of this yesterday when burning brush piles, lighting matches in the wind). Nor am I maintaining that modern transportation, medicine, methods of production and so on are "bad." I am glad to have a gas heater this winter, since I can't cut wood. Yet I am not saying I am a better human being this winter, when I have more "leisure," than I was last winter when I did a lot of chopping. Nothing wrong with the chopping either. What I question is the universal myth that technology infallibly makes everything in every way better for everybody. It does not.

Modern medicine is certainly a good thing. Thank God for it. Thank God for the fact that penicillin saves thousands of lives. But let's also face the fact that penicillin saves lives for people whom society then allows to starve because it is not set up to feed them. If it used its technological resources well, society certainly could feed them. In fact it doesn't. Technology comes into a "backward country" with an industrial setup that works fine in an advanced country—and depends for financial support on an advanced country and brings profits back to the advanced country. It may simply dislocate the "backward country" completely. Today twelve percent of the world's population (repeat, *twelve percent*) live in the appalling shanty towns and *poblaciones* that are seen in the outskirts of South American, African and Asian cities. What is technology doing for these people? It is not creating work for them, but is developing more and more labor-saving methods of production because technology in our society is not in the service of people but in the service of profit. What I am criticizing then is the myth that this kind of "labor-saving" technology will turn the world into a paradise. It will not. Look what technology is doing to Viet Nam!!!

On the other hand, I am quite willing to admit that the resources are there and that things *could be* quite other than they are. Technology could indeed make a much better world for millions of human beings. It not only can do this, but it must do it. We have an absolute obligation to use the means at our disposal to keep people from living in utter misery and dying like flies. Note: there has never been such abject misery on earth as that which our technological society has produced along with the fantastic plenty for very few. What I am "against" then is a complacent and naïve progressivism which pays no attention to anything but the fact that wonderful things can be and are done with machinery and with electronics. Even more wonderful things might be done. But in our present setup, the chances of them getting done are not as good as these people seem to think.

We face an utterly self-defeating and even absurd situation. A critic [Michele Murray] took me to task for saying in the book that "the realm of politics is the realm of waste." It is and always has been. When a human question becomes a "political issue," unfortunately the human problem gets shoved into the background, human hopes are derided and ignored, money passes from hand to hand and a lot of noise is made in the press, and the human problem may or may not even be touched. Witness [President Lyndon B.] Johnson's great "war on poverty." It is a sheer insult to the people living in our Eastern Kentucky Mountains. All the attention and money are going not to help them but to exterminate innocent non-combatants in Viet Nam and to enrich the big corporations that are making higher profits now than they ever did before.

In our technological world we have wonderful methods for keeping people alive and wonderful methods for killing them off, and they both go together. We rush in and save lives from tropical diseases, then we come along with napalm and burn up the people we have saved. The net result is more murder, more suffering, more inhumanity. This I know is a caricature, but is it that far from the truth?

What is my answer? I don't have one, except to suggest that technology could be used entirely differently. But the only way it ever will be is to get it free from this inescapable hang-up with profit or power, so that it will be used for people and not for money or politics. The essential message of an encyclical like *Mater et Magistra* or the Council Constitution *Gaudium et Spes* adds up to this: technology has given us the means to alleviate human misery, but the profit system makes it practically impossible to use the means effectively. The myth of technology (as distinct from the reality) serves the religion of profit vs. people. He who swallows the myth is serving that religion.

Sorry for this long tirade, but I thought it was worthwhile to make this point clear. Obviously I have no intention whatever of turning the clock back to the Middle Ages, though there are people around who want to do that too.

And so we turn our eyes to the great feast of Christian hope: the Resurrection. Too often the Passion and Resurrection of the Lord have been used in the past to canonize earthly injustice and despair: the old business of saying "Yes, you are getting a dirty deal, but just offer it up and you will be happy in heaven." The real root of Christian hope is the presence of the Risen Lord among us and in us by His Spirit which is the Spirit and power of love. The power of the Resurrection is the power of love that is stronger than death and evil, and its promise is the promise that the power of this love is ours if we freely accept it. To accept it is not just a matter of making a wish, but of entire and total commitment to the Law of Christ which is the Law of Love. Let us realize this, and believe it, and pray for one another. Let us be one in this love, and seek to make all men one in it, even here on earth. And if technology helps to express the creative power of love, then all the better: it will give glory to God and have its own place in the Kingdom of God on earth. But technology by itself will never establish that Kingdom.

10 BARBARA HUBBARD   *Barbara Hubbard was director of the Center of American Living in New York City. Merton was a recipient of her "Center Letters," which invited more than a thousand individuals to reflect on the future of humankind and the planet. In his response to Hubbard, Merton insists on the necessity of an "ecological consciousness."*

DECEMBER 23, 1967

Thanks for your letter. In the midst of the welter of Christmas I'll try to get a few thoughts on paper before I forget everything.

1) There can be no question whatever that mankind now stands at one of the crucial thresholds of his existence. In some sense it is the most crucial, since his entire future is to a great extent in his own hands. In the sense that he can determine that future, but not in the sense that he knows entirely what he is doing since he cannot foresee all the results of his decision. And also it will do him no good to hang back or try to avoid the decision, because even not deciding is a decision and will have its own (I think unfortunate) results.

2) Man now knows enough to determine his own future without knowing quite what all the implications are going to be. That is of course characteristic of human acts and human freedom. What is new is that now man can decide not just for himself and his immediate entourage as individuals, but he can decide for the whole race. He can commit the future to a certain quality of life—or no life at all.

3) It seems to me that we must not be too naïve about this situation. The fact that it is excitingly new should not blind us to the other fact that man is still acting in the same wrong ways that he should have learned to avoid. In

other words, we have to face the new without forgetting crucially important lessons from the past. Our decision must be a life-affirming and loving one: but a life-affirming decision is not likely to emerge from a thought system that is largely programmed by unconscious death drives, destructiveness, greed, etc. And yet it still can, if we take account of a few vital and by no means new imperatives: to refrain from the wanton taking of life, to avoid selfish greed and the exploitation of others for our own ends, to tell the truth (and that goes for governments and corporations as well as for individuals), to respect the personal integrity of others even when they belong to groups that are alien to us, etc., etc.

4) We must face the challenge of the future realizing that we are still problems to ourselves. Where the religious dimension enters in is not just in pious clichés but in a radical self-criticism and openness and a profound ability to *trust* not only in our chances of a winning gamble, but in an inner dynamism of life itself, a basic creativity, a power of life to win over entropy and death. But once again, we have to pay attention to the fact that we may formulate this in words, and our unconscious death-drive may be contradicting us in destructive undertones we don't hear.

In other words, we have all got to learn to be wide open, and not get closed up in little tight systems and cliques, little coteries of gnostic experts. . . . Your work in bringing people from different fields together is symptomatic. It shows the realization of one of our greatest needs: a real expansion of communication to its worldwide limits. I wish you success.

FEBRUARY 16, 1968

About our "birth into space": one reason why I am perhaps a bit backward about joining spontaneously and articulately in the celebration of a space age mystique is that I am not properly informed. Perhaps you can help me there. I do get the sense of immense technical skill and virtuosity and the opening of fabulous new horizons. But since my knowledge is largely based on magazines that I leaf through in the tedium of a doctor's office, I also get an impression of commercialism, hubris, and cliché, which frankly turns me off. I realize that this is a by-product which really has nothing to do with the seriousness of scientific exploration. There is another dimly sensed aspect of space flights as a sort of cosmic and ritual shamanic dance by which I could conceivably be turned back on. . . .

All I am saying is that I am really not ready to speak on this subject.

Here is another aspect of the situation. The future depends very much on what we are thinking and doing *now*. Let me suggest a perhaps new and offbeat approach to what we are thinking now, ethically. I detect two broad kinds of ethical consciousness developing (over and above the sclerotic fixation on norms that are given by the past): (1) a *millennial* consciousness, (2) an *ecological* consciousness. The millennial consciousness is like this: all that has happened up to now has been at best provisional and preparatory, at worst a complete mess. The real thing is about to happen: the new creation, the millennium, the coming of the Kingdom, the withering away of the State, etc. But if you want to enter into the Kingdom there are certain things you have to do. They consist partly in acts which destroy and repudiate the past (metanoia, conversion, revolution, etc.) and partly in acts which open you up to the future. If you do these things, the big event will happen. This consciousness is found in Marxism, in Black Power, in Cargo Cults, in Church *aggiornamento*, in Third World revolutionary movements, but also doubtless in esoteric movements within the establishment, management, science, etc., which are all beyond my simple ken. The ecological consciousness says: look out! In preparing this great event you run the risk of forgetting something. We are not alone in this thing. We belong to a community of living beings and we owe our fellow members in this community the respect and honor due to them. If we are to enter into a new era, well and good, but let's bring the rest of the living along with us.

In other words, we must not try to prepare the millennium by immolating our living earth, by careless and stupid exploitation for short-term commercial, military, or technological ends which will be paid for by irreparable loss in living species and natural resources. This ecological consciousness can be summed up in the words of Albert Schweitzer: to wit, "life is sacred . . . that of plants and animals [as well as that of our] fellow man." And the conservationist Aldo Leopold spoke of a basic "ecological conscience," the source of an ethic that can be stated in the following expansion of the Golden Rule: "A thing is right when it tends to preserve the integrity, stability, and beauty of the biotic community. It is wrong when it tends otherwise."

The scientific exploration of space and of other planets—I say scientific, not military—can be seen in itself as neutral, neither millennial nor ecological. Since it reaches *outside* the natural ecological environment of our earth and becomes independent of it to a great extent, it tends to function in a different climate of thought. Nevertheless, as some scientists have reminded us, the ecological implications of interplanetary flight could be enormous.

My suggestion is this. The space age can be dominated by millennial thinking or by ecological thinking. If the millennial predominates, it may lead to ecological irresponsibility. If it does, then in terms of Leopold's "ecological ethic," it would be "wrong." That wrong can be prevented by a deepening of the ecological sense and by a corresponding restraint and wisdom in the way we treat the earth we live on and the other members of the ecological community with which we live.

The ecological consciousness is not predominant, to put it mildly, in business, in the armed services, in government, in urban and suburban life, in the academy. It tends to receive some notice from humanist philosophers, artists, psychoanalysts, poets, conservationists, hippies, etc. I regret to say that it is something about which the Church apparently couldn't care less, at least today. But in the past people like St. Francis of Assisi have stood for it in a primitive sort of way.

Well, not to draw this out too long: it seems to me that the important thing is to avoid a shallow millenarianism as we enter the space age, and retain a solid ecological consciousness. Then we will be all right. I suggest creating and distributing a new button with the following message: "Put Flower Power into Space."

TO ETHEL KENNEDY   JUNE 22, 1968, [FOLLOWING
                    SENATOR ROBERT F. KENNEDY'S ASSASSINATION
                           IN LOS ANGELES ON JUNE 5, 1968]

. . . Really it is hard to say anything that is capable of measuring the shock and sorrow of Bobby's tragic immolation. Nowadays we tend to expect almost anything. But there was something particularly awful and traumatic about this, just because Bobby represented a very real hope for the whole country and for the world. He was the only one with a real chance who might also have done something very definite for peace. And now it looks as if we will be faced with a completely illusory choice at the polls—so much that I wonder if I'll vote at all. At least for the Presidency.

It has been a shock for everyone and I think you must have felt that the dimensions of your personal sorrow were multiplied in all directions. But that does not make it any easier to have to go through all that you and the family have suffered. . . .

Naturally I have said Masses for Bobby and I remember all of you at the altar. More and more we are forced to realize that God is our only real hope in the stark mystery of what we are all up against. Certainly we know that all will be well, but the ways in which He makes it well are apt to be difficult for us. Courage and peace be with you. My love to all the family, and God bless you. . . .

TO FRIENDS   MIDSUMMER 1968

. . . Several magazines asked me to write something concerning the assassination of Robert Kennedy. I refused because I am a bit suspicious of what seems to me to be a growing ritual cycle: murder, public acts of contrition, deploring violence, gestures of appeasement, then everything goes on unchanged and presently there is another assassination. The cycle continues. The sickness seems to be so deep that ritual expressions of sorrow, horror, astonishment, etc., have just become part of a general routine. At such a time perhaps silence is more decent. Certainly the sense of shock is real. People are indeed horrified by the fact that nothing is safe, and that the *least safe* are the people, the values, that we admire, love and rely on the most. In a word we are beginning to sense in our society a tendency to harm and to destroy the very things we claim to need and admire. The Kennedys (for all that they had enemies and critics) did offer something of an image of what Americans like and approve of: what they identify with. The fact that this is precisely what is most menaced, and menaced from *inside our society,* not outside it, is what is significant. It is not enough to say that the assassins of both Kennedys were in some sense "un-American." They emerged from a society which made their crime easy. In the case of Dr. King, evidence seems to suggest that there was indeed a conspiracy and that the assassin was after money that had been explicitly *offered* to anyone who would get Dr. King out of the way. In any event, this is my comment: the problem of violence in our society is now critical, and it is not just a problem of a few psychopaths or rebels. The violence that threatens us to the point of possible self-destruction is endemic in the whole of society, and more especially in the establishment itself, the military, the police, the established forces of "order"—they are all infected with a mania for overkill, rooted in fear. The future promises an era of force, suspicion, terrorism with more or less futile acts of protest, violently repressed. Unless we get some really intelligent and creative leadership, our future as a democracy is not bright. . . .

: . . I am against war, against violence, against violent revolution, for peaceful settlement of differences, for non-violent but nevertheless radical change. Change is needed, and violence will not really change anything: at most it will only transfer power from one set of bull-headed authorities to another. . . .

But the problems of man can never be solved by political means alone. Over and over again the Church has said that the forgetfulness of God and of prayer are at the root of our trouble. This has been reduced to a cliché. But it is nevertheless true. And I realize more and more that in my own vocation what matters is not comment, not statements of opinion, not judgments, but prayer. Let us pray for one another and try in everything to do what God asks of us.

TO VICTORIA OCAMPO   JULY 14, 1968

. . . The violence in this country and its moral disorientation are indeed disturbing. The wanton and useless destruction of life is something much more unacceptable than the fact of death itself. My own hope is that in spite of everything good will come out of what we are undergoing, though I do not see much evidence of it.

Unlike Camus, I believe in a Providence which will bring out of suffering the victory of mercy: but this does not absolve us from the necessity of courage. . . .

THE RACE QUESTION

TO JAMES BALDWIN   *Born and raised in Harlem, novelist and essayist James Baldwin drew on his own experience of racism and discrimination in twentieth-century America. Merton wrote to Baldwin after reading excerpts of* The Fire Next Time *in the* New Yorker. *In a letter to Sister Therese Lentfoehr, Merton lauded Baldwin's book as "powerful and great."*

[N.D.; CA. FEBRUARY 1963]

You cannot expect to write as you do without getting letters like this. One has to write, and I am sure you have received lots of letters already that say better than I can what this will try to say.

First of all, you are right all down the line. You exaggerate nowhere. You know exactly what you are talking about, and as a matter of fact it is really news to nobody (that is precisely one of your points). I have said the same myself, much more mildly and briefly, and far less well, in print so it is small wonder that I agree with you.

But the point is that this is one of the great realities of our time. For Americans it is perhaps the crucial truth, and all the other critical questions that face us are involved in this one.

It is certainly matter for joy that you have at least said so much, and in the place where you have said it. It will be read and understood. But as I went through column after column [in the *New Yorker*] I was struck, as I am sure you were, by the ads all along each side of your text. What a commentary! They prove you more right than you could have imagined. They go far beyond anything you have said. What force they lend to all your statements. No one could have dreamed up more damning evidence to illustrate what you say.

Sometimes I am convinced that there cannot be a way out of this. Humanly there is no hope, at least on the white side (that is where I unfortunately am). I don't see any courage or any capacity to grasp even the smallest bit of the enormous truth about ourselves. Note, I speak as a Catholic priest. We still see the whole thing as a sort of abstract exercise in ethics, when we see it at all. We don't see we are killing our own hope and the hope of the world.

You are very careful to make explicit the non-Christian attitude you take, and I respect this because I understand that this is necessary for you and I do not say this as an act of tolerant indulgence. It is in some sense necessary for me, too, because I am only worth so much as a priest as I am able to see what the non-Christian sees. I am in most things right with you and the only point on which I disagree is that I think your view is fundamentally religious, genuinely religious, and therefore has to be against conventional religiosity. If you do not agree it does not matter very much.

The other day I was talking to an African priest from Ghana. The impression I always get in talking to Africans is that they have about ten times as much reality as we have. This of course is not an accurate way of speaking: I think what it really expresses, this "sense," is the awareness of complementarity, the awareness of a reality in him which completes some lack in myself, and not of course an intuition of an absolute ontological value of a special essence. And I think as you yourself have suggested, that this is the whole story: there is not one of us, individually, racially, socially, who is fully complete in the sense of having in himself *all* the excellence of all humanity. And that this excellence, this totality, is built up out of the contributions of the particular parts of it that we all can share with one another. I am therefore not completely human until I have found myself in my African and Asian and Indonesian brother because he has the part of humanity which I lack.

The trouble is that we are supposed to be, and in a way we are, complete in ourselves. And we cherish the illusion that this completeness is not just a potential, but that it is finally realized from the very start, and that the notion of having to find something of ourselves only after a long search and after the gift of ourselves to others, does not apply to us. This illusion, which makes the white man imagine he does not need the Negro, enables him to think he can treat the Negro as an "object" and do what he likes with him. Indeed, in order to prove that his illusion is true, he goes ahead and treats the Negro in the way we know. He has to.

At the heart of the matter then is man's contempt for truth, and the substitution of his "self" for reality. His image is his truth. He believes in his specter and sacrifices human beings to his specter. This is what we are doing, and this is not Christianity or any other genuine religion: it is barbarity.

We cannot afford to have contempt for any truth, but least of all for a truth as urgent in our lives as this one. Hence, I want to give you all the moral support I can, which isn't much. I know you are more than fatigued with well-meaning white people clapping you on the shoulder and saying with utmost earnestness, "We are right with you," when of course we are right with ourselves and not in any of the predicaments you are in at all. What I will say is that I am glad I am not a Negro because I probably would never be able to take it: but that I recognize in conscience that I have a duty to try to make my fellow whites stop doing the things they do and see the problem, or a surge of optimism, because I am still convinced that there is almost nothing to be done that will have any deep effect or make any real difference.

I am not in a position to be completely well informed on this issue, anyway. If you think of anything I ought to know about, I would be grateful if you put it in an envelope and send it down. I hope your article will have done some good. The mere fact that truth has been told is already a very great good in itself.

TO LESLIE DEWART   [N.D.; BETWEEN MAY 10 AND JUNE 28, 1963]

... Take the race question in the U.S. We are now in the middle of a real American revolution, just as real as the one in 1776, and perhaps destined to have an even more decisive importance. This too is a "micro-cosmic" situation, another apocalyptic sign like the Cuban revolution. What has the Church done? She has made token and symbolic gestures of good will and justice. She has integrated schools and colleges in many areas. She has been *less* prejudiced than most of the other sectors of white society, and she has roundly condemned racial injustice on paper. She has shown good will and motherly concern. Apart from that, she has taken a safe position, neither too much of this nor too much of that, and has carefully avoided signs of haste in getting anywhere. Whatever may be the merits of the various arguments for a more radical approach, it is certain that the Church has striven, as much as possible, to avoid every kind of risk, anything that might compromise her stable and quasi-respectable status in the South. In other words, she has made sure that the Catholic did not fall back into the same gehenna as the Negro, and did not become, with him and the Jew, bottom man on the totem pole. To guarantee this, it was necessary that no priest be seen on a freedom ride, that Catholics as Catholics should be kept out of anything messy (jails, sit-ins, etc.), and that the Church remain in the background. While of course retaining its influence over souls.

But what is happening is that there is extraordinary life surging up in the Negro community all over the U.S. In some of its forms this life is magnificently and explicitly Christian (Martin Luther King and his non-violent movement). But in other places the movement is anything but Christian, and reflects disillusionment and disgust with Christian values and claims, whether Catholic or Protestant. It is not very hard to detect the irrationality, the fanaticism, and the potential cataclysmic violence contained in the new Negro racism. But it is not enough to detect this and deplore it, and then withdraw into a defensive, truculent, or even repressive position, using violence and hate against violence and hate. Yet this is the risk we run if we refuse to see to what extent our own vagueness, indecisiveness, and lack of creative initiative has engendered Negro violence.

What has happened is that the Church, in order to retain its respectability in the South, has risked losing the Negro entirely, not only in America but perhaps even to some extent in Africa. In other words, where there is life, where there is a real movement indicating the course of history (and Pope John somewhere said that we have to listen to the voice of history because it is the voice of God), where this voice is heard Catholics don't listen, because, with all the good will in the world they *cannot* listen. We cannot listen, because, after centuries of Holy Roman Empires and the rest, we cannot look upon history otherwise than as a force sustaining the Church's power to reach and *control* souls. The sin, hidden but real, is in this concept of the *absolute need for external control* over souls in order to save them. . . .

TO DAME MARCELLA VAN BRUYN   OCTOBER 15, 1963

. . . You evidently do not know about the events in the American South, and everywhere in this country. I think it is something you *should* know because it is terribly symptomatic of the spirit of the age. The Negroes are theoretically "equal" to the whites in this country, but in fact of course they are not allowed to share the same restaurants, hotels, public services and whatnot. They are rigidly segregated in their living quarters and even in schools (in the South). In the last few years they have given up waiting for the white people to apply the laws that exist granting them their rights, and have started to agitate for their rights themselves. The resistance has been "nonviolent" (rather like Gandhi's approach) and in most cases very spiritual and religious in its base. One of the leaders is a Protestant pastor, Martin Luther King (a Negro), who is a very courageous and I think quite edifying Christian. The "Children of Birmingham" were schoolchildren who, in one of the Southern cities, went in procession to the City Hall, as an act of protest against the condition of the Negroes. The police would not let them carry on the procession, and stopped them with high-pressure fire hoses, turned Alsatian police dogs on them, beat them and threw hundreds of them in prison for "rioting." It was a great act of injustice on the part of the police, but the wonderful good order of the children and their indomitable religious spirit of charity, and their lack of resentment, was really a wonderful thing. It moved the whole country and the whole world. Since that time however things have not got better. In September, four such children were killed when white people bombed a Church (!) where the children were at Sunday School. There has been much criminal violence on the part of the whites, and the police are hand-in-glove with them. No one is ever caught or punished for these things, only the Negroes are put in jail as soon as they dare to manifest any spirit of protest. It is a most serious injustice, and as such it is something that needs to be known by contemplatives and remembered in their prayers and penances, because reparation is urgently needed. Also it is a very serious moral problem for this country. It is so complex that it is beyond the serious efforts of the Government to handle properly, and I personally believe that it is going to take on the proportions of a revolution, it is so serious. It may have disastrous effects. So pray for us. . . .

TO ROBERT LAWRENCE WILLIAMS   *Robert Lawrence Williams, a young black tenor, asked Merton to write a series of poems on faith and brotherhood. He planned a concert for the benefit of the Foundation for the Education of Black Students at which he would sing these poems set to music. Merton wrote eight "Freedom Songs" for Williams. The concert Williams had hoped for never materialized, but the "Freedom Songs," which Williams never got to sing, were performed at the National Liturgical Conference in Washington, D.C., on August 20, 1968, as a memorial tribute to Martin Luther King Jr.*

MARCH 21, 1964

Thanks for your letter and for your request, which I hope I will be able to fulfill. I have been giving it quite a bit of thought, and I really do want to do anything I can to help. But also I want to do only what is worthwhile. . . .

It seems to me that anything I do must be an authentic expression of the Negro's struggle for his rights, and not just a friendly expression of concern by someone who lives comfortably looking on. A lot would then depend on who will be writing the music, who will be singing, and so on. I think that ideally speaking we should aim at a collaboration in which the music would be in the Negro tradition, and I would contribute words that would be (I hope) appropriate. When I say Negro tradition I mean, in this case, something between spirituals and the blues, and it seems to me that the jazz element is essential.

APRIL 23, 1964

. . . I fully understand how important it is for you to stress the fact that the Negro is fully an American and that he has helped to build up this country. I could see my way to writing an article on this, for instance. But with a poem, a song, it is a little different, as I myself am not that much of an American. I am on the contrary more of a European. I was born [in France] and largely brought up abroad, though my mother was from Ohio. Still, I don't have that deep feeling for the land and the continent that you have, and consequently I find it hard to identify with you on this point, poetically. . . .

The only thing I have written for you so far is this piece based on the Prophet Michaeas (Micah).

I will keep thinking about these various ideas and will get to town to hear a lot of spirituals in the library: that will help. I find myself here without material that suggests anything concrete. . . .

. . . Even though the civil rights bill has passed, and that at least is something, there is going to be need of Freedom Songs for many a day yet, I fear. There is a deep, deep wound, and it is not healing. . . . A long and thankless task is ahead and we may not be able to do much. But the important thing is communication, openness, understanding, willingness to listen. . . .

. . . The big problem you run into in dealing with white people is that, in this matter, no doubt they are sympathetic, but they aren't black, and because they aren't, they don't know what it feels like and they are not able to enter into the experience except abstractly. Hence they may have good intentions, but these will lead nowhere or will easily peter out. There is nothing to back them. In the long run, if you could get a really concerned Negro composer it would be much more effective. . . .

. . . You must realize that it is the ordinary way of God's dealings with us that our ideas do not work out speedily and efficiently as we would like them to. The reason for this is not only the loving wisdom of God, but also the fact that our acts have to fit into a great complex pattern that we cannot possibly understand. I have learned over the years that Providence is always a whole lot wiser than any of us, and that there are always not only good reasons but the very *best* reasons for the delays and blocks that often seem to us so frustrating and absurd. This applies certainly to anyone who has done what he can, though it obviously does not justify complete passivity in political affairs, such as the civil rights struggle. But even then, obstacles have a meaning. . . .

. . . I wish the American white people were capable of realizing how much the Negro can and does contribute to making American culture an authentic reality in its own right. Failure to realize this is not only an added injustice, but it deprives America of advantages it would otherwise enjoy.

I also want to say how happy I was that the Nobel Peace Prize was awarded to Dr. King. This is, or at least can be, something very significant for the whole civil rights movement. I am more and more hopeful that, in spite of all the frustrations and delays, truth and justice will come out on top, and that significant steps can continue to be made. But certainly much more depends on the courage and resourcefulness of the Negro than on the initiative of the white people, unfortunately. How sad it is to have to continue to admit this. . . .

DECEMBER 21, 1964

. . . You are right about the reactions of people, composers, who are on the lookout for money and prestige. It is true also that people are frightened of the civil rights cause. But that is no credit to them at all, and has nothing to do with the matter: except that of course anyone who is not committed would hardly be able to do a good job in writing the music. Never mind, though, I can tell you from long experience that when God wills to bring fruit from a work, He makes it wait and puts all sorts of obstructions in the way, or lets them be put there, in order to really bring the thing to maturity. I am sure it will work this way. Do not worry, Freedom Songs will be needed for a long time to come, I am afraid. . . .

JANUARY 29, 1965

. . . You are so right about the difficulty of communication. I suppose it is in large part a failure of the white imagination, first of all. Then when one is prosperous and comfortable, he becomes insensitive to the needs and sufferings of others; and then finally there is just the simple mendacity of the press seeing only one side of things and eventually distorting news to fit the one-sided view. . . .

The tragedy is that when people have warm and generous hearts, and reach out impulsively to what ought normally to be a warm human response, and then meet with incomprehension, in the end the frustration gets to be just too much. The Negro is a warm and generous person, and he looks first of all for a human response. The white man is more calculating and he looks for a good deal, a return on his investment. This is nothing to be proud of. It is the source of the trouble. The refusal to be human with one's fellow man, and the insistence on treating him as an object to be used for profit and pleasure, covering this up with a superficial friendliness: that is the tragedy of the white man. But it is not his tragedy because he is white. It is his tragedy because he is rich. All rich people, irrespective of color, tend to get that way, and when the black man gets rich, as he one day will, and when he gets power, he will tend to be the same. But, I hope, in a warmer and more lavish kind of society. . . .

MAY 27, 1965

. . . There is a Vietnamese Buddhist who has been fasting, in Brooklyn, in protest against the violence exerted against his innocent fellow citizens and the North Vietnamese civilians. He has not had solid food since March. He will probably soon die, since he has vowed not to eat until there is a cease-fire and negotiation in Vietnam. Few people in this country even give the man a thought. His actions have nothing to do with business so why notice them? But this is typical of the whole plight of all the colored races in the world. They try to enter some kind of human dialogue with the white races, and the answer is "You are just not *there.* We will only allow you to have existence on our terms, you have to conform to what our fantasy says about you. We will not admit that you are real."

. . . I want with all my heart to say something for the Negroes everywhere and to join my voice to theirs. It is one of the few honorable things I can think of at the present time. Every day I am ashamed of being a white man, and I suppose that is only just, since the white people have contrived for generations to make Negroes ashamed of their gift from God, their own skin. As if there were something wrong with it. How stupid people can be. . . .

MAY 1, 1967

. . . The behavior of so many white Catholics has effectively silenced me and deprived me of any possibility of giving you advice about the Church. All I can honestly say is that the decision is yours, and that the Church has to some extent forfeited the right to demand loyalty of her black children since she has not lived up to her role of mother in their regard. I speak now of the Church as institution. Invisibly, the union of believers who really obey God is another matter. . . . The answer is true faith in God and a really obedient heart that hears and follows His voice, careful not to be deceived. Let us pray for each other that we may always follow that voice: we will remain in a secret, underground way, united.

Robert, I have no illusions about the future. Many chickens are coming home to roost in the white man's parlor. Some of them are going to be pretty large chickens, and some of them are going to have the manners of vultures. Too bad. The white man thinks himself sincere and honest, but he will gradually begin to find out what a con man he has been. It is a pity that you have run into such things: people who think themselves disinterested and idealistic can be in reality the crassest kind of operators, and never realize it. That is the pity of so many Catholics: in the name of God and the Church they are ruthlessly ambitious, aggressive, arrogant, self-seeking characters. They cannot see it. But these traits are universal, unfortunately, and if we imagine that they belong only to this or that group, then we never get out of confusion. However, I admit that for the time being the white man is the one who is getting all the prizes in this contest.

On August 29, 1967, Williams wrote a moving letter to Merton in which he said he could not leave the Church even though she had not been a mother to her black children.

SEPTEMBER 5, 1967

I was happy to get your letter—a very moving and deep letter too. It shows once again that the Spirit and the Church are far beyond any lines of division that human beings can think up for themselves. And it shows too that the Church can no longer continue to be a "white" Church. And God will not let her do so. It is up to you not just to be part of a "white" Church but to help make the Church what she is really meant to be. Christ in the world today is not white, nor black either: but He is certainly present and suffering in the black people and colored people of the earth. The white world is purely and simply under judgment. And they don't know it.

On March 23, 1968, Williams replied to a letter of Merton's that is missing in which Merton apparently said what had happened (namely, that Williams never got to sing the songs Merton wrote for him) was the will of God. Williams disagreed: "I no longer believe in you or your white Christianity. I believe in the sweet, kind, humble little Jesus who came to teach us how to live."

TO MARTIN E. MARTY   *Martin E. Marty, well-known author in the field of religious literature, longtime associate editor of the* Christian Century, *and professor at the University of Chicago, wrote a strongly critical review of Merton's* Seeds of Destruction, *taking issue with "Letters to a White Liberal," in which Merton questioned the sincerity of the white liberal's commitment to reforms that would actually benefit black people. When the real crisis came, Merton maintained, the self-interest of the white man would take over. Marty pictured Merton safe behind his monastery walls, attempting to pose as a white James Baldwin. Two and a half years later, in the August 30, 1967, issue of the* National Catholic Reporter, *Marty wrote an open letter to Merton in which he apologized for having put down* Seeds of Destruction. *With most of the summer of 1967 past, he said, we can now "see that you were correct." He wrote: "Recently I have had occasion to reread the book. What bothers me now is the degree of accuracy in your predictions and prophecies in general. At the time you seemed to be trying to be a white James Baldwin. Now it seems to me that you were 'telling it as it is' and maybe 'as it will be.'" Signing his letter "your regained admirer and friend," Marty suggests that Merton might try his hand at what could be called "Seeds of Hope."*

SEPTEMBER 6, 1967

I long ago learned to live with the idea that I was half crazy. Lately, seeing the reaction of some people to my more recent books, I have become resigned to the possibility that I am completely crazy. Your open letter awakens in me the hope that I am only half crazy after all. Restored to where I thought I was, I am reassured. Thank you for your generosity. . . .

This is not the reply you suggested in your closing lines, only a spontaneous reaction of friendship and common concern: not a scenario, but perhaps a few hopeful questions, based on a warm agreement with your own tentative approach—I like the whole picture of tolerance, "play" not being too deadly serious, keeping creative possibilities open even when events are most destructive. I agree with you, it does no good to be too raffishly apocalyptic at this point. It only adds to the violence where there is already more than enough. I still think, though, that what I said four years ago needed to be said, and said perhaps in that provocative way. Today there is plenty of provocation everywhere, and I aim at provoking no one if I can help it.

When I say we are in for a hell of a time in this country I am not being apocalyptic: just saying what everyone now realizes. If my doubts about the viability of optimistic liberalism are greater now than they were before, it is because such liberalism presupposes a situation that can be controlled by reasonable policies. There has been a shaking of foundations: just a beginning. Reasonable control is not something we can rely on. Nor even reasonable dialogue. We are not even going to find things fitting the names we have been accustomed to give them. We are in a great crisis of meaning. The fact that the racial identity of the Negro is now a central question is only a small part of it. Now more than ever generalizations, particularly old and familiar generalizations, are going to be dangerous. Perhaps we must now all be very careful to explain ourselves when we say "the Negro" or "the liberal." What Negro, and what liberal? And what radical?

I should imagine this summer's crisis has done a lot of winnowing among liberals, driving a great many to the right and a few to a hesitant left that is not quite there. I don't know, I am just guessing. I imagine, though, that there must be a few liberals around who are now fully convinced of the need for a new politics in this country. The old two-party system was finished decades ago. Perhaps there is some hope that out of this hot summer we may at last get the serious beginnings of a really effective radical coalition where, in spite of all the black separatism that is announced by "the Negro," there may in fact be collaboration between white and black on the left toward peace, new horizons, constructive change—not without a little more shaking of the foundation. This is perhaps the only hope of a third way, something other than complete anarchy on the one hand or a police state on the other.

I happened to be in Louisville right after the Detroit riots—and right after there was supposed to be a riot in Louisville itself. (The riot did not

take place.) All the Negroes I met were being not only friendly but vocif-
erously friendly. I did not feel that they were tense and mad, but relaxed
and confident. It was the kind of feeling you used to get on the campus at
Columbia the morning after we had burned down the Barnard fence. Not
a sense of animosity and racial war. Obviously, I must follow my own rule
and not generalize from this very limited experience, but I am quite sure
that it is very important, at the moment, not to lump "the Negro" into one
mad red-eyed monster with a Molotov cocktail in his hand. Nor to panic
at the thought that the Negro's hate of the white man has now reached the
point where it is completely irreversible and be assuaged only by everybody's blood. This is just not true of "the Negro" in general, only a small
minority. And in that small minority, the hate of the white man tends to be
first of all a hate of white society, its institutions, its self-image, its property,
its pretensions. I don't condone the senseless murder of firemen who are
trying to put out blazes started by rioters: but still, it is the fireman as symbolic of white institutions and not the fireman purely and simply as white
man that is being shot at.

In my opinion, the intransigence of the Black Power people is first of all
aimed at one point: getting white liberals and radicals too off the back of
the Negro activist so that the Negro can function freely by himself. Once
this is quite clear, and I think it is now abundantly clear to everybody, if the
white liberal or radical is willing to cooperate with the Negro *independently,*
and *completely out of his way,* without trying to dominate the Negro and
make up his mind for him about *anything,* the chances are that his support
will be accepted. But it will be accepted grudgingly, without thanks, without
demonstrations of wonderment and pleasure: it will be accepted merely as
what is due. If this could have begun four years ago on these clear grounds
of understanding, we would be better off today. I do not say we would not
have had the Newark and Detroit riots. These were inevitable, and more like
them are inevitable. The injustice and cruelty which are by now endemic
beneath the surface of our bland and seemingly benign society are too deep
and too serious to be cured by legislation, even if by some miracle the legislation were to mean anything in practice. This is all going to have to come
out the hard way, and in my opinion (forgive the slight twanging of those
apocalyptic wires) the un-Christianity of American Christianity is going to

be inexorably exposed and judged: mine, perhaps, included. The form this Judgment will take will, first of all, be the panic, the hate, the violence, and the fanaticism of people who, calling themselves Christians, will resort to killing in "self-defense" because they are so obsessed with the fear that what they believe in—the affluent society—is being menaced by revolution. It is significant that the TV set, fancy clothes, furniture, liquor and of course weapons are so central in the rioting and looting of the ghetto. This is a religious war over what we all, white and black, really believe in!

It is here that I return to one of my more obvious suggestions. We Christians, some of us at least, were and are anxious to support the Negro non-violent movement for civil rights which is now, if not completely a thing of the past, at least seriously diminished in significance. But what about a white non-violent response to Negro violence? Strangely enough that has not been much preached, though in fact it has been practiced. I think for instance of Msgr. Robert Fox and his people in the Puerto Rican riots in East Harlem. Processions with flowers and lights, songs, in the streets on the nights of rioting certainly did a great deal to keep things calm. But of course the great thing is for this witness to be unambiguous, and it is hard for the clergy to be unambiguous insofar as the priest, like it or not, is aligned with the cop and the National Guardsman as a defender of the establishment. Christian non-violence in the presence of Negro violence must first of all mean a complete dissociation from and repudiation of an "order" which defends the money of the slum landlord and the white businessman against the people who are exploited by them in the ghetto. We have to clearly recognize that this order is disorder, and join the Negro in protesting against it. Such sentiments are by no means popular among Catholics today, but I submit they must be made and aired, and I think you will agree they are not apocalyptic. I am certainly all for your idea that in our search for ways of keeping elements of reason and humanity alive in an ugly and destructive situation, we can best study the ways of flower power. You do not use that expression which is already perhaps a bit outworn (it takes anything about six weeks to become phony in America today). But in conclusion, I take this opportunity to say precisely where I myself stand.

I am not convinced that Stokely Carmichael is the incarnation of Satan. I do not go along with violence, but I do not recognize in myself the slightest right to impose non-violence on the Negro. It is up to him to choose his own policies. I do not personally believe that there is much chance of the United States handing over Alabama to the Negro, though I wish it were possible. If non-violence is, as I think it is, a Christian duty in a time like this (because it is the only way to keep open really reasonable and creative possibilities in the mess that is to come), I think that we white Christians should get busy and find out about using it. But we must not use it for the interests of the white against the Negro. We must use it, as it is meant to be used, for truth, and for the good of everybody. To begin with, it must be used to keep open possibilities of authentic human communication when the bullets are flying.

My position is on the Christian non-violent left, particularly that seg ment of it which is occupied by Dorothy Day, the Catholic Peace Fellowship and people like Joan Baez. We are not liberals. We are still, I suppose, Christian anarchists, except that the term has no political relevance whatever. But the Christian anarchist remains—unlike the liberal—clearly non-identified with established disorder. Or at least he tries to. In so doing, he may exasperate everyone, but perhaps sometimes he may see an opening toward peace and love even when the sulphur and brimstone are at their worst, and others have given up trusting in anything except weapons. . . .

TO JUNE J. YUNGBLUT   *June J. Yungblut and her husband, John, directed the Quaker House in Atlanta, Georgia. In 1966, they served in South Africa for the Friends of the World Committee. In 1968, John Yungblut was attempting to arrange a retreat at Bellarmine for Martin Luther King Jr. when King was assassinated.*

MARCH 29, 1968

. . . I'll send another copy of *Nat Turner*. Thanks for passing the first one along to Martin King. I hope he can come, and will do what I can to make it worthwhile if he does: but also feel acutely that I have absolutely nothing to say and am probably not expected to say much of anything. Just be around. . . .

Dr. Martin Luther King Jr. was assassinated in Memphis on April 4, 1968.

APRIL 5, 1968

By a strange coincidence, I happened to be out in Lexington [with Donald Allchin] when Martin was shot and I heard all the news at once, instead of remaining for a day or more without finding out. What a terrible thing: and yet I felt that he was expecting it. In fact, almost at the very time of the murder I saw the TV film of his speech the previous night and heard what he said, in the place where we were eating a sandwich before starting home. A few moments later, the news came through on the car radio.

This all means something more serious than we can imagine. But he, at any rate, has done all that any man can do. It will be to his glory.

Could you please pass on the enclosed note to Mrs. King? [*See below.*] I don't have their address.

TO CORETTA SCOTT KING   *Coretta Scott and Martin Luther King Jr. were married in 1953. She shared his passion for racial justice and his commitment to nonviolence.*

APRIL 5, 1968

Some events are too big and terrible to talk about. I think we all anticipated this one: I am sure he did. Somehow when John Yungblut spoke of Martin coming here for a brief retreat before the big march, I had the awful feeling that it might be a preparation for something like this. It was to be Memphis instead of Washington—or somewhere else on the way.

Let me only say how deeply I share your personal grief as well as the shock which pervades the whole nation. He has done the greatest thing anyone can do. In imitation of his Master he has laid down his life for his friends and enemies. He knew the nation was under judgment and he tried everything to stay the hand of God and man. He will go down in history as one of our greatest citizens.

My prayers are with you and with him. May he find the rest and reward which God has promised to all who trust in His mercy. This morning my Eucharistic offering will be for him and for you.

On April 6, June wrote that she and other friends of the Kings had been at Coretta's house since the assassination. The Ebenezer Baptist

Choir was singing and praying. Coretta had gone to Memphis for Dr. King's body. When she returned, "she spoke for a moment to each of us. She put her arms around me and held me a long time. Neither of us said anything."

TO JUNE YUNGBLUT   APRIL 9, 1968

Today is the day of the funeral. The other day I offered Mass for Martin, and two Anglican friends [Donald Allchin and an Anglican seminarian] joined me there. Yesterday I got your most moving letter and the note too. I was just on my way to Louisville, where I met a musician from Boston who had planned some time ago to come down and go over some songs of mine he had set to music. The songs were biblical "Freedom Songs" and were to have been first presented at the Liturgical Conference this summer at which Martin was to have been present, I understand. The music for them is powerful and they are quite effective. As Dr. Peloquin and I (he is the musician, fairly prominent at least in Catholic circles) went over them, we both agreed that they should not wait until August, but should be presented as soon as possible on TV and as a memorial to Martin. What we really need is a good strong Negro voice—someone like Harry Belafonte. . . . I thought maybe you down there might speak to Belafonte or someone similar about the possibility of doing these songs. I'm sending the music of a couple of them, and also the text of my own poems—of which four out of eight are being used. I'll mark which ones. You and Coretta and anyone else likely to be interested might look them over. The music is somewhat arty and difficult but also basically popular, though not too "churchy." I think the whole project has possibilities. My only difficulty was that even in the August presentation Peloquin was thinking of a white singer. To my mind, that's out. One young Negro tenor was originally very interested and in fact started the whole thing, but Peloquin feels that this man's voice is not strong enough. And Peloquin does not seem to have other contacts.

These have been terrible days for everyone, and God alone knows what is to come. I feel that we have really crossed a definitive line into a more apocalyptic kind of time—the recent years were bitter enough, but mostly as anticipations of what now seems to be realizing itself. We will need a lot of faith and a new vision and courage to move in these new and more bitter realities. . . .

June wrote on April 11 about the funeral. She told how Ralph Abernathy's children asked if it was all right to hate the assassin. Dr. King's two children (Martin and Dexter) both answered: "No, Daddy said not to hate anyone."

In a letter of March 28, 1968, Robert Williams apologized to Merton for his recent letter. He suggested that Peloquin should go ahead with the songs: "Mr. Peloquin has probably worked hard on the songs and he deserves the fruit of his efforts. The poems are too beautiful to stick them away in a closet."

TO ROBERT WILLIAMS   APRIL 1, 1968

Your letter which I received Sunday meant more to me than I can ever say. It is one of the most noble I ever got from anyone. If it made me happy, it was above all because I was relieved to think that the bitterness had gone from your own heart and that I was not causing you pain. I am sorry if there was any harshness in my own letter. . . .

Well, here is the situation. Peloquin has really put out an awful lot of work on the songs. I don't know yet how good it is, but I do realize that we cannot prevent him from producing them without a very serious reason to the contrary. All my own income from the songs will go to your African students. Peloquin also said that he would give half of his income. I don't think this is all going to amount to a very large sum, but I hope it will at least be useful. But in any case, you control the literary rights and anything that comes from the publication of the songs (my text, not the music) will be yours. . . .

APRIL 15, 1968

I know you said you didn't want to hear more about the songs, but there is one development I think you ought to know. I have sent my texts together with the music of two of them to Mrs. Martin Luther King, through a mutual friend [June Yungblut], who is very close to them. I thought there could be no more fitting use for the songs than to have them first presented as a memorial to the martyr for non-violence and civil rights. She is considering this, in the midst of all the other distractions and business by which she is assailed. If the songs can be presented as a small tribute to this greatest of Americans, in this tragic moment, I think you will feel as I do that something worthwhile has come out of our trouble and work after all. . . .

TO FRIENDS   PASCHAL TIME 1968

. . . First of all, the tragic death of Dr. Martin Luther King coincided in a significant way with Passiontide and Easter this year. I was in rather close touch with these events as Dr. King had been tentatively planning to make a retreat here before the "Poor People's March." The day before his death a friend of his and mine [June J. Yungblut] wrote from Atlanta: "Martin is going to Memphis today; he is going cold into a hot situation, and I wish he were going to Gethsemani instead . . ." but it is evident that Dr. King was expecting something and went to meet it with his eyes open. His final speech was certainly prophetic in its way. I believe he felt the best thing he could do would be to lay down his life not only for Black people but for the whole country. He always hoped to preserve the country from senseless violence that would be merely destructive, and may have hoped that sacrifice of his life would bring home to people the need for a fully Christian solution of the grave problems we all face. I believe the Black people understood this better than the white. Too many whites think that non-violence may be all right for Negroes but see no reason to practice it themselves. And of course non-violence has been to some extent abandoned and discredited. It should be remembered that in the rioting that has happened and will continue to happen, there is always violence on *two* sides. Few people seem to realize that most of those killed in riots are Negroes killed by whites, and not the other way round.

Since this assassination the race situation in this country is probably worse, and we do not yet know what the summer will bring: but there is no point in letting ourselves be governed by fear. If we think in terms of objective rights and wrongs, we will see that the Negroes of this country are still trying to get what is due to them, and though the mass media try to make a sensational story out of everything, and thereby distort the perspective, we still must try to look at things as they are. . . .

TO JUNE J. YUNGBLUT   MAY 23, 1968

I am writing this in the awareness that you are in the middle of everything now in the Poor People's March, but the letter will reach you perhaps when things are over, or less active. Meanwhile my prayers are with you and all who have gone to Washington, and especially Coretta and all the others who are leading it. I came close to some of it when I was in New Mexico, and talked to people who had been at the big rally in Albuquerque the day before. I just missed it in Louisville on the way back. . . .

One other thing. Those most moving telegrams you sent (in response to the death of Dr. King). I would very much like to use one of them in *Monks Pond*—the anonymous one from "Humbleness Nobody US Latin," which is to me as moving as the speech of Sacco-Vanzetti. I think it would not be wrong, as the message was anonymous and its intention was to be a sort of public witness. If Coretta would permit it, I want to use this in the next issue of *Monks Pond*. . . .

TO ROBERT WILLIAMS   JULY 16, 1968

. . . You are of course right to say that the failure of your plans, which were so beautiful and idealistic at the start, is partly because you are black. You are right also in saying that no white man can really understand all that a black man has to go through in a racist society. I don't deny that. On the other hand, you must not think that white people have it all the way they like just because they are white. I happen to be able to understand something of the rejection and frustration of black people because I am first of all an orphan and second a Trappist. As an orphan, I went through the business of being passed around from family to family, and being a "ward," and an "object of charitable concern," etc. etc. I know how inhuman and frustrating that can be—being treated as a thing and not as a person. . . .

As a Trappist, I can say I lived for twenty-five years in a situation in which I had NO human and civil rights whatever. Anything I got I had to beg for in an ignominious way. But I also had luck, as some do. I may be a success of sorts, but I can tell you what it amounts to: exactly zero. Sure, you run into a lot of praise, but you run into a lot of criticism, blame, jealousy, hatchet jobs and raw deals. In the end, a successful person is no better off than anybody else, as far as real gains are concerned. He may have a lot of apparent advantages, but they are canceled out by so many other things. Of course, I admit, some people are satisfied with success, a good image, and a fair amount of money. You would not be any more than I am. You are a different kind of person. For that very reason you cannot do the mean and ruthless things that have to be done in the jungle of contemporary life; you are not the kind of person that just ignores the rights of others.

In the end what really matters is not race, or good breaks, or bad breaks (though these are certainly important) but who you are as a person. And if you have real quality as a person (which you do, let me tell you), it does not matter whether the market is interested. The market does not know real quality, it just guesses sales value.

. . . I wanted to try to say what was in my heart. I know it is not adequate and I have no illusions about glossing over the immense difficulties of the world we live in. But ultimately it all gets down to the individual, the person, and to each one's relation with his neighbor. Even if society itself is racist, in the end what is decisive is not that we are black and white but that we are people. And members of our own race can be to us as wolves or tigers—as well as saints and angels. . . .

PART 7

Networking for Peace

The Struggle against War and Other Forms of Violence and Oppression

"As for writing: I don't feel that I can in conscience, at a time like this, go on writing just about things like meditation, though that has its point. . . . I think I have to face the big issues, the life-and-death issues. . . ."

—To Dorothy Day, August 23, 1961

W hen, in the early sixties, Merton began to speak out in a flurry of published works against war and on behalf of peace and the practice of nonviolence, his letter writing played a key role in the effort. Not only did the letters he received keep him informed about the growing threat of war and the emerging peace movement, but the letters he wrote served as a way for him to network for peace and to support the way of nonviolence. Merton himself recognized the potential of his letters on these subjects to promote the peace effort when he mimeographed and distributed collections of his "Cold War Letters" and included some of those letters as "Letters in a Time of Crisis" in *Seeds of Destruction*.

This section features selections from Merton's letters to James H. Forest and Daniel Berrigan as well as excerpts from Merton's correspondence with Dorothy Day, Hildegard Goss-Mayr, Wilbur H. ("Ping") Ferry, and John C. Heidbrink. Together, these letters tell the story of Merton's commitment to peace and nonviolence.

TO JAMES H. FOREST   *James Hendrickson Forest, born in 1941 in Salt Lake City, Utah, was at the age of twenty discharged from the U.S. Navy as a conscientious objector. He joined the staff of the Catholic Worker, which ran a house of hospitality for unemployed and homeless persons. It also published a pacifist magazine,* The Catholic Worker, *of which Forest became editor. For him this was the beginning of a lifelong commitment to peace and nonviolence. He published a number of articles by Merton and several times visited him at Gethsemani. He helped found the Catholic Peace Fellowship (CPF). His correspondence brought him more than eighty letters from Merton.*

AUGUST 9, 1961

... This morning I said the Mass in Time of War. Might as well face it. It is a very good formulary. Nowhere in it are the promises of blessings upon the strong and the unscrupulous or the violent. Only suggestions that we shut up and be humble and stay put and trust in God and hope for a peace that we can use for the good of our souls. It is certainly not a very belligerent Mass, and it asks no one to be struck down. But it does say that we don't have to worry too much about the King of Babylon. Are we very sure that he has his headquarters in Moscow only? ...

OCTOBER 21, 1961

Your letter of the 17th or rather 18th reached me today. I had not received the previous one to which you refer, and so was a bit in the dark, though I did hear about the *America* article [by L. C. McHugh, S.J., defending a people's right to use arms if necessary to prevent neighbors from entering their air-raid shelter] which seemed to me to be in many ways completely scandalous. Not that men renounce the right to defend themselves, but it is a question of emphasis and viewpoint. Are we going to minimize, and fix our eyes entirely on the lowest level of natural ethics, or are we going to be Christians and take the Gospel seriously? This is a matter of extreme importance, because never has the Church and the Christian world (so called) been so grimly and terribly under judgment. Now is the chance for us to be Christians, and it may be the last chance. If we let this go, the world may be destroyed or, more likely, it may be handed over to the secular messianism which will take over the task we have let fall from our hands and perhaps accomplish it with grim and inhuman efficiency, producing universal peace at the price of liberty, intelligence, faith, spirit, and everything that is valuable in man, reducing us to the level of ants and robots. . . .

. . . I do not deny that when one is not able to practice non-violence, violent defense is legitimate and even necessary. But what I do assert is that the Church, the clergy, the Catholic lay apostle, the Catholic teacher, the Catholic intellectual have a serious obligation today to investigate the meaning and the feasibility of non-violent defense not only on the individual but on the national level. If we fail in this obligation we are very probably lost. And we *are failing* in it. . . .

OCTOBER 29, 1961

I want to get this text ["The Machine Gun in the Fallout Shelter"] to you so that you can at least read it. I am trying to get it through the censors if possible for the November issue. I have begged them to be cooperative if possible, but this means nothing. I don't think most of them have the slightest idea of the import of what is taking place, or if they do they have perhaps cultivated a kind of holy callousness that does not seem to me to have much to do with the Gospel of Christ or the spirit of the Church. . . .

. . . He [Abbot James Fox] . . . said it would be all right for me to be a sponsor of the Pax movement in America. I think this is very important and I am very eager to help out. You understand my inevitable limitations, however. . . .

. . . There is one loophole in the censorship statute that leaves me a little liberty of action. When a publication is very small and of very limited influence (and this is not defined), articles for it do not need to be censored. Father Abbot has decided that we can regard the publication of the FOR [Fellowship of Reconciliation] as falling under this category. . . .

. . . Do not worry about the change of title for the articles [from "The Machine Gun in the Fallout Shelter" to "Shelter Ethics"], I understand all right. No problem, as far as I am concerned. I can also understand that since my viewpoint was not precisely that of the editorial policy of *CW*, Dorothy [Day] might want to clarify somewhere along the line. Technically I am not a pure pacifist in theory, though today in practice I don't see how one can be anything else since limited wars (however "just") present an almost certain danger of nuclear war on an all-out scale. It is absolutely clear to me that we are faced with the obligation, both as human beings and as Christians, of striving in every way possible to abolish war. The magnitude of the task cannot be allowed to deter us. Even if it seems impossible, we must still attempt it. This demands of course a spirit of faith. Without the religious dimension, even pacifism and non-violence are relatively meaningless. One cannot have non-violence that makes sense if one does not also have faith in God. This of course complicates matters tremendously, because of the scandal that so many who claim to believe in God enlist Him in their wars. God is always the first one to be drafted, and this is a universal stumbling block. . . .

The letters in reply to the McHugh article are really good. I enjoyed reading that page of *America* [issue of November 25, 1961, giving reactions to the McHugh article], and it made the air seem a little fresher. The off-key note in McHugh's reply, which shows he is a "realist" and thinks the Sermon on the Mount after all sentimental, seems to cinch the argument as far as I am concerned. . . .

DECEMBER 20, 1961

. . . Good news. Fr. Abbot said if I wrote a *letter* any time, it could go in without censorship. This does not mean a flood of eight-page letters, but anyway if I do have anything special to say, you can quote any letter without further formality. . . .

JANUARY 5, 1962

. . . *Commonweal* asked me for an article for Christmas. I sent it to the censor in October. It still hasn't been passed. One censor vetoed it, and it has been in the hands of a third for some time. . . . That is the kind of thing one has to try to be patient with. It is wearying, of course. However, it is all I can offer to compare with what you people are doing to share the lot of the poor. A poor man is one who has to sit and wait and wait and wait, in clinics, in offices, in places where you sign papers, in police stations, etc. And he has nothing to say about it. At least there is this element of poverty for me too. The rest of what we have here isn't that hard or that poor. . . .

[COLD WAR LETTER 25] JANUARY 29, 1962

It is really quite providential that the Peace article ["Nuclear War and Christian Responsibility"] I wrote for the *Commonweal* Christmas issue was held up (by the censors) and is now appearing this week [February 9, 1962], in conjunction with the General Strike for Peace. I do hope it helps even a little bit. Anyway, my heart goes with it, and I am with you all in spirit. . . .

My Mass on February 1st, the Feast of St. Ignatius Martyr of Antioch, will be for all of the strikers everywhere in the world and for all who yearn for a true peace, all who are willing to shoulder the great burden of patiently working, praying and sacrificing themselves for peace. . . . Really we have to pray for a total and profound change in the mentality of the whole world. . . . Hairshirts will not do the trick, though there is no harm in mortifying the flesh. But vastly more important is the complete change of heart and the totally new outlook on the world of man. We have to see our duty to mankind as a whole. . . .

. . . We all have the great duty to realize the deep need for purity of soul, that is to say the deep need to possess in us the Holy Spirit, to be possessed by Him. This takes precedence over everything else. If He lives and works in us, then our activity will be true and our witness will generate love of the truth, even though we may be persecuted and beaten down in apparent incomprehension. . . .

[Cold War Letter 31] February 6, 1962

. . . One of the most problematical questions about non-violence is the inevitable involvement of hidden aggressions and provocations. I think this is especially true when there are a fair proportion of non-religious elements, or religious elements that are not spiritually developed. It is an enormously subtle question, but we have to consider the fact that in its pro-vocative aspect, non-violence may tend to harden the opposition and con-firm people in their righteous blindness. It may even in some cases separate men out and drive them in the other direction, away from us and away from peace. . . .

March 21, 1962

. . . One has to learn to see the significance of one's apparent uselessness and not be driven to frustration by it. The uselessness, the inactivity, the frustration are deliberately assumed as an important part of non-violent resistance. . . .

[Cold War Letter 69] April 29, Low Sunday, 1962

. . . Now here is the ax. For a long time I have been anticipating trouble with the higher Superiors and now I have it. The orders are, no more writ-ing about peace. This is transparently arbitrary and uncomprehending, but doubtless I have to make the best of it. I am hoping to get the book [*Peace in the Post-Christian Era*] through on the ground that it is already writ-ten. Of course the order does not apply to unpublished writing, but I have to be careful even with privately circulated stuff, like the mimeographed material. So for one thing please do not under any circumstances publish anywhere anything I write to you on this subject or on non-violence etc. It will only make it impossible to do whatever still remains possible. Besides, the order is not yet absolutely beyond appeal and I can perhaps obtain some slight modification of it. But in substance I am being silenced on the subject of war and peace. . . . It reflects an insensitivity to Christian and ecclesiastical values, and to the real sense of the monastic vocation. The reason given is that this is not the right kind of work for a monk, and that it "falsifies the monastic message." Imagine that: the thought that a monk might be deeply enough concerned with the issue of nuclear war to voice a protest against the arms race, is supposed to bring the monastic life into *disrepute*. Man, I would think that it might just possibly salvage a last shred of repute for an institution that many consider to be dead on its feet. . . .

. . . The monk is the one supposedly attuned to the inner spiritual dimension of things. If he hears nothing, and says nothing, then the renewal [of the Church] as a whole will be in danger and may be completely sterilized. But these authoritarian minds believe that the function of the monk is not to see or hear any new dimension, simply to support the already existing viewpoints precisely insofar as and because they are defined for him by somebody else. . . . The function of the monk . . . then becomes simply to affirm his total support of officialdom. He has no other function, then except perhaps to pray for what he is told to pray for: namely the purposes and objectives of an ecclesiastical bureaucracy. The monastery as dynamo concept goes back to this. The monk is there to generate spiritual power that will justify over and over again the already predecided rightness of the officials above him. . . .

Now you will ask me: How do I reconcile obedience, true obedience (which is synonymous with love), with a situation like this? Shouldn't I just blast the whole thing wide open, or walk out, or tell them to jump in the lake?

Let us suppose for the sake of argument that this was not completely excluded. Why would I do this? For the sake of the witness for peace? For the sake of witnessing to the truth of the Church, in its reality, as against this figment of the imagination? Simply for the sake of blasting off and getting rid of the tensions and frustrations in my own spirit and feeling honest about it? . . .

I am where I am. I have freely chosen this state, and have freely chosen to stay in it when the question of a possible change arose. If I am a disturbing element, that is all right. I am not making a point of being that, but simply of saying what my conscience dictates and doing so without seeking my own interest. This means accepting such limitations as may be placed on me by authority, not merely because it is placed on me by authority, and not because I may or may not agree with the ostensible reasons why the limitations are imposed, but out of love for God who is using these things to attain an end which I myself cannot at the moment see or comprehend. . . .

[CA.] JUNE 14, 1962

. . . I appealed the case of my book to the General of the Order, but he repeated his order firmly and clearly: I am to publish nothing more on war and peace. I was denounced to him by an American abbot who was told by a friend in the intelligence service that I was writing for a "communist-controlled publication" (*The Catholic Worker*). You didn't know you were communist-controlled, did you? . . .

Forest wrote that he thought Merton, in his efforts to please the censors, was bending over backward and not really saying what he meant.

JULY 7, 1962

Thanks for your long letter, and the remarks on the book. That just goes to show what a mess one gets into trying to write a book that will get through the censors, and at the same time say something. I was bending in all directions to qualify every statement and balance everything off . . . In the long run the result is about zero. . . .

Gordon Zahn is quite right about it being the layman's responsibility, and about the fact that laymen have the leeway. After all, there is not that much the bishops can do to you guys. . . .

. . . We are mimeographing an enlarged edition of the "Cold War Letters," and I will send you a few. No objections to it going to Europe where people are more intelligent about the peace issue, generally, than here. . . .

I am joining the FOR [Fellowship of Reconciliation] officially, anyway, as a rather obvious thing to do. Reading a ms. of Father [Alfred] Delp who was killed by Hitler. A tremendous document. It will come out next year, I think, and you will see. . . .

NOVEMBER 7, 1962

. . . The ambiguity of so many Catholics on the war question, or worse still the frank belligerency of the majority of them, is a very serious symptom of spiritual sickness in our society. It is a mark of the failure of Catholics to meet the spiritual challenge of the times. . . .

The real issue is then the recognition of the individual conscience to assess the *facts* of the case, as well as the principle of the just war. To say that the clergy can tell the laity they are obliged to fight because the Pentagon or *Time* magazine says so, this is to me a total default of Christianity, a surrender to the worst kind of secularism, a handing over of the Christian conscience in servitude to nefarious and anonymous secular power. And we have good reason to believe that in the exercise of that power the morality to which we hold is ignored and sometimes derided. It is certain that some of those who have the greatest power, some of the button pressers, frankly consider the moral issue "irrelevant" in nuclear war. All that matters is to "get them first." To make the Christian conscience subservient to the decisions of such people is a crass betrayal. . . .

JANUARY 17, 1963

. . . I think it would be good if the non-violent movement could get a more and more solid foundation, and deeper roots, spiritual roots. . . . We have really got to work on the theological and spiritual bases for *ahimsa* and tie them in with the Gospel in a way that leaves no doubt as to the Christian *obligation* in this regard. . . .

... Hence the importance of non-violent people who are really conscientious objectors not only to nuclear war but to *everything* that leads to it or goes with it in the same general atmosphere of violence and criminality. I think the perspectives of the non-violent have to be enlarged in all directions, so that it becomes a genuine and profound spiritual movement, and a force for *life* in a really rotting and corrupt world. ...

... I am happy about the encyclical [*Pacem in Terris*] saying clearly that it is "impossible for war to be an instrument of justice" in the context of nuclear armaments. The Pope is lucky he does not have to be approved by the censors of our Order, he would never get by them! ...

... I think I told you I wrote to the Abbot General and said it is a good thing Pope John didn't have to get his encyclical through our censors: and could I now start up again? I will let you know what happens. ...

... Yes, the loss of Pope John is great, but he did an astonishing work in four and a half years. The Holy Spirit really moved in him, and I hope this will be true at the conclave and in the next Pope, whoever he may be. I have always liked Montini, but I suppose he has had people against him from way back. Lercaro might be good. But I think it would probably be best if we got another like Pope John, a dark horse who was not thought to be too progressive. ...

... A group of Hibakusha [Hiroshima victims on tour for peace] came through here Saturday. I had them up at the house and we talked a bit but they were rushed away before we could really get down to anything interesting. Yet they are the people I have most enjoyed meeting for a long time. Rare ones that seemed to be worth talking to. I read them a poem (of which

I do not yet have copies but I will send one when I do) and one of them, an old lady, very sweet and quiet, left me a folded paper crane. I loved them.

. . . I am reading some fantastic stuff on Islam by Louis Massignon, and Buddhist books which I now have to review for [the] magazine of the Order. I am reviewer in chief of Buddhist, Hindu, etc. etc., bks. Something I would not have expected from our magazine a few years ago, and who knows it may yet get sat on. We shall see. . . .

JULY 22, 1964

. . . Because a few people in America want power and wealth, a lot of Vietnamese, Chinese, and Americans have been and will be sacrificed. It is a complete travesty of justice and right and liberty. I do not think it can meet any of the requirements of the traditional "just war." Please keep me posted on this. . . .

SEPTEMBER 1, 1964

. . . I know the situation in Vietnam is completely poisonous. In a way it makes me much more disgusted and depressed than the tests and so on did because here the folly of it and the crass, brutal untruth of it is spelled out so much more obviously in so much more human detail. The injustice of it is so flagrant and so absurd, and what is worst is the *refusal* to see it. . . .

OCTOBER 2, 1964

Thanks for the letters and all the things sent. I am sorry I forgot about the name business. I was thinking about it, and actually I want to help, so I suppose you might as well use my name for the Peace Fellowship along with the others if it is any use. The only thing is that I do agree in feeling that it is sort of a useless gesture. . . .

OCTOBER 21, 1964

. . . I am so happy about Martin Luther King [getting the Nobel Peace Prize]. That is magnificent and I think it will do much for the race situation, in that it will restore a lot of confidence in his leadership. Or at least I hope so. . . .

*From November 18 to 20, a meeting took place at Gethsemani for
leaders in the peace movement. Forest was among those present for
the meeting.*

DECEMBER 9, 1964

... Living more in solitude I see more clearly how real it is that there are
so to speak nests in our minds, where death hatches all kinds of eggs. One of
the great and awful realities of the time is this infestation of man by a very
active and very prolific force of evil. ...

MARCH 13, 1965

Thanks for sending along the clippings about Selma. There does not
seem to be much hope of very encouraging news these days. I suppose this
sort of thing is going to drag on for a long time, now here and now there.
As to Vietnam, the Pentagon crowd really seems to want a regular war out
there, but there is not much taste for it among the people as far as I can see,
so this may be holding things back a little. All we need is the sinking of the
Maine or another Pearl Harbor. ...

[TELEGRAM] NOVEMBER 11, 1965

Just heard about suicide of Roger La Porte. While I do not hold Catholic
Peace Fellowship responsible for the tragedy current developments in peace
movement make it impossible for me to continue as sponsor for fellowship.
Please remove my name from list of sponsors. Letter follows.

NOVEMBER 11, 1965

This is a bitter letter to have to write. This morning, after receiving the
news of the suicide of Roger La Porte, which I heard of quite by chance, I
had to send you a telegram asking to remove my name from the list of sponsors of the CPF. I know of course that the CPF is not encouraging people to
burn themselves up. Unfortunately, however, the CPF is in the middle of a
peace movement in which, rightly or wrongly, with good intentions or not I
don't know, there is something that looks to me to be a little pathological.

As you know, I am not sufficiently well informed to make clear judgments
of this or that policy, for instance the burning of draft cards. Certainly protest

is called for, and it may very well be that this precise form of protest is what is called for at the moment. I do not know. Maybe I am wrong in thinking that it is harming the peace movement rather than helping it, and that it is in fact fanning up the war fever rather than abating it.

But this suicide, coming on top of the other one in Washington and of so many other things which are disturbing and equivocal, leads me to make the regretful decision that I cannot accept the present spirit of the movement as it presents itself to me. . . .

. . . The whole thing gives off a very different smell from the Gandhian movement, the non-violent movement in France and the non-violence of Martin Luther King. Jim, there is something wrong here. I think there is something demonic at work in it. This suicide of a Catholic ex-seminarian (I was told) does not make sense in terms of a Christian peace movement. . . .

. . . I am strictly out of touch with what you are doing, and yet my name is being used, and by its use kids are likely to get drawn into something that seems to me to have something very bad around the edges of it. I have no way of helping anyone to stay with what is good and avoid what is bad, I cannot be there and talk or advise. Hence there remains only one thing for me to do, that is to withdraw my name from the list of sponsors. So please take me off the list.

The spirit of this country at the present moment is to me terribly disturbing. . . . This whole atmosphere is crazy, not just the peace movement, everybody. There is in it such an air of absurdity and moral void, even where conscience and morality are invoked (as they are by everyone). The joint is going into a slow frenzy. The country is nuts.

For people to avail themselves of their right to conscientious objection which the Council has, thank God, finally acknowledged: that is what ought to be done. Instead, this business of burning oneself alive. What in heaven's name is the idea of that? It will only neutralize all the work that has been done and all the gains that have been made. What on earth are the American bishops going to make out of that?

I am sorry, Jim, I must ask you to take my name off that list. Naturally I will do anything I can to be of help, if you need me for anything. This does not mean a complete repudiation of the CPF or anything of the sort. . . .

... If I thought of getting my name off your list of sponsors, it was chiefly because of the embarrassment caused me by the inevitable fact that I am automatically blamed for whatever is done in your area of the peace movement, which means in practice for anything done by a Catholic Worker member too.

I am perfectly willing to leave the thing hanging in the balance for a while, so as not to create the impression that I am publicly denouncing you or throwing a wrench in your good work. But in any case I must sooner or later get in a position where it is clear that I am *not* accountable for what my friends do, and that I don't necessarily advocate all that is done by them.

Do you see my position? I think it would be clear and acceptable to all if it were understood that I was withdrawing from all such involvements, formally, without repudiating anyone personally. And without repudiating the movement. . . .

. . . All I ask is that people should never be led to assume that I am personally behind a specific project or demonstration inspired by a recent event of which I may have no knowledge. In other words, I am behind the pastoral aims of the CPF all the way, and insofar as you are implementing the teaching of the Church on peace. . . .

. . . I still do not think that the dramatic and provocative type of witness is what we most need now, in the sphere of Catholic peace witness. On the contrary, I think what we need is massive and undramatic apostolic work to clarify the Church's teaching and get it thoroughly known. . . .

. . . The next thing is I think to begin a study of the pervasive violence that is everywhere in our thinking. This is the thing that I think is most dangerous, and humanly speaking I think it makes one almost despair of this nation being a peaceful one: we are a nation addicted to images of violence, brutality, sadism, self-affirmation by arrogance, aggression, and so on. . . .

On February 15 Forest wrote that he was in a bleak mood; no one seemed to be listening to CPF: "I feel like an ant climbing a cliff, and even worse, for in the distance there seems to be an avalanche. . . . Perhaps you have some thoughts that would help?"

FEBRUARY 21, 1966

Thanks for the letter and for the awful, and illuminating, enclosure. I can well understand your sense of desperation. And the "bleak mood." And also I am glad that you wrote about it. As you say, there are no clear answers, and you can guess that I don't have magic solutions for bleak moods: if I did I would use them on my own which are habitually pretty bleak too. But that is just part of this particular life and I don't expect much else.

Actually, I would say one thing that probably accounts for your feelings, besides all the objective and obvious reasons, you are doubtless tired. I don't know whether you are physically tired or not but you have certainly been pouring your emotional and psychic energy into the CPF and all that it stands for, and you have been sustained by hopes that are now giving out. Hence the reaction. Well, the first thing is that you have to go through this kind of reaction periodically, learn to expect it and cope with it when it comes, don't do things that precipitate it, without necessity (you will always have to).

And then this: do not depend on the hope of results. When you are doing the sort of work you have taken on, essentially an apostolic work, you may have to face the fact that your work will be apparently worthless and even achieve no result at all, if not perhaps results opposite to what you expect. As you get used to this idea you start more and more to concentrate not on the results but on the value, the rightness, the truth of the work itself. And there too is a great deal has to be gone through, as gradually you struggle less and less for an idea and more and more for specific people. The range tends to narrow down, but it gets much more real. In the end, as you yourself mention in passing, it is the reality of personal relationships that saves everything.

You are fed up with words, and I don't blame you. I am nauseated by them sometimes. I am also, to tell the truth, nauseated with ideals and with causes. This sounds like heresy, but I think you will understand what

I mean. It is so easy to get engrossed with ideas and slogans and myths that in the end one is left holding the bag, empty, with no trace of meaning left in it. . . .

This country is SICK, man. It is one of the sickest things that has happened. People are fed on myths, they are stuffed up to the eyes with illusions. They CAN'T think straight. They have a modicum of good will, and some of them have a whole lot of it, but with the mental bombardment everybody lives under, it is just not possible to see straight, no matter where you are looking. The average everyday "Catlick" is probably in worse shape than a lot of others. He has in his head a few principles of faith which lend no coherence whatever to his life. No one has ever sought any coherence from him or given him the idea that he needed any. All he has been asked to do has been to measure up to a few simple notions about sexual morality (which he may or may not quite make, but anyway he knows where he stands—or falls on his face) and he has been taught that the cross and sacrifice in his life mean in practice going off to war every twenty years or so. He has done this with exemplary, unquestioning generosity, and has reaped the results: a corresponding brutalization, which is not his fault and which he thinks has something to do with being a real human being. In this whole area of war and peace, no matter what the Council may have said about it the average layman and the average priest are all alike conditioned by this mentality. Furthermore, when it is a question of a kind of remote box score of casualties which gives meaning to life each day, they no longer think of the casualties as people, it is just a score. Also they don't want to think of them as people, they want *casualties,* they want somebody to get it, because they have been brutalized and this is a fully legitimate way of indulging the brutality that has been engendered in them. It is not only for country, it is even for God. . . .

So the next step in the process is for you to see that your own thinking about what you are doing is crucially important. . . . All the good that you will do will come not from you but from the fact that you have allowed yourself, in the obedience of faith, to be used by God's love. Think of this more and gradually you will be free from the need to prove yourself, and you can be more open to the power that will work through you without your knowing it.

The great thing after all is to live, not to pour out your life in the service of a myth: and we turn the best things into myths. If you can get free from the domination of causes and just serve Christ's truth, you will be able to do more and will be less crushed by the inevitable disappointments. Because I see nothing whatever in sight but much disappointment, frustration, and confusion. I hope we can avoid a world war: but do we deserve to? . . .

NOVEMBER 16, 1966

. . . You are right, Jim, about all the "hate LBJ" stuff. The thing this Vietnam war is proving is that this whole country is rotten with violence and hate and frustration and this means the peaceniks as much as everybody else. We just don't know what peace and love *mean*. The only ones who have really done anything are Martin Luther King and those who worked so hard as it in the South—and a few others who have tried here and there in various ways and for various causes. . . .

FEBRUARY 23, 1967

. . . I am convinced that now is the time for CPF to really catch on if it is going to. This is the *kairos*. It must not be missed. This is the moment to connect with the people all over the place who are potentially interested and get them doing something.

Get them specifically talking and acting where they are, and explaining the fundamental of a Catholic peace movement in the simplest and most universal terms: *Pacem in Terris,* the Council on war, [Austrian conscientious objector Franz] Jaegerstaetter, Pope Paul, etc. . . .

And then the moral issue spelled out: this is a world in which power rules by indiscriminate nihilistic terror and depends on the cooperation of "ordinary decent people" to do it, and the "ordinary decent people" come through with flying colors, giving their docility and even their lives, in order that brutality may continue and grow worse—threatening the survival of the human race itself. . . .

JUNE 17, 1967

. . . Thanks for your last letter. I am glad everything went off all right, and I was with you in spirit on Pentecost which was a big day down here as my old friend Dan Walsh was suddenly ordained, in his sixties, with all sorts of dispensations, and there was a lot of celebrating. In fact I celebrated on too much champagne, which is a thing a Trappist rarely gets to do, but I did a very thorough job. At one point in the afternoon I remember looking up and focusing rather uncertainly upon four faces of nuns sitting in a row looking at me in a state of complete scandal and shock. Another pillar of the Church had fallen. . . .

APRIL 6, 1968

. . . Terrible about Martin Luther King [assassinated April 4]. But I guess it was expected. I almost have the feeling he *wanted* it: even get the temptation to think that in a kind of desperation he realized that martyrdom was the most efficacious thing left for him. That the March wouldn't work. . . .

AUGUST 5, 1968

. . . I'd be interested in your piece on the spiritual roots of revolution. For my part—as usual I am half in touch and half out of it—I hear a lot of political talk about revolution coming in and it sounds highly irresponsible and calculated to do nothing but get a lot of people's heads knocked off for no purpose whatever. More and more I see the thing in terms of a kind of post-political eschatology which in any case I cannot articulate. . . .

SEPTEMBER 1968

From Redwoods, California

We are at the meeting at Redwoods in an atmosphere of love and peace. Thinking much of you and praying for you. Pray for us.

TO DANIEL BERRIGAN   *Daniel J. Berrigan entered the Jesuits and taught at Le Moyne College in Syracuse, New York (1957–63). One of the founders of the Catholic Peace Fellowship, he participated in a number of antiwar demonstrations. In 1968 he joined his brother Philip and seven others in the burning of draft records in Catonsville, Maryland. Convicted in October 1968, he went underground for a time. He was finally apprehended by federal agents in*

August 1970. Paroled in February 1972, he resides in New York City and is still very much involved in the cause of peace and social justice.

NOVEMBER 10, 1961

I am very glad to hear that the Pax movement is getting started in this country and that you are part of it. So am I. We are perhaps very late. Nor should it be regarded as much of a consolation that we are able in some way to salve our consciences by doing something at this hour, even though ineffectual. We must desire to be effective. The greatness of the task is appalling. At moments it seems we are in the middle of a total apostasy, an almost total apostasy from Christ and His teaching. It is not comforting to read the prophets in our night Office these days.

With New Directions I am trying to get up a little paperback anthology of good strong articles by all kinds of people about peace. Can you suggest anything? I am getting together things like that Jerome Frank article on "Breaking the Thought Barrier," something by Erich Fromm, Lewis Mumford. . . .

Next year you and some other peace people must come down, and we must get together a bit. Do you think you can do this—in the spring, perhaps, or the early summer? . . .

DECEMBER 7, 1961

. . . I have asked Father Abbot if we could have you down to give some talks to the novices and students next summer. He said yes. Hence I am inviting you to come down and give us three talks at least, one a day, on perhaps the main problems confronting the Church in America at the present moment. And what ought to be done about them. . . .

MARCH 10, 1962

My correspondence is a kind of Sisyphus act: rolling the boulder up the hill and then having it roll down again. The boulder is way ahead of me at the moment and I am only just getting around to your letter(s). . . . I am preparing a bunch of talks on the Prophets and in doing this I am getting much deeper into the Bible. Frankly I have been inhibited by the fact that for a long time there was nothing but Catholic material on the Bible around the monastery. Now that we have much of the best of Protestant books available, it is a different story. . . .

I am not sure I know what you mean about the Benedictine approach in prayer. . . . If you mean the Cassian-like desert solitary stuff, this is Benedictine in its way, Cistercian in its way, I don't know what it is. But really it is Oriental and when seen in the Oriental context, I think such objections as you may have to it, vanish. There is an absolute need for the solitary, bare, dark, beyond-concept, beyond-thought, beyond-feeling type of prayer. Not of course for everybody. But unless that dimension is there in the Church somewhere, the whole caboodle lacks life and light and intelligence. It is a kind of hidden, secret, unknown stabilizer, and a compass too. About this I have no hesitations and no doubts, because it is my vocation; about one's own vocation, after it has been tested and continues to be tested, one can say in humility that he knows. Knows what? That it is willed by God, insofar as in it one feels the hand of God pressing down on him. Unmistakably. . . .

JUNE 15, 1962

. . . My peace writings have reached an abrupt halt. Told not to do any more on that subject. Dangerous, subversive, perilous, offensive to pious ears, and confusing to good Catholics who are all at peace in the nice idea that we ought to wipe Russia off the face of the earth. Why get people all stirred up? . . .

In a letter of June 14, 1963, Berrigan wrote of his desire to go to Birmingham, Alabama, to take part in a civil rights demonstration. His Superiors were opposed to his going. In the letter he muses about the question of civil disobedience and Church disobedience. "Is this wild talk?" he asks.

JUNE 25, 1963

. . . I am still not able to give a final and satisfactory answer one way or the other. I think that such an answer is not yet possible. We are going to have to grope our way with a great deal of prudence (the supernatural kind) and attention to grace. I will just jot down some of the different aspects of the matter as they occur to me.

1. Most important of all: you do have to consider the continuity of your work as a living unit. You must be careful not to rupture that continuity in

a violent and drastic way without having an exceptionally grave reason and a rather evident sign that this is required precisely of *you*. . . .

2. What are the reasons for wanting to get in there with the movement for racial justice? Setting aside the obvious and indisputably valuable ones which stem from personal conscience and the need to affirm an honest and loyally Christian position, there is also the matter of bearing witness to the fact that the Holy Roman Catholic Church is not, much as one might be tempted to think so, ossified and committed to the status quo, but that she is really alive and means to do something about justice. . . .

3. Certainly I think that the only thing to do is to scout around and canvass the best Catholic opinion in Europe. Get in touch with Fr. Régamey, O.P., who has been slapped down a lot about the peace issue and is into non-violence and probably civil disobedience. . . .

4. One has to consider that no matter how far one goes now, it is not going to be far enough. I mean that the racial movement is entering a revolutionary and perhaps soon violent stage. Hence to build your hopes around the kind of actions that would have been fully valid up to recently, when they involved a very drastic separation, is to cut yourself off when you need to be able to hang on to something. We need to see what is coming next, I am afraid. I don't mean prosperity about [sic] the corner. I mean violent revolution around the corner. . . . I really think that at the present moment you can do more by talking and writing than by anything else. . . .

What is the contemplative life if one doesn't listen to God in it? What is the contemplative life if one becomes oblivious to the rights of men and the truth of God in the world and in His Church? Answer: listen to the Superior and shut up because the Superior is God. My own Abbot always manages to show just enough good will and tolerance on the crucial issues to keep me hesitant about the next drastic step; but I think that in my own case everything indicates my staying put and waiting. Nothing else is definite enough and writing does get someplace. When it gets past censors or around them. . . .

MAY 18, 1964

. . . Other day a group of Hibakusha, survivors of the atomic bombing at Hiroshima, stopped here. Such good, beautiful, beat-up people. I think they are being well received on their peace pilgrimage. . . .

... I have more hope for the intellectuals of South and Latin America than for almost anyone. There are great hopes of life and truth there and a real freedom of spirit, a real "spirituality" and not this phony curled-up-in-the-shell stuff. ...

AUGUST 4, 1964

... Really I have been blessed with special graces. So I should complain? However at the same time I realize that I am about at the end of some kind of line. What line? What is the trolley I am probably getting off? The trolley is a special kind of hope. The streetcar of expectation, of proximately to be fulfilled desire of betterment of things becoming more intelligible. ... Point one, things are not going to get better. Point two, things are going to get worse. ... Point three, I don't need to be on the trolley anyway. ... You can call the trolley anything you like. I have got off it. You can call the trolley a form of religious leprosy if you like. It is burning out. In a lot of sweat and pain if you like but it is burning out for real. ... As a priest I am a burnt-out case, repeat, burnt-out case. So burnt out that the question of standing and so forth becomes irrelevant. I just continue to stand there where I was hit by the bullet. And I will continue to stand there, saying Mass. Not that Mass doesn't mean a thousand times more. You know what I mean. But I have been shot dead and the situation is somehow different. I have no priestly ax to grind with anyone or about anything, monastic either. This has got a bit of burning out to do yet, though. The funny thing is that I will probably continue to write books. And word will go round about how they got this priest who was shot and they got him stuffed sitting up at a desk propped up with books and writing books, this book machine that was killed. I am waiting to fall over and it may take about ten more years of writing. When I fall over, it will be a big laugh because I wasn't there at all. ...

I am sick up to the teeth and beyond the teeth, up to the eyes and beyond the eyes, with all forms of projects and expectations and statements and programs and explanations of anything, especially explanations about where we are all going, because where we are all going is where we went a long time ago, over the falls. We are in a new river and we don't know it. ...

NOVEMBER 11, 1964

Could you be prepared to more or less lead a discussion at one of the sessions? General topic: spiritual root of protest. Take any angle you like. I will give it from monastic-desert viewpoint.

The meeting took place at the Abbey of Gethsemani from Wednesday, November 18, to Friday, November 20, 1964. It was apparently a bit more structured than Merton originally intended. The guidelines he eventually proposed included: (1) the topic: "Our common grounds for religious dissent and commitment in the face of injustice and disorder"; and (2) a structure for the meeting: "It is suggested that at each of our meetings someone act as leader of the discussion, after himself starting off with a talk on any aspect of the question that seems relevant to him. E.g., Wednesday morning: T. Merton, 'The Monastic Protest: The Voice of the Desert'; Thursday morning, A.J. Muste; Thursday afternoon, John H. Yoder; Friday morning, Fr. Daniel Berrigan, S.J."

FEBRUARY 26, 1965

. . . Things are moving along quietly and in a certain amount of confusion, but with the Holy Spirit I hope making sense underneath it all. It is definite that I am to be allowed a chance to try a crack at real hermit life. That will be after I have finished out the year as novice master. Meanwhile I am in the cottage a lot more, and actually living pretty much as a hermit right now, except to come down for work in the novitiate and for some of the offices. I know I can cook, anyway. So provided enough cans of beans are sent my way, I can probably survive. . . .

On October 15, 1965, David Miller, a young Catholic Worker who had been a student of Berrigan's at Le Moyne College, defied Selective Service law and burned his draft card. Less than a month later, on November 6, 1965, Roger La Porte, also a Catholic Worker, immolated himself on the steps of the United Nations Building as a protest against the war in Vietnam. Merton was very disturbed by this "suicide" and sent telegrams to Jim Forest and Dorothy Day. In the telegram to Jim Forest he asked that his name be removed from the list of sponsors of the Catholic Peace Fellowship. Daniel Berrigan celebrated a memorial service for La Porte, describing La Porte's action as a proclamation of life. Under pressure from Cardinal Spellman, Berrigan was "exiled" to South America.

NOVEMBER 19, 1965

Today your letter came, with one from Jim and also one from Dorothy Day. It was a great relief to hear your human voices. I don't think you have any idea what a distorted and kooky picture of things I have been getting here. More than ever I am dependent on fragments and bits of gossip that blow in the window, and what had been blowing in lately came on winds of much alarm from people who were very disturbed by everything. On top of that the tragic death of Roger La Porte. I will write to Jim and tell him of the things I am sorry for having done, the first being the very unreasonable act of immediately sending that telegram, as a kind of emotional reaction. It was a reflex of shock. . . .

In any case let me be clear about this: I really don't mean to blame the Catholic Peace Fellowship or to "blame" anyone. Jim's letter and enclosures threw a lot of sane light on the situation, and cleared up a lot of my questions. Certainly it never was and never will be a question of a personal repudiation of Jim, Tom, etc. . . . Thanks for your letter and for the moving, difficult words at the liturgy for Roger. Don't think I am blind to the great spirit of charity and understanding that is evident in all of you, in all this. It is really very striking. It gives me hope that you can bear with me in my own difficulties and lunacies. And really I think you don't need me that much. I am pretty sure that I have outlived my active usefulness and that I can serve you much better by being a halfway decent hermit. . . .

FEBRUARY 14, 1966

. . . The problem of authority and obedience has to be handled with delicacy and understanding. For many reasons. First of all there is a lot of emotional power pent up in lay people and just ordinary frustrated religious and it is looking for an outlet. Just an outlet. And this is not enough. What is demanded is a real renewal. . . .

While in fact there are a lot of Superiors who think themselves infallible, and are absolutely incapable of understanding what it means to really find out what their subjects need and desire (they consult only yes-men or people who have made the grade by never rocking any boats), there is a new bunch coming up that sincerely wants to help change things, but obviously can't do everything they would like to do either. And then there are the good Joes who want to go along wherever the Church seems to be going even if they don't really understand what it is all about. If all these are treated as if they were purely and simply reactionary tyrants, then there will be a real mess for sure. In your position, if you really clarify a true and indisputably Christian position, these open-minded Superiors will give you credit for it, even though the others may play every kind of dirty trick in the book. The moment of truth will come when you will have to resist the arbitrary and reactionary use of authority in order to save the real concept of authority and obedience, in the line of renewal. This will take charismatic grace. And it is not easy to know when one is acting "charismatically" when one is surrounded with a great deal of popular support on one side and nonsensical opposition on the other. . . .

. . . In either case let us work for the Church and for people, not for ideas and programs. . . .

SEPTEMBER 18, 1966

. . . As you know I am supposed to be cut off as to communications from M. but maybe you could take care of the enclosed—I'd be most grateful. Going back to the possibility of your coming down, I see the 13th is a Thursday and I was thinking in terms of weekend. But if you are here Friday 14th that will be great. Stay over Saturday too if you want. . . .

In the fall of 1967 Berrigan was invited to become associate director of United Religious Work at Cornell University. He was asked to teach a seminar on nonviolence and religious traditions. He wrote asking Merton for help in planning this seminar.

Here is some stuff I dug out of the pile. Not much, if any, about non-violence but some on Zen and so on. I'll have the bookstores send along *Mystics and Zen Masters*. Not much specifically on non-violence there but one essay is kind of background for it and might be of use: "Pilgrimage to Crusade." . . .

. . . I'm glad you're at Cornell. It's a good place. Stay away from Catlicks, they are poison. . . .

Reaction to the airmail special about Phil [Berrigan] and the group that wants to get violent [toward "idolatrous" things, not persons]. This will help me clarify my own ideas too. . . .

a. Ethically and evangelically we are getting toward the place where we have to be able to define our limits. I don't say violence against property is off-limits. It certainly seems to me that killing people *is*. But if it comes to burning buildings, then people are going to be in danger and whoever is involved is going to be partly responsible for people getting destroyed even on his own side in a way that the non-violent resister would not be responsible. . . .

b. Politically: are we just getting involved in a fake revolution of badly mixed-up disaster inviting people who are willing to do anything absurd and irrational simply to mess things us, and to mess them up especially for the well-meaning "idealists" who want to run along proving that they are such real good hip people?

c. Psychologically: how nuts is the whole damn business?

In my opinion the job of the Christian is to try to give an example of sanity, independence, human integrity, good sense, as well as Christian love and wisdom, against all establishments and all mass movements and all current fashions which are merely mindless and hysterical. . . . The most popular and exciting thing at the moment is not necessarily the best choice.

I don't say any of this comes anywhere near applying to the situation Phil speaks of, I have no real idea whether that is sane or nutty: I am just talking in terms of the whole situation judged by the smell of the smog that reaches me down here. . . .

NOVEMBER 27, 1967

. . . Here is a little background on present conditions here. The present Abbot is retiring. No idea who the next one will be, but I want to give him every possible chance to be different. In particular I want to see if he will not be a lot more open than this one about letting me get a little more freedom of movement, which I could certainly use to advantage. . . .

. . . Trouble about the Abbot who is retiring here is that he will stay around and continue to influence things indirectly. He has a very snappy-looking hermitage going up on a distant hill. It is out in moonshine country, too. Place where the local boys have orgies, and you find all the bushes full of beer cans with bullet holes through them. . . .

FEBRUARY 8, 1968

: . . Looking at the thing from my own viewpoint, and having given it some thought: if I had a choice and had to decide it myself, I would also be against any form of public appearance. . . . I think it is necessary for me to stay out of the lecture circuit and campus appearances, much more some of the other things (N.Y. appearances, etc.) that would necessarily follow. I don't think I can do what God and the Gospel demand of me personally unless I maintain the special kind of conditions I have been chosen for, that have been wished on me, and that I myself have chosen and prefer.

As regards peace movements, etc.: my job continues to be putting it on paper as best I can, I think, and, by letter or otherwise, helping individual C.O.'s with advice. In this last connection I want to maintain a kind of clarity, focused on the right and duty of a priest to give such advice even to people who "resist" the law, and that giving such advice does *not* constitute civil disobedience, but the ordinary job of any priest. It seems to me that this point is very important indeed and it may be in danger of getting lost. One of my own functions, as I see it, is to keep it from getting lost. That helping a man form his own conscience is a priest's duty, and how the man forms his conscience even if it is formed in a way that is socially unacceptable, does not alter the right and duty of the priest to help him follow his conscience. And that society has no business whatever interfering in this area. Which is why it must remain clearly a private and personal affair. . . .

A month later, on May 17, 1968, Daniel and Philip Berrigan and seven others broke into the Selective Service offices in the Knights of Columbus building in Catonsville, Maryland. They seized the 1-A files of potential draftees from several cabinets, carried them to the parking lot, and burned them in wire baskets with napalm made from instructions given in a military manual.

The nine were imprisoned, then released on bail. The trial was set for October 5, 1968. Philip Berrigan wrote to Merton—who was in Alaska at the time—asking him to be present as a witness at the trial.

TO PHILIP BERRIGAN   SEPTEMBER 30, 1968

Your letter finally caught up with me in Alaska, but I am moving on.

Impossible to get to trial. I am going to India in October and am busy raising money for it now. I wish you all luck. . . .

TO DOROTHY DAY   *One of the truly influential persons in the history of American Catholicism in the twentieth century, Dorothy Day exercised a prophetic role in the American Church, combining a radical position on social issues with a conservative and unquestioning theology of Church and sacraments. A deep concern for the poor and needy led her and Peter Maurin to found the Catholic Worker movement. Her total commitment to nonviolence was a source of inspiration for many, including Thomas Merton, who often wrote for* The Catholic Worker, *the journal she founded. His reverent affection for her finds expression in his letters to her. At one point Merton wrote, "If there were no Catholic Worker and such forms of witness, I would never have joined the Catholic Church."*

AUGUST 17, 1960

. . . We should in a way fear for our perseverance because there is a big hole in us, an abyss, and we have to fall though it into emptiness, but the Lord will catch us. Who can fall through the center of himself into that nothingness and not be appalled? But the Lord will catch us. He will catch you without fail and take you to His Heart. Because of the *prayers of the poor.* You are the richest woman in America spiritually, with such prayers behind you. You cannot fail even if you try to. The mighty prayers of the poor will embrace you with invincible strength and mercy and bear you in spite of everything into the Heart of God. Those prayers are His own arms. I have immense faith in the prayers of the poor: ask them for me too please. God bless you, in Christ. . . .

AUGUST 23, 1961

. . . God always makes it possible for me to say what seems to be necessary, and hence there is no question that I am completely in His hands where I am and that I should therefore continue as I am doing. But why this awful silence and apathy on the part of Catholics, clergy, hierarchy, lay people on this terrible issue on which the very continued existence of the human race depends? . . .

. . . As for writing: I don't feel that I can in conscience, at a time like this, go on writing just about things like meditation, though that has its point. I cannot just bury my head in a lot of rather tiny and secondary monastic studies either. I think I have to face the big issues, the life-and-death issues: and this is what everyone is afraid of. . . .

SEPTEMBER 22, 1961

. . . Actually it [the article Merton sent to her] is a chapter from *New Seeds of Contemplation*. This is a rewriting of the old *Seeds* which preserves practically all the material that was there before and adds a whole lot more. Most of this material is new, though there are a few paragraphs from the old version. . . .

[COLD WAR LETTER 86] JUNE 16, 1962

. . . Yesterday I mailed to you a copy of the book which is not to be published, *Peace in a Post-Christian Era* [*Peace in the Post-Christian Era* (2004)]. My Superiors, having been alerted by zealous individuals in this country, felt that I was "going too far" and getting away from the contemplative vocation into "dangerous ground," etc., etc. . . .

It is no use speculating too much about the world situation, but it is certainly a very risky one. The whole word is under judgment, and one feels it keenly. . . . I think the evil in us all has reached the point of overflowing. . . .

AUGUST 11, 1962

. . . I am sorry that Pax is not shaping up to anything. I suppose it is a manifestation of our confusion and helplessness. We Catholics are so frustrated and passive that we no longer know how to begin to do the things we really ought to do. It saddens one: I should talk, you must be much more saddened by it than I could ever be, since I am away from most of it. . . .

JULY 16, 1965

I was very glad indeed to get your letter. It came at a good time, I had just been reading and enjoying Karl Stern's new book, *The Flight from Woman,* which is excellent. And I am always very glad to hear from you. I think often of you and pray often for you and the CW. Jim Douglass and his wife were here the other day speaking of you. . . .

NOVEMBER 22, 1965

. . . My main reaction has been to try to withdraw further from the peace movement and from the appearance of being publicly involved in it, and this too was unfortunate, because Jim Forest and above all John Heidbrink interpreted this as a knife in the back, and so on (since I said I would prefer to be no longer on the list of sponsors of the Catholic Peace Fellowship). They think I am doing this out of fear, and I know I cannot really expect them to take the slightest interest in the peculiar problem I have trying to live an authentic life of solitude (which I certainly think will do more for the peace movement than anything I write). However, we will work this out quietly I hope, and come to some conclusion. John Heidbrink by the way in a long letter argued that my whole monastic life was a pure evasion, that I ought to be back in the world leading a life of authentic involvement like himself, etc. etc. Don't worry, I have heard enough of that to know what I think of it. I am more determined than ever on my present course, in spite of what they may think about it, in fact their opposition is to me another reason to continue obeying God rather than man. . . .

DECEMBER 20, 1965

Thanks for your very good letter. I reached what I thought would be a fair solution with the CPF: I would continue to be their sponsor insofar as I heartily approve their pastoral activities for objectors, etc., and it would be understood in some way (by a statement or something) that I did not make myself responsible for every political act of theirs. I haven't heard, but I should think that would be acceptable. . . .

About Dan Berrigan: I guess you and I are a bit old-fashioned, but I agree with you. I wrote a quiet letter to his Provincial, not protesting the decision but just saying that I had full confidence in Dan as a fine priest who was doing much good, and got a courteous reply. Quite possibly there was a little string pulling behind the scenes to get him out of NY but I don't see that he will suffer much from the transfer and will probably come back better than ever. I have had enough in twenty-four years of monastic life to know that even if certain measures of Superiors may be a little unfair, one never loses anything by obeying, quite the contrary, and God sometimes reserves special gifts and an extra fruitfulness for us, something we could not have gained without this sacrifice. I hope Dan is taking it well and I am sure he is. . . .

DECEMBER 29, 1965

. . . To me the Catholic Worker stands for something absolutely unique and alive in the American Church. It would be hard to put into words how much it means to me, for so many personal reasons: it stands for my own youth and for the kind of influences that shaped my own life thirty years ago. It happened that I went to Friendship House [in Harlem] rather than CW because I was at Columbia, FH was just down the hill and so on. But CW stands for so much that has always been meaningful to me: I associate it with similar trends of thought, like that of the English Dominicans and Eric Gill, who also were very important to me. And Maritain. And so on. Catholic Worker is part of my life, Dorothy. I am sure the world is full of people who would say the same. . . .

If there were no Catholic Worker and such forms of witness, I would never have joined the Catholic Church. . . .

SEPTEMBER 12, 1966

. . . I have taken a permanent commitment to live in the hermitage for the rest of my life, insofar as I can (of course if I get incapacitated I can go to the infirmary). So please pray that I may carry this out as God wants. When one is entirely on his own, I find that curious mistakes become possible. But with the guidance of grace and normal good will they do not have effects that are too terrible. Pray for me, then, and I keep you and the *CW* in my prayers and thoughts always. . . .

FEBRUARY 9, 1967

Thanks so much for your good note of January 29th. I have read your piece in the latest *CW* on Cardinal Spellman and the war. It is beautifully done, soft-toned and restrained, and speaks of love more than of reproof. It is the way a Christian should speak up, and we can all be grateful to you for speaking in this way. It *has* to be done. The moral insensitivity of those in authority, on certain points so utterly crucial for man and for the Church, has to be pointed out and if possible dispelled. It does not imply that we ourselves are perfect or infallible. But what is a Church after all but a community in which truth is shared, not a monopoly that dispenses it from the top down. Light travels on a two-way street in our Church: or I hope it does. . . .

AUGUST 18, 1967

. . . The hermit life is no joke at all, and no picnic, but in it one gradually comes face to face with the awful need of self-emptying and even of a kind of annihilation so that God may be all, and also the apparent impossibility of it. And of course the total folly of trying to find ways of doing it oneself. The great comfort is in the goodness and sweetness and nearness of all God has made, and the created *isness* which makes Him first of all present in us, speaking us. Then that other word: "Follow. . . ."

TO HILDEGARD GOSS-MAYR   *Hildegard Goss-Mayr was born in Vienna in 1930. From her childhood she was strongly influenced by the peace activities of her father, Kaspar Mayr, who had been converted to nonviolence during the First World War and who became editor of a small but influential journal,* Der Christ in der Welt. *Hildegard and her husband, Jean Goss, who died in 1991, were active in promoting the nonviolent message of the Gospel in Eastern and Western Europe, in Latin America, and in the Philippines. With a number of other women (including Dorothy Day), Hildegard was in Rome during the Second Vatican Council. The women managed to get their materials on war, peace, and nonviolence to the theologians and the Council Fathers. On September 13, 1966, Merton wrote, "Hildegard Goss-Mayr is my candidate for sainthood in this day (along with Dorothy Day and a few others like that)."*

[COLD WAR LETTER 19] JANUARY 1962

... I have been waiting for some time to get the documents which were sent under separate cover. I have not yet received these but at least I want to send a word of acknowledgment for your letter. It is very good to be in touch with you. I will send you a few things which you may or may not be able to use in *Der Christ in der Welt.* I can read German sufficiently well to profit by this if you send it.

It is sometimes discouraging to see how small the Christian peace movement is, and especially here in America where it is most necessary. But we have to remember that this is the usual pattern, and the Bible has led us to expect it. Spiritual work is done with disproportionately small and feeble instruments. And now above all when everything is so utterly complex, and when people collapse under the burden of confusions and cease to think at all, it is natural that few may want to take on the burden of trying to effect something in the moral and spiritual way, in political action. Yet this is precisely what has to be done.

... I think your efforts to state the questions clearly and place them before the Church, particularly before the Council, is of the greatest importance....

... I would say that at the moment we have to understand better than we do the cold-war mentality.... The great danger is that under the pressures of anxiety and fear, the alternation of crisis and relaxation and new crisis, the people of the world will come to accept gradually the idea of war, the idea of submission to total power, and the abdication of reason, spirit and individual conscience. The great peril of the cold war is the progressive deadening of conscience....

... I am glad you are there at the Council, and that your proposals will have a hearing. Archbishop Roberts tells me he is hoping to get an official approval for conscientious objection. I think this is a very good approach, and most important. It is absolutely terrible that Catholics today should be forced into wars that are almost certain to be immoral, just because the hierarchy may be willing, if not eager, to accept the lies of the military as to the probable character of the war.... It is all very simple. Our missiles will aim at their missile bases and knock them all out before they can aim at our cities. This is considered to be the acme of morality....

About the American bishops: I have not much information. Most of them would simply not understand the problem, I am afraid. Archbishop Flahiff of Winnipeg, Canada, is a bright and understanding new bishop, and a friend of good friends of mine. He is a good prospect. You must see him. Also Fr. Stransky on the Secretariat for Christian Unity, whom I know. Also Bishop Wright of Pittsburgh, very good. Perhaps Cardinal Ritter of St. Louis, who was a pioneer in race relations here. I think he is open-minded....

... Incidentally, I suggest you go see our Abbot General, Dom Gabriel Sortais, and give him a strong push in favor of my writing about peace. He is reasonable enough, but is also under pressure from a lot of silly and unreasonable people....

... It seems to me that the arguments about the morality of nuclear war by Catholic theologians, even by the Popes, all seem tacitly to assume that the atom bomb or the H-bomb are simply bigger and more powerful versions of what we already know. Those who have said that this constitutes an "essentially new kind of war" have doubtless used this phrase more rhetorically than theologically. But as a matter of fact the entire rationale of war is completely altered by the present state of arms production and the arms race....

I have by the way mimeographed some more copies of my unpublished book on peace [*Peace in the Post-Christian Era* (2004)].... I can send more now if you need them. Do you think it advisable to send any copies to any bishops? . . .

DECEMBER 17, 1962

Under separate cover I am sending you three envelopes full of materials more or less related to the question of nuclear war.

In one is the book *Breakthrough to Peace* in which I have an essay on "Peace: A Religious Responsibility," which is pretty much a summary of what I have had to say on the subject. The introduction to that book, which I also wrote, is useful perhaps as a summary of the *status questionis.*

The most complete text I have written is that of the book *Peace in a Post-Christian Era* [*Peace in the Post-Christian Era* (2004)], which is not published, but I am sending you a mimeographed copy. I believe I sent you a copy before this but I am not sure. In any case I shall send some more copies by sea mail, and you can share them with others who may be interested. Together with this book, I am sending one or two other essays, like that entitled "Target Equals City." . . .

First of all, it is most important for the Church to recognize clearly that the presence of nuclear weapons in the world has *essentially* changed the whole problem of war. The whole question must now be rethought in the light of an essentially new situation, which has never existed before. This is more even than a new set of circumstances which alter the same sort of war we have always known. War itself has completely new implications and a totally new character. Hence it is of no use discussing traditional ideas of the just war in a situation where the whole concept of war has been fundamentally altered. . . .

I am convinced that in this question of nuclear war the Church confronts an issue similar to that which arose in the case of Galileo, but one with much more momentous consequences for man. I feel that the Church is in serious danger of making the same kind of error that was made in the case of Galileo, through failure to understand the nature of the question, and judging it in an unrealistic way, having no real relation to the issue. It was possible to err in Galileo's case, and still avoid destruction. Error in this matter may involve the Church in the most ghastly tragedy of human history, indeed a tragedy of possibly eschatological proportions. . . .

. . . You are certainly right that a theology of peace needs to be developed. . . .

. . . It should be clear that the Christian objector is also one who dedicates himself to a positive action based on redemptive love, ordered toward world peace. This is the great weakness of the peace movement in the United States: it is purely a movement of protest, often without even a solidly rational basis, against the evil of war. Unfortunately some of the elements in the peace movement are so weak, morally (and notoriously), that the whole idea of pacifism is discredited by their presence. I certainly recognize the need for a clear statement of the positive theology of love in connection with the question of war and peace. . . .

Hildegard Goss-Mayr wrote that she and Jean planned to spend a year in Brazil helping to form groups in support of non-violence. They wanted to get others involved. Dorothy Day had agreed to come for at least part of the time. Would it be possible for Merton to join them?

. . . I very much regret my inability to respond to your offer. It would give me great joy to do so if I thought it were God's will. Probably I am not worthy of the favor. But I can at least associate myself very closely with you in prayers and I may also be able to help you through friends in Brazil. As for the volunteer you seek, Dorothy Day will probably know the best one for you. I think personally it would be less ambiguous if he were a European or Latin American. If you ever go to Central America I have a lot of friends in Nicaragua who might be interested in such a project. . . .

. . . The great March on Washington was in many ways triumphant, and it was certainly a magnificent expression of restraint, dignity, good order. The nobility of the thousands of Negro participants was evident in the highest degree, and when they "thanked the white people" who were there, one of my friends broke down in tears. Really, for the whites who participated, it was a very great grace, and something they needed. Indeed they needed this chance to give some sign of repentance, much more than the Negro needed to have them there. In fact, politically, the presence of these white people was perhaps not entirely an advantage to the Negro because it tended to confuse the real situation just a little. Everything that tends to preserve the atmosphere of illusion, the false optimism which supposes that the Negro has a place all ready for him in white America, once more strengthens the inertia of those attached to a status quo in which, in fact, the Negro has no place whatever. He is an outcast. You would be horrified to know to what extent even in the Negro ghettoes the Negro is oppressed and exploited by white men, even to the extent that it is very difficult for a Negro to own a store or run a business of any consequence even in the Negro ghetto, and the white shopkeepers bleed him with usury. This situation is very grave indeed and it is slowly creeping toward revolution of the violent kind, I very much fear. Yet the greatness of people like Martin Luther King is something to hope in and trust in. God can certainly use such men to work miracles, and perhaps He will. Indeed He already has.

Fr. Häring was here and we had a wonderful talk, all too short. He said he would read my peace book and try to intervene with Dom Gabriel. Unfortunately, I am afraid Dom Gabriel is too obsessed with the foreign policies of de Gaulle, and can never admit the possibility of disagreement on this matter of the bomb. It must not be condemned, according to him, even though *Pacem in Terris* is so clear on the subject. . . .

In October 1965, Hildegard Goss-Mayr, accompanied by Jim Douglass, visited Merton at Gethsemani. In the following letter Merton replies to her letter of October 25, 1965, in which among other things she asked him if he would be willing to be on the editorial board of Der Christ in der Welt.

NOVEMBER 10, 1965

. . . As usual I do not have too much information about what goes on but I hear that the atmosphere in this country is getting to be quite tense. One can see so clearly that the real trouble here is the lack of spiritual roots.

This country would not be so unreasonable and so prone to violence if it were more firmly based in a spiritual tradition and had a few more solid principles to go by. That is easy enough to say, but what one can do about it is another matter. I think that actually the peace-movement people are not helping much, except that they are making a strong protest, which is all right. But what we need is a peace movement that will help the country to actually understand and want peace, and that is quite another matter. Burning draft cards will not bring this about, it only upsets a lot of poor confused people who are not capable of seeing what it means: except to interpret it as another threat in a time when they feel themselves already gravely threatened by millions of communists behind every tree. . . .

DECEMBER 8, 1965

. . . It is true that I have had a little difficulty about adjusting my position as a solitary with the publicity that is connected with the peace movement. My name is still used and newspaper articles give the impression that I am somehow actively involved in actions about which I know nothing whatever. Hence I finally decided to ask Jim Forest to make it clear that I am *not* involved in any of the political activities of the CPF but that I still morally support their spiritual and pastoral aims. . . .

JANUARY 14, 1966

It is the feast of St. Hilary, Doctor of the Church, who said: "The best way to solve the problem of rendering to Caesar what is Caesar's is to have nothing that is Caesar's." This is a good day then to send you the essay on "Demut," which turned out to be really an essay on the beatitude of the Meek, as applied to Christian non-violence. Since I really do not know what I am talking about, it is rather presumptuous to write on such subjects, but anyway I have done so. I hope what I have said makes sense. . . .

There are hopes now that the Vietnam War may reach the conference table, thanks largely to the efforts of Paul VI. Something to be very thankful for. I have not any recent news, but I hope all will be going well and that the Pope's wishes for peace in the New Year (which we all share) may be granted. You will know better than I what chance there is of all this working out. . . .

... The spring is really lovely here, but how can one enjoy it when things get worse and worse in Vietnam? There is a certain feeling of desperation among some in the peace movement when they see that they get nowhere with their efforts: but perhaps they ought to realize that efforts against war are not always popular in a nation which is at war, and it is a good thing that there is as much conscientious opposition as there really is here. But I wish the end were in sight. . . .

TO WILBUR H. ("PING") FERRY   *Wilbur H. Ferry was vice president of the Center for the Study of Democratic Institutions in Santa Barbara, California. Merton's letter of September 18, 1961, initiated a lengthy correspondence that proved lasting and mutually enriching. Ferry sent him much reading material and introduced him to authors such as Jacques Ellul, Lewis Mumford, and I. F. Stone. A frequent visitor to Gethsemani, he helped Merton to get some of his writings distributed at a time when the censors of the Order were limiting the subjects Merton was allowed to write about. In 1968, Ferry saw Merton to the plane that would take him to Asia.*

SEPTEMBER 18, 1961

For a long time I have been meaning to write this letter to you, ever since my friend and publisher, James Laughlin, of New Directions, has spoken to me about the work you and Dr. Hutchins are doing at Santa Barbara. Through his intervention and by your kindness I have now received many of the pamphlets published by the Center and have read many of these with great interest. I knew before this the one called "Community of Fear," which is certainly one of the most pointed and articulate statements of our present danger. . . . It seems to me that our deep-rooted addiction to the kind of narcotic thinking induced by mass media has gone very far in blinding even those who are supposed to be in a position to see, understand and decide our destinies. . . .

In any case as one who is at the same time a priest, a member of a monastic order, and a citizen of the country which still prides itself on being the model and defender of democracy, I believe it is a moral issue of the greatest importance which faces me along with everybody else: and that most of us are not even regarding it as a moral issue at all. As if politics and ethics had nothing whatever to do with one another, and indeed as if ethical considerations were completely irrelevant, or at best subjective, only, in their relevance. . . . I feel that too few of the religious spokesmen of our time, and every minister is such a spokesman, have faced the question of war and peace, except in a very general way. "Peace is desirable." . . .

DECEMBER 21, 1961

. . . I am having a bit of censor trouble. This makes me think that one way of getting some of my stuff around would be to let you people mimeograph it and circulate it with your material. Would you consider this in some cases? This would not require censorship. I have, for instance, some copies of letters to people—to make up a book called "Cold War Letters." Very unlikely to be published (!). I'll get them typed up and you can judge whether you would think it worth circulating some of them. Happy New Year to all of you. . . .

JANUARY 18, 1962

. . . I have given up guessing what will happen soon. I have little confidence in Kennedy, I think he cannot fully measure up to the magnitude of his task, and lacks creative imagination and the deeper kind of sensitivity that is needed. . . . What is needed is really not shrewdness or craft, but what the politicians don't have: depth, humanity and a certain totality of self-forgetfulness and compassion, not just for individuals but for man as a whole: a deeper kind of dedication. Maybe Kennedy will break through into that someday by miracle. But such people are before long marked out for assassination. He does not strike me as so marked. At least not for that kind of reason.

[COLD WAR LETTER 48] MARCH 6, 1962

. . . The first and greatest of all commandments is that America shall not and must not be beaten in the cold war, and the second is like unto this that if a hot war is necessary to prevent defeat in the cold war, then a hot war must be fought even if civilization is to be destroyed. . . .

MAY 8, 1962

... J. is worried about "Original Child Bomb" [Merton's grim poem on the bombing of Hiroshima] not getting any attention and finally it transpired that the bookstores were putting it with the juveniles, Peter Rabbit, etc. My comic book. . . .

JUNE 12, 1963

... You are right about the race thing. . . . There is going to be an awakening. But a lot of people do not want that kind of awakening, I am afraid. Still, it has to come. I too am afraid there is going to be a real revolution and real violence. There already is a revolution. Martin Luther King started it off, and in a way that was admirable. But the less admirable ways are certainly going to take over, and the confusion is going to be tremendous. . . .

JULY 1, 1964

... One book you must read if you have not already is *The Pilgrim* by [Michael] Serafian, about Pope Paul and the Council. Thesis that Pope Paul's curial instincts took over and he sacrificed [Cardinal Augustine] Bea and the Johannine drive to the conservative pressures against them, then went on pilgrimage as a surrogate for the non-achievements of the second session. . . . The thing is now so constructed that perhaps the Papacy has come to depend to a great extent on machinery like that of the H. Office, and the Office crowd is serenely convinced that it has to arrogate to itself all the powers of the Pope even against the Pope himself, becoming in the end the real seat of infallibility. This means of course that infallibility becomes organized and to some extent anonymous (no longer a charism but an institution) and of course that means one thing: totalism and the monolith. . . .

DECEMBER 9, 1966

Joan [Baez] and Ira [Sandperl] were here yesterday—got here late and had all too little time, but it was wonderful to have them, and I enjoyed every minute of it. Thanks again for sending them. I think they got something out of being here and I know I profited greatly from meeting them and having them here to talk to. Joan is a person of total integrity and purity of heart:

one of those rare people who keep things from falling apart . . . they are an inspiration. . . .

. . . Thanks for the *Observer* piece on or of Fr. [Charles] Davis. As far as I can see his points are unassailable. Authority has simply been abused too long in the Catholic Church and for many people it just becomes utterly stupid and intolerable to have to put up with the kind of jackassing around that is imposed in God's name. It is an insult to God Himself and in the end it can only discredit all idea of authority and obedience. There comes a point where they simply forfeit the right to be listened to. . . .

. . . I am going to Indonesia, God willing, in November. That is the one thing definite about Asia so far. Bangkok still undecided. Doesn't matter. Indonesia is a good start, and I presume after that at least Japan.

It seems to me that the best thing would be for me to come out to Santa Barbara before my flight to the Indies and we could take a week or so to look at the Coast. Then perhaps when I came back I could hole in for that retreat I am hoping to make early next year. That's the way it seems to make sense at the moment and the way I think the Abbot would tolerate it. . . .

Great! Will fly to Santa Barbara I hope on Sept. 30 and will let you know when my flying saucer touches down. As to the trip—yes I do plan to stay at the Redwoods convent when I get there, as I have a meeting of nuns (and will have to be there about the 9th I guess). But fine if your wife comes along. Addition of feminine wisdom will doubtless help find even better hideout. . . .

. . . My journey before Santa B. takes me, guess where, to Alaska. I have been assigned an impossible flight with a three-hour wait at Los Angeles. . . . I have a flight to Santa Barbara via Los Angeles from Anchorage. . . .

[ANCHORAGE] SEPTEMBER 26, 1968

. . . It is quite possible that if and whenever I get back from Asia, I may end up here. Local bishops xtreley [extremely] friendly and generous and everybody very helpful. Lots of little lost islands and spots like fishing villages with two Catlick families who'd be glad to have Mass on Sundays, wonderful lost towns with no road to them only reachable by plane or boat, places turned upside down by tidal wave and earthquake and moved to another spot etc. The mountains are the finest I have ever seen anywhere. It is a GREAT land. Today off to Juneau and SE Alaska and then back to Anchorage for the nunnies. . . .

[OBEROI GRAND HOTEL, CALCUTTA] NOVEMBER 11, 1968

Hastily sending back the transcript which I only received today. Hope changes are OK. I had a marvelous eight days at Dharamsala in the Himalayas—three long talks with the Dalai, who is a great guy. All pure gold. And met many other lamas; also they are all on to something deep, which must not get out! Very good stuff. Great people. . . .

TO JOHN C. HEIDBRINK   *John Heidbrink, after his studies in Texas, in Bern, Switzerland, and at Harvard University, became Presbyterian chaplain at the University of Oklahoma, where in 1967 he participated in one of the earliest student sit-ins. He joined the Fellowship of Reconciliation (FOR) and worked at the FOR center in Nyack, New York. He assisted Daniel Berrigan and Jim Forest in setting up the Catholic Peace Fellowship (CPF). He admired Thomas Merton and carried on an extensive correspondence with him from 1961 to 1967.*

[COLD WAR LETTER 2] OCTOBER 30, 1961

Thanks for your good letter of October 25. I am glad Dorothy Day and the *CW* got in touch with you. I am very anxious to be in touch with anyone who is working for peace at this hour. I do not think that Catholics realize the situation at all. They seem to be totally unaware of the gravity of the hour spiritually speaking, quite apart from the physical danger. It may very well be that we are faced with a temptation to a total interior apostasy from Christ, while perhaps maintaining an exterior rectitude of some sort. This is frightful. In this event, I feel that the supreme obligation of every Christian, taking precedence over absolutely everything else, is to devote himself by the best means at his disposal to a struggle to preserve the human race from annihilation and to abolish war as the essential means to accomplish this end. . . .

DECEMBER 2, 1961

. . . Do please all of you at the FOR consider Gethsemani a place where you will always be welcome. If you want to be sure to see me, let me know a week or so in advance and I will get permission. I cannot always guarantee to see people at short notice. . . .

MAY 30, 1962

. . . The Abbot General has just vetoed a book of mine about nuclear war, just as the last page was typed on stencils. I will run a few copies off anyway and my friends can see it. But it must not be published. I have been told that I must cease writing and publishing on "controversial subjects" that have "nothing to do with the monastic life." There is no alternative but to accept the decision, which I do. . . .

SEPTEMBER 25, 1962

Thanks for your good letter . . . We will look forward to seeing you October 15th. I am sending in the signed application for membership in the FOR. As I consider the principles set down, the aims of the Fellowship, it is difficult to see how I can do anything but join. [At this time, FOR was considered a *protestant organization which Catholics simply did not join.*] . . .

On the other hand it would not be the desire of my Superiors to have this act of mine publicized, even for the benefit of a just cause like this. So long as I am just "there" and one of you, without any special attention being drawn to the fact, I think everyone will be acceptable to them. Otherwise they might complain. . . .

APRIL 9, 1963

. . . It would be better if a group of ten or so simply came down and spent a few days in the quiet of the monastery, in meditation, attending such offices as they would like, and devoting most of the afternoons to discussion and exchange of ideas. This last part would be under my aegis, I suppose. I have a suitable place for it, and can arrange the time fairly conveniently in the afternoon. My mornings are usually pretty well taken up with the novices. Naturally, three days is a rough idea of what might be feasible, and would fit my own plans for afternoons. But if anyone wanted to stay longer, that would be all right. . . .

MAY 9, 1964

. . . What I would prefer to do would be simply to say: suppose two or three of those concerned drop down here for an informal visit sometime in November, preferably not on a weekend. We could certainly discuss "spiritual roots of protest" in a very informal way, and if Dan is there the discussion would certainly be lively and fruitful. But let us not try to plan a formal session, and I will go along with the idea. I would tend to set the maximum at about six. . . .

NOVEMBER 26, 1964

By now you may have heard reports from others of the retreat last week. I think we all felt it was a great experience . . . certainly I think we were in contact with reality and truth in a way that is not met with every day. Thanks be to God for it. I would sum it up in two words: (a) a sense of the awful depth and seriousness of the situation; (b) a sense of deeper and purer hope, a hope purified of trust in the technological machinery and the "principalities and powers" at work therein. . . .

NOVEMBER 20, 1965

Yesterday I got very good letters from Dan and Jim and answered them immediately. Today I received yours, which set me back a bit, but came clearer on a second reading. . . .

The problem is simply this: when people burn draft cards or themselves (and I appreciate your analysis of Roger La Porte's tragic act [self-immolation for peace] and its implications for society), I hear about it if at all from someone who is very upset by it, and who may or may not represent someone else who is even more upset and who in addition holds me in some way accountable if the people are Catholics. . . . Since I am not able to keep up with these things and since it is no longer possible for me to be making all kinds of pronouncements about them, I would appreciate not being expected to. . . .

I appreciate your frankness, John. And I see the ambiguities of my life well enough, I assure you. But this is the life I have to live whether people accept it or not. It is not that I disbelieve or distrust Jim and the others in their engagement in the CPF: it is myself that I disbelieve and distrust in that context. . . .

PART 8

Keeping Faith in Times of Change

Merton's Reflections on the Catholic Church

"The church needs Christians with independent and original thought, with new solutions and with the capacity to take risks."

—To Cintio Vitier, August 1, 1963

A convert to Roman Catholicism, Merton remained always the faithful Catholic even as, in the sixties, he became its incisive critic. Although there is no single correspondence dedicated to the subject of "Church," Merton's reflections on the Catholic Church, expressing both his faithfulness and his frustration, appear throughout his correspondence as he shares his vision of Church with friends, fellow writers, theologians, and others who wrote to him. Merton anticipates and monitors the progress of the Second Vatican Council; he decries the failure of Church leaders (excepting the popes) and fellow Catholics to speak out on war; and he expresses hope that all Christians will recognize their unity with one another, a unity greater than any differences among them. Along the way, Merton addresses issues of tradition and renewal, obedience and authority, institutionalization, and tensions within the Catholic Church. For Merton, "keeping faith" is not simply a matter of preserving the past. As the letters excerpted in this section illustrate, Merton was committed to honoring the past while also imagining and embracing a vision of Church at once faithful to the Gospel and courageously responsive to "the signs of the times."

TO MRS. LEONARD *Mrs. Leonard was Paul Tillich's secretary. Merton had sent the theologian a copy of the limited edition of his book* Prometheus [: A Meditation], *published by Victor Hammer. Mrs. Leonard wrote to tell Merton that Paul Tillich "had read and enjoyed" the book.*

JUNE 20, 1959

. . . For some time past the thought has been growing on me more and more that since Christianity is simple life in Christ, a life that we all share, then the more we can be conscious of that sharing and rejoice in it together, the more we will be Christians and the more we will be one in Him. And I do feel that what we all have in common is so much greater and more important than what we do not have in common, at least dogmatically and juridically. There is One Christ on earth when Christians really will to be one in mind and heart, in Him. The institutional differences are there, and they are unfortunate, but they are not stronger than charity. That is the best formula I can think of for Christian unity, and I have a strong suspicion that it has something to do with the Gospels. The rest follows from this, and must, if anything is to follow at all.

TO CZESLAW MILOSZ   MAY 6, 1960

. . . Friendship is the first and most important thing, and is the true cement of the Church built by Christ. . . .

TO ARCHIMANDRITE SOPHRONY *A priest of the Orthodox Church, Archimandrite Sophrony lived in a monastic house in England together with six monks. He is known for his books on Eastern Christian spirituality.*

JANUARY 26, 1961

. . . I received with much joy your friendly letter of October and the ship-ment of books and articles, all of which I have read. I have also been moved by the simplicity of your gracious letter and by all you have told me about your monastic experience in England. . . .

First of all, your book about the Staretz Silouane [a spiritual guide, highly regarded by Orthodox Christians] offers a striking example of a sanctity that is monastic, authentic and traditional, and also belongs to our time. I find there the mark of a contemporary holiness: this vision of the "dark side" of wisdom, this hope that struggles with despair, this feeling of being in hell. This is the "dark side" of the truth, the beauty of a wisdom which seems to be hidden in the chaotic disorder of sin. Oh, how discouraging it sometimes is to see what little good, true good, one is capable of. How false and disgusting so much conventional piety appears to be. Though the omnipresence of lies and of the Devil may frighten us, we must not sur-render to tragedy. With the simplicity of the Staretz Silouane we must "keep our hearts in hell and not despair." It is not the lies we should see, but the truth with its darkened face, so like the Servant of the Lord who has no beauty, who is neither noble nor great, yet who comes forth like a shoot from the parched earth. And at the same time it is the Beauty of God who is always playing in the world before the Face of the Father. . . .

But above all, I enjoyed your article on the Unity of the Church. I am under the impression that you did not quite succeed in saying all that you wanted to; but you have certainly sketched the beginnings of a doctrinal approach that I find very attractive. I confess quite simply that I very much admire the truth of this beautiful doctrine and that I have many times thought of it myself. Above all, I try to live out the consequences of that doctrine, namely, to unite in myself all Christian truth and all Christian love so that every Christian, and indeed everyone who is authentically in Christ, might take flesh in my life, or at least in my love. We must love the truth wherever it is found; we must go straight to the truth without wanting to glance backward and without caring about what school of theology it represents. The Church must truly be our Mother, which means that she must be the Church of the love of Christ; she must welcome us with a mother's love that shares her wisdom with us. You surely know the distress that one must experience in seeking to find the truth of love instead of the truth of formulas . . . and of laws, of programs, of projects. . . .

I like everything you tell me about your small community. I pray for you at the Divine Liturgy. I am going to say the Jesus-Prayer for a while for you and in union with you with the hope that I may come to understand it more deeply. . . .

TO LAWRENCE FERLINGHETTI *Lawrence Ferlinghetti, American beat poet and publisher of City Lights Books, published Merton's Auschwitz poem, "Chant to Be Used in Processions Around a Site with Furnaces." However, as the flowing excerpt shows, their correspondence was not limited to literary matters and publishing issues.*

AUGUST 2, 1961

. . . Look, I don't give you the gotta go to confession right away routine. What is vitally important is that you should be a Christian and as faithful to the truth as you can get. This may mean anything but resembling some of the pious faithful. But I don't have to tell you, because you know, that there is only one thing that is of any importance in your life. Call it fidelity to conscience, or to the inner voice, or to the Holy Spirit: but it involves a lot of struggle and no supineness and you probably won't get much encouragement from anybody. There is a dimension of Catholicism, mostly French and German, which gives a little room for growth like this. But you have to find it as best you can. I can't necessarily tell you where to look or how much of it you have found already. The start of it all is that none of us really have started to look. But the mercy of God, unknown and caricatured and blasphemed by some of the most reputable squares, is the central reality out of which all the rest comes and into which all the rest returns.

TO JUSTUS GEORGE LAWLER   *Justus George Lawler was an editor at Herder and Herder. He also edited the journal* Continuum.

[COLD WAR LETTER 60] MARCH 1962

. . . Your article on the Bishops is very timely and I appreciate it fully having just finished [Hans] Küng's remarkable book on the Council [*The Council, Reform, and Reunion*]. How right you are. I am so afraid that the concept of "renewal" will turn out to be nothing more than a tightening of the screws on the poor rank-and-file religious, clergy, and layman who have been hog-tied for so long. This Council is going to have to be a proof that we are not just a monolithic organization, because that is how such organizations renew themselves: by tightening their grip on the rank and file and re-asserting the perpetual rightness of the managers. If that happens this time, so help us, it will be one of the most horrible scandals that ever took place. It will be a disaster. That, principally, is the object of my prayers; that it will be a real renewal, or a step toward it. But honestly, I am scared. I ought to have more faith, one might say. It is not exactly that. I am scared because in a way I think we have deserved to come out in our true light. We have deserved the fate of efficiency for good and all. But God is merciful. He can save us from an endless succession of Good Joe Bishops whose greatest concern is to keep up a perpetual flow of innocent Irish drolleries about Pat and Mike and never say a serious word about anything except that so-and-so's marriage case is hopeless. . . .

TO CATHERINE DE HUECK DOHERTY   *Russian-born Catherine de Hueck Doherty established Friendship House in New York City in Harlem, where Merton volunteered in 1941 after hearing the Baroness speak at St. Bonaventure University. She and her husband, Eddie Doherty, founded a community of prayer and training for the lay apostolate at Madonna House in Cambermere, Ontario.*

[COLD WAR LETTER 79] JUNE 4, 1962

. . . The thing that eats one up is the anguish over the Church. This of course leaves me inarticulate because I know that anyone can show where and how and why I am not a good Catholic, a good Christian, a faithful member of Christ. And yet there is this conviction that the Church is full of a terrible spiritual sickness, even though there is always that inexpressible life. . . .

It is at such a time as this that one has to have faith in the Church, and the fact that we suffer from the things that make us suffer, the fact that we cannot find the way out of the suffering, is perhaps a sign of hope. I do not pretend to understand the situation or to analyze anything. Your answer is correct. What is wanted is love. But love has been buried under words, noise, plans, projects, systems, and apostolic gimmicks. And when we open our mouths to do something about it we add more words, noise, plans, etc. We are afflicted with the disease of constant talking with almost nothing to say. . . .

TO JOHN HARRIS   *John Harris, a schoolteacher in England, wrote to Boris Pasternak after reading* Dr. Zhivago. *Pasternak responded and asked him to contact Thomas Merton, "whose precious thoughts and dear bottomless letters enrich me and make me happy." Merton sent Harris a mimeographed copy of the "Cold War Letters" (the short version) as a present upon his entry into the Catholic Church.*

[COLD WAR LETTER 83] JUNE 8, 1962

. . . What can I tell you about the Church? You have been very patient with her human deficiencies, and that patience is also her gift. Your letter reflects the extraordinary serenity with which the new convert accepts *everything*. And one has to. In a sense it is true that one only comes in with blinders on, blinders one has put on and kept on. One has to refuse to be disturbed by so many things. And you are right in the refusal. These are temporal and absurd things which, in the eschatological perspectives, which are the true ones, must vanish forever along with many other things that are more precious and far from absurd in themselves.

The Church is not of this world, and she complacently reminds us of this when we try to budge her in any direction. But on the other hand we also are of the Church and we also have our duty to speak up and say the Church is not of this world when her refusal to budge turns out, in effect, to be a refusal to budge from a solidly and immovably temporal position. And that is the trouble with this war business. The Church's voice is clear enough, but the people who are responsible for applying Catholic principles to political action are acting in a way that is more secular than sacred. The current war ethic is pagan and less than pagan. There is very little of Christianity left in it anywhere. The truth and justice have been drained out of it. It is a lie and a blasphemy, and this has to be said. Not by you. But certainly if I have felt obliged to say it, I have been left without alternative. The urgency with which I have shouted what I wanted to say is due to the fact that I knew I would not go on shouting for very long and indeed the shouting is already over. You may perhaps see an issue of *Blackfriars* one of these days with the last echo of my outcry. I have written a whole book [*Peace in the Post-Christian Era*], but it has all been forbidden without even going to the censors. I have just been instructed to shut my trap and behave, which I do since these are orders that must be obeyed and I have said what I had to say. I will send you a mimeographed copy of the book if I can. Meanwhile with the letters of course you can use them discreetly, and I see no objection to their being quoted in class in a private school.

But to get back to you and Emy, I am so happy for you. You will have the grace to see through all that is inconsequential and unfortunate in the Church. She is still the Church, the Body of Christ, and nobody can change that, not even some of those who imagine themselves to represent her perfectly when they have simply twisted her teachings to suit their own secularism. Be true to the Spirit of God and to Christ. Read your Prophets sometimes, and go through the Gospels and St. Paul and see what is said there: that is your life. You are called to a totally new, risen, transformed life in the Spirit of Christ. A life of simplicity and truth and joy that is not of this world. May you be blessed always in it, you and the children. I send you all my love and blessings.

TO E. I. WATKIN　　*British author, philosopher, and linguist E. I. Watkin was received into the Catholic Church in 1908. Watkin saw Christianity as a credible alternative to the prevailing philosophies, valuing especially the inner spiritual truth of Christianity.*

NOVEMBER 15, 1962

I owe you three letters: and I do at least want to say how much I appreciate your warm and generous lines. They convince me more and more that the true reality of the Church is precisely what the Gospel said it is: the communion of "saints" in the Holy Spirit. Let us dare to call ourselves saints because we know well enough that we are sinners and poor, and that we cannot possibly have any good that is not in and from Christ. But that in Him and from Him and with Him we have immense riches, which are, however, not our making but His gift. . . .

JANUARY 11, 1963

. . . I agree with your remarks about the Church. The problem is much deeper than many people seem to imagine, though the possibilities of renewal, with people like Pope John available, are great. Still I think the approach is not radical enough. Or at least, we do not know as yet how radical it is, because for all the enthusiasm of some theologians, and I am enthusiastic with them, the first session did not really get down to the roots. Liturgy is all very well, but it is not the root problem. Nor is the schema on revelation. The great problem is the fact that the Church is utterly embedded in a social matrix that is radically unfriendly to genuine spiritual growth because it tends to stifle justice and charity as well as genuine inner life. . . .

TO VICTORIA OCAMPO　　JANUARY 13, 1963

. . . Victoria, I do not really have the feeling that we are searching for God by different ways. At root one searches for God by only one way, i.e. in following the truth with all the sincerity of one's conscience. Is it not a fact that we are on the same path after all? I feel myself to be very close to you. There are not two Gods—mine and yours. But we have all lived in different circumstances, and God alone sees our hearts. Who knows if he does not

take more satisfaction in yours than in mine? These questions are meaningless because we do not know what he does with them. . . .

TO E. I. WATKIN   HOLY THURSDAY 1963

. . . I do think Pope John has been entirely providential, a great and fine
Pope, and so much better than the last one. He has shown that a little initiative at Rome can really work great changes in the general atmosphere, not
only of the Church, but of the whole West. . . .

MAY 7, 1963

. . . There is no question that the mystics are the ones who have kept
Christianity going, if anyone has. . . .

TO LESLIE DEWART   [N.D.; BETWEEN MAY 10 AND JUNE 28, 1963]

. . . We are very good at coming out with declarations and resolutions,
usually a little late. When it has become quite evident that a situation is
unjust, and when it is clear that the "safer" liberal elements have recognized
the injustice, some Bishops or some Catholic association will produce a
declaration deploring the injustice. And indeed some attempt may be made
to tackle it. But on the whole the church is too cautious, too inert, and too
slow to have a really creative influence in social affairs. She never leads. She
always follows, often with rather pathetic attempts to scramble onto the
back of somebody else's bandwagon. One gets the feeling that she is not so
much concerned with burning social questions as with showing the masses
she is really on their side—while at the same time not antagonizing those in
power, unless they are Communists.

In one word: the Church is involved in the political life of the world but
not as a creative or constructive force. When a showdown comes she tends to
become reactionary because she is too often committed to the status quo. . . .

. . . Here is one of the great weaknesses of the Church today. We seem
to be incapable of thinking of the Church's work for the salvation of souls
except in terms of her *power over* souls—that is to say, except in terms of
control.

Hence an appalling vicious circle. We believe that in the Church is our salvation. But how can the Church save men if she does not get to them before anybody else? How does the Church save men if she does not begin to control them from the cradle on? If I do or say or think anything that tends to weaken this all-important control, I am sinning against the faith, endangering my soul and the souls of thousands, millions, whole nations. Thus it becomes necessary *first of all, before anything else* (since faith is after all the *initium salutis*), to accept and defend certain pragmatic positions which guarantee, or seem to guarantee, this control, this access to "souls," this power over souls. . . . But of course is it the power to teach, rule, and sanctify which God gave His Church? Well, is it? Have we perhaps lost our true perspective on the teaching, ruling, and sanctifying power of the Church? Have we secularized that perspective? Have we secularized it so completely that defense of the faith means defense of certain very worldly compromises and *deals* made by the hierarchy in the worldwide struggle for power? What happens, in that event, is that in order to safeguard and defend the faith, indeed my immortal soul, I have to accept them as if they were of faith. In other words the real test of my Catholicity comes to be not my belief in God, or in Christ and His teachings, His Church and her Sacraments, so much as my commitment to extremely pragmatic and often very short-sighted views which have been dreamed up in chanceries and sacristies. I have to go along with policies that are often so inert, so blind, so stupid that they utterly stifle the true life of the Church and make it *impossible* for the most clear-sighted and courageous of her members to do anything that will further the real manifestation of the truth and char-ity of Christ in the world. Thus it is that at a time when the Popes have pleaded for creative social action, for a really living apostolate, for social justice, for international collaboration, for peace, etc., the Catholic press comes out everywhere with enthusiastic editorials about all these things in the abstract, while in the concrete everybody who tries to do anything really serious about them is blocked, silenced, and forbidden to act. All the energy of the best-intentioned and most zealous Christians then blow off in symbolic and image-making inanities, in campaigns and movements which mobilize the great religious publicity machine and involve every-body in senseless, futile, and exhausting collective rituals which, in the end, produce nothing. And behind all this spurious Pentecostal wind one can hear, if he listens carefully, the hideous merriment of demons.

We are living in a condition of endemic self-contradiction and frustration which is extremely dangerous, because each new move, each new spasm that goes through the Body of the Church makes us momentarily hope and imagine that we have not stifled the Holy Spirit: but then we discover, once again, or are in danger of discovering that we really have. (His voice, after all, is not easy to silence.) Then a new and more violent spasm becomes necessary, lest we hear Him and live.

Each new spasm aggravates all the problems we are trying to solve, both our own and those of the "world" we are meant to save. Each new self-contradiction, each new retreat from truth, each new abandonment of a position that was, for a moment, almost conquered, each new retreat into the old after proclaiming our advance into the new, leaves us more discredited in the eyes of a world that has *long since ceased to be interested in our inner contradictions.* . . .

TO NAPOLEON CHOW   MAY 14, 1963

. . . I am very much in agreement with your opposition to the kind of myopic Catholic policies which prevail everywhere, in North America as well as in Latin America. Here of course the situation is in many ways worse, as regards the majority.

The Cuba revolution has brought out the essential weakness of Catholic social action. I am very much afraid that we are sentimentalists, and our revolutionary aspirations tend to be infantile. The Catholics of Cuba for the most part, as I understand it, generously helped [Fidel] Castro in the beginning. But when the time came for the testing of the spirits the depth of the Catholic understanding of the Cuban revolution was found to be inadequate. There was not sufficient strength to advance in positive competition with the Marxists, and the Catholics, particularly the hierarchy, fell back immediately upon a negative position of anti-Communist protest, making exceedingly unrealistic *demands* for a total anti-Communism on Castro's part, as a sign of "good faith" etc. Then, as Castro naturally let himself be more and more forced into the position where he had to choose, he chose

Communism. Then the Cuban Church tended more and more to equate the cause of Christ with the cause of the United States: result, the collapse of what might have been the beginning of a genuine "third force" and a real revolution. Naturally, the influence of the U.S. and of mass opinion fabricated in the U.S. has been largely responsible for this.

Underneath this is the weakness of Catholic thought and of the Catholic spirit. In our thought, we are too abstract, in a sense too idealistic, and too ready to fall back on abstract constructions, unable to grasp pragmatic political situations in their reality. Spiritually we are weakened by profound sentimentalism which vitiates our charity. I believe that the renewal of Christianity must take place in every sphere simultaneously, in the spiritual as well as the political. It is no use to advance purely in one direction.

At the same time I think it would be very wise to avoid everything that precipitates political issues by prematurely making them *problems of conscience* before they really are such. This innate *fear of being wrong* and the terror that every false step may mean the collapse of our faith, is the greatest weakness of Catholics today.

It also seems to me that the protest of the beatniks, while having a certain element of sincerity, is largely a delusion. It is a false revolution, sterile and impotent, and its few flashes of originality, its attempts to express compassion, only increase the delusion. I am afraid the beats are to a great extent infantile. Yet this much can be said for them: their very formlessness may perhaps be something that is in their favor. It may perhaps enable them to reject most of the false solutions and deride the "square" propositions of the decadent liberalism around them. It may perhaps prepare them to go in the right direction. I think the beats have contributed much to the peace movement in the U.S., in their own way, and they are often quite committed to the only serious revolutionary movement we have: that for the rights of the Negro. So there are points in their favor, even though they are amorphous and often quite absurd.

Politics are of vital importance. The Catholic in Latin America who refuses a priori to have anything to do with politics of any kind, is doing more to destroy the faith than the Catholic who does not refuse, if necessary, to make common cause with the most radical elements. Incidentally Communism is no longer truly radical in any case, though doubtless in

Latin America the Communists are probably a powerful force for radical action, since the situation favors their approach tremendously.

. . . Our world is in very bad shape, in the sense that the irresponsible ones who have in their hands the greatest power, do not have mentalities that inspire confidence. . . .

TO CINTIO VITIER   AUGUST 1, 1963

. . . Do not feel that the difficulties under which you labor are making your lives less significant. On the contrary, all Christians are everywhere in a kind of exile and it is necessary for all to realize this. The greatest danger is identification of the Church with a prosperous and established economic and cultural system, as if Christ and the world had finally settled down to be friends. The Church needs Christians with independent and original thought, with new solutions and with the capacity to take risks. It is unfortunate that in Latin America, Christianity tends to identify itself with the policies of the State Department in Washington. The fact that the President of this country happens, at the moment, to be Catholic, is not a matter of great significance as far as the policies of the country itself are concerned: they are determined not by religion but by the interests of business. The Church is being purified of such connections, but the purification has hardly begun. You should not be in confusion or in doubt, but open your hearts to the Holy Spirit and rejoice in His freedom which no man can take from you. No power on earth can keep you from loving God and from union with Him. Nor need you depend on the devotionalism of the past. The Lord is near to you and lives in you. His Gospel is not old and forgotten, it is new, and it is there for you to mediate. By His grace you can still come to the sacraments of the Church, and rejoice that you are in the Body of Christ. And you have your fellow Christians and all of Cuba to love. . . .

TO E. I. WATKIN   DECEMBER 12, 1963

. . . The question of liturgy is of course a very complex one, and I think it is going to disturb very many people on both sides of the question. The adaptation is not going to be easy, nor is the sweeping optimism of liturgical reformers always a guarantee of the greatest intelligence. I am afraid that inevitably much that is good will be lost, and needlessly lost, and this will be very sad. . . . However, it is certain that there must be a warmer and more intelligent relationship between what goes on at the altar and what is done by the people. . . . It is also easy for us to understand the Middle Ages and to feel our deep indebtedness to them, and to realize the continuity of our experience with that of the Middle Ages. A vast majority of Christians in our day cannot do this, unfortunately. . . .

I have been asked to write some notes on a notorious play [Rolf Hochhuth's *The Deputy*] which treats Pius XII as a renegade for not having openly protested against the mass murder of Jews by Hitler. The play is mediocre and heavy-handed, and there is obviously an air of resentment and prejudice everywhere in it, and yet after all one can see something of a justification for this viewpoint, in its essence. The idea that a Pope should put first of all the "duty" of retaining political advantage and power, and that the "good of souls" depends on this, is something that we cannot deny exists in Rome, and furthermore the play makes a great point of the fact that the whole Catholic notion of obedience and authority has come to be something dependent on this concept of power. In other words, obedience is something that ultimately has a political use: it makes the members of the Church pliant instruments of policy. This can be seen to have utterly shocking consequences. And amusing ones, for instance, in the curial indignation over the mere idea of reform. The shocked exasperation of the curial party when the bishops actually dared to question the value and honesty of certain curial procedures, and the flagrant opposition of the Curia to the Pope's own wishes, have been quite striking in the last Council session. Obviously for the Curia obedience means nothing outside the context of their *own* power. They obey a Pope as long as he plays their game. Only that. Apparently the definition of Papal infallibility in Vatican I was really understood as a definition of curial omnipotence. . . .

TO GORDON ZAHN   *Sociologist and pacifist Gordon Zahn's postdoctoral study and research in Germany resulted in his book* German Catholics and

Hitler's War *(1962). While in Germany, he also learned of Franz Jaegerstaetter, an Austrian peasant who courageously refused to fight in Hitler's war and was tried and beheaded. Zahn wrote the story of Jaegerstaetter, entitled* In Solitary Witness.

DECEMBER 13, 1963

. . . As to Hochhuth: yes, I have read the play [*The Deputy*] and have dashed off some notes on it which George Lawler says he wants to include with some other notebook excerpts in *Continuum.* I am sending you a Xeroxed copy of the notes. . . .

As to the play, I think it is awful: at least to read. Hochhuth strikes me as somewhat sick, not that I blame him for that. However, the question he raises is an important one, and though he has been grossly unjust to Pius XII (after all, there is no hint whatever of the real greatness of the man in the play), yet I think that the Vatican is at fault, and the hierarchy too, for favoring that kind of abominable and moss-grown concept of authority and of obedience. Here Hochhuth has something to be said for him. When such a temptation is presented to him, how can one blame him for taking it? There has been so much sickening nonsense about Pius XII, and such obviously interested efforts to promote him as a saint, that no one can blame this man for saying he does not agree. And after all, it is his business as well as ours, because if we set someone up as a saint we have to justify our choice to an extremely demanding and critical world. Here is one case where the world has decided to speak up, and we must admit that there is a foundation to the protest, though it is a pity that Pius XII should be so blackened as a person. Frankly, though the play raises this issue, it does not seem to me to treat it in a satisfactory manner and I do believe that it will not do anyone any good. It will confirm those who hate the Church in their prejudices, and it will not help Catholics to think about this real problem, so in the end I would be sorry to see it played: yet, on the other hand, do we really have a full right to demand that it be kept off the stage, and is it wise to attempt this? . . .

TO JOHN J. WRIGHT   *Ordained to the priesthood in 1935, John J. Wright became bishop of Springfield, Massachusetts, and later of Pittsburgh. He par-*

ticipated in the Second Vatican Council. He and Merton exchanged letters on Gaudium et Spes, *the Council's* Pastoral Constitution on the Church in the Modern World.

January 10, 1964

... It seems to me that the Church today faces a great "temptation" which arises out of the last thousand years or so of her history: that of too closely identifying her policy in affairs of diplomacy etc. with her mission to save souls, and of tending to seek obedience in these matters of policy just as if they did in fact involve the salvation of souls. I call this a temptation, but others like the German playwright Hochhuth (most unjustly, I think,) have accused the Church of yielding to it. So it is a problem. ...

TO KARL RAHNER *Merton wrote to the renowned Roman Catholic theologian Karl Rahner, who was one of the leading lights of Vatican II, after reading his book,* The Christian Commitment.

March 16, 1964

I do not know whether you read English but I thought you might be interested in an article ["The Monk in the Diaspora"] which took, as its starting point, your diaspora idea in the new book *The Christian Commitment.* I have also done a review of the book ["Rahner's Diaspora"], which I will send you if and when it gets published. But meanwhile I wanted to let you have a copy of this article. Reading your book from the monastic point of view, I was especially happy with your discerning insistence on the *person* as opposed to the rather naive and sweeping collectivism that sometimes passes for pastoral theology today. Needless to say, I am in hearty agreement with your book and share with you the deep concern for a new and less rigidly institutional view of the Church, the concern that has been raised by the situation of the Church in her true "diaspora," the countries where unpleasant realities must be faced (and are not always faced). ...

I will not lengthen this letter without need, but I thought, Father, that a word from a fellow disciple in a distant country would be of some cheer and encouragement to you. I too am often discouraged in encounters with the obtuseness of certain critics and censors, and find myself in a position where I am forbidden to speak on one of the most urgent issues of the time:

nuclear war. In this country where so many theologians are proposing complacent and totally un-Christian arguments in favor of the bomb, I am not permitted to speak out against it. I do ask you to pray for me, and for us all. I will of course remember you in return. With most cordial and fraternal good wishes for Easter.

TO WILLIAM DUBAY   *William DuBay was ordained a Catholic priest in the diocese of Los Angeles in 1960. He defied his cardinal's ban on preaching about discrimination and civil rights and wrote to Pope Paul VI asking that the cardinal be removed from office for "gross malfeasance" and "abuses of authority" in his failure of leadership against discrimination. Although DuBay complied when he was required to renew his promise of obedience to the Cardinal, he published a book,* The Human Church, *without being granted the imprimatur. In February 1966, he was suspended and forbidden to exercise his priestly functions.*

MAY 14, 1964

. . . Yes you are absolutely right about rights within the Church. The right to have an opinion as a member of the people of God, a right to participate in the life of the people of God, and not just by hymn singing. This is one of the most important things about renewal. Without it, no real renewal. The fact that along with Vatican II there has been a lot of discussion and new ideas have reached a lot of ordinary Christians, this is already something, but not much. It is not just a matter of ideas "reaching ordinary people" but recognizing that "ordinary people" may have some ideas of their own which may be important for the whole Church. And they are entitled to something more than misinformation or withheld information, or tricky and deceptive information. I agree with you that the Catholic liberal is content to make pious statements about "roles" to be assigned and to avoid the issue of changing structures. . . .

TO DANIEL J. BERRIGAN   JUNE 30, 1964

. . . I just finished *The Pilgrim* by Serafian, on the Council. It is really a smasher, much better than the gossip columns of Xavier Rynne, much deeper, much more serious and much more sobering. I had not realized what a beating [Cardinal] Bea took at the last session and what this really represented. This curial thing is really disastrous, and it threatens the whole structure of the church, and maybe, one thinks, this is providential. . . . I wonder if we are really going to have to get along without a structure one of these days. Maybe that will be good, but Lord it will be rough on most people. Maybe less rough on you and me, with all the welts we have acquired in the machinery. More and more I come to think we are living in one great big illusion. Centuries of triumphalist self-deception. The late Middle Ages, with all their sores, were more real. . . . Everything is all twisted up and the worst thing is the facade of smoothness over all the busted iron and the fragments of a building that has perhaps fallen in. But where it has fallen God will build and is building. The front is man's work and that will really cave in. Who worries about that? We must learn not to, and even, when necessary, give it a good shove. Mitres, croziers, rings, slippers, baubles, documents, seals, bulls, rescripts, indults. . . . Have a good time on your trip.

TO PABLO ANTONIO CUADRA   JUNE 30, 1964

. . . With the frustration of the progressive hopes in the second session of the Council and realization that in spite of all the fuss made the accomplishments of the Council have been relatively superficial and trivial, one has to face the fact that the Church is and remains in severe crisis. All the discussion and publicity do little or nothing to change this fact, and the various movements (including the monastic movement) do not seem to be profoundly real, or as real as they claim to be. Yet there is something there, God alone knows what. I personally think that we are paralyzed by institutionalism, formalism, rigidity and regression. The real life of the Church is not in her hierarchy, it is dormant somewhere. There are all kinds of signs of awakening, but which of them can be accepted as real? I think we need a deep enlightenment and liberation from cultural and intellectual habits, from spiritualities, from pious attitudes, from social prejudices, and perhaps the liberation must reach the proportions of an explosion before it will be genuine. Yet I realize that a human approach to this is futile, and that we are all waiting for something we know not. The real movement will start of itself, and I am convinced that the great areas of new life are to be sought in South America (Central America too), Africa, and Asia perhaps. It would be wonderful to participate to some small extent in the beginnings of the awakening. Perhaps that is why preference should always be given to the voice of the *criollos*. Perhaps I will write you further about this. Today is hot and it has been a long day, so I must end this letter. . . .

TO RAFAEL SQUIRRU   *Argentinean poet and critic Rafael Squirru was director of Cultural Affairs for the Organization of American States. In his letter to Squirru, Merton distinguishes between "European" and "universal" Catholicism.*

JULY 12, 1964

Many thanks for your little book on the "New Man." I have read it carefully and with pleasure and want to congratulate you on it. I especially liked the essays on the poet and on the role of the intellectual. It seems to me that this little book represents a vitally important trend of thought, and you know of course how much I agree with it. The thinking of the public, especially in the "great powers," seems to me to be hallucinated by the unreal concept of what one might call an Atlantic gigantism (except that it would have to include Russia and even China). The belief that the only kind of thinking that is real and meaningful is that which is associated with European and North American thought patterns, extending this also to Chinese Marxism. But this cerebration leaves out most of the human race, most of its needs, most of its aspirations. It has proved itself completely incapable of really solving the problems of man and is now increasingly incapable even of defining them.

It might seem scandalous for me, a priest of the Catholic Church, to admit such things, as it is naturally assumed that Catholicism is simply one aspect of this whole European pattern of thought. Unfortunately that is true of the Catholic "ideology" in its European dress. But there is more to Christian faith than this limited ideology, and true Catholicism (which has yet to rediscover itself in our age, I think) is indeed universal. Where there has been a failure has been precisely in the imposition of the limited (the

European) as "Catholic" or universal. I think the Council is partly beginning to be aware of this, but only partly. It is very dim.

Meanwhile the great task for the Catholic and the humanist and indeed the honest man in this hemisphere is to work for a mutual understanding and spiritual communication between the North and the South. A tremendous task, so neglected and so misunderstood that it seems at times impossible. Fortunately books like yours and articles like some of those in *Americas* are there to give one hope. And Miguel Grinberg with his fantastic movement. And the voices of the Latin American poets and artists. . . .

TO MRS. MYCOCK   APRIL 2, 1965

Your supposition that if I wrote that book (*The Seven Storey Mountain*) again today I would speak differently of Anglicans was both charitable and correct. My thought at the time of writing was hardly matured and I just said what came to mind, as people so often do, and more often in those days. It is, unfortunately, so easy and so usual simply to compare the dark side of someone else's Church with the bright side of one's own. Thank heaven we are getting over that now, I hope.

Needless to say, I regret having offended you, and as to the injustice I may have done to Anglicans, there are, I hope, ways in which I have since been gradually repairing it.

As to the effect my book may have had on anyone's hopes of an "ultimate reunion of Christianity," all I can say is that we are all up against a huge accumulation of injustices, faux pas, errors, cruelties, iniquities, on every hand, and there can be no hope of reunion unless these are seen for what they are, admitted, accepted, understood, painfully atoned for, replaced by the opposites. Reunion is not something that will painlessly happen. It depends on us, and even to some extent on you, not to say me. The best we can do at this moment is to be prepared to understand and tolerate a great deal that is utterly regrettable, and try as far as possible not to add more to the accumulation. At the moment, I can hope for your forgiveness, and assure you of my own contrition and of my prayers.

TO RICHARD BASS   *Richard Bass invited Merton "to say a word" to Bass'*
fellow parishioners belonging to the Guild of St. Paul.

APRIL 5, 1965

. . . One thing that converts have is that they have had to accept the
Church with a rather clear view of some of her shortcomings, culturally,
etc., and they have learned that these things do not matter. When cradle
Catholics suddenly become panicky about these shortcomings, there is
surely no need for the panic to affect us. But we can work peacefully and
calmly to make things better where we can.

In a word, what it comes down to is gratitude to the Lord, who has called
us into His true Church, and a real love and devotion to the Church, to
whom we owe everything. We can have this, and still not go in for foolish
and servile routines of "triumphalism" in an effort to make out that there
is never anything left to be desired. The Church is Christ, often a wounded
and bleeding Christ, surely more often bleeding than glorious, in this age of
history. Let us be very careful and faithful about avoiding everything that
makes the wounds of division bleed more. I think that is going to be a very
crucial point to keep in mind in the next few years. And let us meanwhile all
pray for one another that we may be faithful and strong.

TO GABRIELLE MUELLER   MAY 10, 1965

. . . The only advice I can give you is to seek God with sincere faith and
concentrate on the essentials: His redemptive and merciful love to all men,
His goodness to you in particular, the indications of His will for you as
shown in your own life, the grace of Baptism you have received, by which
Christ dwells in your heart, and the fact that you have received the Holy
Spirit, the Spirit of Love, which helps you to understand and love others in
spite of their faults and limitations, in spite of the harm they may do to you.
These are the realities of the Christian life and the Church will fit into this
pattern if you seek first the Kingdom of God and can stand on your own
feet. . . .

TO GEORGE BERNARD FLAHIFF   *George Bernard Flahiff became arch-*
bishop of Winnipeg, Manitoba, in 1961 and was made a cardinal of the Roman
Catholic Church in 1969.

JULY 17, 1965

. . . If we are going to get anywhere in the modern world, obviously
Christians are going to have to make new judgments in new situations, and
in order to do this they must be free to protest, in the name of Christian
conscience and of the Gospel, when mere acceptance and submission might
in effect mean cooperation with a power structure showing demonic tendencies (as in the case of Hitler's Germany). Where, as in the case of Germany again, the whole thing was decided beforehand by Church authority,
the Christian conscience was silenced and men simply had to submit to
what was objectively a great wrong, and they participated in this wrong,
thinking they were obeying God.

I think this is much the same kind of problem we face with Schema
13 [an early draft of Vatican II's *Pastoral Constitution on the Church in the
Modern World*]: and the most important thing, it seems to me, is not necessarily to lay down a hard-and-fast rule this way or that, even about the
bomb, but rather to make clear that there must be plenty of leeway for new
and creative decisions, and hence also for protest and for resistance (of a
non-violent and pacific kind) when the power structure arrogates to itself
decisions which are not acceptable to the Christian conscience. . . .

TO JOHN J. WRIGHT   JULY 17, 1965

I realize that it was perhaps presumptuous of me to draft the enclosed
notes [on Schema 13], which I have sent to *Commonweal.* I am not yet certain they will be published, and I have no doubt some of the bishops will
not like them. But on the other hand there is such a thing as public opinion
in the Church, and now, if ever, is the time for it to be articulate. . . .

Thanks for your long letter. It was a good idea to write and express your feelings exactly as they are. The real notion of the Church depends on the possibility of frank exchange and a genuine quest for truth. For my part, in a day or two I will be at the anniversary of my baptism again (almost thirty years now) and the vivid memory of these days keeps alive in me gratitude for my faith and for the Church.

It is certainly true that when I joined the Catholic Church I was myself fed up with the superficial hymn-singing vernacular worship that I had grown up with, and deeply attracted to the austere, traditional Latin liturgy of Roman Catholicism. I was even more attracted to it in the monastery and I grew up in it as a monk, so that now when I see even the monks discarding Gregorian and Latin I realize that it is a great loss, for monks at least ought to be able to keep alive this ancient tradition so valid in itself.

But at the same time, Rita, I have been able to swallow my own reactions and have come to see how much real value and grace comes to the new generation from the changes. There is no question that their hearts are really in all this and that there will be a true deepening of faith. Hence I am willing to sacrifice my own feelings and enter into the spirit of the new, and I must admit that this sacrifice has been a grace for me too. After all, the heart of our religion is love and sacrifice of ourselves for the good of others. Naturally when we cannot see it as a good for anyone, then the sacrifice becomes impossible. And here is where the great temptation lies. And it is an awfully hard thing. Do not think I reprove you and condemn your ideas. I know too well how difficult a position is yours.

So be patient and have courage and realize the difficulty you are in. There is *no substitute* for the Sacraments of Holy Church when you can easily get to them. I pray that it may not become too hard for you.

In a time of crisis like this there will be many conflicts of opinions on every level, religion, politics, and everywhere. Whatever may happen let us remember that persons are more important than opinions and that what counts is the immortal soul, not this or that idea concerning what ought to be done, for example, in Vietnam. Let us always give the other side the benefit of the doubt and credit others with good will even when they seem to be heading in a very wrong direction.

For my part, though I tend to go along with the modern views and on some points am probably what you would call very radical, I still want above all to try to be a bridge builder for everybody and to keep communication open between the extremists at both ends. That is an awful task, and I don't expect to get anywhere. But let us all try to keep the lines of communication open, especially among fellow Catholics. So much depends on it.

TO LORD NORTHBOURNE   *Lord Northbourne sent a copy of his book* Religion in the Modern World *to Merton, and Merton sent Northbourne an essay,* "The Church and the 'Godless' World," *an analysis of* Gaudium et Spes: Pastoral Constitution on the Church in the Modern World.

FEBRUARY 23, 1966

. . . I have written a commentary on the Council's *Constitution on the Church in the Modern World*. This was done not because I particularly wanted to do it, but because it was needed and asked for by [the London publisher] Burns and Oates. I am very much afraid that the job is unsatisfactory in many ways. At least I am not at all satisfied with it. The basic purpose of the Constitution is one that I obviously agree with: the maintaining of reasonable communication between the Church and the world of modern technology. If communication breaks down entirely, and there is no hope of exchanging ideas, then the situation becomes impossible. However, the naive optimism with which some of the Council Fathers seem to have wanted a Church entirely identified with the modern scientific mentality is equally impossible. I have said this in the end as conclusively as I could, with respect to one issue in particular. But in any case if I can get some copies made of the text I will send you one. There might be a few points of interest in it. I am of course very much concerned with one issue which is symptomatic of all the rest: nuclear warfare. It is true that one should not focus on one issue so as to distract attention from the entire scene in all its gravity. I think I have touched on a few other things as well, but have certainly not done a complete job, and have tried to be conciliatory in some ways. In a word, I am not satisfied with it and perhaps few others will be. . . .

TO DOLORES   NOVEMBER 16, 1966

... I guess the Church is going to go over some bumps, and if the institution gets a bit shaken, I think I will be secretly glad. It needs to be. But the Holy Spirit will not sleep and neither will redemptive love. May they both wake and act in us always.

TO FRIENDS   SEPTUAGESIMA SUNDAY 1967

... There has been a lot of talk about Fr. Charles Davis and his farewell to the Church. Note, his problem was church authority, not celibacy. He could conceivably have left the priesthood and got married with a dispensation. In a long statement which was front page news in England, he made some very drastic criticisms of the abuse of authority in the Church. I do not think these criticisms were altogether baseless or unjust. The present institutional structure of the Church is certainly too antiquated, too baroque, and is so often in practice unjust, inhuman, arbitrary and even absurd in its functioning. It sometimes imposes useless and intolerable burdens on the human person and demands outrageous sacrifices, often with no better result that to maintain a rigid system in its rigidity and to keep the same abuses established, one might think, until kingdom come. I certainly respect Fr. Davis's anguish—who of us does not sometimes share it? But I cannot follow him in his conclusion that the institutional Church has now reached the point where it can hardly be anything other than dishonest, tyrannical, mendacious and inhuman. He feels he has a moral obligation to leave the Church and he offers this theological justification for his decision.

I hope most of us Catholics have learned by now that this kind of decision on the part of one of our brothers merits our compassion and understanding, not fulminations against heresy and bad faith. One can feel Fr. Davis is still a brother without coming to the same conclusions as he did.

I have in fact just been reading Romano Guardini's excellent little book on Pascal [*Pascal for Our Time*]. He analyzes the "demon of combativeness" in Pascal—a demon which is no prerogative of Jansenists. At times one wonders if a certain combativeness is not endemic in Catholicism: a "compulsion to be always right" and to prove the adversary wrong. A compulsion which easily leads to witch-hunting and which, when turned the wrong way, hunts its witches in the Church herself and finally needs to find them in Rome. There are always human failures which can be exploited for this purpose. Pascal nearly went over the falls completely but he recognized the destructiveness of his own inner demon in time, and knows enough to be silent and to believe. And to love. The story of his death is very moving.

There comes a time when it is no longer important to prove one's point, but simply to live, to surrender to God and to love. There have been bad days when I might have considered doing what Fr. Davis has done. In actual fact I have never seriously considered leaving the Church and though the question of leaving the monastic state *has* presented itself, I was not able to take it seriously for more than five or ten minutes. It is true that if I had at one time or other left the Church, I would have found scores of friends who would have approved my action and declared it honest and courageous. I do not claim any special merit in having decided otherwise. Nor does a decision for Christian obedience imply an admission that I think authority has always been infallibly just, reasonable or human. Being a Catholic and being a monk have not always been easy. But I know that I owe too much to the Church and the Christ for me to be able to take these other things seriously. The absurdity, the prejudice, the rigidity and unreasonableness one encounters in some Catholics are nothing whatever when placed in the balance with the grace, love and infinite mercy of Christ in His Church. And after all, am I not arrogant too? Am I not unreasonable, unfair, demanding, suspicious and often quite arbitrary in my dealings with others? The point is not just "who is right?" but "judge not" and "forgive one another" and "bear one another's burdens." This by no means implies passive obsequiousness and blind obedience, but a willingness to listen, to be patient, and to keep working to help the Church change and renew herself from within. This is our task. Therefore by God's grace I remain a Catholic, a monk and a hermit. I have made commitments which are unconditional and cannot be taken back. I do not regard this position as especially courageous: it is just the ordinary stuff of life, the acceptance of limits which we must all accept in one way or another: the acceptance of a sphere in which one is called to love, trust and believe and pray—and meet those whom one is destined to meet and love.

More and more I see the meaning of my relationships with all of you, and the value of the love that unites us, usually unexpressed. This is the area in which the term "union in Christ" really means most to me, though some of you are not enrolled in the Church.

More and more since living alone I have wanted to stop fighting, and arguing, and proclaiming and criticizing. I think the points on which protest has been demanded of me and given by me are now well enough known. Obviously there may be other such situations in the future. In a world like ours—a world of war, riot, murder, racism, tyranny and established banditry—one has to be able to stand up and say NO. But there are also other things to do. I am more and more convinced of the reality of my own job which is meditation and study and prayer in silence. I do not intend to give up writing, that too is obviously my vocation. But I hope I will be able to give up controversy some day. Pray for me. When one gets older (Jan. 31 is my fifty-second birthday) one realizes the futility of a life wasted in argument when it should be given entirely to love. . . .

TO WILBUR H. FERRY   JANUARY 19, 1967

. . . Thanks for the *Observer* piece on or of Fr. [Charles] Davis. As far as I can see, his points are unassailable. Authority has simply been abused too long in the Catholic Church and for many people it just becomes utterly stupid and intolerable to have to put up with the kind of jackassing around that is imposed in God's name. It is an insult to God Himself and in the end it can only discredit all idea of authority and obedience. There comes a point where they simply forfeit the right to be listened to.

On the other hand, I regret that poor D. had to get pushed so far. It doesn't help the rest of us much. If everyone with any sense just pulls out, then that leaves the curial boys in full command of the field with the assurance that they are martyrs to justice or something. The real problem remains the reform of the Church people who remain inside. And if there can only be a little agreement on a more reasonable and free approach, something can be done. With super-organization and over-control, the whole works is doomed. . . .

TO ROSEMARY RADFORD REUTHER   *At the time that she and Merton were corresponding, Rosemary Radford Reuther was on the faculty of Howard University in Washington, D.C. She first wrote to tell Merton that she had heard of his interest in her article on Gabriel Vahanian and offered to send him the manuscript of her book* The Church Against Itself. *Though their correspondence spanned little more than a year, it was a spirited theological, and sometimes personal, exchange.*

JANUARY 29, 1967

. . . To begin with the Church: I have no problem about "leaving" or anything. My problem with "authority" is just the usual one and I can survive it. But the real Church. I am simply browned off with and afraid of Catholics. All Catholics, from [Alfredo] Ottaviani to [William] DuBay, all down the damn line. There are a few Catholics I can stand with equanimity when I forget they are Catholics, and remember they are just my friends, like Dan Berrigan and Ed Rice and Sister Mary Luke and a lot of people like that. I love the monks but they might as well be in China. I love all the nice well-meaning people who go to Mass and want things to get better and so on, but I understand Zen Buddhists better than I do them and the Zens understand me better. But this is awful because where is the Church and where am I in the Church? You are a person who might have an idea of the Church that might help me and that I might trust. An idea of the Church in which projects and crusades (ancient or modern) or ideas (new or old) or policies or orthodoxies (old or new) don't stand in the way between people. Is the Church a community of people who love each other or a big dogfight where you do your religious business, seeking meanwhile your friends somewhere else?

Could you suggest something good on this? I haven't been reading Catholic stuff, books or magazines, for a long time (except recently Guardini on Pascal). I'd be perfectly content to forget I am a Catholic. I suppose that is bad faith, because meanwhile I continue in a monastery and a hermitage where I am content with life and the institution is supporting me in this. . . .

. . . But I do wonder at times if the Church is real at all. I believe it, you know. But I wonder if I am nuts to do so. Am I part of a great big hoax?

I don't explain myself as well as I would like to: there is a real sense of and confidence in an underlying reality, the presence of Christ in the world which I don't doubt for an instant. But is that presence where we are all saying it is? We are all pointing (in various directions) and my dreadful feeling is that we are all pointing wrong. Could you point someplace for me, maybe?

FEBRUARY 14, 1967

Many thanks for your very good letter. It was what I needed, a sign that someone was there and that my own struggle with the institution was not madness, *hubris* or something. I do see, as you do, how demonic it can be. Your ms. [*The Church Against Itself*] is fine on that. I agree with you all along about the hardening of the Church as institution and idol and its becoming against what it ought to be a sign of. If we and others see this problem—and it is pretty terrible—then there *is* something going on, anyway, and if there is smoke going up here and there that is something. I also think we will be a very scattered Church for a while. But as long as I know what direction seems to be the one to go in, I will gladly go in it.

So, in your book first of all: what you say about the Church as happening clicks perfectly. I really think what I really wanted to know most of all was that my own personal "sense" of when Church happens was not just self-deception—at least not purely so. Because if that is where God speaks and the Spirit acts, then I can be confident that God has not abandoned us. Not left us at the mercy of the princes of the Church.

What I don't know about is the Christology. I am not arguing about it. It is just that my coming into the Church was marked by a pretty strong and dazzled belief in the Christ of the Nicene Creed. One reason for this was a strong reaction against the fogginess and subjectivity and messed-upness of the ideas about Christ that I had met with up and down in various kinds of Protestantism. I was tired of a Christ who had evaporated. But that is not what is bugging me and I will see about it all if I get to reading [Alfred] Loisy. What does bother me theologically (I am not enough of a theologian to be really bothered by theological problems) is the sense that, when you go back into the history of the Church, you run into a bigger and bigger hole of unconscious bad faith, and at that point I get rather uneasy about our dictating to all the "other religions" that we are the one authentic outfit that has the real goods. I am not saying that I want to be able to mix Christianity and Buddhism in quantities to suit myself, however. Far from it. I think you got me wrong on that. . . .

TO FRIENDS   EASTER 1967

. . . A friend wrote quoting a line of verse [by T.S. Eliot]: "In the juvescence of the year came Christ the Tiger" and wondered if Easter was going to be like that. There is an inner strength which is "ours" yet "not ours," which can be for us or against us, depending on whether we resolve to face it and submit, or seek to evade and resist it. Easter is the season of that strength (and Easter is all year round, really). At Easter we resolve liturgically and communally to "face it" and to join this Tiger who is then our Tiger and our Lamb. (I am thinking of the two great Blake poems: "Tyger Tyger burning bright. . . .") [Both poems are called "The Tyger"] There is no joy but in the victory of Christ over death in us: and all love that is valid has something of that victory. But the power of love cannot "win" in us if we insist on opposing it with something else to which we can cling, on which we trust because we ourselves can manipulate it. It all depends [on] who is in control: our own ego, or Christ. We must learn to surrender our ego-mastery to His mastery. And this implies a certain independence even of apparently holy systems and routines, official "answers" and infallible gimmicks of every kind. Easter celebrates the victory of love over everything. *Amor vincit omnia.* If we believe it we still understand it, because belief is what opens the door to love. But to believe only in systems and *statements* and not in *people* is an evasion, a betrayal of love. When we really believe as Christians, we find ourselves trusting and accepting *people* as well dogmas. Woe to us when we are merely orthodox, and reject human beings, flesh and blood, the aspirations, joys and needs of men. Yet there is no fruit, either, in merely sentimental gestures of communion that mean little, and seek only to flatter or placate. Love can also be tough and uncompromising in its fidelity to its own highest principles. Let us be united in joy, peace and prayer this Easter and always. "Fear not" says Jesus. "It is I. I am with you all days!"

TO FRIENDS   PENTECOST [MAY 14] 1967

. . . I think everyone is looking for a less systematic and less rigid kind of Church structure, something that leaves room for a more charismatic kind of religion, and this gave some of us a small glimmer of hope.

. . . There is everywhere a kind of hunger for the grace and light of the Spirit in forms that can be actually *experienced.* One hears a great deal of movements that can be called in a broad sort of sense "Pentecostal" even though they do not restrict themselves simply to far-out Protestant groups by any means. I am often asked what I think about all this. I cannot really judge from hearsay, but at any rate the phenomenon represents a real spiritual hunger, just as the craze for LSD represents a real hunger for experience—I hasten to add that I don't think an LSD trip is the answer for most of us! Personally, my own life and vocation have their own peculiar dimension which is a little different from all this. I have always tended more toward a deepening of faith in solitude, a "desert" and "wilderness" existence in which one does not seek special experiences. But I concur with these others in being unable to remain satisfied with a formal and exterior kind of religion. Nor do I think that a more lively liturgy is enough. Worship and belief have become ossified and rigid, and so has the religious life in many cases. The idea that "the Church" does all your thinking, feeling, willing, and experiencing for you is, to my mind, carried too far. It leads to alienation. After all, the Church is made up of living and loving human beings: if they all act and feel like robots, the Church can't experience and love on their behalf. The whole thing becomes an abstraction. Certainly it is fine that now the liturgy is becoming more spontaneous, more alive, and people are putting their hearts into it more. (I am not saying it was not possible to enter into the old Latin liturgy, but it was hard for many.) But we need a real deepening of life in every area, and that is why it is proper that laypeople and others who have been kept in subordinate positions are now claiming the right to make decisions in what concerns their own lives. This is also true in religious orders. As long as everything is decided at the top, and received passively by those at the bottom, the vocation crisis will continue. There is no longer any place in our life for a passive and inert religiosity in which one simply takes orders and lets someone else do all the thinking. Those who fail to accept such a situation are not rebels, most of the time, they are sensitive and intelligent human beings who protest against a real disorder and who have a right to be heard. . . .

TO A PRIEST   MAY 20, 1967

Sorry to have let your poignant letter go without answer for so long. I should have got right down to it then and there, but you know how it is. So many immediate demands, and I hate to answer a letter like that from the top of my head.

Of course now we all have very much the same problem. There is so much that is sick and false in our institutions. Submission is canonized and all opposition is suspect. There is a machinery that grinds everyone to powder. Then, as you say, the effect is that when we finally open our mouths we are so wrought up that we explode, and that, too, is held against us. From my own experience, I would suggest several things:

1. No point in direct confrontation when it is hopeless. You don't have any obligation to speak out if it just means you will have your face kicked in—except in an extreme case. In the ordinary routine struggles, silence is preferable, and then go ahead and do what you have to do without asking. Just do it, and let them figure it out afterwards.

2. Things are never quite as hopeless as they appear to us in our moments of crisis. Unexpectedly a good Bishop appears or someone open-minded is on the scene when needed and things just clear up, at least to some extent. Or you get support. If you have been patient, and stuck to your principles without making a federal case out of them, your turn will come.

3. In things like the wrestling with censors, I have always stood up for my rights and for my work. Often decisions against me have been reversed when I least expected. (A censor declared that *The Seven Storey Mountain*

should be put on the shelf for twenty years. Fortunately it had already been accepted by the publisher. . . .)

4. Seek some company with like-minded people and work together with them. That gives a better understanding of problems.

5. In ordinary conversation with people who are suffering, the best thing is to be quite frank about abuses and injustices and not to defend what is moribund and indefensible. Try to be as realistic about it as possible, and help as much as you can, without raising hopes of an impossible solution.

If you are frank in expressing your contrary opinion and yet accept obedience when it is imposed, they will soon come to respect you and will not use you as a stooge, should they be tempted to do so.

TO FRIENDS   ADVENT-CHRISTMAS 1967

. . . About religious renewal: obviously it is slower and more complicated than most of us would like. It is a pity that so much useless and misleading fuss is made about it in the papers: people's hopes are raised beyond measure then crushed by some conservative, then raised again by someone else. For my own part I am keeping out of all the political maneuverings that are involved, even in my own Order. I am not trying to sell anybody anything. My part in renewal, as far as this community is concerned, is to be a hermit. That too is a full-time job.

I do not have enormously sanguine hopes about what is likely to be accomplished all of a sudden in monastic renewal. I do think that a lot of the hopes are deceptive and sometimes silly: but the long term view seems to me to be quite good. A new generation is sooner or later going to take over, and I think the youngest generation in religion and elsewhere (those born about 1940–47) look very good indeed. The old guys like me have had it anyway, and as for the ones in between—well, let's hope they make out. They have a fifty-fifty chance, maybe. As for the ultra-conservatives, I am afraid I gave up worrying over them long since. There is nothing to be done about them, or about people who insist on filling the air with lamentations about everything as if the Church were just about to go over the falls and as if there were ten commandments under every bed. To be frank I think a lot of what is said and done is truly pathetic, but it is not worth paying attention to. It is God's Church, and I assume He knows what to do with it. For all I know He may be quite willing and ready to let a lot of dead wood fall off the tree without the slightest attempt to save it. Christ in the Gospel told us long ago that the branches of the vine would have to be pruned off. That may apply to some religious institutions. I can think of plenty of Catholic publications that could do the world a favor by going out of business. Others are trying hard to look alive, and I wish them luck: same way with colleges and schools. . . .

. . . The times are difficult. They call for courage and faith. Faith is in the end a lonely virtue. Lonely especially where a deeply authentic community of love is not an accomplished fact, but a job to be begun over and over: I am not referring to Gethsemani, where there is a respectable amount of love, but to all Christian communities in general. Love is not something we get from Mother Church as a child gets milk from the breast: it also has to be *given*. We don't get any love if we don't give any. And fear, suspicion, the sense that we have often been "had" and may well be "had" some more in the future, understandably restrain the spontaneity of love at times. So in the end we have to hope mightily in God who sent His Son in to the world to bring out not just optimism and good business but the only chance of man's making it at all.

Christmas, then, is not just a sweet regression to breast-feeding and infancy. It is a serious and sometimes difficult feast. Difficult especially if, for psychological reasons, we fail to grasp the indestructible kernel of hope that is in it. If we are just looking for a little consolation—we may be disappointed. Let us pray for one another, love one another in truth, in the sobriety of earnest, Christian hope: for hope, says Paul, does not deceive. A blessed and joyous Christmas to all of you.

TO CZESLAW MILOSZ · MARCH 15, 1968

Let me reassure you. There was absolutely nothing wounding in your letter. Anything you may be tempted to think about the Church, I think myself, and much more so as I am in constant contact with all of it. The boy scout atmosphere, the puerile optimism about the "secular city" and all the pathetic maneuvers to be accepted by the "world"—I see all this and much more. And I also get it from the other side. Conservative Catholics in Louisville are burning my books because I am opposed to the Vietnam War. The whole thing is ridiculous. I do think however that some of the young priests have a pathetic honesty and sincerity which is very moving. Beyond that, I have nothing to say. And I have a thick skin. You can say absolutely nothing about the Church that can shock me. If I stay with the Church it is out of a disillusioned love, and with a realization that I myself could not be happy outside, though I have no guarantee of being happy inside either. In effect, my "happiness" does not depend on any institution or any establishment. As for you, you are part of my "Church" of friends who are in many ways more important to me than the institution. . . .

PART 9

Seeking Unity Beyond Difference

Engaging in Interreligious Dialogue

"I believe that the only really valid thing that can be accomplished in the direction of world peace and unity is. . .the formation of men [and women]who. . .are able to unite in themselves and experience in their own lives all that is best and most true in the great spiritual traditions."

—To Doña Luisa Coomaraswamy, January 13, 1961

For Thomas Merton, interreligious dialogue began simply with a candid and respectful exchange of letters with partners who were almost always as well rooted in their religious and mystical traditions as he was in his. Merton recognized that such dialogue—whether with representatives of Western or Eastern traditions—was grounded in the capacity to listen as well as to speak. His interest in the dialogue lay more in the things that united people than in what divided them.

Sharing religious experience was more fruitful, he believed, than discussing differing doctrinal formulations (though such discussion did have its own importance). To John Whitman Sears, Merton wrote:

> I believe in the importance not so much of abstract notions as of living human dialogue. I have come to see that perhaps the most fruitful things we can do today are in the realm not of 'proving' this or that, or of 'convincing' anyone, but simply of communicating more or less validly with someone else on a level of genuine interest and in a matter of importance. . . (November 12, 1962).

This section highlights, first of all, letters to scholars of two religions that trace their origin back to Abraham: Judaism (Abraham Heschel, Erich Fromm, and Zalman Schachter) and Islam, with an emphasis on Sufism (Abdul Aziz, Herbert Mason, and Louis Massignon). This is followed by letters to well-known scholars of the following Eastern religions: Buddhism, including Zen (Daisetz T. Suzuki, Thich Nhat Hanh, and Marco Pallis), Chinese Taoism (John C. H. Wu), and Hinduism (Amiya Chakravarty and Doña Luisa Coomaraswamy, who was preparing an edition of her husband, Ananda K. Coomaraswamy's writings).

TWO ABRAHAMIC RELIGIONS

Judaism

TO ABRAHAM HESCHEL *A highly respected Jewish scholar, Abraham Heschel was forced to flee Germany by the Nazis. He taught at a Hebrew school in Cincinnati and then at Jewish Theological Seminary in New York City, where he completed his teaching career. He is a well-known and widely read author.*

DECEMBER 17, 1960

It was a real pleasure for me to get your good letter of October 23rd and the package of books, which are to me full of very satisfying intuitions and statements. It is an added satisfaction to have these books here at hand and to be able to meditate on them in a leisurely fashion, instead of rushing to get them back to the library.

I think the one that really appeals to me the most of all is *God in Search of Man.* I do not mean that I think it contains all your best and deepest thought, but it is what most appeals to me, at least now, because it has most to say about prayer. This is what I can agree with you on, in the deepest possible way. It is something beyond the intellect and beyond reflection. I am happy that someone is there, like yourself, to emphasize the mystery and the Holiness of God.

There are so many voices heard today asserting that one should "have religion" or "believe," but all they mean is that one should associate himself, "sign up" with some religious group. Stand up and be counted. As if religion were somehow primarily a matter of gregariousness. . . .

Needless to say, I look forward eagerly to your book on the Prophets. This fall I went through Amos carefully with my novices. It is a frightening accusation of our own age, with its prosperity, its arrogance and its unbelief. And its poverty, its injustice and its oppression. And now we are in the season when, in our liturgy, Isaiah is read daily, a season of longing for the fulfillment of divine promises, those promises which are so infinitely *serious,* and which are taken so lightly. Nor are these expectations fulfilled, for Christians, at Christmas merely. That too is another expectation. I believe humbly that Christians and Jews ought to realize together something of the same urgency of expectation and desire, even though there is a radically different theological dimension to their hopes. They remain the same hopes with altered perspectives. It does not seem to me that this is ever emphasized. . . .

It is a great pleasure to have received your fine book on *The Prophets*. I have been anticipating this for a long time, and my anticipation is not disappointed. You take exactly the kind of reflective approach that seems to me most significant and spiritually fruitful, for after all it is not the Prophets we study but the word of God revealed in and through them. They offer us examples of fidelity to Him and patterns of suffering and faith which we must take into account if we are to live as religious men in any sense of the word. . . .

. . . We have the bad habit of thinking that because we believe the prophecies are fulfilled, we can consider them to be fulfilled in any way we please, that is to say that we are too confident of understanding this "fulfillment." Consequently, the medieval facility with which the Kingdom of God was assumed to be the society inherited from Charlemagne. And consequently the even more portentous facility with which Christians did exactly what they accused the Jews of having done: finding an earthly fulfillment of prophecy in political institutions dressed up as theocracy. . . .

Abraham Heschel visited Merton on July 13, 1964.

JULY 27, 1964

Shortly after your visit, that warm and memorable occasion, which was a real and providential gift, I wrote this letter to Cardinal Bea. . . .

JULY 14, 1964

Your Eminence Cardinal Augustine Bea:

Yesterday I had the very great pleasure of speaking at some length with Rabbi Abraham Heschel who visited us briefly here at the monastery. He spoke much of his hopes and fears for the Council and of course spoke very much of Your Eminence and of the Jewish Chapter, which we all have so closely at heart, and concerning which we share a certain sadness, not devoid of hope.

Naturally, one such as I, who am very far from the scene, can offer no constructive help save that of prayer. But this may turn out in the end to be more efficacious than other means. . . . It is true that the Chapter can do much for the Jews, but there is no question that the Church herself stands to benefit by it spiritually in incalculable ways. I am personally convinced that the grace to truly see the Church as she is in her humility and in her splendor may perhaps not be granted to the Council Fathers if they fail to take account of her relation to the anguished Synagogue.... The deepest truths are in question. The very words themselves should suggest that the *ekklesia* is not altogether alien from the *synagogue* and that she should be able to see herself to some extent, though darkly, in this antitypal mirror. But if she looks at the picture, what she sees is not consoling. Yet she has the power to bring mercy and consolation into this mirror image, and thus to experience in herself the beatitude promised to the merciful. If she forgoes this opportunity out of temporal and political motives (in exactly the same way that a recent Pontiff [Pius XII] is accused of having done) will she not by that very fact manifest that she has in some way forgotten her own true identity? Is not then the whole meaning and purpose of the Council at stake? These are some of the thoughts that run through my mind as I reflect on the present situation in the Church of God. I dare to confide them to Your Eminence as a son to a Father.

Would it not perhaps be possible, theologically as well as "diplomatically," to meet the objections raised by those who fear to alienate the Moslems? . . . Christians and Jews together in the Koran occupy a privileged position as "people of the book" and as spiritual descendants of Abraham. Perhaps this common theological root in the promises made to Abraham might bear fruit in a Chapter on anti-Semitism oriented to peace with *all* Semites and then with special emphasis on the relation of the Church and Synagogue and at least an implicit recognition of the long-standing sin of anti-Jewish hatred among Catholics. . . .

On September 3, 1964, Abraham Heschel mailed a mimeographed statement about the declaration at the Council on the Jewish-Christian relationship. The original statement, he said, had been in almost all respects a monumental declaration. Since the last session of the Council, reports had come to him that the statement had been rewritten in a way that made it ineffective and even offensive to Jews. It was said to state that "the Church expects in unshakable faith and with ardent desire the union of the Jewish people with the Church." Dr. Heschel pointed out that he had repeatedly said to leaders at the Vatican (and he had been received in audience by Paul VI): "I am ready to go to Auschwitz any time if faced with the alternative of conversion or death." He also pointed out that no such expectations had been expressed by the Church regarding Islam. He hoped that the coming session of the Council would eradicate tensions between Catholics and Jews.

SEPTEMBER 9, 1964

Your mimeographed bulletin referring to the revised Jewish Chapter has just reached me.

It is simply incredible. I don't know what to say about it.

This much I will say: my latent ambitions to be a true Jew under my Catholic skin will surely be realized if I continue to go through experiences like this, being spiritually slapped in the face by these blind and complacent people of whom I am nevertheless a "collaborator." If I were not "working with" the Catholic movement for ecumenical understanding, it would not be such a shock to take the three steps backward after each timid step forward. . . .

TO ERICH FROMM   *Psychoanalyst, philosopher, and anthropologist Erich Fromm (1900–1980) was born in Frankfurt, Germany, and trained as a psychoanalyst in Berlin. In 1934 he left Nazi Germany and came to New York City. He taught at the National University of Mexico, Cuernavaca. He also kept a New York office, where he spent two months each year. One of his chief concerns was the adjustment of individuals to society.*

OCTOBER 2, 1954

Some time ago when I was reading your *Psychoanalysis and Religion*, I thought I would write you a letter. Now that I am in the middle of *Man for Himself* and am hoping to get *Escape from Freedom*, I think I shall put a few of my thoughts on paper and send them to you.

. . . I would like to say that I notice a profound agreement between the psychoanalyst and the Catholic priest on some very fundamental points. I believe that this agreement ought to be noticed and emphasized, because I feel that our two vocations in a sense complete and assist one another. I also feel that there is much in Christian tradition that fits in very well with the general tendency of writers like [TK] Horney and yourself.

The reason for this is that Christianity is fundamentally humanistic, in the sense that its chief task is to enable man to achieve his destiny, to find himself, to be himself: to be the person he is made to become. Man is supposed to be God's helper in the work of creating himself. *Dei adjutores sumus.* Salvation is no passive thing. Nor is it an absorption of man into a kind of nonentity before the face of God. It is the elevation and diviniza-tion of man's freedom. And the Christian life demands that man be fully conscious of his freedom and of the responsibility it implies. . . .

At a time like the present, when over vast areas of the earth systems of thought and government are tending to the complete debasement of man's fundamental dignity as the image of God, it seems to me important that all who take to heart the value and the nobility of the human spirit should realize their solidarity with one another, and should be able to commu-nicate with one another in every way, in spite of perhaps grave doctrinal divergences. . . .

Finally, on one point I think you are definitely wrong. I do not see how you can consider that mystical religion is indifferent on the question of the objective existence of God. Jnana yoga and perhaps Buddhism are more or less atheistic, but the majority of true mystics stand or fall with the exis-tence or nonexistence of God. Besides there is, it seems to me, the absolute ontological impossibility of anything existing if God does not exist. . . . I think what you are really saying is that true mysticism does not know God after the manner of an object, and that is perfectly true. God is not expe-rienced as an object outside ourselves, as "another being" capable of being enclosed in some human concept. Yet though He be known as the source of our own being, He is still *das ganz Andere.* . . .

NOVEMBER 14, 1961

. . . Catholics in the United States are very silent and inarticulate on this most urgent question, but a small Catholic peace movement is at least starting. I am one of the sponsors, though I don't have much freedom of action where I now am. In Europe Catholic thought has been much more articulate and Cardinal Ottaviani, who is very high up in the Roman Curia and is in fact the head of the Holy Office (and something of a shellback, to tell the truth), has pronounced very strongly for the total abolition of war, asserting that nuclear war is not just a more intense form of the traditional warfare but a new species of war which does not admit to any of the conditions that make war morally permissible. To tell the truth, I believe the Holy See ought frankly to pronounce a condemnation of nuclear war. Whether this can be expected or not is another matter. I don't think Pope John would hesitate if it were up to him alone. The irony of it is that the integrist faction in Rome, which is most insistent on Papal infallibility, is actually against the Council, which gives more importance to the ideas of the bishops as a body. And the Pope himself is the one who wants the Council. A paradoxical development of Vatican centralism. . . .

[COLD WAR LETTER 5] DECEMBER 1961

. . . The situation certainly makes the psalms we chant in choir each day most eloquent. Erich, I am a complete Jew as far as that goes: I am steeped in that experience of bafflement, compunction and wonder which is the experience of those who have been rescued from tyranny, only to renounce freedom and in confusion and subjection to worse tyrants, through infidelity to the Lord. For only in His service is there true freedom, as the Prophets would tell us. This is still the clear experience of the Jews, as it ought to be of the Christians, except that we were too sure of our freedom and too sure we could never alienate it . . . If only Christians had valued the freedom of the sons of God that was given them. They preferred safety and the Grand Inquisitor.

The Catholics in the peace movement we are now starting are not the most influential in the country by any means, quite the contrary. Some of us are of an already notoriously pacifist group, the Catholic Worker, tolerated by all as a sign that we can find a mansion for beats in the Church as well as for the respectable. There are few priests, no bishops. . . .

OCTOBER 8, 1963

. . . I agree with you perfectly about the "unconscious faith" of so-called atheists and the unconscious infidelity of supposedly religious people. This of course is the great thing a priest has to contend with, not only in others but also in himself. The key is of course, as Kierkegaard saw, the question of conformism and security. When one becomes a "believer" in a well-established and accepted group, he no longer needs the concern and the risk of freedom that are demanded in real faith. Fortunately for us in the Church, there is that other element, the Holy Spirit's action and grace, which keep working to break the institutional crust. . . .

JANUARY 15, 1966

. . . You will be interested to know that I have moved out of the monastery to live in the woods as a hermit, remaining under the jurisdiction of the monastery. I go down once a day, take one meal there, and give one class a week on anything I like. At the moment I am giving conferences on the poetry of Rilke, but I cover a lot of other areas and hope to give a few lectures on Sufism, then Celtic monasticism and so on. As to the solitary life, it is to my mind a very valid experiment. . . .

On August 25, 1966, Fromm sent this interesting comment: "I understand very well about your need for meditation and delving into reality. I try to do this in my own much more limited way, and to meditate an hour each morning. . . . I find tremendous rewards of new insights and new strengths; I am sometimes surprised how, even at my age of 66, and after so many years of being occupied with the analysis of others and myself, I still discover the many veils and blindfolds and the increasing happiness when more and more falls off."

OCTOBER 13, 1966

. . . I am thriving in the hermitage: it is the ideal milieu for me, out in the woods, plenty of silence and inner freedom. I am not cut off in an artificial way from other people: occasionally I have a visitor for a day or two at the monastery and can keep human that way, and I also participate a little in some of the monastery activities, giving a course on this and that—for a while lectured on Marx. Now I am talking on modern poets. Really I feel much more human and natural on my own than when tied up in the routines of an institution. Here I don't have to play any part at all . . . I just live.

TO ZALMAN SCHACHTER   *Born in Poland in 1924 and interned in a prison camp by the Vichy French government, Zalman Schachter came to the United States in 1941. He was ordained a rabbi in 1947 and taught at the University of Manitoba in Winnipeg, Canada. In 1968 he received a doctorate from Hebrew Union College in Cincinnati. His interest in the mystical aspects of Judaism created an obvious affinity with Merton. During his stay in Cincinnati, Rabbi Schachter visited Merton several times.*

[COLD WAR LETTER 37] FEBRUARY 15, 1962

. . . The Jews have been the great eschatological sign of the twentieth century. That everything comes to depend on people understanding this fact, not just reacting to it with a little appropriate feeling, but seeing the whole thing as a sign from God, *telling* us. Telling us what? Among other things, telling Christians that if they don't look out they are going to miss the boat or fall out of it, because the antinomy they have unconsciously and complacently supposed between the Jews and Christ is not even a very good figment of the imagination. The Suffering Servant is One: Christ, Israel. There is one wedding and one wedding feast, not two or five or six. There is one bride. There is one mystery, and the mystery of Israel and of the Church is ultimately to be revealed as One. As one great scandal maybe to a lot of people on both sides who had better things to do than come to the wedding.

And of course it is in no sense a matter of shuttling back and forth institutionally. Each on our side must prepare for the great eschatological feast on the mountains of Israel. . . .

When the Christians began to look at Christ as Prometheus. . . . You see what I mean? Then they justified war, then they justified crusades, then they justified pogroms, then they justified Auschwitz, then they justified the bomb, then they justified the Last Judgment: the Christ of Michelangelo is Prometheus, I mean the Christ in the Sistine Chapel. He is whipping sinners with his great Greek muscles. "All right, if we can't make it to the wedding feast (and we are the ones who refused), we can blow up the joint and say it is the Last Judgment." Well, that's the way it is the Judgment, and that's the way men judge themselves, and that's the way the poor and the helpless and the maimed and the blind enter into the Kingdom: when the Prometheus types blow the door wide open for them. . . .

Islam (with an emphasis on Sufism)

TO ABDUL AZIZ   *A native of Karachi, Pakistan, Abdul Aziz, educated at the University of Karachi, held a government job in the Office of the Collector of Customs. He dedicated his life to a study of mysticism, especially Sufism. Favorably impressed by Merton's* Ascent to Truth, *and on the advice of Louis Massignon, he wrote to Merton. This was the beginning of a long and fruitful relationship by correspondence that lasted from 1960 to 1968.*

NOVEMBER 17, 1960

It was a pleasure for me to receive your good letter and I am certainly grateful to our mutual friend Louis Massignon for referring you to me. Thank you for your very kind words concerning the *Ascent to Truth.* As you expressed some interest in the things I write, I have sent to you under separate cover two packages of books of mine which I hope you will accept as a gift. They include most of those you ask for. *The Seven Storey Mountain* is the original edition of *Elected Silence,* and it is a longer, more complete version. There are some passages on contemplation in the later sections of *The Sign of Jonas* and I also included two little books on monasticism. I hope you can find something in these books that may be of interest to you. As to *Seeds of Contemplation,* the reason why I have not added this to the others is, frankly, shame. The book was written when I was much younger and contains many foolish statements, but one of the most foolish reflects an altogether stupid ignorance of Sufism.*. . .

---

* In *Seeds of Contemplation* (published 1949), Merton speaks of "the sensual dreams of the Sufis" as a "poor substitute" for the true contemplation that is found only in the Church. Actually, in this letter he seems to have forgotten that in the December 1949 reprint he had eliminated the reference to the Sufis.

...I am also well acquainted with Jalalu'l Din Rumi, who is to my mind one of the greatest poets and mystics, and I find his words inspiring and filled with the fire of divine love. I am also tremendously impressed with the insights into the mysticism of Islam that I have been able to attain through the medium of Louis Massignon's writings. I believe that it is of the greatest importance for these writings to be studied and made known everywhere and I am sure your work is one that will be blessed with great fruitfulness. I should be very glad indeed to make known to you any possible sources in Western mysticism. In return, if you can help me to widen my knowledge and understanding of Sufism I would be deeply grateful to you. . . .

As one spiritual man to another (if I may so speak in all humility), I speak to you from my heart of our obligation to study the truth in deep prayer and meditation, and bear witness to the light that comes from the All-Holy God into this world of darkness where He is not known and not remembered. The world we live in has become an awful void, a desecrated sanctuary, reflecting outwardly the emptiness and blindness of the hearts of men who have gone crazy with their love for money and power and with pride in their technology. . . .

JANUARY 30, 1961

. . . You ask for some information about our life here. . . . This monastery is a contemplative community, that is to say we are monks who live strictly enclosed within our monastery and do not go outside into the world except for very exceptional reasons. We keep a strict rule of silence, not speaking to one another except when it is essential. Our life is devoted to prayer, and we live under a relatively strict discipline of poverty and obedience. Of course, like all Christian monks, we are obligated to chastity. I say our poverty is relatively strict: we possess nothing at all, but the standard of life in the monastery would not appear poor to a resident in Pakistan though it is relatively poor in America. That is to say we lack many of the comforts and conveniences that American people regard as necessities, and we live by our manual labor and the produce of our farm. Our clothing is poor and simple, and our food also. The diet is vegetarian.

. . . I am allowed by the Father Abbot to spend a certain part of the day, often an entire afternoon, in a little house in the woods where there is complete silence and isolation, and it is possible to give oneself completely to meditative prayer. I feel that in some respects our situation is a little analogous to that of the Sufis in their relation with the orthodox Moslem community with its emphasis on legal observance. . . .

MAY 13, 1961

. . . I especially appreciate what you said about remembering me in prayer on the "Night of Power" since I have read about this in [Titus] Burckhardt. I have been remembering you in prayer as the days go by, and will keep you especially in mind on the feast of Pentecost, May 21st, in which we celebrate the descent of the Holy Ghost into the hearts and souls of men that they may be wise with the Spirit of God. It is the great feast of wisdom. . . .

. . . . Let us in any case have great love for Truth and open our hearts to the Spirit of God our Lord and Father, Compassionate and Merciful. He alone is Real, and we have our reality only as a gift from Him at every moment. And at every moment it is our joy to be realized by Him over an abyss of nothingness: but the world has turned to the abyss and away from Him Who Is. That is why we live in dreadful times, and we must be brothers in prayer and worship no matter what may be the doctrinal differences that separate our minds. . . .

SEPTEMBER 24, 1961

. . . It is my belief that all those in the world who have kept some vestige of sanity and spirituality should unite in firm resistance to the movements of power politicians and the monster nations, resist the whole movement of war and aggression, resist the diplomatic overtures of power and develop a strong and coherent "third world" that can stand on its own feet and affirm the spiritual and human values which are cynically denied by the great powers. . . . May the Lord give us peace and spare us to serve Him in joy and understanding. May He bless us in wisdom and may the light of His countenance shine upon us. . . .

. . . We are about the same age, perhaps almost exactly the same age [Abdul Aziz had written that he was forty-six years of age and unmarried]. I am now forty-seven. I was born in France, educated in France, England and America. My outlook is not purely American and I feel sometimes disturbed by the lack of balance in the powerful civilization of this country. It is technologically very strong, spiritually superficial and weak. There is much good in the people, who are very simple and kind, but there is much potential evil in the irresponsibility of the society that leaves all to the interplay of human appetites, assuming that everything will adjust itself automatically for the good of all. . . . I entered the monastery twenty years ago, and am the novice master here. I believe my vocation is essentially that of a pilgrim and an exile in life, that I have no proper place in this world but that for that reason I am in some sense to be the friend and brother of people everywhere, especially those who are exiles and pilgrims like myself. . . .

December 26, 1962

. . . The departure of Louis Massignon is a great and regrettable loss. He was a man of great comprehension and I was happy to have been numbered among his friends, for this meant entering into an almost prophetic world, in which he habitually moved. It sees to me that mutual comprehension between Christians and Moslems is something of very vital importance today, and unfortunately it is rare and uncertain, or else subjected to the vagaries of politics. I am touched at the deep respect and understanding which so many Moslems had for him [Massignon], indeed they understood him perhaps better than many Christians. . . .

I am not surprised at your great interest in St. John of the Cross. The question of detachment depends it seems to me first of all on self-knowledge. Or rather the two are mutually interdependent. One must know what are the real attachments in his soul before he can effectively work against them, and one must have a detached will in order to see the truth of one's attachments. . . . Exterior detachment is easier: it is a matter of renouncing comforts and gratifications of the sensual appetites, and this renunciation is of course essential. . . . One must handle this question with prudent discretion. But inner detachment centers around the "self," especially in one's pride, one's desire to react and to defend or to assert "self" in one's own will. This attachment to the self is a fertile sowing ground for seeds of blindness, and from this most of our errors proceed. I think it is necessary for us to see that God Himself works to purify us of this inner "self" that tends to resist Him and to assert itself against Him. . . .

JUNE 2, 1963

. . . As you say, the differences begin with the questions of soteriology (salvation).* Personally, in matters where dogmatic beliefs differ, I think that controversy is of little value because it takes us away from the spiritual realities into the realm of words and ideas. In the realm of realities we may have a great deal in common, whereas in words there are apt to be infinite complexities and subtleties which are beyond resolution. It is, however, important, I think, to try to understand the beliefs of other religions. But much more important is the sharing of the experience of divine light, and first of all of the light that God gives us even as the Creator and Ruler of the Universe. It is here that the area of fruitful dialogue exists between Christianity and Islam. I love the passages of the Quran which speak of the manifestations of the Creator in His Creation. . . .

OCTOBER 18, 1963

. . . The one thing which we must absolutely confess without any hesitation is the supreme transcendent Unity of God, and the fact that there is no other with Him or beside Him. He has "no helper." The work of creation and of the salvation of man is entirely His work alone. The manner in which Christianity preaches salvation in and through Christ must not obscure this fact which is basic to the Christian faith, as it is to Islam. The fact is that we believe, as you know, that Christ is not a being outside of God who is His helper. It is God in Christ who does the work of salvation. But here we come to the enormous difficulty of stating in technical terms the

---

* In a letter of April 4, 1963, Abdul Aziz had detailed the beliefs of Islam. It inculcates, he said, "individual responsibility for one's actions and does not subscribe to the doctrine of atonement or the theory of redemption."

incarnation without making Christ something separate from God, when in fact the humanity of Christ is "an individual" human nature. This is beyond me for the moment, but I will try to think about it in terms that would be meaningful to you. . . .

I perfectly agree that any man who in his heart sincerely believes in God and acts according to his conscience, with all rectitude, will certainly be saved and will come to the vision of God. I have no doubt in my mind that a sincere Muslim will be saved and brought to heaven, even though for some reason he may not subjectively be able to accept all that the Church teaches about Christ . . . This also applies to Jews, Hindus, Buddhists and in fact to all sincere men. I think that all men who believe in one God Who is the Father of all and Who wills all to be saved, will certainly be saved if they do His will. This is certainly the teaching of the Catholic Church. . . .

JUNE 28, 1964

. . . In your letter of last August you referred to a statement of Pope Pius XI about the question of the salvation of non-Christians.* I do not know if I ever commented on this, but I think I did. In any case, it should be perfectly clear that Christian doctrine on this point is in accord with common sense and the ordinary religious feeling of all believers: obviously the ultimate destiny of each individual person is a matter of his personal response to the truth and to the manifestation of God's will to him, and not merely a matter of belonging to this or that organization. Hence it follows that any man who follows his faith and his conscience, and responds truthfully and sincerely to what he believes to be the manifestation of the will of God, cannot help being saved by God. There is and can be no question in my mind that every sincere believer in God, no matter what may be his affiliation, if he lives according to his belief will receive mercy and, if needed, further enlightenment. How can one be in contact with the great thinkers and men of prayer of the various religions without recognizing that these men have known God and have loved Him because they recognized themselves loved by Him? It is true that there are different ways to Him and some are more perfect and more complete than

---

* Pius XI had said to the apostolic delegate to Libya: "Do not think you are going among infidels. Muslims attain to salvation. The ways of Providence are infinite."

others. It is true that the revelation given to the "People of the Book," Christians, Jews and Muslims, is more detailed and more perfect than that given through natural means only to the other religions....

DECEMBER 9, 1964

... When is Ramadan in 1965? I would like to join spiritually with the Moslem world in this act of love, faith and obedience toward Him Whose greatness and mercy surround us at all times, and Whose wisdom guides and protects us even though, in the godlessness of the world of men, we are constantly on the edge of disaster ... I see more and more clearly that even the believers are often far short of having true faith in the Living God. The great sin remains idolatry, and there is an idolatry of *concepts* as well as of graven images....

NOVEMBER 7, 1965

... Well, my friend, we live in troubled and sad times, and we must pray the infinite and merciful Lord to bear patiently with the sins of this world, which are very great. We must humble our hearts in silence and poverty of spirit and listen to His commands which come from the depths of His love, and work that men's hearts may be converted to the ways of love and justice, not of blood, murder, lust and greed....

JANUARY 2, 1966

... The main thing I can tell you without difficulty is the outline of my daily life in the hermitage.

The hermitage is ten minutes' walk from the monastery in a hidden place in the woods....

I go to bed about 7:30 at night and rise about 2:30 in the morning. On rising I say part of the canonical Office consisting of psalms, lessons, etc. Then I take an hour or an hour and a quarter for meditation. I follow this with some Bible reading and then make some tea or coffee, with perhaps a piece of fruit or some honey. With breakfast I begin reading, and continue reading and studying until sunrise. Now the sun rises very late, in summer it rises earlier, so this period of study varies but it is on the average about two hours.

At sunrise I say another Office of psalms, etc., then begin my manual work, which includes sweeping, cleaning, cutting wood, and other necessary jobs. This finishes about nine o'clock, at which time I say another Office of psalms. If I have time then I may write a few letters, usually short (today is Sunday and I have more time). After this I go down to the monastery to say Mass, as I am not yet permitted to offer Mass in the hermitage. Saying Mass requires an altar, an acolyte who serves the Mass, special vestments, candles and so on. It is in a way better to have all this in the monastery. It would be hard to care for so many things and keep them clean in the hermitage. After Mass I take one cooked meal in the monastery. Then I return immediately to the hermitage usually without seeing or speaking to anyone except the ones I happen to meet as I go from place to place (these I do not ordinarily speak to as we have a rule of strict silence). (When I speak it is to the Abbot, whom I see once a week, or to someone in a position of authority, about necessary business.)

On returning to the hermitage I do some light reading, and then say another Office about one o'clock. This is followed by another hour or more of meditation. On feast days I can take an hour and a half or two hours for this afternoon meditation. Then I work at my writing. Usually I do not have more than an hour and a half or two hours at most for this, each day. Following that, it being now late afternoon (about four) I say another Office of psalms, and prepare for myself a light supper. I keep down to a minimum of cooking, usually only tea or soup, and make a sandwich of some sort. Thus I have only a minimum of dishes to wash. After supper I have another hour or more of meditation, after which I go to bed.

Now you ask about my method of meditation. Strictly speaking I have a very simple way of prayer. It is centered entirely on attention to the presence of God and to His will and His love. That is to say that it is centered on *faith* by which alone we can know the presence of God. One might say this gives my meditation the character described by the Prophet as "being before God as if you saw Him." Yet it does not mean imagining anything or conceiving a precise image of God, for to my mind this would be a kind of idolatry. On the contrary, it is a matter of adoring Him as invisible and infinitely beyond our comprehension, and realizing Him as all. My prayer tends very much toward what you call *fana*. There is in my heart this great thirst to recognize totally the nothingness of all that is not God. My prayer is then a kind of praise rising up out of the center of Nothing and Silence. If I am still present "myself" this I recognize as an obstacle about which I can do nothing unless He Himself removes the obstacle. If He wills He can then make the Nothingness into a total clarity. If He does not will, then the Nothingness seems to itself to be an object and remains an obstacle. Such is my ordinary way of prayer, or meditation. It is not "thinking about" anything, but a direct seeking of the Face of the Invisible Which cannot be found unless we become lost in Him who is Invisible. I do not ordinarily write about such things and I ask you therefore to be discreet about it. But I write this as a testimony of confidence and friendship. It will show you how much I appreciate the tradition of Sufism. Let us therefore adore and praise God and pray to Him for the world which is in great trouble and confusion. I am united with you in prayer during this month of Ramadan and will remember you on the Night of Destiny. . . .

JANUARY 16, 1968

. . . About reading in solitude [this in reply to Abdul Aziz's question about whether reading is a hindrance to interior detachment for one living a solitary life], I have the following remarks to make:

First, it is true that one who is learning to meditate must also learn to get along without any support external to his own heart and the gifts of God. Hence it is good for such a one to have to remain in silence without reading or even using vocal prayers sometimes, in order to come to terms with the need for inner struggle and discipline. On the other hand this not a universal rule. There are times when it is necessary to read, and even to read quite a lot, in order to store up material and get new perspectives. In the solitary life, however, though one has a lot of time for reading, it becomes difficult to read a great deal. One finds that in a couple of hours he reads only a few pages. The rest of the time is spent in reflection and prayer. It becomes difficult to absorb more than this. Moderate reading is, however, normal. Provided that more time is spent in prayer and meditation than in reading. . . .

To HERBERT MASON   *Noted author and translator Herbert Mason, professor of history at Boston University, is well known for his narrative versions of the epic* Gilgamesh *as well as* The Death of al-Hallaj. *As a youth of twenty-six in 1959, he came under the influence of Louis Massignon, then seventy-six, the distinguished professor emeritus of the College de France, a master of the Arabic language and of Muslim studies. They became close friends. It was Mason who interested Merton in Massignon. In 1982 Mason published his translation of Massignon's greatest work,* The Passion of al-Hallaj.

JUNE 6, 1959

Your paragraph on Prometheus echoes very exactly and sums up what I have been driving at . . . It is the great mystery of grace. Not grace in the sense of a kind of theological gasoline that you get by performing virtuous actions (that is the sin we commit!), but grace in the fact that God has given Himself completely to us already. Completely. But we have to enter into the darkness of His presence. Not tragic darkness, just ordinariness: but above all what does not appear to be religion. . . .

. . . The journey is present every day. Better, the voyage. The nothing which happens every day has to be an adventure, and it is. To be Prometheus and to be on a voyage is almost the same thing. It is out of the nothing, the void, of our own self that we freely create the paradise in which we walk with God. This act of creation is—grace. It is all a gift. Grace out of nothingness. . . .

AUGUST 24, 1959

One of the most fascinating things I have had my hands on in a long time is that offprint of Louis Massignon about the Seven Sleepers.* It is tremendous, and I want to know more about all those places and things. . . .

Louis Massignon wrote me a letter a long time ago and I was always wanting to answer it. He is a terrific person, from what I know of him, and because of him I have wanted for ten minutes to learn some Oriental languages. Do tell him that I am full of an impassioned interest in the Seven Sleepers and that I send him my good wishes and pray for him. . . .

---

* According to a sixth-century legend, seven Christians in Ephesus took refuge in a cave during the persecution of Decius. God put them to sleep. Two hundred years later they awoke to find their city Christian.

SEPTEMBER 3, 1959

. . . The main purpose of this immediate reply is that I want to say how deeply moved I am at this idea of Louis Massignon's that salvation is coming from the most afflicted and despised. This, of course, is the only idea that makes any sense in our time. It is the key to our time or to any other time. It is the great idea of the Bible, the Prophets, everything. I have been obsessed with it for a long time. . . .

. . . I want to put something about Hallaj in the book I am writing, and have nothing at hand. Can you lend or send me anything? The book is all about inner experience, intuition, the inmost self that sees in and through our whole being, and not just through intellectual constructions—which too often are a veil between us and experience, deliberately woven to frustrate immediate experience. . . .

NOVEMBER 14, 1959

. . . I received Louis Massignon's further brochures on the Seven Sleepers. All that material is really fascinating. . . .

. . . One of the functions of our "remnant" is to recognize the supreme value of the useless. That too is certainly part of the message of the Seven Sleepers. They just slept. . . .

CHRISTMAS EVE 1959

. . .I just want to say that your last poem, about the Seven Sleepers and Brittany, moved me very much, and I think it is one of the very finest. It has a great deal in it. Thank you for sending it. I like its dark and austere character. . . .

The other day I happened to have a chance to see the old Shaker settlement near Lexington [Kentucky]. Only buildings, of course, nobody there since 1910. It was sad and moving. It was once an intense and rather wacky spiritual center, but I think it was very significant. The truth and simplicity of their handiwork remains to bear witness to something tremendously genuine in their spirit. For some reason it made a similar intuitive impression on me to that made by the story of the Sleepers. The spirit of these people was very alive in their building—the one I went into, the only one I could get into, had a marvelous double winding stair coming out in the mysterious pale light of a small dome at the top of the house. The silence, light, and effect were extraordinary. There were some empty rooms at the top of the house, and I went into them to taste the silence—sunlit windows, looking out on the bleak fields and a huge Lebanon cedar, with the wind in it. You would like the place. . . .

. . . You know I have the greatest respect for every insight of Louis Massignon, and I have no doubt first that he is right about our hope being to unite with the Arabs, and second about his fear that this will not be done and that consequently God will search "Jerusalem with lamps" as the prophet said. It will be a trial by fire. I doubt if America will suffer Communism exactly, unless we are beaten in a war. But God alone knows what is going to happen. . . .

I have not had any direct contact with the Negro problem in the South, but I was hoping that a Protestant Negro minister [Martin Luther King Jr.] who is in the forefront of the non-violent resistance movement would show up here. He may still do so and I would have an opportunity to speak with him. . . .

. . . The thing to remember is that in non-violence the important thing is *not* the reaction of the people, the effect on the onlookers, or the use the demonstration can be put to by the papers. That would put non-violence on the same vulgar plane as the other cheap tricks of politicians. It was not the effect on people of Gandhi's fasts that were efficacious, but the fasts themselves. They have their own spiritual effect, quite apart from what people may think, or how they may react. . . .

Poor Pasternak has died. His story has ended and remains to be understood. There again, the newspapers raised so much dust and smoke that no one could see what it was all about. . . .

Let us think more about the role of America in all this. I have been feeling rather negative and discouraged, but I realize how little I see and understand. All I know is that I have an overwhelming feeling that we are missing the boat because we have been blinded by money and the love of material things. . . .

JULY 5, 1960

. . . I will write to Louis. I keep him in my prayers and will send him St. Peter Damian's prayer to the Seven Sleepers. . . .

JANUARY 14, 1961

. . . Louis told a Moslem in Pakistan to write to me, Abdul Aziz. I have two fine letters from him. It looks as though I am being drawn into Louis' Moslem circle after all. The circle of the poor, the outcast. That is good. . . .

. . . I think more and more of simply being in contact, in friendship, with people of the Orient and of Islam. There is nothing I can do for them, or "do for" anybody. Who are we that we wake up in the morning expecting ourselves to "do something for" somebody or for "the world"? I can only try to be someone for them. This I very much want to be. And the doing part need only be an expression that I am there. This is very much the Foucauld universal brother idea, I think . . . I think the only thing that will help is being a more or less helpless brother, in Christ. Even a rather silent one, because I cannot write as much as I would like to all the people. . . .

[COLD WAR LETTER 52] MARCH 9, 1962

. . . I absolutely agree with you on the danger of non-violent and civil-disobedience movements that go ahead irresponsibly. There is a great danger of opportunism and improvisation here too, especially as a lot of them are young and lack perspective. There must be non-violence, and this is one of the only solutions. But precisely it must be real, mature, well-prepared, disciplined non-violence. And for this we are by no means ready. There is every danger that resentment, immature rebelliousness, Beatnik non-conformism, and so on may be taken automatically to be charismatic just because they are opposed to what is obviously stuffy and inert. And cruel.

. . . It requires a great deal of spiritual wisdom and formation to do this kind of thing. I am afraid that the little bud of non-violence that is beginning to show itself in this country may be killed by discredit, through the inexperience of its proponents. And through their obvious spiritual eclecticism, immaturity, instability, and so on. Yet on the other hand some of the kids from the Catholic Worker were down here and they are in general very solid. Or so I think. Especially Jim Forest seems to me to have considerable possibilities. He is in jail now, and perhaps ought not to be there. I mean he perhaps precipitated things in a way that should not have been done. Yet they have a refreshing hopefulness and energy. This seems to have been lost in the years after the war and is coming back at last, but perhaps too late. . . .

NOVEMBER 17, 1962

Thank you for informing me so promptly of the solemn news of Louis' death. I had been thinking of him lately and praying for him . . . I suppose it was in the logic of things that this great man should go to his rest. And yet we cannot afford to lose people like him. There are too few, and they are not being replaced. May he pray for us and watch over us and obtain for us the light and the strength to follow in his footsteps. We will understand later his greatness better than we do now. . . .

TO LOUIS MASSIGNON   *An outstanding Christian scholar of Islam, especially in its mystical expression (Sufism), Louis Massignon was raised in an atmosphere of traditional nineteenth-century French Catholic piety. Very early he was attracted to the ninth-century Sufi mystic of Baghdad, al-Hallaj, whose identification of himself with the divine Reality led to his martyrdom. Massignon's dissertation at the Sorbonne was titled "The Passion of al-Hallaj." Married and with three children, he received permission from Pope Pius XII to be ordained a priest in the Melkite rite. He believed in the "substitution mystique," compassion that takes on the sufferings of another and transfers them to oneself. Hallaj gave the name* badal *to this spiritual practice. Massignon's interest in this practice led to the formation of the sodality of the Badaliya, among whose most illustrious members was Cardinal Montini, who became Pope Paul VI.*

MARCH 18, 1960

How can I begin to write you a letter about the amazing book of the prayers and exhortations of Hallaj [*Akhbar al-Hallaj*, third edition, in Arabic, with Massignon's French translation]? I think it is tremendous. In many ways the rude paradoxes are striking in the same way as Zen. But there is the added depth and fire of knowledge of the one God. There is the inexorable force of sanctity. The sense of the Holy that lays one low: as in Isaiah. To read Hallaj makes one lament and beat his breast. Where has it gone, the sense of the sacred, this awareness of the Holy? What has happened to us? . . .

May the Lord give me the grace to be worthy of such a book, and to read it with a pure and humble heart, as I hope I have been doing. May I have ears to hear this voice, so alien to our comfortable and complacent piety. . . .

Often I read your little leaflet on Charles de Foucauld [*Plus qu'un anneau sur le doigt* . . . "More than a ring on the finger"]. It moves me deeply. I am very sad at the lack of seriousness of my life compared with the lives of the men who have really listened to the word of God and kept it. I have not sought Him as I should!

Tomorrow, in my Mass for the Feast of St. Joseph, I will remember you very especially, Louis. I am more and more convinced of the rightness of your spiritual intuition and of the direction in which you travel: the way of mystery and risk, and of fervor.

With warm good wishes and prayers for a holy Easter. God bless you.

MAY 12, 1960

. . . On June 3rd I shall be saying Mass for you and for all your intentions.

Do you know the prayer to the Seven Sleepers composed by St. Peter Damian? If not I'll send it to you.

I like al-Hallaj more and more each day. . . .

JULY 20, 1960

For a long time I have practically written no letters because I have been trying to finish a long article and also to read proofs of a new full-length book, along with other duties. Hence I have had to let your letters go, and I am very sorry. However, I have copied out the prayer by St. Peter Damian and I hope it will reach you by the 27th [feast of the Seven Sleepers]. Though if you are going to Vieux Marché [a tiny Breton village] for the Pardon [the Breton word for "pilgrimage"], it will be too late. I wish I could be there with you, and I envy you. I know you will pray for me. I will remember you in a very special way in my Mass that day. . . .

I cannot thank you too much for the latest issue of the *Les Mardis de Dar el Salam* [regularly published papers that grew out of mutual-goodwill and common-interest sessions held at an ecumenical center called Dar el Salam, which means "the house of peace"]. Is there some way in which I could get all of them, I mean all the back issues? Could you have them sent to me? My [French] publisher, Albin Michel, will take care of the expense and will charge it to me. I think the issue you sent me is full of the most wonderful things and I was above all deeply moved by your own short meditations on the desert and the God of Agar and Ishmael. They are wonderful, and especially the fragments.

Louis, one thing strikes me and moves me most of all. It is the idea of the "*point vierge, ou le désespoir accule le coeur de l'excommunié*" ["the virginal point, the center of the soul, where despair corners the heart of the outsider"]. What a very fine analysis, and how true. We in our turn have to reach that same "*point vierge*" in a kind of despair at the hypocrisy of our own world. It is dawning more and more on me that I have been caught in civilization as in a kind of spider's web, and I am beginning to say "No" louder and louder, though surrounded by the solicitude of those who ask me why I do so. There is no way of explaining it, and perhaps not even time to do so. . . .

OCTOBER 29, 1960

. . . I have been wanting to write to you. I have not had time to write anything adequate. Today at least I can tell you that Herbert [Mason]'s message reached me and I, with the monks, am praying for your "Isaac" whom God asked of you and whom you surrendered to Him. [The reference is to Massignon's eldest son, Yves, who died at the age of twenty.]

Louis, in the presence of the darkness, the cloud of falsity and pretense, of confusion, of evasion, of desecration, one grows more and more to distrust words, to distrust even human communication itself. There grows in my heart a need to express something inexpressible, and I do not dare to find out what it might possibly be. So I can only fall back on half-articulate utterances. Forgive the lack of meaning.

First I struggle in my heart with the mystery and the need of peace, peace for the world. As a priest and a monk I must be a man of peace. I tell myself that there must be some truth in that idea. But in fact we are surrounded by and committed to a climate of violence. This is to me a terrible problem. Pray that I may be worthy to face it before the Lord of mercy and peace. . . .

EASTERN RELIGIONS

Buddhism

TO DAISETZ T. SUZUKI   *Acclaimed scholar of Zen Buddhism Daisetz T. Suzuki taught at universities in Japan, Europe, and the United States. His widely read books include* Introduction to Zen Buddhism *and* Mysticism: Christian and Buddhist. *Merton had invited Suzuki to write an introduction for a book of the sayings and stories of the Desert Fathers. Suzuki responded with an essay on Paradise, and Merton wrote an essay in response. The censors of the Order objected to this kind of dialogue, and the essays were not included in* The Wisdom of the Desert. *The essays by Merton and Suzuki were published in* New Directions 17 *and in* Zen and the Birds of Appetite. *In June 1964, Abbot James Fox permitted Merton to travel to New York City to meet with the ninety-three-year-old Suzuki.*

MARCH 12, 1959

Perhaps you are accustomed to receiving letters from strangers. I hope so, because I do not wish to disturb you with a bad-mannered intrusion. I hope a word of explanation will reconcile you to the disturbance, if it is one. The one who writes to you is a monk, a Christian, and so-called contemplative of a rather strict Order. A monk also, who has tried to write some books about the contemplative life and who, for better or worse, has a great love of and interest in Zen.

I will not be so foolish as to pretend to you that I understand Zen. To be frank, I hardly understand Christianity. And I often feel that those who think they know all about the teachings of Christ and of His church are not as close to the target as they think. And I think, too, that many of the Americans who are excited about Zen are perhaps dealing with something in their own imagination, and not with a reality. . . .

All I know is that when I read your books—and I have read many of them—and above all when I read English versions of the little verses in which the Zen masters point their finger to something which flashed out at the time, I feel a profound and intimate agreement. Time after time, as I read your pages, something in me says, "That's it!" Don't ask me what. . . . I have my own way to walk, and for some reason or other Zen is right in the middle of it wherever I go. So there it is, with all its beautiful purposelessness, and it has become very familiar to me though I do not know "what it is." Or even if it is an "it." Not to be foolish and multiply words, I'll say simply that it seems to me that Zen is the very atmosphere of the Gospels, and the Gospels are busting with it. It is the proper climate for any monk, no matter what kind of monk he may be. If I could not breathe Zen I would probably die of spiritual asphyxiation. But I still don't know what it is. No matter. I don't know what the air is either.

. . . Enclosed with this letter are a couple of pages of quotations from a little book of translations I have made [*The Wisdom of the Desert*]. These are translations from the hermits who lived in the Egyptian deserts in the fourth and fifth centuries A.D. I feel very strongly that you will like them for a kind of Zen quality they have about them. If you agree that they are interesting and that they show this particular quality, I wonder if you would let me send you the complete manuscript, which is quite short, and if you would do me the very, very great honor of writing a few words of introduction to it. . . . I cannot assure you too strongly of my conviction that a preface from you would be a great and estimable favor. To be plain, I can think of no one more appropriate for the task, because in all simplicity I believe that you are the one man, of all modern writers, who bears some resemblance to the Desert Fathers who wrote these little lines, or rather spoke them. I do hope you will be able to say yes to this clumsy request of mine. . . .

APRIL 11, 1959

What a pleasure to receive your kind reply to my letter. I was very happy to learn that my suppositions had been correct, and that you were indeed interested in the Zen-like sayings of the Desert Fathers. . . . And one of the things the Zen masters and Desert Fathers share, among so many other qualities, is their quiet humor, blended with spiritual joy that transcends difficulties and sufferings.

Therefore I am sending on to you the manuscript which has received the provisional title of *The Wisdom of the Desert*. . . .

. . . We in the West are ready to talk about things like Zen and about a hundred and one other things besides, but we are not so eager to do the things that Zen implies: and that is what really counts . . . At the moment, I occasionally meet my own kind of Zen master, in passing, and for a brief moment. For example, the other day a bluebird sitting on a fence post suddenly took off after a wasp, dived for it, missed, and instantly returned to the same position on the fence post as if nothing had ever happened. A brief, split-second lesson in Zen. If I only knew some Japanese I would put it into a haiku . . . the gist of it would be that the birds never stop to say "I missed" because, in fact, whether they catch the wasp or not, they never miss, and neither does Zen. We in the West are the ones with the hit-or-miss outlook on life, and so we hit and we miss. And in both cases the results are likely to be tragic. I fear our successes more than our failures.

And now for your deeply moving and profoundly true intuitions on Christianity. I wish I could tell you with what joy and what understanding I respond to them. We have very much the same views, and take the same standpoint, which is, it seems to me, so truly that of the New Testament. I am sending you an article on Easter . . . Behind it is the same paradox you bring out in the words "we are innocent because of our sinfulness." That in fact is one of the great Christian paradoxes, one that has preoccupied thinkers like St. Augustine, Dostoevsky, St. Paul and a thousand others. . . .

In your phrase "God wanted to know Himself, hence the creation," you touch upon a most interesting theological idea that has been developed by some Russian Orthodox thinkers and which has deep consequences and ramifications. The Russian view pushes very far the idea of God "emptying Himself" (kenosis) to go over into His creation, while creation passes over into a divine world—precisely a new paradise. Your intuition about paradise is profoundly correct and patristic. In Christ the world and the whole cosmos has been created anew (which means to say restored to its original perfection and beyond that made divine, totally transfigured). The whole world has risen in Christ, say the Fathers. If God is "all in all," then everything is in fact paradise, because it is filled with the glory and presence of God, and nothing is any more separated from God. Then comes the question whether or not the Resurrection of Christ shows that we had never really been separated from Him in the first place. Was it only that we *thought* we were separated from Him? But that thought was a conviction so great and so strong that it amounted to separation. It was a thought that each one of us had to be a god in his own right. Each one of us began to slave and struggle to make himself a god, which he imagined he was supposed to be. Each one slaved in the service of his own idol—his consciously fabricated social self . . . This is Original Sin. In this sense, Original Sin and paradise are directly opposed. In this sense there is exclusion from paradise. But yet we are in paradise, and once we break free from the false image, we find ourselves what we are: and we are "in Christ."

. . . The Christ we seek is within us, in our inmost self, *is* our inmost self, and yet infinitely transcends ourselves. We have to be "found in Him:" and yet be perfectly ourselves and free from the domination of any image of Him other than Himself. You see, that is the trouble with the Christian world. It is not dominated by Christ (which would be perfect freedom), it is enslaved by images and ideas of Christ that are creations and projections of men and stand in the way of God's freedom. But Christ Himself is in us as unknown and unseen. We follow Him, we find Him (it is like the cowcatching pictures) and then He must vanish and we must go along without Him at our side. Why? Because He is even closer that that. *He is ourself.* Oh my dear Dr. Suzuki, I know you will understand this so well, and so many people do not, even though they are "doctors in Israel." . . .

As you know, the problem of writing down things about Christianity is fraught with ludicrous and overwhelming difficulties. . . . Everyone is preoccupied with formulas. Is this correct, is this absolutely in accordance with such and such a formula? Does this fit the official definitions? Etc. . . .

Meanwhile you see that I enjoy talking with you of these things, and I assure you I will be very happy to hear how the ideas develop. And for the rest, we are in paradise, and what fools would we be to think thoughts that would put us out of it (as if we *could* be out of it!). One thing I would add. To my mind, the Christian doctrine of grace (however understood—I mean here the gift of God's Life to us) seems to me to fulfill a most important function in all this. The realization, the finding of ourselves in Christ and hence in paradise, has a special character from the fact that this is all a free gift from God. With us, this stress on freedom, God's freedom, the *indeterminateness* of salvation, is the thing that corresponds to Zen in Christianity. The breakthrough that comes with the realization of what the finger of a koan is pointing to is like the breakthrough of the realization that a sacrament, for instance, is a finger pointing to the completely spontaneous Gift of Himself to us on the part of God—beyond everything high or low, everything spiritual or material. . . . I like to see this freedom of God at work outside of all set forms, all rites, all theology, all contemplation—everything. But the rites and contemplation and discipline have their place. In fact they are most important.

And now one more thing. . . . I want to speak for this Western world which has been and is so utterly wrong. This world which has in past centuries broken in upon you and brought you our own confusion, our own alienation, our own decrepitude, our lack of culture, our lack of faith. And worst of all, that we have shamed the Truth of Christ by imposing upon you our own confusion as if it came from Christ. . . . If only we had thought of coming to you to *learn* something. There are some who want to do this now, but perhaps it is too late. The victims of Hiroshima and Nagasaki are before me and beside me every day when I say Mass. I pray for them and I feel they intercede for me before God. If only we had thought of coming to you and loving you for what you are in yourselves, instead of trying to make you over into our own image and likeness. . . . The fact that you are a Zen Buddhist and I am a Christian monk, far from separating us, makes us most like one another. How many centuries is it going to take for people to discover this fact? . . .

OCTOBER 24, 1959

Your article arrived very promptly—yesterday, when I returned to the monastery, it was already here. I have read it twice carefully and intend to study it much more, in fact I am having one of the novices copy it so that there will be no danger of losing the material. As you suggested I have modified a word here and there, and I will send you a copy of the slightly emended version. I will speak of the emendations in a moment.

But first of all I want to thank you for a really excellent and stimulating study. It is very fine indeed, and is to me one of the most significant short pieces of yours that I have read in very many ways. I am thoroughly pleased with it. But I feel in order to give it the full impact which it deserves, I will have to write a further text, to explain and integrate your own study in the whole plan.

Your commentary is excellent, but I am convinced that most readers will have no grasp of its real and intimate relation to the Desert Fathers, and will think it is a rather "unrelated' excursus on Zen, which of course is not the case at all. Hence, in order that they may grasp the import of your distinction between innocence and knowledge, which is so fundamental for the Desert Fathers and for ancient Christian tradition, I will absolutely have to bring to light some clear Christian texts which show conclusively that what you are saying really belongs to the authentic Christian tradition; it is not merely something that you, as a Buddhist, have read into it through Eckhart. Your use of Eckhart of course puts the whole study on a much more sophisticated level than the Desert Fathers' sayings originally suggest, since the Desert Fathers were really only simple Egyptian peasants—at least the ones quoted in these stories. . . . Nevertheless they were all distinctly aware of this vocation to recover the paradisiacal innocence of Adam, and to do so by the kind of emptiness and poverty which you so perfectly describe, the only distinction being that they were less subtle about it than Eckhart or the Zen masters, and tended to see the thing more in objective, symbolic terms. Your point about the contrast of knowledge with innocence is deeply rooted in the tradition of the early Christian centuries and I shall adduce texts to show this. So my plan is to have your study and my comment follow *The Wisdom of the Fathers,* as a second section of the book, a kind of dialogue between East and West. Thus it is no longer a question of a simple preface. . . .

One more small point—where I have presumed to change one word of your text. I think that on page one your use of the word "mythical" for the Christian concept of God will lead to serious misunderstanding and will make many readers miss the point of your study. . . . I would suggest a use of the term "analogical." This means that we describe something that we do not and cannot know directly, by a reference to something that we do know. The terms "being," "power," "love," "wisdom," etc., applied to God are all *analogies.* We know what being, power, etc., are in the world of experience, but the things that we thus know are so infinitely far from the "being," etc., of God that it is just as true to say that God is "no-being" as to say that he is "being." This you will find in St. Thomas, the traditions of Pseudo-Denys etc.—in other words, in Eckhart's main sources. I would heartily recommend the use of the words "analogy" and "analogical," as thoroughly acceptable to Christian theologians, while "mythical" will give them all a fit of apoplexy. . . .

JUNE 11, 1964

I am really delighted to hear that you are in this country and that it is possible for me to meet you. I have received a special permission from my Father Abbot to travel to New York especially for this purpose, but I must ask you not to let this be too widely known. Obviously if your immediate companions know it, that is fine. But it should not become generally known around New York as this would cause difficulties. . . .

Looking forward to a very pleasant visit with you. . . .

OCTOBER 14, 1964

. . . Don't forget that you were going to write out a few Japanese characters for me with a brush. I will put them up in the hermitage. And did any of the pictures taken by Mihokosan get developed? Are there copies? I would like very much to have one.

P.S. If you write out something in Japanese, please be sure to say what it is, and again I will be most grateful. The memory of our happy visit [at Columbia in June] remains as a joy and a wonder.

MARCH 4, 1965

This year's Sengai Calendar reached me somewhat late with its intimations of the treasure ship heaped high with treasures from abroad. A few days later came a treasure indeed: your calligraphy, a presence of great beauty and strength which I have given a place of honor in the hermitage. It transforms all around it. Everything about the gift was admirable, and I am most honored and delighted to receive such a thing from Japan and from you. It is to me a deep bond with a world and tradition which I greatly love and admire. It is above all a special reminder of you whom I venerate. . . .

MAY 3, 1965

I have been reading a remarkable passage in a Syrian Christian thinker of the fifth century, Philoxenus. In fact I think *Holiday* magazine sent you an issue in which I had an article ["Rain and the Rhinoceros"] which refers to him. I think you will especially like this passage which discusses the *simplicity* which is a prime essential of spiritual life, and which was "normal" to Adam and Eve in paradise. Hence it is a description of the "paradise life" of prajna and emptiness.

Here is what he says. After saying that God was with them and "showed them everything": "They received no thought about Him into their spirit. They never asked: Where does He live, who shows us these things? How long has He existed? If He created all, was He Himself created? By whom? And we, why has He created us? Why has He placed us in this paradise? Why has He given us this law? All these things were far from their minds, because simplicity does not think such thoughts. Simplicity is completely absorbed in listening to what it hears. All its thought is mingled with the word of him who speaks. It is like the little child, completely absorbed in the person speaking to it." . . .

I think that Buddhism is very aware of this, and it is therefore aware of that which is the intimate ground of all knowledge and all faith. And to the extent that Christian faith is unaware of this, it lacks some of the reality which it ought to have. However, I think it is there in the depths both of Christianity and Buddhism. . . . In any event, there is only one meeting place for all religions, and it is paradise. How nice to be there and wander about looking at the flowers. Or being the flowers.

TO THICH NHAT HANH   *Forced to flee his home during the Vietnam War, Thich Nhat Hanh headed the Vietnamese Buddhist Peace Delegation. John*

Heidbrink brought the Buddhist monk to visit Merton at Gethsemani in May 1966. In his journal. Merton noted that "Nhat Hanh is first of all a true monk . . . and you can see that his Zen has worked." After the visit, Merton wrote a short essay entitled "Thich Nhat Hanh Is My Brother."

JUNE 29, 1966

I suppose you are probably back in Vietnam by now. I thought of you today because I finished your excellent little book on Buddhism today. It is really a good book and I especially liked the chapters about contact with reality and on the way to live the inner life.

You know that the FOR [Fellowship of Reconciliation] people have nominated you for the Nobel Peace Prize. I have written a letter in support of the nomination and hope you get it. It would certainly be very satisfying to us all if you did.

It was a great pleasure to have you here and I hope you will return sometime and stay longer. . . . More of your own work ought to be translated into Western languages. I think you make very clear what Buddhism really is. And I certainly feel very strongly as you do that the essential thing is to escape ignorance and the inevitable suffering that follows from it by a real contact with things as they are, instead of an illusory relationship with the world. I think your problems with conservative and formalist religiosity are very much the same as ours in the Catholic Church. It is the same everywhere. A new mentality is needed, and this implies above all a recovery of ancient and original wisdom.

TO MARCO PALLIS   *Born in Liverpool, England, in 1895 of Greek parents, Marco Pallis was a mountain climber and a student of Tibetan art, religion, and culture. His most famous book,* Peaks and Lamas, *was first published in 1939. His contact with Pallis helped prepare Merton for his visit to Tibetan monks on his Asian journey.*

1963 [PROBABLY JULY]

. . . I read your book several years ago and found it very congenial indeed. I certainly envy you your experience with Tibetan monasticism. . . .

To my mind the meeting of Eastern and Western philosophy and mysticism is a crucially important matter. My general feeling is that the work that has been done so far, and the kind of thing I myself might be able to participate in, is not thorough enough and too intuitive. Of course a sapiential approach must be intuitive. But a great deepening is necessary. The task of getting to know the Eastern literature thoroughly is immense, and I do not have any Oriental languages. I might say, however, that I have a deep affinity and respect for Buddhism, and I think that I am as much a Chinese Buddhist in temperament and spirit as I am a Christian. I don't find any contradiction in matters of "faith" as I see it. But of course I say this without having an expert knowledge of the literature, and perhaps it is only irresponsibility and impressionism. I think one can certainly believe in the revealed truths of Christianity and follow Christ, while at the same time having a Buddhist outlook of life and nature. Or in other words, a certain element of Buddhism in culture and spirituality is by no means incompatible with Christian belief. . . .

EASTER 1965

. . . I agree entirely that one must cling to one tradition and to its orthodoxy, at the risk of not understanding any tradition. One cannot supplement his own tradition with little borrowings here and there from other traditions. On the other hand, if one is genuinely living his own tradition, he is capable of seeing where other traditions say and attain the same thing, and where they are different. The differences must be respected, not brushed aside, even and especially where they are irreconcilable with one's own view. . . .

. . . There is every solid reason even within the framework of Catholic orthodoxy to say that all the genuine living religious traditions can and must be said to originate in God and to be revelations of Him, some more, some less. And that it makes no sense to classify some of them as "natural." There is no merely natural "revelation" of God, and there is no merely natural mysticism (a contradiction in terms). However, this whole business of natural and supernatural requires a great deal of study. . . .

NOVEMBER 14, 1965

. . . Your very good letter of last August, about your walking trip to Switzerland and the visit of Aelred Graham, was much appreciated and I have just reread it. It came, as a matter of fact, just when I was preparing to move out from the monastery to a hermitage to begin my vanaprastha, which is, I hope, definitive. I have been at it three months, and it is a splendid form of life. But three months have taught me many things and show me that I have more to learn, in order to get on the way without ambiguities. Well, that is what solitude is for and I am learning to be patient with the long task of gradually peeling off non-essential things. . . .

. . . Life at the hermitage is peaceful and assumes a clear direction. One sees the way more clearly, and as you say, it is a great help to know that there are companions here and there. There is nothing whatever of any importance except this quest for inner truth, the truth that one "is" without being able to see it because we have all covered it over with the results of our selfish and deluded acts. The enormity of the task is great, yet simple, and one may have great desire and great hope of going on with the help of the Holy Spirit, in finding the path by His light in darkness. The path that leads home to Him in ourself, and the path which is also Himself. ("I am the way, the truth and the life.") . . .

In October 1965 Pallis sent Merton a beautiful eighteenth-century Greek icon of the Madonna with four saints in attendance on her.

DECEMBER 5, 1965

Where shall I begin? I have never received such a precious and magnificent gift from anyone in my life. I have no words to express how deeply moved I was to come face to face with this sacred and beautiful presence granted to me in the coming of the ikon to my most unworthy person. At first I could hardly believe it. And yet perhaps your intuition about my karma is right, since in a strange way the ikon of the Holy Mother came as a messenger at a precise moment when a message was needed, and her presence before me has been an incalculable aid in resolving a difficult problem [the action of Roger LaPorte in immolating himself for peace]. . . .

But that is all business. Let me return to the holy ikon. Certainly it is a perfect act of timeless worship, a great help. I never tire of gazing at it. There is a spiritual presence and reality about it, a true spiritual "Thaboric" light, which seems unaccountably to proceed from the Heart of the Virgin and

Child as if they had One heart, and which goes out to the whole universe. It is unutterably splendid. And silent. It imposes a silence on the whole hermitage. . . .

Thank you, dear friend, for such a generous and noble gift. . . .

TO FRIENDS   PASCHAL TIME 1968

. . . As you know I am very interested in dialogue between Christianity and Asian religions, especially Buddhism. Also for almost a year I have been lecturing on Sufism, the mystical side of Islam, to the monks here. It is very revealing. For a long time Christians have too readily assumed that other religions had little "depth." This is entirely wrong. I think today we need to be more aware than we are of the real depth of the other major religions and the "mystical" side of their experience. Especially is this true when in some ways it can be said that the Western trend is toward activism and lack of depth. . . . Genuine progress must take place on a much deeper level—and will doubtless do so.

As Pentecost draws near, let us reflect a little on the reality of the Spirit who is truly given to us as to a Church that is called to be in every sense prophetic and eschatological: a sign of Christ which is at once a sign of supreme hope and a sign of contradiction. We all have work to do if we are to measure up to this vocation.

Chinese Taoism

TO JOHN C. H. WU   *Scholar, diplomat, professor, and writer John C. H. Wu studied law in Europe and the United States, worked as a lawyer and judge in Shanghai, and after his conversion to Christianity served as Chinese delegate to the Vatican. Merton wrote to Wu seeking guidance in the study of Oriental philosophy. They soon became collaborators as Wu assisted Merton in crafting his own renderings of selections from Chuang Tzu (published as* The Way of Chuang Tzu) *by sending Merton four different translations of the texts and adding his own literal translations. Among Wu's writings are* Beyond East *and West and* The Golden Age of Zen, *for the latter of which Merton wrote an introduction.*

MARCH 14, 1961

Father Paul Chan wrote to me some time ago saying that he had kindly spoken to you about a project of mine which came to his attention, through a letter I had written to Archbishop Yu Pin. So you are already acquainted with the fact that I have been for some time persuaded of the immense importance of a prudent study of Oriental philosophy by some of us in the West, particularly in the kind of perspective that guided some of the early Church Fathers in their use of Platonism, and St. Thomas in his use of Aristotle. . . .

Where shall I begin? The one concrete thing that Father Chan seized upon in my letter to Archbishop Yu Pin was the tentative project of a selection from Chuang Tzu which New Directions would like to publish. But this is perhaps premature. I don't know if you saw a raw attempt of mine to say something about Chinese thought in *Jubilee* ["Classic Chinese Thought"]. It may have seemed articulate but I am sure you would have realized that I have only the most superficial grasp of the Confucian Classics, which is what I was mainly talking about. I do think it would be important perhaps for me to read some more and if possible discuss the Four Classics with you, on the most elementary level, like any Chinese schoolboy of the old days. I would like to really get impregnated with the spirit of the Four Classics, which to my mind is perfectly compatible with Christian ethics, and then go on to what really attracts me even more, the mysticism of the early Taoists. Then after that I might be able to talk sense about Chuang Tzu, and if you are still interested, we could do an original translation of the things we selected. I have the Legge translation here which looks suspiciously doctored to me.

I would be interested in your reaction, and would welcome any suggestions as to how to proceed and what to read now. And then, when you are free, I would like to invite you down to Gethsemani for a few days or a week. . . .

Replying on March 20 to the above letter, John Wu praises Merton's grasp of the Chinese way of thinking and indicates that he would be delighted to cooperate with Merton in a translation of Chuang Tzu. He writes: "I have come to see that Chuang Tzu is neither a pantheist pure and simple nor a theist pure and true, but a mixture of the two—a prototype of what von Hügel calls panentheism. . . . Only a man like yourself steeped in the works of the great Christian mystics can know what Lao Tzu and Chuang Tzu were pointing at, and how utterly honest and correct they were."

APRIL 1, 1961

Your wonderful letter was a joy and an encouragement. I have no more doubts about the project being willed by God. It has the marks of the Holy Spirit's action upon it everywhere, doesn't it? The way you received the suggestion and your wonderful response is all the evidence one needs. I am sure we will go on to work together very happily and fruitfully. . . .

So let us then proceed with love for the God Who manifested His wisdom so simply and so strikingly in the early Chinese sages, and let us give Him glory by bringing out the inner heart of that wisdom once again. One of the defects of a wrong kind of supernaturalism is that by rejecting those wonderful natural wisdoms that came before Christ and cried out for fulfillment in the Gospel, they set aside the challenging demands which would make us Christians strive for the highest purity of our own spiritual wisdom. And then, while claiming to be supernatural, we live on a level that is in some way *below* nature; the supernatural becomes the unnatural "sanctified" by legalistic formulas and appeals to gestures and rites whose inner meaning is not understood. And the whole thing is kept going by the magic formula *ex opere operato*. . . .

I am so happy you are doing a study of Chuang Tzu, and I look forward to reading it, avidly. I am more and more struck by the profundity of his thought. He is one of the *great* wise men: I will not say "philosophers" in the speculative sense, for his wisdom has a marvelous wholeness, and that is what makes it seem "simple." Indeed it is simple, but at the same time utterly profound. I think he has in him an element which is essential to all true contemplation, and which is often lacking in Western "contemplatives." His grasp of the fact that most of what is done in the name of "perfection" is actually perversion. His respect for the wholeness of reality which cannot be seized in a definition. The real meaning of *nature*. One must respect nature before one can rise out of it to be a person. Certainly he is well prepared for the "true light" which shines out in the Resurrection of Christ. The wisdom of Chuang Tzu demands the Resurrection, for the Resurrection goes beyond all moralities and moral theories, it is a totally new life in the Spirit. . . .

God bless you, belatedly, on your birthday this Holy Week. I will be keeping you in my Easter Masses and ask the Lord to give you every blessing and joy and to keep ever fresh and young your "child's mind" which is the only one worth having. May He grant us (as you so well say) to be both inebriated and sober in Christ, Confucians and Taoists. It is all-important for us to *be* in Christ what the great sages cried out to God for. May our studies help us to live what they hoped for, and may we be able to bring to the Orient hope and light, which by right is theirs: for Christ rose up in the East, and we sing to Him "*O Oriens*" in Advent. . . .

APRIL 11, 1961

Thank you for your very good letter, for the Giles translation which I have now received and which is clear, idiomatic English, throwing light on Legge's more cautious and careful translation. Thanks above all for the first sample of your own translation. I like the almost poetic form and think we ought to use that often. I will discuss the details later—whether for instance it is better to use "benevolence" or "humanity," etc. . . .

I enjoy Chuang Tzu more and more. The liberty of spirit he seeks is found truly in St. Paul's Epistles and in St. John. We underestimate St. Paul. We do not realize what a liberation he went through and how carefree and undetermined a Christian really should be, with no care save to listen to the Holy Spirit and follow wherever He beckons! Let us seek more and more to do this in the gaiety and childlike joy of Chuang Tzu. I think spiritual childhood must be characteristically Chinese grace. . . .

APRIL 21, 1961

Many thanks for your good letter. . . . There are so many fine things in your book (*Beyond East and West*). I especially enjoy the notations from your diary that are being read now. The community was in a state of near riot when you described your marriage. I am in love with your parents. The book is most enjoyable and moving. . . .

MAY 19, 1961

Forgive me for the delay in writing to you. I have been busy finishing up my course in mystical theology and various other tasks and now I have a little time to "return to the roots" and let the things that are more important come to the surface. Your manuscript on St. Therese I consider one of these "more important" things. . . .

Now I enjoy the quiet of the woods and the song of birds and the presence of the Lord in silence. Here is Nameless Tao, revealed as Jesus, the brightness of the hidden Father, our joy and our life. . . .

AUGUST 12, 1961

. . . I am reading Paul Sih's book about China at the moment. It is very clear and informative, and tells me a lot of things about which I knew nothing. When we are up against a monster propaganda machine, the task is discouraging, but we must nevertheless stick to the truth. The trouble is that there is also a monster ambiguity to deal with at the same time, as though the propaganda machine had not only changed the "truths" but even changed the "truth" itself. As if it had somehow created a new kind of truth, in the face of which all former truths, however true, become irrelevant. This is the problem.

. . . Before I can attempt to do anything myself with Chuang Tzu I am going to have to learn two hundred fundamental ideograms. I don't think I can honestly approach the task otherwise. I need to orient myself somewhat in the Chinese text, which I am so glad to have. I have to make at least some kind of gesture at thinking through the ideograms and not just through sentences in Western languages. Can you suggest the best collection of ideograms for a beginner? Or is there some other approach? . . .

On November 28 Dr. Wu wrote that he had just received Merton's book The New Man. *It is, he says, "a living synthesis of East and West. . . . It seems to me that you read contemplatively. You are so deeply Christian that you cannot help touching the vital springs of other religions."*

DECEMBER 12, 1961

... I think my time would probably have been spent better with Chuang Tzu, except that I cannot see my way to doing this at the moment. Perhaps after a couple of months, when I have settled my mind as to exactly what line I ought to take and how to clarify that position. . . .

. . . Someone has recently sent me a marvelous book, *Poems of Solitude*, a collection including Juan Chi, Pao Chao, Wang Wei, Li Ho and Li Yu. Maybe you are right about my being Chinese, because this kind of thing is just what makes me feel most happy and most at home. I do not know whether or not I am always happy with mystical writings that are completely out of touch with ordinary life. On the contrary, it seems to me that mysticism flourishes most purely right in the middle of the ordinary. And such mysticism, in order to flourish, must be quite prompt to renounce all apparent claim to be mystical at all: after all, what difference do labels make? I know you agree, for this is what St. Therese so well saw. And by the way, how are you coming along with that book?

Your remarks on *The New Man* obviously made me very happy. What nicer compliments could any man have than to be told he has approached something which is the object of his greatest admiration and respect? To have been told that the book has a really Oriental quality is all the reward I ask for having written it, because I know that there is in the fact of having written it a value that cannot be taken away. I hope you will like the *New Seeds of Contemplation*, which will reach you soon. . . .

[COLD WAR LETTER 82] JUNE 7, 1962

... I hesitate to send you the enclosed angry and bitter poem ["A Picture of Lee Ying"]. It is savage, and its savagery hits everything in sight, so that it is not kind to anyone, even to the poor and desperate Chinese girl whose picture broke my heart and suggested the poem. I wish I could have said something full of mercy and love that would have been worthy of the situation, but I have only used her plight to attack the hypocrisy of those who find no room for the Chinese refugees, and who always have a very good reason. And the sad plight of a whole society which nods approval, while pronouncing a few formulas of regret. . . .

Many thanks for your two letters, and above all, thanks for coming. It was certainly a grace to have you here, a grace for me and a grace for us all. Therefore we hope you will return soon. And I am sure you will do that, now that you know what to expect: our disappearances and appearances, the long silences, the informality, and everything else down to Father Abbot's coy jokes about picture cards in the envelopes. This is just the way we are.

. . . Then I am preoccupied because one of my novices tells me that I have a neighbor: a snake has taken up residence in the woodshed up the Hill. I don't want to disturb him. I knew he was there, since he left his skin on the woodpile. I did not know he was a permanent resident. He appears to be harmless. Yet I don't like to be pulling apart the woodpile and suddenly have a family of snakes fall out all around me. So I will have to get together with Tao and wait for something to work itself out. Maybe I will just talk to him reasonably, or maybe we will just settle down and be neighbors. I hate to kill even a snake, and anyway there seems to be no real reason for killing this one.

I thought I would finally type out one of the "versions" I did after Chuang Tzu. Very much "after," I fear. But anyway, it no longer even pretends to be a serious rendering. I might insert it in a collection of poems I am getting together, as an experiment.

. . . I also enclose a poem, landscape, especially with a quail in it. The quail, as I seem to remember, is also a bird loved by Chuang Tzu. The quail is called, popularly, "bobwhite" around here. I thought you might like this. . . .

John Wu takes issue with Merton for calling his translation "after Chuang Tzu." He writes on July 17: "You have taken him by the forelocks not by the tail. I swear that I am not flattering when I say that this is exactly what Chuang Tzu would write had he learned English."

DECEMBER 20, 1962

I was so happy to get your letter this morning. I am putting aside all others to answer you immediately: such is the power of Chuang Tzu and Tao to get action out of one buried in the inertia of too much activity. The very name of Chuang Tzu restores me to sanity, at least momentarily. . . .

Insanity. Anything but his quiet debunking view is plain insanity. Even within the framework of the Gospel message there is too much temptation to forget what Jesus Himself warned at every step. One thing is necessary. Christianity as it has developed in the West, including monasteries of the West, has become a complex and multifarious thing. It takes Chuang Tzu to remind us of an essential element in the Gospel which we have simply "tuned out" with all our wretched concerns. The whole Sermon on the Mount, for instance. And the Discourse of the Last Supper. Even the central message of the Cross and the Resurrection. And the crib full of straw, in which the Lord of the world laughs and says "You should worry!" . . .

JUNE 23, 1963

. . . Thank you for the note on No Mind. Yes, the term Unconscious is misleading, and very much so. The thing is to get a real equivalent to the direct awareness *in depth,* the pure and complete immediacy implied by it. The problem of English terms like "no reflection" is that they seem to imply a kind of sensible quietism, a *surface* intuitiveness, more or less a rest in the immediacy of *sense* experience. That is of course only the least part of it. On the other hand we are bedeviled with the Platonist prejudice against senses, so that when it becomes an interior quietism of the zazen type, then some are satisfied with that. The old forced duality. And how they like to force it. . . .

JANUARY 31, 1965

Look how much time has passed since I received your letter and the chapter on Hui Neng [in Dr. Wu's book *The Golden Age of Zen*]. Time does not obey me, it will not stop for my convenience. This is very strange, but I must put up with it, even though time obeys everybody else. I will have to picket time for this unfairness.

Really I enjoyed your chapter on Hui Neng very much, as it has much new material and I like your insight about the quiet revolution on p. 10. Your pages bring out more of the real importance of Hui Neng. I like the concept of playful Samadhi, which comes very naturally from you. . . .

At every turn, we get back to the big question, which is the question of the person as void and not as individual or empirical ego. I know of no one in the West who has treated of person in such a way as to make clear that what is most ourselves is what is least ourself, or better the other way round. It is the void that is our personality, and not our individuality that seems to be concrete and defined and present etc . . . But the West is so used to identifying the person with the individual and the deeper self with the empirical self (confusing the issue by juggling around a divided "body and soul") that the basic truth is never seen. It is the Not-I that is most of all the I in each one of us. But we are completely enslaved by the illusory I that is not I, and never can be I, except in a purely fictional and social sense. And of course there is yet one more convolution in this strange dialectic: there remains to suppress the apparent division between empirical self and real or inner self. There is no such division. There is only the Void which is I, covered over by an apparent I. And when the apparent I is seen to be void it no longer needs to be rejected, *for it is I.* How wonderful it is to be alive in such a world of craziness and simplicity. . . .

John Wu wrote on May 11, 1965: "I have just read your nosegay of poems called The Way of Chuang Tzu. *I am simply bewitched. If Chuang Tzu were writing in English, he would surely write like this."*

JUNE 9, 1965

What a wonderful letter that was! It was a pure delight, and it made me so happy that I had been insane enough to go ahead with the work of Chuang Tzu. To have one such reader would be enough! And to encounter living in you the spirit of Chuang Tzu himself with such liveliness and force is, I must say, an experience. . . .

We will need illustrations, as New Directions wants to make a rather lavish book out of it. My idea is that perhaps some very fine free ancient calligraphy, perhaps something with some of the more important ideograms like Tao, wu wei and so on. I do have a little book where some Chinese drawings of trees, people and so on are found. They are adequate but not exciting. . . .

Naturally, I want to dedicate the Chuang Tzu book to you. So I hope you will accept, indeed I will not permit you to refuse: then your name will appear on a good blank page and we will all fly away on the back of the same dragon.

JULY 22, 1965

. . . You will be pleased to hear the news: the Chuang Tzu book was not only passed with honors by both censors, but one of them even asked to keep the ms. For a good long time so that he might study it and use it more. So you must have said a good strong prayer and the Holy Spirit must have breathed over the waters of argument. In fact, though, now that I know who did the censoring, I can see they would be open to something like this. There are others who would have had seven kinds of fits. . . .

In a letter of November 19, Dr. Wu says that he is going to Taiwan in the spring. Then, writing on November 24, he expresses his joy at receiving the completed text of The Way of Chuang Tzu: *"I have come to the conclusion that you and Chuang Tzu are one. It is Chuang Tzu himself who writes his thoughts in the English of Thomas Merton. You are a true man of Tao just as he is. You have met in that eternal place which is no place and you look at each other and laugh together . . . The spirit of joy is written over all the pages."*

DECEMBER 3, 1965

. . . As to what you said about the book, well, all I can say is that if Tao did the job through me, it was done in the usual way: without my knowing a thing about it. All I know is that in the beginning especially I was doing a job for which I felt no capacity whatever, and in the end, while I still felt I had no capacity it did not make any difference, I was having a lot of fun. As to attributing it to me, well, you can do so if you like, maybe Tao is playing games and acknowledging who did the work in this particular way. Who am I to interfere with Tao? . . .

John Wu wrote on December 17, 1965, that Merton's name in Chinese was Mei Teng, which means "silent lamp."

DECEMBER 28, 1965

Your letter and poem reached me on the Feast of St. Thomas, just as I was about to go to say Mass for Asia and all my Asian friends and for my own vocation to see things Asian in their simplicity and truth, if possible. So it was moving to be "baptized" in Chinese with a name I must live up to. After all, a name indicates a divine demand. Hence I must be Mei Teng, a silent lamp, not a sputtering one. Over these quiet feast days . . . I have been in the woods just staying quiet. And since the earth is one, I think I have plenty of Asia under my feet. The thing is to recognize it. This is the only real contribution I have to make to a tormented political situation. Instead of fighting Asia, to be it. And stubbornly, too. . . .

Hinduism

TO DOÑA LUISA COOMARASWAMY *Born of Jewish parents in Argentina, Doña Luisa Coomaraswamy came to the United States at the age of sixteen. She was working as a photographer in Boston when she met and married Ananda K. Coomaraswamy in 1931. He was a renowned scholar of Indian, Persian, and Islamic art. After his death in 1947, Doña Luisa began putting together a definitive collection of her husband's writings. Although she died before finishing the project, Roger Lipsey brought out a two-volume set of Ananda K. Coomaraswamy's papers in 1977.*

JANUARY 13, 1961

. . . Ananda Coomaraswamy is in many ways to me a model: the model of one who has thoroughly and completely united in himself the spiritual tradition and attitudes of the Orient and of the Christian West, not excluding also something of Islam, I believe. This kind of comprehension is, it seems to me, quite obligatory for the contemplative of our day, at least if he is in any sense also a scholar. I believe that the only really valid thing that can be accomplished in the direction of world peace and unity at the moment is the preparation of the way by the formation of men who, isolated, perhaps not accepted or understood by any "movement," are able to unite in themselves and experience in their own lives all that is best and most true in the various great spiritual traditions. Such men can become as it were "sacraments" or signs of peace, at least. Our task is one of very remote preparation, a kind of arduous and unthanked pioneering.

I certainly feel that I owe very much to AKC as his book *The Transformation of Nature in Art,* when I was doing my thesis on Blake years ago, was decisive in leading me to take the right turn in life and to set my feet upon the spiritual road, which led to the monastery and to the contemplative life. . . .

. . . It is not that I want to write about AKC but rather that I want to enter contemplatively into the world of thought which, as you so rightly say, is for all of us, is not any private property of his, but which nevertheless had to be opened to us by him. . . .

FEBRUARY 12, 1961

. . . We have here a record of some Indian religious music, in the Folkway series, and I enjoy it very much, especially some of the popular legends, like the one about the Black Parrot. But the chanting of the Vedas, of which a sample is given, was the thing that really first opened up the Upanishads to me. The *way* in which the words are chanted shows the spiritual character of Hindu singing and reflects the spiritual understanding of breath that is exposed in the Upanishads. I am now finishing the Brihad Aranyaka Upanishad and it is tremendous. . . .

. . . [AKC] just was a voice bearing witness to the truth, and he wanted nothing but for others to receive that truth in their own way, in agreement with their own mental and spiritual context. As if there were any other way of accepting it. But no, this awful mistake of the West, which is certainly not a "Christian" mistake at all, but the fruit of Western aggression, was the idea that one had to "convert" the East and make it change in every way into a replica of the West. This is one of the great spiritual crimes of man in its own unconscious way and we are only beginning to reap the fruit of it in China, the Congo, etc. . . .

TO AMIYA CHAKRAVARTY *Amiya Chakravarty was born in India in 1901. He studied in India and at Oxford University and taught at Boston University, Smith College, and the State University of New York at New Paltz. A distinguished poet, philosopher, and scholar, he also served as an adviser to the Indian delegation at the United Nations, a delegate to UNESCO, and literary secretary to Indian poet Rabindranath Tagore. While teaching at Smith College, Chakravarty arranged an evening colloquium on Merton for his students.*

JANUARY 21, 1967

. . . Thanks for letting me know about the discussion at Smith. I feel honored—and also I am not humble enough to take these things gracefully and therefore I am also a little confused . . . I would like to say that I hope it does not take on the aspect of a personality cult. I think the girls at Smith are wise enough to avoid that . . . So, apart from that, I am happy with the idea, and it is to me a way of being in contact with others like myself, with kindred interests and concerns, people who look for something more in life than plenty of food, comfort, amusement and money. In fact I suppose that some of them feel as I do that American life can at times take on the aspect of an appalling wilderness. I am certainly not one of those who, on supposedly "Christian" motives, preach submission to this state of affairs. What does matter, however, is not just protest and discontent, but the love which is beyond all that. May that love grow in all of us. It is the one thing necessary. Give them, then, my love.

On March 29 Chakravarty wrote: "We had the great evening. It began late in the afternoon, but the students and faculty carried on till past dinnertime. We were immersed in the silence and eloquence of your thoughts and writings. . . . The young scholars here realize that the absolute rootedness of your faith makes you free to understand other faiths. . . . Your books have the rock-like inner strength which sustains the Abbey of Gethsemani, which can challenge violence and untruth wherever they may appear."

APRIL 13, 1967

I have put off answering until a moment of quiet, an afternoon that is almost as hot as summer. For a writer there is surely not much that can be more rewarding than the fact of being really read and understood and appreciated. After all, the great thing in life is to share the best one has, no matter how poor it may be. The sharing gives it value. Often when I reread things I have written I find them so bad that I am irritated with myself: of course this is only vanity. But once I realize that they have meant something to someone they acquire something of the other person's value and meaning. What you read and liked of mine I shall like better now because you have all enjoyed them: I will like them because of all of you. I will like them because they are more yours than mine.

. . . I do really have the feeling that you have all understood and shared quite perfectly. That you have seen something that I see to be most precious—and most available too. The reality that is present to us and in us: call it Being, call it Atman, call it Pneuma . . . or Silence. And the simple fact that by being attentive, by learning to listen (or recovering the natural capacity to listen which cannot be learned any more than breathing), we can find ourself engulfed in such happiness that it cannot be explained: the happiness of being at one with everything in that hidden ground of Love for which there can be no explanations.

I suppose what makes me most glad is that we all recognize each other in this metaphysical space of silence and happiness, and get some sense, for a moment, that we are full of paradise without knowing it. . . .

OCTOBER 11, 1967

. . . I was interested and gratified to know from you that Dr. Radhakrishnan knew and liked my work. It is always a joy to me to feel that my writings have made friends for me in Asia. More and more I feel that Asia is in so many ways more congenial to me than the West. . . .

JUNE 14, 1968

. . . And now, good news. Though it is not certain that I shall attend the meeting at Bangkok I have received permission to go and preach a retreat at our Cistercian monastery in Indonesia. This will give me also an opportunity to visit some non-Christian monasteries in SE Asia and in Japan. That is what I'd like to plan. In Japan I want most of all to visit Suzuki's friends and associates. They are presumably at Otani University. Have you any suggestions? And I'd like to see a couple of good Zen monasteries and meet some Roshis . . . Is there anything you know of at or near Singapore? Anything you know of in Java (which is where our monastery is)? . . . (I am not planning on going to India this time, though if it were possible to make a retreat in the Himalayas I'd certainly be most tempted to change all plans and go there. But as I am too arthritic to be a caveman, it would have to be in a cottage of sorts!!!) . . .

AUGUST 31, 1968

. . . Things seem to be shaping up very well for India. I have, I think, a good chance of entrée to some of the Tibetan Buddhist monasteries and hope to stay at Darjeeling after the meeting to see those in that area. I hope to go to Nepal and also to go over and meet the Dalai Lama at Mussoorie. . . .

POSTSCRIPT

A LETTER FROM ASIA TO FRIENDS [NEW DELHI, INDIA] NOVEMBER 1968

This newsletter is not a reply to mail because I have not been getting mail on this Asian trip. . . . I have received permission to be absent from my monastery for several months, chiefly because I was invited to attend a meeting of Asian Catholic abbots in Bangkok and give a talk there. Since this gave me an opportunity to be in Asia, I have been permitted to extend the trip a little in order to learn something about Asian monasticism, especially Buddhist. I will be visiting our Cistercian monasteries in Indonesia, Hong Kong, and Japan and giving some talks there. Apart from that, the trip is not concerned with talking but with learning and with making contact with important people in the Buddhist monastic field. I am especially interested in Tibetan Buddhism and in Japanese (possibly Chinese) Zen. (Maybe there are still some Chinese Ch'an [Zen] centers in Taiwan.) I hope to see John Wu in Taiwan.

I am writing this in New Delhi, the capital of India, an impressive city which I like very much. My first contact with India was at Calcutta, which, no matter how prepared you may be, is always a shock. The poverty and misery are overwhelming there—and even more so in rural India. Some towns are indescribable. This morning I went to put a small coin into the hands of a beggar and saw he was a leper whose fingers had been eaten away. . . . It's like that. People sleep in the streets—some have never had a house to live in. People die in the streets. In Calcutta you walk out the front door of your hotel on the "best" street in the city and find a cow sleeping on the sidewalk. . . .

Bangkok was the worst place for traffic I ever saw; no lights, you just step on the gas and race five hundred other cars to the crossing. The main rule of Asian driving seems to be: never use the brake, just lean on the horn. It is wildly exciting. Especially in the Himalayas, where you whiz around corners at dizzy heights and speeds and meet these huge buses coming the other way painted to look like dragons. Usually the road is just about one lane wide anyway, but somehow one manages. I am still alive.

. . . The main point of this letter is to tell you something about my con-tacts with Tibetan mysticism and my meeting with the Dalai Lama in his new headquarters, high on a mountain at Dharamsala, which is an over-night train trip from Delhi, up in the Himalayas. (The Himalayas are the most beautiful mountains I have ever seen. There is something peculiar about the light there, a blue and a clarity you see nowhere else.) I spent eight days at Dharamsala making a kind of retreat, reading and meditating and meeting Tibetan masters. I had three long interviews with the Dalai Lama and spoke also with many others.

The Dalai Lama is the religious head of the Tibetan Buddhists and also in some ways their temporal leader. As you know, he had to escape from Tibet in 1959 when the Chinese Communists took over his country. There are many Tibetan refugees living in tents in the mountains, and many also forming colonies on tea plantations. I have seen monastic communities on these plantations. The Dalai Lama is much loved by his people, and they are the most prayerful people I have seen. Some of them seem to be praying constantly, and I don't mean monks. Lay people. Some always have rosaries in their hands (counting out Buddhist mantras), and I have seen some with prayer wheels. It is customary in the West to laugh at prayer wheels, but the people I have seen using them looked pretty recollected to me. They were obviously deep in prayer and very devout.

The Dalai Lama is thirty-three years old, a very alert and energetic person. He is simple and outgoing and spoke with great openness and frankness. He is in no sense what you would expect of a political émigré, and the things he said about Communism seemed to me to be fair and objective. His real interests are monastic and mystical. He is a religious leader and scholar, and also a man who has obviously received a remarkable monastic formation. We spoke almost entirely about the life of meditation, about *samadi* (concentration), which is the first stage of meditative discipline and where one systematically clarifies and recollects his mind. The Tibetans have a very acute, subtle, and scientific knowledge of "the mind" and are still experimenting with meditation. We also talked of higher forms of prayer, of Tibetan mysticism (most of which is esoteric and kept strictly secret). In either case the highest mysticism is in some ways quite "simple"—but always and everywhere the Dalai Lama kept insisting on the fact that one could not attain anything in the spiritual life without total dedication, continued effort, experienced guidance, real discipline, and the combination of wisdom and method (which is stressed by Tibetan mysticism). He was very interested in our Western monasticism and the questions he asked about the Cistercian life were interesting. He wanted to know about the vows, and whether the vows meant that one became committed to a "high attainment" in the mystical life. He wanted to know if one's vows constituted an initiation into a mystical tradition and experience under a qualified master, or were they just "equivalent to an oath"—a kind of agreement to stick around. When I explained the vows, then he still wanted to know what kind of attainment the monks might achieve and if there were possibilities of a deep mystical life in our monasteries. I said well, that is what they are supposed to be for, but many monks seem to be interested in something else. . . . I would note, however, that some of the monks around the Dalai Lama complain of the same things our monks do: lack of time, too much work, inability to devote enough time to meditation, etc. I don't suppose the Dalai Lam has much time on his hands, but in the long talks we had on meditation I could see that he has certainly gone very thoroughly and deeply into it and is a man of high "attainment." I have also met many other Tibetans who are very far advanced in a special type of Tibetan contemplation which is like Zen and is called *dzogchen*. . . .

I have also had some contact with the Sufi tradition (Moslem), which has penetrated India in the Delhi area (which used to be capital of the Mogul empire and is still quite Moslem). I met an expert on Sufism who told me of the meetings at which the Sufis of this area use singing to induce contemplation, but I have not been to any of them. . . .

In summary, I can say that so far my contacts with Asian monks have been very fruitful and rewarding. We seem to understand one another very well indeed. I have been dealing with Buddhists mostly, and I find that the Tibetans above all are very alive and also generally well trained. They are wonderful people. Many of the monasteries, both Thai and Tibetan, seem to have a life of the same kind that was lived, for instance, at Cluny in the Middle Ages: scholarly, well trained, with much liturgy and ritual. But they are also specialists in meditation and contemplation. This is what appeals to me most. It is invaluable to have direct contact with people who have really put in a lifetime of hard work in training their minds and liberating themselves from passion and illusion. . . . Talking with them is a real pleasure. . . .

I hope you will understand why I cannot answer my mail these days. I am entirely occupied with these monastic encounters and with the study and prayer that are required to make them fruitful. . . . I also hope I can bring back to my monastery something of the Asian wisdom with which I am fortunate to be in contact—but it is something very hard to put into words.

I wish you all the peace and joy in the Lord and an increase of faith: for in my contacts with these new friends I also feel consolation in my own faith in Jesus Christ and His indwelling presence. I hope and believe He may be present in the hearts of us all.

Index